Longevity Risk

Longevity Risk

Edited by Emma McWilliam

Published by Risk Books, a Division of Incisive Media Investments Ltd

Haymarket House
28–29 Haymarket
London SW1Y 4RX
Tel: + 44 (0)20 7484 9700
Fax: + 44 (0)20 7484 9797
E-mail: books@incisivemedia.com
Sites: www.riskbooks.com
       www.incisivemedia.com

© 2011 Incisive Media Investments Ltd

ISBN 978-1-906348-53-3

British Library Cataloguing in Publication Data
A catalogue record for this book is available from the British Library

Publisher: Nick Carver
Commissioning Editor: Lynette Kubale
Managing Editor: Lewis O'Sullivan
Designer: Lisa Ling

Copy-edited and typeset by T&T Productions Ltd, London
Printed and bound in the UK by PrintonDemand-Worldwide

Conditions of sale

All rights reserved. No part of this publication may be reproduced in any material form whether by photocopying or storing in any medium by electronic means whether or not transiently or incidentally to some other use for this publication without the prior written consent of the copyright owner except in accordance with the provisions of the Copyright, Designs and Patents Act 1988 or under the terms of a licence issued by the Copyright Licensing Agency Limited of 90, Tottenham Court Road, London W1P 0LP.

Warning: the doing of any unauthorised act in relation to this work may result in both civil and criminal liability.

Every effort has been made to ensure the accuracy of the text at the time of publication, this includes efforts to contact each author to ensure the accuracy of their details at publication is correct. However, no responsibility for loss occasioned to any person acting or refraining from acting as a result of the material contained in this publication will be accepted by the copyright owner, the editor, the authors or Incisive Media.

Many of the product names contained in this publication are registered trade marks, and Risk Books has made every effort to print them with the capitalisation and punctuation used by the trademark owner. For reasons of textual clarity, it is not our house style to use symbols such as TM, ®, etc. However, the absence of such symbols should not be taken to indicate absence of trademark protection; anyone wishing to use product names in the public domain should first clear such use with the product owner.

While best efforts have been intended for the preparation of this book, neither the publisher, the editor, the authors nor any of the potentially implicitly affiliated organisations accept responsibility for any errors, mistakes and or omissions it may provide or for any losses howsoever arising from or in reliance upon its information, meanings and interpretations by any parties.

There is considerable variability surrounding future changes in longevity, and the influences on future experience are numerous and complex. Any estimates and examples presented are illustrative only and not intended to provide, nor should they be interpreted as providing, any facts regarding, or prediction or forecast of, the likelihood that they will be representative of actual experience. This publication is intended solely for educational purposes and presents information of a general nature. It is not intended to guide or determine any specific individual situation and persons should consult qualified professionals before taking specific actions.

Contents

About the Editor   vii

About the Authors   ix

Foreword   xvii
Baroness Sally Greengross
International Longevity Centre (ILC-UK)

Introduction   xix
Emma McWilliam
Milliman

PART I   SETTING THE SCENE   1

1   **Ageing Populations and Changing Demographics**   3
Edouard Debonneuil, Lise He, Jessica Mosher, Nathalie Weiss
Groupe AXA

2   **Magnitude of the Longevity Issue: The Market Opportunity and Capacity**   45
Ed Collinge, Joseph Lu
Legal & General

PART II   PRICING LONGEVITY RISK   61

3   **Pricing Longevity Risk: Establishing Base Mortality Level**   63
Eli Friedwald
RGA UK Services Ltd

4   **Projecting Future Mortality**   91
Bridget Browne
Partner Reinsurance Europe Ltd

5   **Underwritten Annuities: The Market and Pricing of Longevity Risk**   123
Jason Hurley, Greg Becker
RGA UK Services Ltd

PART III   RESERVING AND CAPITAL REQUIREMENTS   145

6   **Reserving and Regulatory Requirements**   147
Stephen Makin
Stephen Makin Consulting Ltd

| 7 | Economic Capital, Modelling and Longevity Risk
Stephen Makin
Stephen Makin Consulting Ltd | 175 |

PART IV RISK MANAGEMENT AND DE-RISKING   201

| 8 | De-Risking Insured Annuity Portfolios
Robert Bugg, Farzana Ismail, Philip Simpson, Nick Dumbreck
Milliman | 203 |
| 9 | Longevity De-Risking Solutions for Pension Schemes
Norman Peard, James Morris
Credit Suisse | 229 |
| 10 | Hedging Longevity Risk through Reinsurance
Gavin Jones
Swiss Re | 255 |
| 11 | Extreme Mortality Risk as a Natural Hedge?
Alison McKie, Nick Ketley
Swiss Re | 267 |

PART V CAPITAL MARKET DEVELOPMENTS   281

| 12 | Capital Markets and Longevity Risk Transfer
Guy Coughlan | 283 |
| 13 | Longevity Indices
Paul Sweeting
University of Kent | 303 |
| 14 | Legal Considerations for Longevity Risk Transactions
Jennifer Donohue
Cadwalader, Wickersham & Taft LLP | 319 |
| | Index | 343 |

About the Editor

Emma McWilliam is an actuary and consultant with Milliman in London. She has significant experience in the area of annuities and longevity risk, having worked internationally advising clients at insurance companies, reinsurance companies, investment banks and institutional investors.

Emma has particular expertise working on longevity risk related projects. Her work has included advising on the acquisition of blocks of annuity business, setting longevity pricing bases and assisting with the risk management of annuities. She has also reviewed longevity portfolio transfers, undertaken strategic assignments to identify life insurance securitisation opportunities and worked on the development of longevity bond and swap structures for transferring this risk to the capital markets. She is a regular presenter at international industry conferences and has contributed to a number of publications and articles, on a range of subjects including longevity risk, Solvency II and International Financial Reporting Standards.

Emma is a fellow of the Institute of Actuaries, a fellow of the Society of Actuaries and a member of the American Academy of Actuaries. She has more than 15 years' experience in the insurance industry, working as a consultant and at reinsurance companies in the US, Australia, Singapore, Switzerland, Germany, the Netherlands, France and Belgium.

Emma enthusiastically balances her work with the care of her three children. For achieving this, she appreciates the support of Milliman.

About the Authors

Greg Becker is a product development actuary, working for the Reinsurance Group of America (RGA). He is responsible for developing forward-thinking and innovative initiatives in the life, health and longevity space, and co-ordinates the RGA Innovation Centre. His career has been diverse, but always with a strong business and strategic focus while working for a life office, a multi-national strategy consultancy, various startups and non-profit organisations. He holds a BBusSc (Hons) with majors in economics, statistics, business studies and actuarial science from the University of Cape Town, and is an Associate of the Institute of Actuaries.

Bridget Browne is senior lecturer in actuarial studies at the Australian National University in Canberra. Until early 2011 she was life chief pricing actuary at Partner Reinsurance Europe Ltd. In that role she was responsible for pricing of PartnerRe's life portfolio worldwide, in particular their longevity portfolios both standard and non-standard. Prior to joining PartnerRe in Paris in 2002, Bridget worked in the UK, Canada and Australia, her country of origin. She spent 10 years with Zurich Financial Services in a wide variety of financial and economic reporting roles, as well as a short spell with Hazell Carr working on the Pensions Review.

Robert Bugg is a consulting actuary in the London office of Milliman. He has worked on a number of projects involving annuity business and longevity risk transfer solutions, including capital and assumption reviews of annuity writers, reviews of cashflow and mortality projection models, assisting potential buyers of annuity portfolios and compiling reports for investors and trustees on the longevity risk capital held by an organisation providing de-risking solutions to the defined-benefit pension industry. Robert assisted in the development of Milliman's stochastic longevity tool, REVEAL, and has co-authored a number of publications covering the areas of longevity risk and Solvency II. Robert has also been involved in a number of mergers and acquisitions covering protection, investment and annuity business. He is currently involved in the design of a Solvency II internal model for a major with-profits company. Robert holds an MMath in mathematics from the University of Oxford, and is a fellow of the Institute and Faculty of Actuaries.

Ed Collinge is the head of capital management for Legal & General's annuity business. Prior to this role he was responsible for the structuring, development and implementation of bespoke solutions for defined-benefit pension schemes, which included longevity risk transfer solutions. Before joining Legal & General in 2008, he was a director in the Lehman Brothers insurance capital markets team, where he focused on implementing insurance related financing solutions, which included life securitisation, reinsurance financing and derivative products. Ed is a fellow of the Institute of Actuaries.

Guy Coughlan was until recently global head of ALM advisory and longevity solutions and co-head of European pension advisory at the London office of US investment bank JP Morgan. On joining JP Morgan in 1994, and over nearly 17 years he was involved in advising corporations, pension funds and insurers on strategic risk management and capital structure. Guy led the development of LifeMetrics, an open-source platform for longevity risk management that includes longevity indices. In 2008 he was involved in executing the world's first longevity hedges using capital markets swaps. He is an active participant in the newly formed Life & Longevity Markets Association (LLMA), a cross-industry body set up to promote the development of the market for longevity risk transfer. He chairs the Technical Committee of the LLMA. Guy holds a BSc degree from the University of Western Australia, a DPhil in physics from Oxford University and an MBA from Henley Business School.

Edouard Debonneuil is head of research & development at AXA Global Life, an actuarial team dedicated to advising AXA entities in the world to define life products and transfer financial risks in an optimal manner. Their advice comes from models and visions of life risks, adapted from external research to each specific case. Longevity is a major topic, in terms of risk assessment, forecast, handling, transfer, community and product positioning. After studies in maths, computer science and finance at the Ecole Centrale Paris, Edouard pursued his MSc and PhD degrees in two directions: biophysics models (UCLA 2003, Pasteur Institute 2006) and biology of ageing (Paris V 2003, Inserm 2006). Before joining AXA in 2009, he worked as an interest rates quant at HSBC in charge of inflation, and he led the creation of actuarial products, mostly longevity derivatives through UK equity release mortgages.

Jennifer Donohue is a partner in the corporate department of the London office of Cadwalader, Wickersham & Taft LLP. Jennifer was called to the Bar of England and Wales and later admitted as a solicitor of the Supreme Court of England and Wales (1992). She was, for a number of years, a senior legal adviser to the Department of Trade and Industry and has subsequently been consulted to advise the UK government and other governments on a number of projects including high profile legislative drafting and UK Financial Investments Ltd (UKFI), which manages the UK government's shareholding in banks subscribing to its recapitalisation fund. She specialises in non-contentious transactional insurance and reinsurance, and has advised insurance companies on mergers and acquisitions, capitalisations, reorganisations, structuring, policy and product development and pre-insolvency strategies such as schemes of arrangement and managed exits such as run off. She worked for several years with PricewaterhouseCoopers on financing solutions. She is currently heavily engaged in finding much needed financing solutions in the insurance and banking sectors based on forensic engineering and modelling that focuses on provisions of regulatory capital and techniques such as the use of derivatives, insurance-linked securities and monetisations.

Nick Dumbreck is practice leader and a consulting actuary with the London office of Milliman. Before joining Milliman in April 2009 he spent 23 years at Watson Wyatt, including seven years as head of the firm's global insurance consulting practice. He began his career at Imperial Life of Canada. Nick advises life assurance clients on a wide range of matters, including mergers and acquisitions and financial management, and he has been heavily involved in the restructuring of the UK life industry over the past 15 years. Nick has been appointed actuary to several life companies in the UK and Ireland, and is actuarial function holder for two UK life companies. He was the president of the Institute of Actuaries from 2006 to 2008. He holds an MA in mathematics from the University of Cambridge.

Eli Friedwald heads a team at Reinsurance Group of America (RGA), which develops mortality, morbidity and longevity bases for use in treaty pricing. Eli joined RGA in 2005, having spent the majority of his career as product actuary at Lincoln Assurance, where he was responsible for the life, investment and pensions ranges. During this period he was involved in the pricing and marketing development of some of the earliest and most innovative universal life, critical illness and long-term care products.

Baroness Sally Greengross has been an independent cross-bench member of the House of Lords since 2000 and chairs four All-Party Parliamentary Groups: Corporate Social Responsibility; Intergenerational Futures: Old & Young Together, Continence Care and Dementia. She is the vice chair of the All-Party Parliamentary Group on Dementia and Ageing and Older People, and is treasurer of the All-Party Parliamentary Group on Equalities. In December 2006, she was announced as a commissioner for the Equality and Human Rights Commission. Baroness Greengross was director general of Age Concern England from 1987 until 2000. Until 2000, she was joint chair of the Age Concern Institute of Gerontology at Kings College London, and secretary general of Eurolink Age. She is chair of the Advisory Groups for the English Longitudinal Study of Ageing (ELSA) and the New Dynamics of Ageing (NDA). She is chief executive of the International Longevity Centre UK, president of the Pensions Policy Institute and honorary vice president of the Royal Society for the Promotion of Health. She holds honorary doctorates from seven UK universities.

Lise He is a life actuary working in the risk management team of the AXA Group in Paris. She is in charge of topics related to Solvency II and the modelling of the internal economic capital for life insurance risks, focusing more specifically on lapse risk. She has also been involved in the development of long term care (LTC or dependency) products in several countries. She previously worked for Scor Global Life in the international research and development team for LTC insurance. Lise is a qualified member of the French Institute of Actuaries, and holds a Masters' degree in economics from the Ecole Nationale de la Statistique et de l'Administration Economique.

Jason Hurley is head of sales and marketing for RGA's UK operation, offering a range of reinsurance solutions. He was instrumental in building the underwritten annuity business in the UK and helped to promote the product in many overseas markets. He is twice winner of the UK Reinsurance Personality of the Year and a frequent speaker at seminars and workshops. He often writes in the trade press and chaired the organising committee of many Institute of Actuaries Health Conferences. Jason previously worked for AMP-NPI in the IFA sales team as their business development actuary, selling Corporate Pension Schemes to the top end of the IFA market, particularly the firms of consultant actuaries. He has also worked for the Actuarial Education Company, and started his career at Sun Life in Bristol, working in marketing, pricing and product development. He qualified as an actuary in 1995.

Farzana Ismail is a consulting actuary with the London office of Milliman. She has significant experience in annuity business, which includes advising buyers and sellers of blocks of annuities, reviewing annuity cashflow and mortality projection models, reviewing payouts on annuity risk transfer transactions from investors' and trustees' viewpoints, undertaking capital reviews of annuity writers and feasibility studies of longevity risk securitisation structures in the UK and Europe. In addition, she has worked on various Solvency II projects, including QIS5, and supported several with-profits actuaries and actuarial function holders for a number of life insurers. Her experience also includes assignments on embedded value and Part VII transfers of life funds, mergers and acquisitions. Farzana holds an MSc from Cass Business School and is a graduate of the London School of Economics and Political Science. She is a fellow of the Institute and Faculty of Actuaries.

Gavin Jones is senior longevity actuary at Swiss Re, where he works within the chief pricing office in the researching, costing, acquisition and management of longevity risk. Before this he worked as mortality research actuary at Prudential, where he co-authored the Staple Inn Actuarial Society paper "Financial Aspects of Longevity Risk". He is a fellow of the Institute of Actuaries and holds a PhD in mathematics from the University of Cambridge.

Nick Ketley is the vice president of the global life & health risk transformation team at Swiss Re in London, focusing on the alternative risk transfer and retrocession of life insurance risks, including longevity. Nick joined the UK reinsurance business of Swiss Re in 2005, initially covering roles in both valuation and pricing. Prior to joining Swiss Re he worked in the financial markets, focusing on the trading and broking of fixed income securities. Nick is a fellow of the Institute of Actuaries and holder of a postgraduate diploma in actuarial science from Cass Business School. He also holds a master's degree in mechanical engineering, manufacture and management from the University of Birmingham.

Joseph Lu is the mortality risk actuary at Legal & General, responsible for the management of mortality risks in the pricing and reserving for annuity businesses. He has been active in working parties relating to longevity risks with The Actuarial Profession in the UK and Society of Actuaries in North America. He has co-authored papers including the Best Sessional Papers of 2004 and 2006, awarded by the Institute and Faculty of Actuaries.

Stephen Makin is an independent actuarial consultant with 15 years' experience in the UK life industry, covering actuarial modelling, product development, commercial transactions, insurance restructuring, asset strategy, longevity research, economic capital and Solvency II. Before starting his own consulting firm, Stephen was Solvency II annuities actuary at Prudential UK & Europe, leading the implementation of Solvency II for their annuity businesses, focusing on developing the internal capital model and associated longevity risk distributions. Prior to that, he was Prudential's head of longevity research. He has published papers and articles on longevity, as well as presenting at actuarial and insurance conferences. Stephen is a fellow of the Institute and Faculty of Actuaries and has a first-class degree in mathematics from The University of Edinburgh.

Alison McKie was appointed as head of the global life & health risk transformation team at Swiss Re in August 2006 to review transformation mechanisms for Swiss Re's life and health business, to support active capital and risk management, including transfer of risk to the capital markets through securitisation and other techniques. Alison joined Swiss Re in 2003 as the finance director for the global life & health business group before being appointed chief financial officer for Swiss Re Life & Health. Alison began her career at PricewaterhouseCoopers. Alison holds an LLB (Hons) from the University of Birmingham and is a qualified ACA.

James Morris works in the longevity markets group at Credit Suisse, and is responsible for originating new longevity and asset risk from pension schemes in the UK. He joined Credit Suisse in March 2009, having spent several years at Dresdner Kleinwort working on the origination of various types of illiquid assets, including insurance risk (both life and non-life). James began his career as a solicitor at Slaughter and May. He holds an MA (Hons) in english literature from the University of Oxford.

Jessica Mosher is a life actuary working in the risk management team of the AXA Group in Paris. She has worked on topics related to Solvency II and the development of the internal economic capital model for life insurance risks, focusing more specifically on pandemics and mortality as well as stochastic longevity modelling. She previously worked for the AXA subsidiary in New York in various pricing and projection roles. Jessica is a fellow of the Society of Actuaries, and holds a BSc in economics from the Wharton School of the University of Pennsylvania.

Norman Peard is an actuary. His career has included roles with leading global actuarial consultants to the insurance and pensions industry, global reinsurers, investment banks and in financial regulation. He has worked to develop and implement non-traditional reinsurance and capital markets based solutions, including insurance-linked securitisation, and has also contributed to the development of policy as to the regulatory treatment of insurance-linked securitisation in the UK as well as broader insurance regulatory policy. Norman was closely involved with the Europe-wide Solvency II project and represented the UK on the Committee of European Insurance and Occupational Pensions Supervisors Pillar 1 Working Group. In his role at Credit Suisse, Norman combines his actuarial, insurance technical, commercial and regulatory experience to develop solutions for capital and risk management for insurance and pensions industry participants. Norman is a graduate of Trinity College Dublin, with an MA and Gold Medal in mathematics. He is a fellow of the Institute of Actuaries, a fellow of the Society of Actuaries in Ireland and an associate of the Society of Actuaries.

Philip Simpson is a principal and consulting actuary in the London office of Milliman. He has significant experience on UK annuity assignments, including advising sellers of blocks on annuities on price and structure, advising new entrants to the longevity market on pricing, underwriting factors and strategy and advising reinsurers on pricing bases and terms of trade. He is the author of three independent expert reports on the reinsurance and transfer of large annuity, having worked with a large investment bank on the development of a UK longevity index, and with a large international investment bank on analysing international longevity trends and correlations. Prior to being a consultant, Philip was a professional reinsurer for 12 years. He is a fellow of the Institute and Faculty of Actuaries and a fellow of the Society of Actuaries in Ireland. He holds an MBA from Edinburgh Business School and a BSc in mathematics and theoretical physics St Andrew's University.

Paul Sweeting is a professor of actuarial science at the University of Kent. Previously, he led the development of longevity reinsurance strategy for Munich Reinsurance, before which he was director of research at Fidelity Investment's Retirement Institute. As well as being a fellow of the Institute of Actuaries, Paul is a fellow of the Chartered Institute for Securities and Investments and a CFA charterholder. He has written a number of articles on longevity-related topics and is a regular commentator on pensions and investment issues.

Nathalie Weiss graduated from the Ecole Nationale de la Statistique et de l'Administration Economique (ENSAE) and is currently working in the risk management team of the AXA Group in Paris. She has worked on topics related to life insurance from both the market and the risk perspective. She has focused more specifically on the subjects of longevity, mortality, long-term care, medical breakthroughs and pandemics, on which she produces regular newsletters. Prior to joining AXA in 2008, she performed economic and statistical studies for the Centre Scientifique et Technique du Bâtiment in Paris.

Foreword

Globally, we are going through an extraordinary demographic transition. It is estimated that there will be 2 billion people over the age of 60 by the middle of the 21st Century, and they will outnumber children (ie, those under 15), for the first time in history. In some countries, such as the UK, we are seeing not just a growth in the numbers of older people but also an increase in the incidence of long-term conditions, including dementia. Over the past 15 years, health services in the UK have seen significant investment alongside further evolutionary reform. Despite these huge improvements, there are marked differences in the health of different groups. Although life expectancy for all people is increasing, inequality in mortality is now greater than at any time since comparable records began, and the higher an individual's socio-economic group, the longer they are likely to live. These demographic realities call for far-reaching work, lifestyle, business and governmental changes, for we are still living with public policies and social infrastructures that were designed for a different time with different demographics.

However, rather than seeing longevity as a burden, we should always celebrate the unprecedented triumph of living in an ageing society. We must all commit to helping this generation and the next live differently, more productively and with greater fulfilment for themselves and society, into their eighties and beyond. We need innovative solutions to improve health and wellness, expand work opportunities and provide ongoing education and financial planning to turn what could be a fiscal and political crisis into platforms for economic growth and intergenerational collaboration. We must ensure the economic and social force of older people is heeded by demonstrating how future society can benefit from being, in all senses of the word, more mature.

If, as it seems, society will be able to provide less of a safety-net for its citizens than previously, then individuals will have to take greater responsibility for planning their own, and their families', health and lifestyle outcomes, both in working life and in old age. As well as managing their wealth, this means taking a sensible approach to lifestyle issues such as obesity, exercise, etc. If these individuals are to cope successfully with this increased exposure to managing their own morbidity, longevity and mortality risks, they will need support from suitable high-quality financial products and services designed to assist them. However, first they will need the appropriate education, information and advice to allow them both to understand the requirement for timely action on their part and to make the right decisions for their own circumstances. For those outcomes to come to pass successfully over the long term, the providers of those products and services will need a comprehensive understanding of how to price and manage the longevity risks we all face. This valuable book goes a very long way towards fulfilling that important need.

Baroness Sally Greengross OBE
Chief Executive, International Longevity Centre (ILC-UK)
Westminster, February 2011

Introduction

Living a long life is a goal common to us all, and for an increasing proportion of us achieving this goal is becoming more likely. This is to be celebrated. However, it also raises challenges regarding how individuals manage their wealth and how society can provide a backstop for those who live beyond their means.

These challenges have been met in recent history through pension and insurance arrangements such as annuities, protection being in place if an individual lives longer than might be expected. This situation, however, becomes a major problem for pension schemes, insurance companies and governments if the majority of the individuals covered live longer than expected. This exposure is known as longevity risk: the topic of this book.

Managing longevity risk requires an understanding of the full gamut of issues from pricing, reserving and capital requirements to risk management and capital market developments. These diverse topics are thoughtfully taken up in this text by leading experts in the field of longevity risk, whose extensive experience cuts across disciplines from (re)insurance to capital markets to law and academia. These varied perspectives give readers a balanced view of the issues in managing longevity risk.

PART I: SETTING THE SCENE

To understand longevity risk it is important to first appreciate the impressive developments in life expectancy and their evolution. With half of babies in certain countries predicted to become centenarians, in Chapter 1 Nathalie Weiss, Lise He, Jessica Mosher and Edouard Debonneuil set the scene for the ageing population, addressing whether there is convergence between countries and considering the impact of environmental, social and medical advancements. With worldwide private pension fund assets in excess of US$22 trillion, Ed Collinge and Joseph Lu then explore in Chapter 2 the magnitude of the longevity issue, capacity for this risk and its market opportunity as well as the array of insurance products and pension schemes containing the risk.

PART II: PRICING LONGEVITY RISK

The lack of a common view on the future development of longevity has forced practitioners to rely on a variety of assumptions in pricing annuity and pension products: an area that has become a key challenge to experts in this field. To make the topic more digestible, we break down the problem into two major items. First, in Chapter 3 Eli Friedwald addresses how to establish base (or current) levels of mortality; then, in Chapter 4 Bridget Browne considers how to project future improvements.

Age and sex are well-established drivers in assessing longevity risk, but other factors also have an impact. With financially secure individuals generally living longer than their less well-off counterparts, consideration also needs to be given to risk factors such as annuity amount, socio-economic class, geographical spread and postcode, as well as to ways in which these factors can be used in predictive pricing. Practitioners use many tools to establish base mortality levels and project future improvements – including graduation techniques, projection methodologies, experience analyses and credibility theory – and these approaches are explored in the context of the underlying population. Specific consideration is also given to situations in which data is often scarce, such as for older ages.

Pricing has also become ever more complex with the introduction of underwritten annuities which use differential pricing for medical conditions (such as cardiovascular risks and cancers) and lifestyle factors (such as smoking and obesity). The advent of this market has a profound selection effect on annuity portfolios and is considered in a discussion by Jason Hurley and Greg Becker, who, in Chapter 5, review the pricing of underwritten annuities and its impact on standard annuity portfolio pricing.

PART III: RESERVING AND CAPITAL REQUIREMENTS

Given the long duration of annuity contracts, holding appropriate reserves and capital is of paramount importance and the cost of capital needs to be reflected in pricing too. Focusing on the requirements for longevity risk, Stephen Makin takes a detailed look at the landscape of changing regulation and capital requirements. While the underlying longevity risk that is borne by insurance companies and pension schemes is fundamentally the same, both are bound by different requirements, which are summarised in Chapters 6 and 7.

Solvency II, the new EU regulatory risk-based solvency requirements for (re)insurance companies, will be a major regulatory change that will have global reach. Therefore, modelling techniques are presented that can be used to assess longevity risk capital as well as concepts of diversification and non-linearity.

Economic capital and enterprise risk management are considered leading frameworks for measuring and managing risk and are explored in the context of longevity risk. Makin ends with a discussion of how longevity risk fits into enterprise risk management and can be used in strategic applications such as capital allocation and de-risking strategies through, say, reinsurance. The goal is informed decision making through the measurement of longevity risk for those needing to manage the risk.

PART IV: RISK MANAGEMENT

Once the level of risk is understood, then, depending on your risk appetite and tolerance for longevity risk, the options available to de-risk need to be understood whether you are the chief financial officer of an insurance company or the trustee or sponsor of a pension scheme. In Chapter 8, Robert Bugg, Farzana Ismail, Nick Dumbreck and Philip Simpson consider the major alternative longevity de-risking methods available to insurance companies, and in Chapter 9 Norman Peard and James Morris focus on those available to pension schemes. Gavin Jones then considers in Chapter 10 the specific options available around reinsurance, and in Chapter 11 Alison McKie and Nick Ketley look at the potential ability to use pandemic risk as a natural hedge for longevity risk.

Key structural decisions for risk mitigation will typically depend on a number of factors, including the risks being transferred, the type of counterparty being engaged and the cost implications of each structure. Bugg *et al* explore the complete spectrum of full portfolio transfer, asset-backed and longevity-swap structures, as well as the form of the solution in terms of parametric (index) and indemnity (customised to scheme experience) based transactions. For pension schemes, Peard and Morris investigate buy-outs, buy-ins and longevity swaps in terms of the mechanics of how they work, their advantages and drawbacks and the relative merits of funded and unfunded transactions. Rapidly evolving market innovations are discussed such as "progressive de-risking" as a route to buy-out and sophisticated variations of longevity swaps with bespoke legs, synthetic buy-ins and insurance-wrapped solutions. Considerations around administration, dealing with both overpayments and late notifications of death and collateral, etc, are also covered.

While insurers and pension schemes are typically the first line of defence for de-risking, the ultimate risk often ends up with reinsurers. Therefore, Jones takes a close look at hedging longevity risk through reinsurance. Asset-backed risk transfer solutions potentially create substantial counterparty credit exposure, which are discussed in terms of practical strategies to reduce this such as novation, collateral and deposit back arrangements. Longevity swaps by design tend to have lower credit and counterparty exposure. The potential restrictions on long-term capacity are discussed in the context of the development of capital market solutions, which would enable insurers and reinsurers alike to manage their aggregate exposures.

It should be remembered that life (re)insurers also write significant volumes of assurance business, making them particularly vulnerable to sudden spikes in mortality from these portfolios. McKie and Ketley take up this issue in their discussion of whether pandemic risk can be considered a natural hedge for longevity risk. Mortality and longevity risk undoubtedly have structural differences, which leads to implications around basis risk associated with different underlying populations and duration mismatch. Yet, extreme mortality risk is also an uncorrelated asset class to longevity risk, and therefore how it can be utilised by an institution as part of a more complete hedging strategy is illustrated in Chapter 11.

PART V: CAPITAL MARKET DEVELOPMENTS

While mortality catastrophe bonds were among the first type of mortality capital market transaction, longevity based capital market transactions are emerging as an opportunity for investors seeking an uncorrelated asset class and an alternative route to de-risking. This development may solve longer term capital issues related to longevity risk by transferring longevity risk from pension schemes and (re)insurers to end investors.

This topic is explored by Guy Coughlan, who discusses in Chapter 12 the key benefits that the capital markets bring in terms of additional capacity, diversity of counterparties, liquidity, fungibiliy and potential for reduced counterparty exposure as well as the respective roles of the market participants from hedgers to investors and financial intermediaries. Building on the concepts explored in Part IV, he takes a detailed look at the specific major hedging solutions available in the capital markets including mortality forwards, survivor forwards and survivor longevity swaps.

Industry initiatives are also important in facilitating the development of a liquid market. Some, such as the launch of a cross-industry trade association, the Life & Longevity Markets Association (LLMA), are summarised in this part of the book. An important role in promoting transactions and raising the awareness of longevity risk has also been played by the launch of a range of mortality and longevity indices, such as the LifeMetrics toolkit, the Credit Suisse Longevity Index and the Deutsche Börse Xpect Index. Therefore, in Chapter 13, Paul Sweeting explores in depth the ideal requirements of indices for mortality- and longevity risk transfer and evaluates the suite of published indices against these criteria.

The transfer of longevity risk has an assortment of potential legal pitfalls, which are discussed in Chapter 14 by Jennifer Donohue, who delves into some of the key legal considerations for both reinsurance and capital markets. As Donohue cautions, experience shows that hastily constructed deals too often carry risks that transacting parties had not considered and are unable to manage.

This chapter brings to a close our appraisal of the challenges of managing longevity risk, but much work still needs to be done. Looking to the future, the magnitude of the exposure is poised to grow. Our ability to refine solutions to meet these challenges is not only a matter of ensuring the stability of the institutions accumulating longevity risk, but also an imperative for supporting the financial needs of the public as they journey into the ever further reaches of old age.

ACKNOWLEDGEMENTS

I would like to say a massive thank you to all of the contributors for their hard work and openness in sharing their personal views on longevity and for preparing many informative examples, illustrations and case studies that enrich the text and help to communicate the key concepts presented in this book.

I would also like to thank those who have actively supported my work on longevity at Milliman, including Harris Bak, Robert Bugg, Neil Cantle, Mary Clare, Matthew Cocke, Joshua Corrigan, Laurent Devineau, Dennis De Vries, Jeff Dukes, Nick Dumbreck, Gary Finkelstein, Martijn Fonville, Dale Hagstrom, Timothy Harris, Farzana Ismail, Al Klein, Nigel Knowles, John McKenzie, Wade Matterson, Scott Mitchell, Silvia Mizzoni, Ken Mungan, Jim Murphy, Padraic O'Malley, Russell Osman, Alan Routhenstein, Steven Schreiber, Philip Simpson, Stuart Silverman, Daniel Theodore and Bruce Winterhof.

Finally, a special thank you also to those who have supported the production of this book in more ways than one, including Lynette Kubale, Nick Carver and Lewis O'Sullivan at Incisive Media, Emma Dain at T&T Productions Ltd, London, Stephen Conwill, Jeremy Engdahl-Johnson and Oliver Gillespie at Milliman, my parents and my husband Brett and my three children, Amy, Sophie and Henry, who are pleased it contains some pictures (albeit in the form of graphs!).

All editor royalties from this publication will be donated to The Anaphylaxis Campaign.

Emma McWilliam
January 2011

Part I

Setting the Scene

1

Ageing Populations and Changing Demographics

Edouard Debonneuil, Lise He, Jessica Mosher, Nathalie Weiss
Groupe AXA

The advancements in longevity in developed countries over the last few decades have been impressive, though these improvements have not affected all countries uniformly. Experts do not agree on what the future holds in terms of longevity. Some demographers estimate that the trend will continue at the pace observed in 2010 or perhaps more steadily than it has, while others argue that life expectancy will increase at a slower rate, stabilise or even decline in some developed countries due to socio-environmental variables. The drivers of longevity remain complex, and the exact consequences of emerging threats such as obesity, electromagnetic waves, genetic engineering, pollution, etc, on life expectancy are heavily debated. Still, living longer may well happen to a degree that will surprise many people.

We begin this chapter by considering the overall trends in longevity in terms of life expectancies at birth and at older ages, and discussing whether there has been convergence among countries and sexes. We then explore the consequences of the ageing population and the increase in the number of centenarians as well as the evolution of the old-age dependency ratio. However, while individuals may be living longer, it is not always clear that the quality of additional years is improving. Comparisons are inevitable, some of which are examined in studies of different countries in terms of morbidity at older ages. We introduce analysis of trends based on the major historical causes of death. The chapter concludes by considering some of the future challenges and opportunities in terms of limits to life expectancies and the impact of environmental, social, dietary and possible medical breakthroughs.

Figure 1.1 Period life expectancy at birth for France from 1816 to 2007

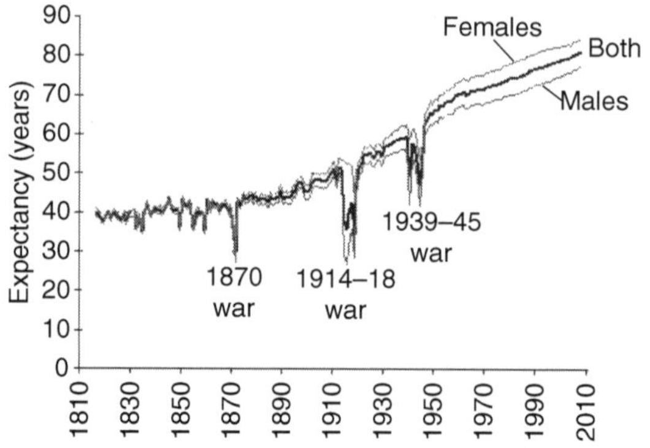

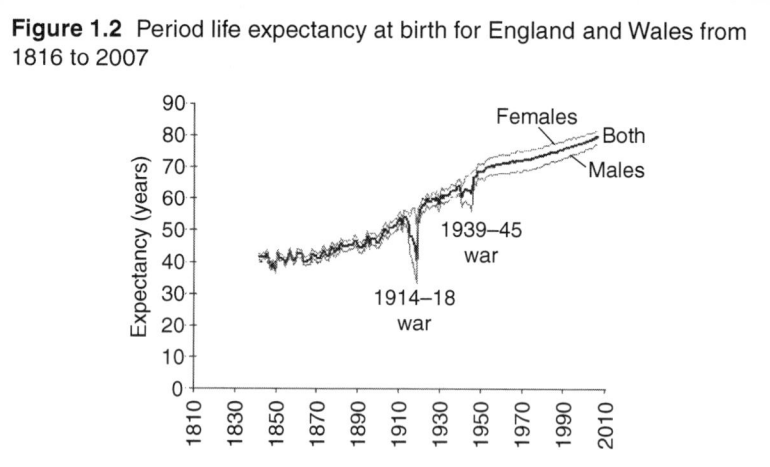

In 1816: 40 (both), 39 (male), 41.1 (female). In 2007: 81.1 (both), 77.4 (male), 84.4 (female).
Source: Human Mortality Database.

Figure 1.2 Period life expectancy at birth for England and Wales from 1816 to 2007

In 1841: 41.7 (both), 40.6 (male), 42.6 (female). In 2006: 79.8 (both), 77.5 (male), 81.7 (female).
Source: Human Mortality Database.

Life expectancy at birth

A study by Vaupel *et al* (2009) predicts that future longevity improvements will allow one-half of the babies born in 2007 to reach the age of 102 in Germany, 103 in the UK, 104 in France and the US and even 107 in Japan. According to Vaupel *et al*, past improvements and the lack of any indication of a slowdown in the progress of life

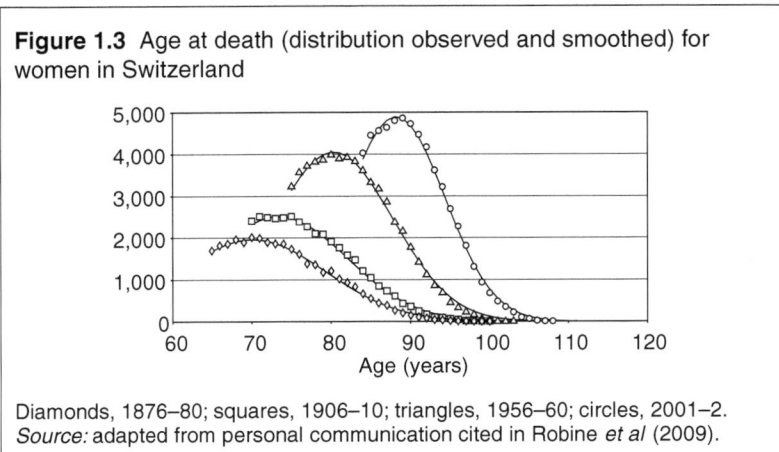

Figure 1.3 Age at death (distribution observed and smoothed) for women in Switzerland

Diamonds, 1876–80; squares, 1906–10; triangles, 1956–60; circles, 2001–2.
Source: adapted from personal communication cited in Robine et al (2009).

expectancy suggest there would be no reason to assume that this progress would not continue.

The trend in increasing life expectancy at birth is shown in Figures 1.1 and 1.2 which introduce the evolution of the "period life expectancy" at birth (in years) for France and for England and Wales, respectively, from 1816 to 2007. The "period life expectancy" at birth for a given year represents the average number of years of life remaining if a group of persons at that age were to experience the mortality rates for that year over the course of their remaining lives.

The figures clearly demonstrate the effects of the Franco-Prussian war of 1870 in France and similarly devastating effects of World War I, the 1918 Spanish influenza outbreak and World War II in both France and England and Wales, among other shocks.

Past stages in the improvement of life expectancy

Over the past 150 years, increases in life expectancies in the "developed" world have occurred at different stages. In the beginning of the period, consecutive increases occurred due to reductions in infant mortality. These increases were followed by an improvement in mortality (ie, reduction in mortality rates) for adults during the middle of the 20th Century, and in more recent years significant improvements in mortality for the elderly. Over the last 20 years or so, the reduction in mortality rates for women over the age of 80 has been the largest contributor to the higher life expectancy observed. The age-specific contributions to record life expectancy resulting

Figure 1.4 Increase in the modal age at death for women in Japan from 1950–1954 to 2000–2004

Source: Cheung and Robine (2007).

Table 1.1 Age-specific contributions to record life expectancy (in %)

Age (years)	1850–1900	1900–1925	1925–1950	1950–1975	1975–1990	1990–2007
0–14	**62.13**	**54.75**	30.99	29.72	11.20	5.93
15–49	29.09	31.55	**37.64**	17.70	6.47	4.67
50–64	5.34	9.32	18.67	16.27	24.29	10.67
65–79	3.17	4.44	12.72	**28.24**	**40.57**	37.22
>80	0.27	−0.06	−0.03	8.07	17.47	**41.51**

From 1850 to 2007, record life expectancy in women was held by six countries: Norway, New Zealand (except Maoris), Iceland, the Netherlands, Sweden and Japan.
Source: Christensen *et al* (2009). Data from Human Mortality Database.

from reductions in death rates at different ages between 1850 and 2007 are illustrated in Table 1.1 for females in the listed countries. The changes in the contributions by age group are highlighted.

An additional illustration of this progression (Robine *et al* 2009) is shown in Figure 1.3, which gives the distribution of age at death in Switzerland over different periods of time. What becomes apparent in the figure is that the curve shifts to the right, with peaks of the numbers of deaths occurring at increasingly higher ages. A similar pattern is also shown for Japanese females in Figure 1.4, which demonstrates that individuals are living longer and the majority of deaths are occurring at older ages than in the past.

These different phases in the evolution of longevity also explain why life expectancy at birth is not always the best indicator of the overall trend, and that the analysis of life expectancy at age 40 and higher could be more relevant, especially for projections related to annuities and pension payments.

Record low levels of mortality are also being reached in some countries around the world at the time of writing. For example, a 2009 study by the UK Office for National Statistics[1] (ONS) shows that in 2008 mortality reached a new low, with the rate of 700 deaths per 100,000 males and 499 deaths per 100,000 females. Over the past 40 years mortality fell by 51% for males and 43% for females. During the 1960s and 1970s, the most significant improvements in mortality (ie, reductions in mortality rates) were recorded for ages between 35 and 59. Between 1980 and 2008, the ages experiencing the largest reductions in mortality rates were those between 60 and 79.

Similar reductions in mortality rates have been observed in other countries too. According to the Institut National d'Etudes Démographiques (INED), the mortality for individuals between the ages of 40 and 70 decreased by approximately 50% (54% for women and 39% for men) throughout Western Europe from 1952 to 2006.

Mortality rates have also continued to decrease over time for ages 80 or older in countries with a high life expectancy, including those countries such as France and Japan that have already experienced extremely low mortality rates for these advanced ages.

International studies by Rau *et al* (2006, 2008) analyse the available demographic data on elderly people for more than 30 countries included in the Kannisto–Thatcher (K–T) database (maintained by the Max Planck Institute for Demographic Research) on old-age mortality. The study confirms that the mortality rates continued to decline at older ages (80 and over). However, it also demonstrates that differences exist among countries: in the US, older age mortality has been stagnant since 1980, while in France and Japan the rate of the decrease of mortality rates at older ages (though already very low) has not slowed down. In Japan, the life expectancy at age 80 in 2008 was 8.5 years for men and 11.4 years for women.

A significant global trend

The trend of increasing life expectancies is generally observed worldwide and has been significant for some countries that have recorded both local and world records. Some examples are given below.

- According to the 2009 Japanese Ministry of Health data on the country's population, life expectancy at birth was slightly more than 79 years for males and 86 years for females: a world record for both sexes. Over one year, the Japanese males gained 37 days of life expectancy and women 22 days.
- In the US, life expectancy surpassed 78 years for the first time in 2008, and was projected to reach 79 by 2015. New mortality tables were then issued to allow for a maximum attainable age of 121.
- Since 1900, life expectancy at birth (for both sexes combined) has doubled in many countries including Spain, Greece, Austria and has exceeded 80 years in 11 countries.
- In Eastern Asia, where the average life expectancy at birth was 45 years in 1950, it is now more than 73 years.
- Significant improvements have also been observed in Latin America, Eastern Europe and in some African countries.

Differences in life expectancies across countries

While the trend of increasing life expectancies is global, there are still many variations that exist between countries.

The Human Mortality Database (HMD)[2] provides useful population data for 37 countries, the majority of which are developed. The database – a result of the collaboration efforts between the Max Planck Institute and the University of Berkeley – can be used for multiple research analyses and comparisons across countries. Chapter 3 explores the types of data and periods of data over which mortality rates are available.

One characteristic of the data is how specific the results are for each country. Table 1.2 shows that over the past 50 years (since 1960), Japan has largely led the improvements in life expectancy at birth for both males and females. Australia and Italy followed for males, and Spain and Italy for females. While some countries such as the US, UK and Belgium have had relatively lower levels of improvements over the same period, they have still experienced improvements nonetheless.

Tables 1.3 and 1.4 provide examples of the country-specificity of improvements in life expectancy for a given age (at birth and at age 65).

Table 1.2 Average annual gain in life expectancy at birth by country (months)

Country	Last available data	Since 1960		Last 10 years	
		Males	Females	Males	Females
Australia	2007	3.0	2.5	4.1	2.8
Belgium	2006	2.3	2.3	3.3	2.1
Canada	2005	2.6	2.4	3.5	2.2
France	2007	2.6	2.8	3.5	2.5
Germany	2008	2.6	2.5	3.4	2.1
Italy	2006	3.0	3.2	**4.2**	**3.0**
Japan	2008	**3.5**	**4.0**	2.5	2.5
Luxembourg	2006	2.8	2.5	4.3	2.6
Spain	2006	2.9	3.3	3.7	2.6
Switzerland	2007	2.7	2.5	3.7	2.4
UK	2006	2.4	2.0	3.6	2.6
US	2006	2.2	1.9	2.8	1.6

Bold denotes the countries with the highest annual gains. For example, in Italy, males have realised an average annual gain of 3 months or a quarter of life expectancy at birth since 1960, and 4.2 months in the last 10 years.
Source: Human Mortality Database.

Is there convergence of life expectancies across countries?

The answer to this commonly asked question is not clear. In some countries, life expectancy has even been decreasing. For example, between 1985 and 2005 Russian males saw a nearly four-year decrease in their life expectancy at birth from 62.7 years to 58.9 years and a nearly one-year decrease from 73.2 years to 72.4 years for females (based on data from the Human Mortality Database). Some reasons cited for the decrease have included the decline in the quality of the health-care system, the consumption of alcohol and a potential degradation of socio-economic conditions. In Africa (particularly in the southern part of the continent), stagnation or even a decline in life expectancy at birth has been observed for several countries due to the AIDS epidemic, which affects many children and young adults. For example, the US Census Bureau estimates the male and female life expectancy at birth in Botswana was 22 and 28 years lower, respectively, in 2006 than it would have been without the mortality due to AIDS (Velkoff and Kowal 2007). In Zimbabwe, life expectancy at birth decreased by 21 years for males and 27 years for females between 1986 and 2006 for the same reasons.

Table 1.3 Period life expectancy at birth by country (years)

Country	Last available data	Life expectancy (males)	Life expectancy (females)	Difference between sexes
Australia	2007	**79.3**	83.8	4.5
Belgium	2007	76.9	82.3	5.4
Canada	2006	78.3	82.9	4.6
France	2007	77.4	84.4	**7.0**
Germany	2008	77.6	82.4	4.9
Italy	2006	78.6	84.1	5.5
Japan	2008	79.3	**86.0**	6.7
Luxembourg	2006	76.7	81.8	5.1
Spain	2006	77.6	84.1	6.5
Switzerland	2007	**79.3**	84.1	4.8
UK	2006	77.5	81.7	4.3
USA	2006	75.5	80.7	5.2

Source: Human Mortality Database (downloaded in June 2010).

Table 1.4 Period life expectancy at age 65 by country (years)

Country	Last available data	Life expectancy (males)	Life expectancy (females)	Difference between sexes
Australia	2007	**18.7**	21.7	3.0
Belgium	2007	17.2	20.7	3.6
Canada	2006	18.2	21.3	3.1
France	2007	18.2	22.5	4.4
Germany	2008	17.3	20.4	3.2
Italy	2006	17.8	21.6	3.8
Japan	2008	18.6	**23.6**	**5.0**
Luxembourg	2006	16.9	20.2	3.3
Spain	2006	17.7	21.6	3.9
Switzerland	2007	18.5	21.9	3.4
UK	2006	17.4	20.1	2.8
US	2006	17.5	20.2	2.7

Source: Human Mortality Database (downloaded in June 2010).

It has appeared at certain times in the past as though life expectancies may be converging across countries but this trend has been short lived. In general, convergence has not occurred, even across developed countries. Figure 1.5 and Figure 1.6 show, for example,

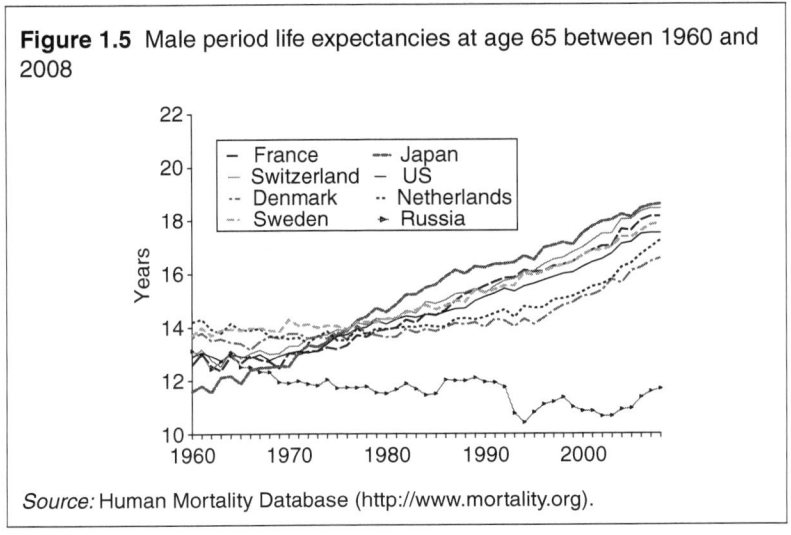

Figure 1.5 Male period life expectancies at age 65 between 1960 and 2008

Source: Human Mortality Database (http://www.mortality.org).

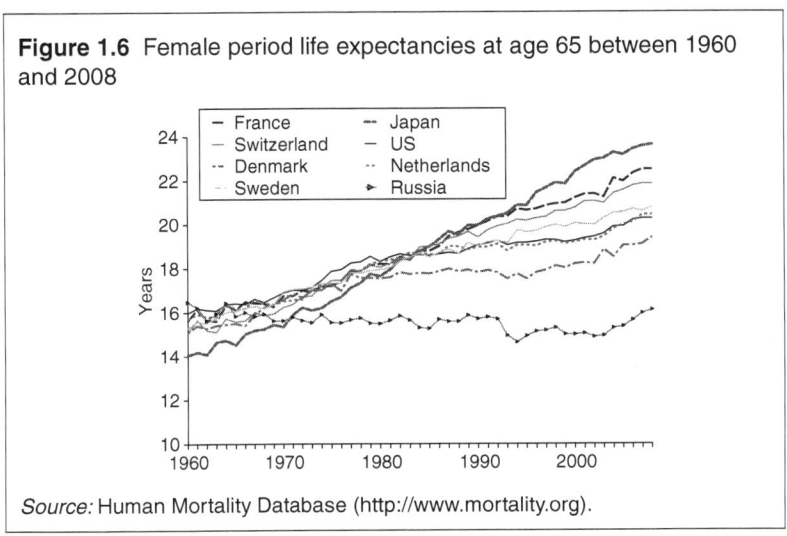

Figure 1.6 Female period life expectancies at age 65 between 1960 and 2008

Source: Human Mortality Database (http://www.mortality.org).

that although life expectancies at age 65 for males and females in seven Western countries appeared to converge until the 1970s and 1980s, they diverged afterwards, with life expectancies continuing to increase in the majority of countries but at different rates.

The study of the evolution of life expectancies at birth in European countries shows, however, that the divergence in life expectancies began much earlier in Europe. By grouping countries into three categories:

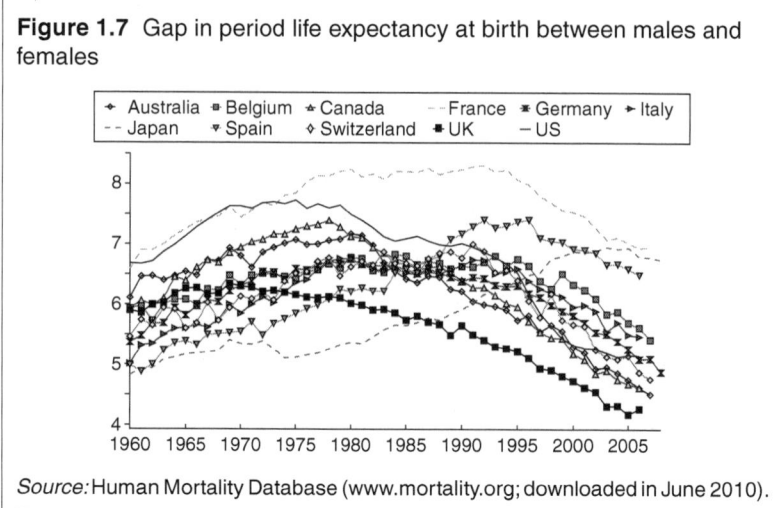

Figure 1.7 Gap in period life expectancy at birth between males and females

Source: Human Mortality Database (www.mortality.org; downloaded in June 2010).

- high convergence, meaning a rapid progression,
- low convergence (low progression) and
- divergent (stable progression, possible regression),

Robine *et al* (2005) showed that the divergence in life expectancies actually started to reappear in 1960. Their analysis also revealed that it is possible for a country to have a low convergence for one sex and a high convergence for the other, as shown for France.

Convergence between males and females

The gap between life expectancies for males and females raises the question of whether there is mortality convergence between the sexes. There is no obvious convergence over time as pointed out in Figure 1.7, which illustrates the gap in period life expectancies at birth between males and females.

In all of the Organisation for Economic Co-operation and Development (OECD) countries shown, females have a higher life expectancy than males at every age. This difference reflects the fact that female mortality rates are lower than those of males for every age group and for most of the main causes of death. The reasons have not been clearly established, although fundamental biology as well as the use of tobacco is often cited. The countries for which the difference between female and male life expectancies is particularly striking are Japan (where in 2008 there was a 6.7-year gap at birth and a 5-year gap at age 65) and France (where in 2007 there was a 7-year gap at birth and 4.4 years at age 65). Not only is the difference between the sexes obvious by country, but the narrowing of the gap also varies greatly. In some countries, such as Australia, the life expectancy of men seems to approach that of women, but in others, such as Japan and also notably ex-USSR countries in Eastern Europe, this situation is not the case.

The cohort effect

Other trends have also emerged in the mortality data of some countries. One such trend, known as the "cohort effect", is where different improvement rates are seen in a generation born within a certain time period compared with those for the generation before or after. This effect is especially evident in the UK, where the generation born between 1925 and 1945 has experienced impressive improvements in longevity, well above those born in previous generations and even those born afterwards. This cohort effect is not homogenous across countries or periods. Biomedical researchers are becoming more and more interested in the cohort effect, which is believed to result from exposure from a young age to certain socio-environmental variables (Willets 2007). The cohort effect is described further in Chapter 4.

Lifestyle drivers

A number of lifestyle drivers of mortality such as socio-economic and lifestyle factors give rise to marked differences in life expectancies not only between countries but also within the same country. The drivers of mortality are considered further in Chapter 3.

In 2008, one study by the World Health Organization (WHO) established, among other things, that a child born in certain suburbs of Glasgow, Scotland, can have a life expectancy 28 years lower than one born just 13 kilometres away, and that adult mortality can be 2.5 times higher in more disadvantaged areas in the UK compared with more well-off areas (World Health Organization 2007). This finding provides evidence about what factors are driving the annuity pricing by postcode in the UK.

The influence of socio-economic inequalities on mortality is supported by numerous other studies. For example, females between the ages of 25 and 59 in England and Wales from disadvantaged classes had a higher rate of mortality over the period 2001–3 than the other classes (Office for National Statistics 2009). In this case, some causes of death are more sensitive to socio-economic variables (such as respiratory illness, gastro-intestinal diseases, blood disorders or lung cancer). However, there are other causes of death which depend less on class. For example, the mortality from breast cancer is similar for women across classes.

Lifestyles

Lifestyles have also been shown to have an impact on mortality. The fact that the citizens of southwest France have a longer life and lower rate of heart attacks despite their consumption of wine and a diet rich in fat (a phenomenon known as the French Paradox) raises the question of the role of nutrition in longevity. Other "longevity diets" that have been studied include those from Crete and Okinawa.

The variables that influence the evolution of longevity are diverse: socio-economic environment, genetic factors, lifestyle (eg, diet, alcohol and tobacco consumption and physical activity). Estimating the magnitude of the contribution of each variable to longevity is difficult.

The WHO has shown that, for retired British residents, tobacco addiction has been one of the main predictive factors in mortality, while moderate consumption of alcohol is a less significant risk factor. This finding may be explained in certain cases by the total avoidance of alcohol for medical reasons being potentially more prevalent among those in poor health. On the other hand, certain components in wine have also been shown to have anti-inflammatory effects.

Diet has also been shown to influence longevity. For example, an American epidemiological study that looked at the effects of nutrition concluded that the consumption of calcium can protect against cancer of the digestive system (Park *et al* 2009; World Cancer Research Fund and American Institute for Cancer Research 2007). Some studies have found a correlation between well-being and happiness and longevity.

CONSEQUENCES: AGEING OF THE POPULATION AND CHANGES IN THE OLD-AGE DEPENDENCY RATIO

The increase in life expectancy combined with the lower birth rate in virtually all countries is driving the overall ageing of the global population. US Census Bureau population data and projections by age group and sex (Kinsella and He 2009) indicate a rather striking trend in the ageing of population for developed countries and to lesser extent for developing countries for the years 1960, 2000 and 2040. The unprecedented growth in older populations shown at the top of each chart in Figure 1.8 reshapes the distribution of population from what had been a well-formed pyramid in 1960 to nearer a column by 2040.

The ageing phenomenon

The increase in the proportion of older individuals relative to the total population appears relentless. The US Census Bureau (Kinsella and He 2009) has projected that in 2040 the portion of the population over the age of 65 will be more than 28% in Western Europe, and (approximately) 25% in Eastern Europe, 20% in North America and Australia, 15% in Asia and South America, 13% in North Africa, 10% in the Middle East and 4% in Sub-Saharan Africa. Furthermore, individuals who are older than 80 will represent increasing proportions, for example, nearly 10% of the total population in Western Europe (compared with around 5% in 2008) and nearly 4% of the Asian population (compared with around 1% in 2008).

The same study estimates that between 2008 and 2040 the population over age 80 will increase by 223%, compared with a 160% increase for the population over 65 years old and a 33% for the global population. The ageing will affect all regions, including Sub-Saharan Africa. In many countries, the population aged over 80 is currently the fastest-growing portion of the total population.

Centenarians

One of the consequences of the increases in life expectancy is an increase in the number of centenarians.

European researchers estimated that the number of centenarians in industrialised countries doubled every 10 years between 1950 and 1990. More than 40,000 centenarians have currently been counted in Japan. Of these individuals, 87% are women (the oldest woman being 114 years old, and the oldest man 112). Similarly, the number of centenarians in France surpassed 20,000 in 2008, from only 200 in 1950. This evolution is observable in the majority of industrialised countries.

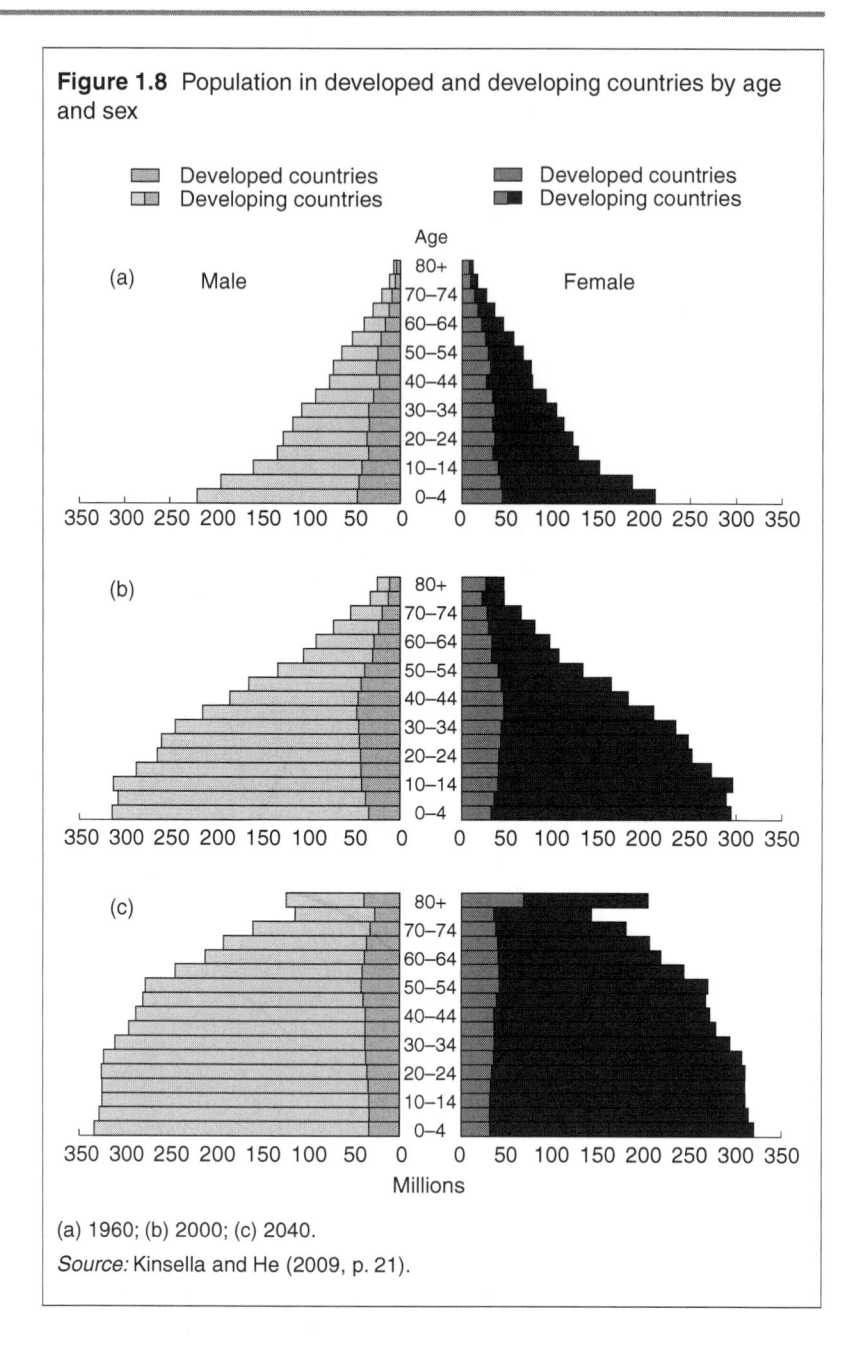

Figure 1.8 Population in developed and developing countries by age and sex

- Developed countries
- Developing countries
- Developed countries
- Developing countries

(a) 1960; (b) 2000; (c) 2040.
Source: Kinsella and He (2009, p. 21).

The United Nations estimated in 2007 that the world population of centenarians was about 270,000 as of 2005 and projected the figure will reach 2.3 million by 2040.

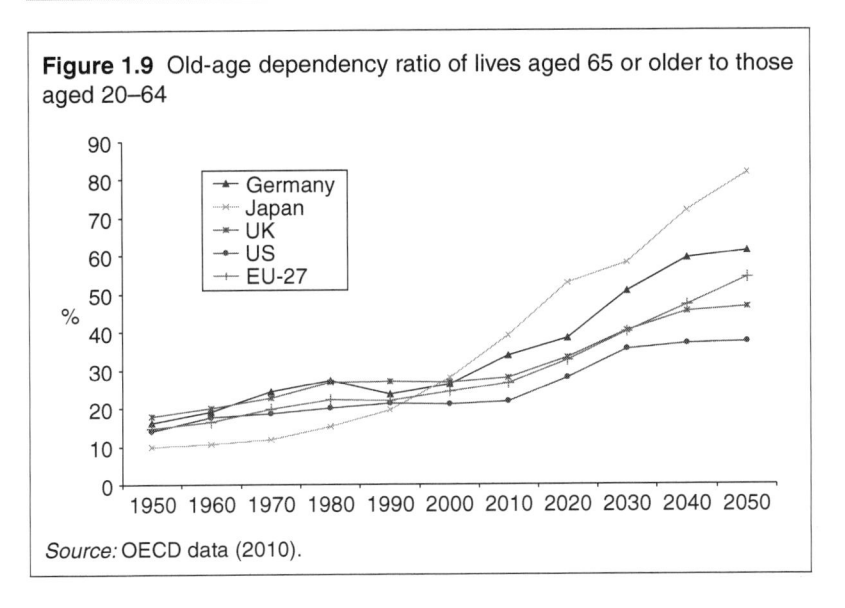

Figure 1.9 Old-age dependency ratio of lives aged 65 or older to those aged 20–64

Source: OECD data (2010).

The old-age dependency ratio

The old-age dependency ratio refers to the proportion of older, generally economically inactive individuals to younger, working-age people and is predicted to continue to grow significantly over the coming years.

The growth in the proportion of people aged 65+ and 80+ undoubtedly has a significant impact on pensions systems worldwide, especially on pay-as-you-go schemes, and also to a certain extent on the health-care systems. For example, researchers in the US (Yang *et al* 2003) estimated that the population aged 80 or older consumes health-care resources (in-patient care and long-term care (LTC) expenditures) disproportionately to its overall population size.

Figure 1.9 illustrates the increase in the old-age dependency ratio for the proportion of individuals aged 65 or older compared with those of working age (20–64) for selected countries as well as the "EU-27" group[3] of countries.

A recent report speculated that in the US ageing could have more consequences than expected (Olshansky *et al* 2009), especially if government projections underestimate the future life expectancy of Americans. For example, the demographic forecasts from the MacArthur Foundation Research Network on an Ageing Society found that by 2050 the life expectancy of Americans may surpass the

Social Security Administration current forecasts[4] by 3.1–7.9 years. If the unanticipated increase were to occur, cumulative outlays for Medicare and Social Security could potentially rise by US$3.2 trillion to US$8.3 trillion over that period.

MORBIDITY

There is no question that people are living longer and longer, which is great news. But a heavily debated point, at least in the countries that have already experienced relatively low mortality, is the quality of the additional years of life. Are the years gained spent in good health, or are they mostly spent struggling with disabling conditions? The answer has direct consequences not only for the individual in terms of quality of life but also for private and public sector organisations in respect to the potential impact on health and care expenditures. The potential increase in life expectancy also has an impact on insurers' product development strategies, which might include the provision of new types of guarantees that are better adapted to the evolving situation. The gains in popularity of critical illness or long-term care products are good examples of insurers' market response.

The absence of a country-by-country consensus on indicators that have comparable underlying definitions of morbidity makes inter-country comparisons difficult. In addition, in most countries the lack of longitudinal surveys with consistent definitions over time makes the measurement of a trend challenging.

Health indicator: disability-free life expectancy

Life expectancy has long been used as an indicator of the health of a population. However, the increase in longevity could also translate into an increase in chronic illness. To reflect the real gains in terms of the health of a population, the concept of "disability-free life expectancy" was introduced in the 1970s. This indicator gives the number of years that a person of a certain age can expect to live without any functional limitation. "Healthy life expectancy" and "active life expectancy" are similar concepts. More recently the term "long-term-care-free life expectancy" was introduced as part of a study performed by the Max Planck Institute.

In addition to traditional life expectancy, these measurements are increasingly part of national population and health surveys. However, when comparing figures between countries or for different periods of time, particular attention should be paid to the definition of disability with respect to the limitation of activity and the level of severity considered. In addition, the interpretation of health conditions differs from one country to another and can also evolve over time.

Assessments of the functional status of a person often use measurements based on the inability to perform "activities of daily living"[5], which refer to basic acts such as hygiene, dressing, eating and moving and/or more complex "instrumental activities of daily living"[6], which refer to acts such as preparing meals, taking medication and managing money among others.

Some projects such as the Survey on Health, Ageing and Retirement in Europe[7] (SHARE) allow the comparison of disability levels among the different countries involved in the project. This project could eventually lead to a harmonised indicator on an international basis.

An estimation of the number of years in good health typically relies on the Sullivan method, a simple static computational method based on mortality tables and the prevalence of disability, which is determined via health surveys, for example, the Eurostat European Community Household Panel[8] (ECHP). Other more sophisticated methods rely on alternative models such as multi-state models, which are much more appropriate in terms of their flexibility to enable the dynamic aspect of disability to be captured through the use of transition probabilities. However, such multi-state models require more detailed data from longitudinal surveys. At present, these surveys only exist in a few countries such as France (the PAQUID[9] survey) and the US (the NLTCS[10]) and are under development in others.

Morbidity comparisons across countries and common findings

Despite some discrepancies in the definition of a disabled condition, many different surveys have been conducted which offer interesting results and some common findings.

Differences between males and females

The differences in morbidity between elderly males and females are quite consistent: women live longer but seem to be more often limited in their activities than men. For females, the additional years of life appear likely to be burdened with disability. Some differences were highlighted in the following studies.

- The PAQUID survey, which followed 3,777 French people aged 65 or older over a 20-year period, found that at age 85, the total life expectancy of females was 6.8 years compared with 4.8 years for males. However, females were only expected to spend 16.6% of those years (1.1 years) active (defined in the study as either full independence or mild disability). On the other hand, at age 85, males were expected to be active for 37.5% (or 1.8 years) of their remaining life. This difference was also observed for ages 65 and 75.

- Similar patterns were observed with National Long Term Care Study (NLTCS) data in the US. Stallard (2008) concluded that at age 65, males spent less than 20% of the residual life expectancy with chronically disabled conditions, while females spent 30% of their remaining years similarly confined.

- A study performed by the Max Planck Institute (Scholz and Schulz 2010) estimated long-term care-free life expectancy (LTCF) using data from the German long-term care insurance system, in which participation is mandatory. It showed that German females have a life expectancy of 82.1 years, of which 78.5 years were in an autonomous state, and males had a lower life expectancy of 76.7 years with their LTCF reaching 74.7 years.

Another study by the Max Planck Institute analysed data from the German Socioeconomic Panel as a way of understanding the influence of sex in the development of health limitations (Doblhammer and Hoffmann 2010). By tracking the mortality and health of people aged 50 or older, researchers found that for age groups where mortality starts to increase more rapidly (60+ years) females are more likely to experience deteriorating health, while males are more likely to die. Whether this well-documented result (see also Oksuzyan *et al* 2008) is due to females' higher capacity to survive or because females are more subject to less fatal chronic diseases has not been established.

Other factors: age groups and socio-economic factors
Morbidity is also linked to age. The PAQUID study found that the inactive life expectancy (defined as moderate or severe disability) decreases more slowly with age than the active life expectancy. At age 65 a male had an active life expectancy of 12.8 years and an inactive life expectancy of 3.3 years, but at age 85 these dropped to 1.8 years and 3.0 years, respectively. A similar phenomenon was observed for women.

To look at the prevalence of dependency, Christensen *et al* (2008) studied a cohort of Danish people born in 1905 over a period of eight years, which allowed them to estimate the physical and mental loss of autonomy between the ages of 92 and 100. Since there was an increase in the probability of loss of autonomy in each additional year of life, but a higher probability of death for those in poor health, the resulting effect was that the proportion of dependants remained at a relatively stable level. This proportion is around 60–70% for centenarians.

Socio-economic variables are also very influential on health. Studies consistently show that the less-educated and the less-wealthy portion of the population not only generally die earlier but also suffer longer from disability. The PAQUID survey reported that more-educated people have a life expectancy longer than those less educated regardless of the ages studied (65, 75 or 85). Moreover, they generally spend a higher percentage of their life expectancy in a non-disabled or mildly disabled state. This finding is especially evident at age 85 when the percentage of a non-disabled or mildly disabled life expectancy was 28.7% for well-educated individuals compared with 15.9% for the less educated.

In 2010, the ONS in the UK published a report on health inequalities (Office for National Statistics 2010), which showed that disability-free life expectancy significantly differs across socio-professional categories and regions. For example, at birth, an English male had a disability-free life expectancy of 62.9 years compared with 59.3 years for a Welshman. An analysis of differences among socio-professional categories also revealed that the higher categories were expected to have a disability-free life more than 13.4 years longer than non-skilled manual labourers. At the age of 65, the gap was still 5.3 years. For women, the difference was smaller but still significant, at 11.1 years at birth and 4.7 years at age 65. The differences between the various socio-professional categories were more marked for disability-free life expectancy than for normal life expectancy.

Differences between countries

Differences in morbidity also exist among countries. A 2008 *Lancet* study (Jagger *et al* 2008) looked at the inequalities in life expectancy and healthy life years at age 50 in the 25 countries of the European Union in 2005 (see also The EHEMU/EHLEIS Team 2009). The results showed that the healthy life expectancy at older ages in Europe varied greatly among countries, with the differences observed in healthy life years being greater than the differences in life expectancies. Males and females aged 50 in Austria were expected to live on average until age 79 and 84, respectively, but only half of their years after the age of 50 were expected to be free from illness. On the other hand, individuals in the UK with a similar life expectancy at age 50 could expect to live about two-thirds of their remaining life in a healthy condition. New entrants into the EU generally experienced lower life expectancy and lower healthy life expectancy compared with established EU countries. The study showed that the countries with a higher life expectancy were not necessarily those in which the population was in the best health. In addition, there were also disparities between men and women across countries.

All of these results give an instantaneous snapshot, but what can we observe about the trends?

Compression or expansion of morbidity?

Three major morbidity trends are possible: There could be

- a compression of morbidity, in which life expectancy without disability increases faster than life expectancy,
- an expansion of morbidity, in which life expectancy increases faster than life expectancy without disability or
- a stabilisation in which both increase at the same rate.

The compression or expansion of morbidity is a heavily debated topic among demographers. National surveys and specific longitudinal studies of the elderly have attempted to answer this question. A decline in disability at older ages was observed in some countries such as in the US during the 1990s, but it does not seem to be a universal trend.

Past trends

It is impossible to cover the vast number of sources that have analysed past trends. Instead a sample of these analyses is provided to give an indication of the work that has been done in the field.

A good place to start is with the 2007 OECD report that assessed the trends in the prevalence of severe disability among elderly people for 12 countries (Organisation for Economic Co-operation and Development 2007) by reviewing past trends and grouping the countries studied into four categories:

- those where the prevalence in disability decreased among the population aged 65 or older in the past 10–20 years (Finland, Denmark, the Netherlands, Italy and the US);
- those where the prevalence had been stable (Australia and Canada);
- those where the rate had increased (Belgium, Japan and Sweden);
- those where no clear trend existed (France and the UK).

In a comparison study by The EHEMU/EHLEIS Team (2009) of the trends in disability-free life expectancy at age 65 in 13 EU countries, the authors distinguished trend scenarios in absolute and relative terms. The former referred to a change in the number of years of disability, whereas the relative compression or expansion related to the change in the proportion of remaining life spent free from disability. The authors introduced an additional scenario of dynamic equilibrium: an increase in the years spent with disability (all levels of severity) and the stabilisation or decrease in the years spent with severe disability. In analysing data from the European Community Household from 1995 to 2001, The EHEMU/EHLEIS Team (2009) also found the trends in health expectancy between 13 EU countries to vary considerably. Austria and Italy demonstrated a clear trend of a compression of disability, while three other countries showed evidence of expansion.

Analysing data from the LTC system in Germany, the Max Planck Institute found that between 1999 and 2005 German men gained nearly two years of life expectancy at birth (2.6% increase), of which 1.7 years (2.3% increase) were in an autonomous state. German women gained 1.3 years (1.6% increase) over the same period, and they were expected to remain autonomous nearly one year longer (1.2% increase).

Finally, the PAQUID survey allows a comparison of the health status for those individuals aged 75–84 between 1998 and 2008 (Pérès et al 2005). In 2008, over 24% of those aged 75–84 were in a totally autonomous state, compared with less than 14% in 1998. This trend was not verified in every country, and even within this cohort the improvements were not homogeneous among males (who experienced improvements mainly related to physical limitations) and females (who experienced large improvements related to mental conditions). The improvements were also larger for highly educated people.

Future trends
If the past trends are subject to debate, the future trends are even more difficult to assess. Some factors, such as improvements in the socio-economic status of new generations of elderly people or a decrease in the number of smokers, could lead to an improvement of health for the elderly. On the other hand, a rise in the prevalence of chronic conditions such as arthritis and diabetes or of obesity could well generate a future increase in disability among the elderly.

Compression or expansion of morbidity is also affected by medical advances. Some drugs and treatments are likely to lower the prevalence and the severity of disability, while others are more likely to extend the lifespan of people in poor health and could therefore increase the prevalence. For example, a therapeutic vaccine against Alzheimer's disease which only slowed the progression of the disease without leading to recovery would not have the same impact on morbidity as, say, a curative vaccine.

Some micro-simulation models have recently been developed to estimate under a number of disease scenarios (SIMPOP[11] by Matthews et al 2009) the number of people aged 65 or older who will be disabled over the next 20 years.

So not only the length of life but also the length of healthy life is an important social trend to consider. Are there specific drivers that we can look at to better understand the broad trends?

ANALYSIS OF THE HISTORICAL CAUSES OF DEATH

The major causes of death contributing to the mortality in developed countries include diseases of the circulatory system and cancers.

Figure 1.10 Major causes of death in the European Union by age: 2001

[Chart legend: Other; External causes of injury and poisoning; Cancer[1]; Diseases of the digestive system; Diseases of the respiratory system; Diseases of the circulatory system. Y-axis: %, 0–100. X-axis: Age group 0[2], 1–4, 5–9, 10–14, 15–19, 20–24, 25–29, 30–34, 35–39, 40–44, 45–49, 50–54, 55–59, 60–64, 65–69, 70–74, 75–79, 80–84, 85+, Total]

[1]Cancer refers to malignant neoplasms including leukaemias and lymphomas.
[2]In the age group 0 (< 1 year), the principal causes of death were "certain conditions originating in the perinatal period" (48%) and "congenital malformations and chromosomal abnormalities" (28%), which are included in "Other". Note: data refer to 25 European Union countries.
Source: Kinsella and He (2009, p. 45), adaptation from European Commission (2007), based on Eurostat mortality statistics.

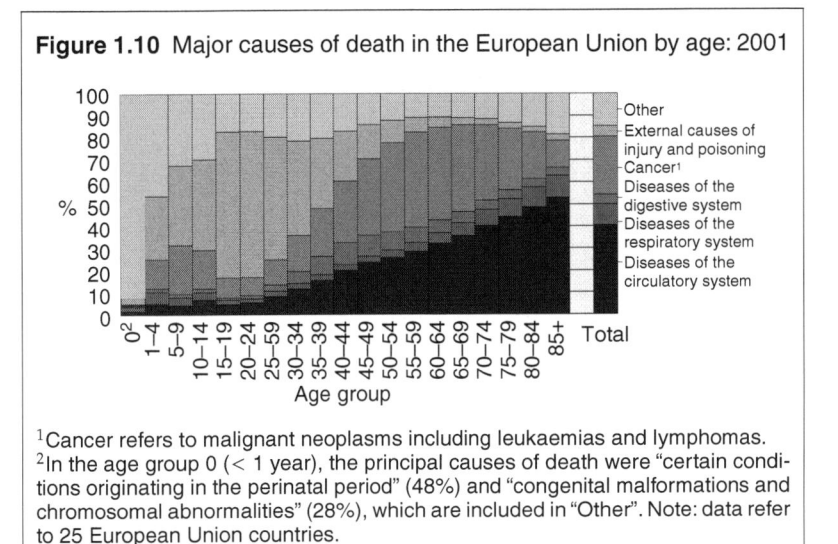

There are also variations by both age and sex in terms of how these have evolved over time. These are explored further below.

The present situation
Developed countries

Figure 1.10 shows the major causes of death in 2001 by age group for the 25 countries, which made up the European Union at that time. Before age 30, the large majority of deaths were due to both external causes of injury and poisoning (eg, accident, homicide, suicide, etc), and "other" causes of death (eg, infectious and parasitic diseases, perinatal deaths, etc). After age 30, cancer-related deaths became more and more significant, especially for ages 50–70, but less so after age 70. Diseases of the circulatory system became the major cause of death at around age 70. The corresponding overall mortality rates by age are shown in Figure 1.11.

Causes of mortality depend not only on age but also on other factors such as sex and period. A survey from INED (Vollset 2008) shows that the decrease in mortality rates observed in Western Europe is largely attributed to the decrease in mortality due to cardiovascular diseases in both sexes. Mortality due to cancer, which had remained stable or had even increased for men before 1990, has since decreased for both sexes. Within any given country, mortality for women is only

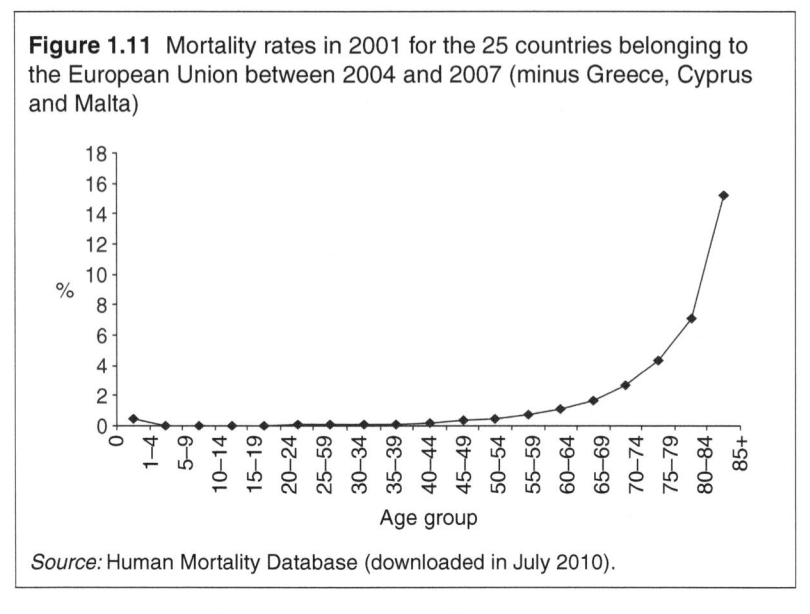

Figure 1.11 Mortality rates in 2001 for the 25 countries belonging to the European Union between 2004 and 2007 (minus Greece, Cyprus and Malta)

Source: Human Mortality Database (downloaded in July 2010).

weakly correlated to mortality for men. Medical breakthroughs are not the only factors in the decrease in mortality rates. Changes in behaviour related to alcohol or tobacco use, physical exercise and nutrition also account for a large part of the observed differences in the evolution of mortality.

Developing countries

In developing countries, diseases such as AIDS, diarrhoea, malaria, measles and pneumonia contribute greatly to mortality. The World Bank estimated that HIV (which caused one in five deaths), and malaria (which caused one in ten deaths), were the two leading causes of death in Sub-Saharan Africa for all ages in 2000. In this region, 46% of deaths occur before the age of 15, 36% between the ages of 15 and 59 and around 18% at age 60 or above.

Historical development of the main causes of death

The evolution of the main causes of death can help to provide an indication of potential future trends. Figure 1.12 shows the dramatic improvements in the mortality rates of adults aged between 40 and 70 over the second half of the 20th Century for 12 countries in Western Europe (Finland, Sweden, Norway, Denmark, Germany, Netherlands, Switzerland, France, UK, Ireland, Spain and Italy). The substantial reduction in the probability of death since 1950 shown for

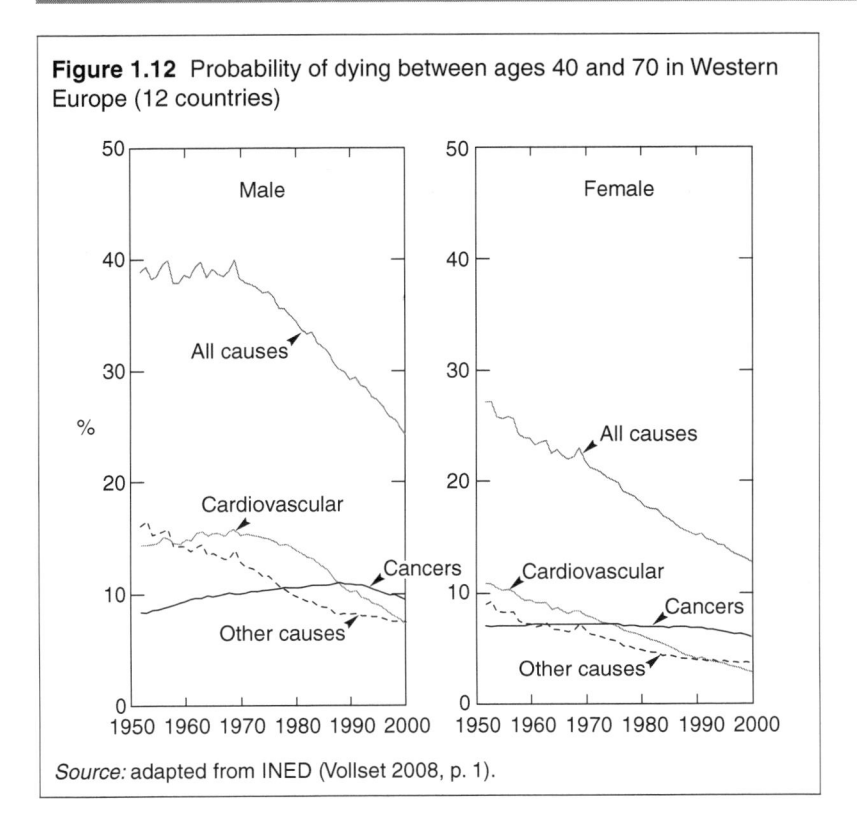

Figure 1.12 Probability of dying between ages 40 and 70 in Western Europe (12 countries)

Source: adapted from INED (Vollset 2008, p. 1).

all causes has largely been driven by similar reductions in mortality from causes of death such as circulatory diseases.

For the UK, a 45% reduction in the overall mortality level (on an age-standardised basis) was observed during the period 1950–99 for both males and females. Mortality related to infectious diseases similarly fell precipitously during the 1950s; by the mid-1960s they represented approximately 10% of what they had been in 1950. Chapter 4 further explores the development of diseases for some major categories over a longer period of time for older ages in the UK.

Circulatory disease

The mortality due to circulatory diseases such as heart, cerebrovascular and hypertensive diseases has decreased dramatically for adults in many countries. For example, in Western Europe, the reduction in circulatory diseases primarily drove the decrease in adult mortality from 1952 to 2001.

The UK has one of the highest mortality rates from circulatory diseases in Western Europe and circulatory diseases are relatively prevalent, but still a general decreasing trend has been observed. Heart disease in males declined slowly between 1950 and 1980, then in the 1980s this trend accelerated. In 1999, mortality from heart disease was half the rate of that in 1950. Mortality from heart disease among females dropped more rapidly compared with males during the 1950s and 1960s and, after levelling out in the 1970s, resumed its decline in the 1980s. The improvement for females over this period was even more impressive than that for males, and by 1999 the mortality rate for heart disease was one-third of its 1950 level.

Cancer

Unlike mortality from circulatory disease, which has improved markedly over the past 50 years, cancer-related mortality remained largely stable until the 1990s: a trend probably largely due to an increase in prevalence.

Across Europe, the INED survey (Vollset 2008) showed the risk of dying from cancer for males aged 40–70 was highest in Southern Europe (France, Italy and Spain) and lower in Northern Europe (Sweden, Finland and Norway) in 2001. However, in 1952, mortality from cancer for males was particularly high in Finland, the UK and Switzerland and low in Italy, Spain and Sweden.

For females, the trends have been different. Over the same period, the highest mortality from cancer was observed in Denmark and the lowest in Spain. In 2001, the countries with the highest female mortality from cancer were those of Northern Europe, with the remarkable exception of Finland.

A study of cancer trends by the UK Office for National Statistics found that the age-standardised mortality from cancer (malignant and non-malignant neoplasms) for both males and females changed relatively little between 1950 and 1999, as mortality largely hovered between 250 and 280 per 100,000 males and between 170 and 180 per 100,000 females. Because of the decrease in deaths due to circulatory and infectious diseases, deaths that occurred as a result of cancer rose proportionally during this time, from 15% to 27% in males and from 16% to 23% in females. For males and females, cancer was the chief cause of death by 1969 and 1995, respectively.

Differences by geography and time periods are driven by the different trends in the prevalence of the disease as well as in survival rates.

Possible improvements in longevity from the diffusion of good practices

With a diffusion of best practices among countries, it would be intuitive to conclude further improvements in longevity could occur over time, and indeed initiatives exist to support and monitor developments in certain major causes of death, which is likely to help this process.

For example, the cancer epidemiology research project EUROCARE-4[12] monitors cancer survival in Europe and allows comparisons to be drawn between the occurrence of and mortality from various types of cancer for several European countries. It also confirms the significant long-observed differences between countries. For example, in France, nearly 59% of women with cancer recover, compared with only 38% in Poland. The most fatal cancer remains lung cancer, which has the highest recovery rate of only 10.3% in France. In addition, significant improvements in mortality were driven by a convergence in these recovery rates, especially in Eastern Europe and the UK.

The UK ONS study (Quinn *et al* 2001) on cancer trends underscores the differences that exist among countries. Notably, the five-year survival for most of the common forms of cancers was lower for patients in the UK diagnosed during 1978–85 than in several comparable European countries. The varying patterns in survival for breast and colon cancer appeared to diverge mostly in the first six months after diagnosis. This is consistent with the hypothesis that international differences exist regarding the advancement of the disease at the time of diagnosis, along with differences in access to the most beneficial treatments.

These differences indicate the possibility that longevity improvements for the most developed countries could increase with the diffusion of good practices in terms of health and alignment in recovery rates for the most common illnesses (cancer, cardiovascular, etc) towards the standards maintained in the highest performing countries.

These analyses of past causes hint at predictions of future mortality, a topic which Chapter 4 explores in more detail.

FUTURE: CHALLENGES AND OPPORTUNITIES
Is there a limit to life expectancy?

Throughout history scientists have attempted to answer this question. Many predictions have been proven wrong, and the answer still remains unknown.

A biological limit?

In 1749, Georges Buffon compared growth and ageing processes in humans and various animals and argued that the duration of life is six or seven times the period of growth, leading to a maximum of one hundred years of life for humans. In 1844 Pierre Flourens revised the coefficients used in Buffon's estimation, which led to an increase of 25 years in Buffon's estimate of the maximum lifespan (Flourens 1850) to 125 years. Made 200 years ago, such estimations are in fact quite close to the current observed age limit and to practices assumed in the insurance industry.

In 1921, the Nobel Prize winner Alexis Carrel found that cells could replicate indefinitely in optimal conditions (Carrel and Ebeling 1921). An experimental error was found, however, and in 1961 Leonard Hayflick showed that cells enter a senescence state after a certain number of divisions (Hayflick and Moorhead 1961), giving rise to the current widely held belief that the human lifespan is limited by this Hayflick limit.

One mechanism was found by Olovnikov (1971) that could explain the Hayflick limit: the extremities of chromosomes, so called "telomeres", which reduce at each cell division up to a limit. But in 1985, the 2009 Nobel Prize winners Elizabeth Blackburn, Carol Greider and Jack W. Szostak discovered that telomere reduction is tightly regulated by the body and that rapidly dividing cells produce abundant "telomerase" which rebuilds the telomeres (Greider and Blackburn 1985). Boosting the telomerase activity would protect against cell ageing, but the consequences would be the risk of proliferation of cancerous cells, which could bypass the Hayflick limit and duplicate without dying. Thus, the apparent delicate equilibrium between telomerase and cancer leaves open the question of a biological limit to human life.

Insight from the oldest old

Frequent, unrealistic claims of extreme old ages require preliminary validation in order to study the very old; this validation is often

Figure 1.13 Number of centenarians in England and Wales

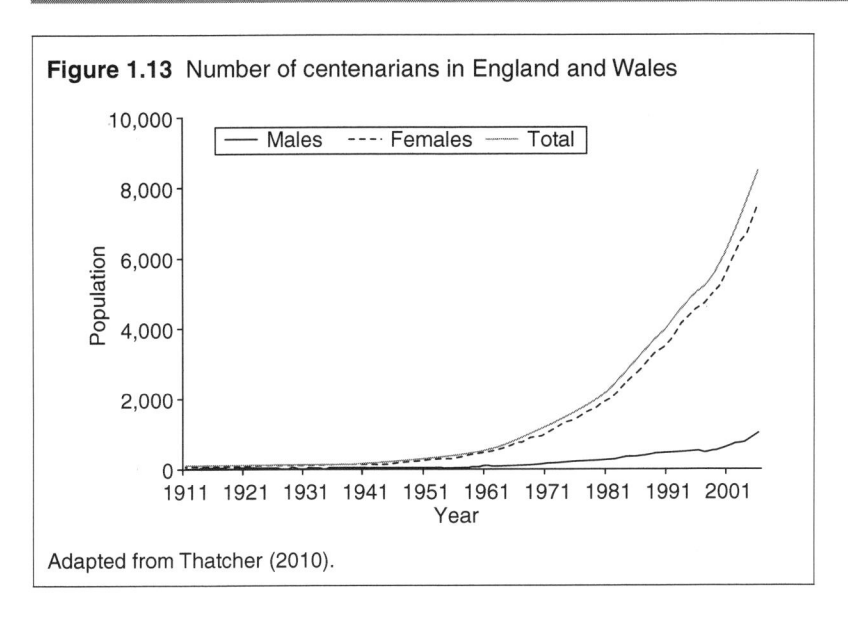

Adapted from Thatcher (2010).

performed by the Supercentenarian Research Foundation, which studies supercentenarians (aged 110 and over). They report that the oldest validated person currently alive is the 114-year-old American woman Eunice Sanborn, born in 1896.[13] The oldest person ever officially recorded was the French woman Jeanne Calment, who died during the summer of 1997 at the age of 122 years, 5 months and 14 days, and the next oldest was the American woman Sarah Knauss, who died in late 1999 at the age of 119 years and 3 months (Jeune *et al* 2010).

Some common features among supercentenarians are that most are women whose ancestors also lived to old ages. Many enjoy indulging in sweets and, moreover, have a strong personality that combines strength of will with friendliness. Behavioural factors apparently do not make all the difference: Jeanne Calment smoked daily and Sarah Knauss did not eat vegetables, suggesting to some that genetics also play an important role. While these women were frail in their last years, they were not suffering from severe illness, so some scientists consider such cases to demonstrate the extreme limit of the human lifespan (Jeune *et al* 2010).

Other views, however, maintain that increases in the maximal lifespan will continue. A stabilisation of the death rates at around 50% has been observed for ages older than 112. Some demographic models also project very large numbers of the "oldest olds" in future

Figure 1.14 Projected numbers of centenarians

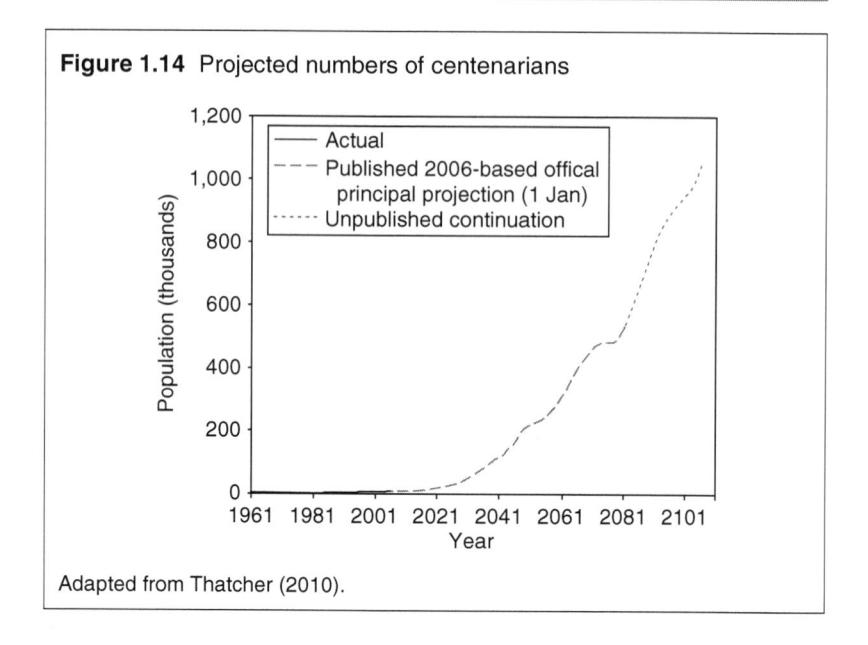

[Chart showing population (thousands) from 1961 to 2101, with three series: Actual, Published 2006-based official principal projection (1 Jan), and Unpublished continuation. Values range from near 0 to approximately 1,200 thousand.]

Adapted from Thatcher (2010).

years. Figure 1.13 shows an exponential growth in the total number of centenarians who were living between 1911 and 2006 and Figure 1.14 shows the projected number of centenarians through 2106.

If the probabilities of dying at high ages remain stable, the number of people aged 112 or older will follow a similar pattern, linearly increasing the theoretical lifespan above age 100 over time. If the mortality were to decrease due to medical advances such as curing the disease TTR amyloidosis, which is often found in autopsies performed on supercentenarians, then the maximum lifespan may increase at an even faster rate.

Evolution of life expectancy: previously underestimated

In the previous discussion we have focused on the maximum lifespan. However, life expectancy still remains much lower than the maximum lifespan, leaving considerable room for life expectancy to increase.

In many countries, life expectancy has consistently been underestimated, and many former actuarial mortality tables have been shown to underestimate the improvements in mortality within one or two decades of being developed.

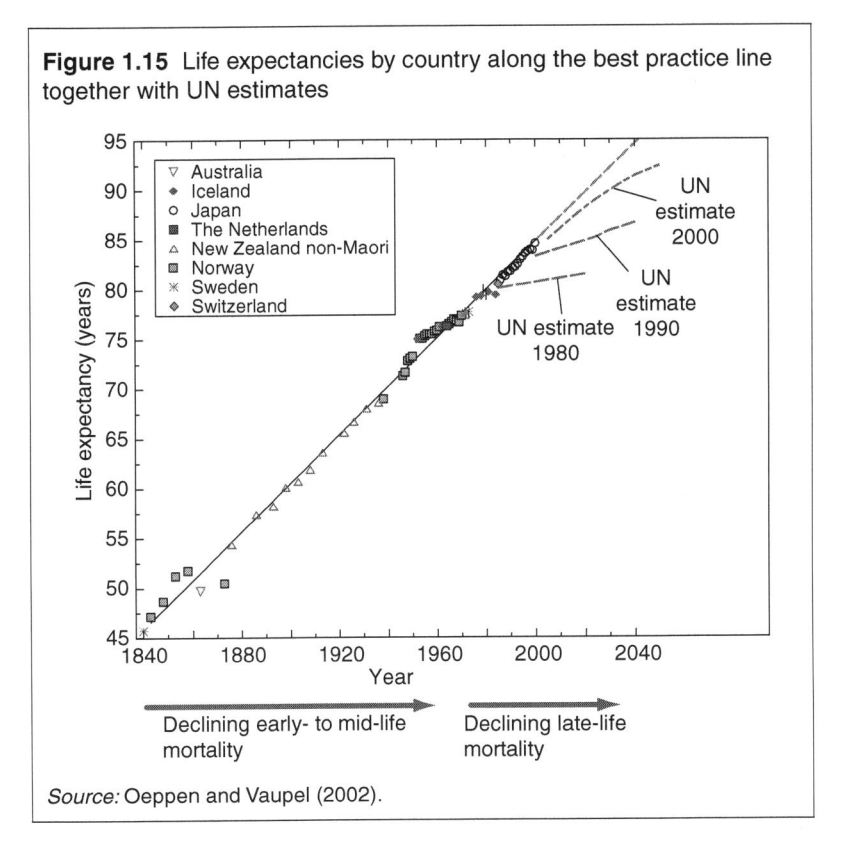

Figure 1.15 Life expectancies by country along the best practice line together with UN estimates

[Chart showing life expectancy (years) on y-axis from 45 to 95, Year on x-axis from 1840 to 2040, with data points for Australia, Iceland, Japan, The Netherlands, New Zealand non-Maori, Norway, Sweden, Switzerland along a best practice line. UN estimates for 1980, 1990, and 2000 are shown diverging below the best practice line. Arrows below indicate "Declining early- to mid-life mortality" and "Declining late-life mortality".]

Source: Oeppen and Vaupel (2002).

Dublin (1928) estimated a lower bound for mortality rates and concluded that the highest achievable life expectancy would be 64.75. At that time life expectancy in the US was 57 years old, and he was not aware that it was already close to 66 for women in New Zealand. The understanding that has since developed regarding international mortality would help to avoid such mistakes. Even so, similar projections based on past mortality rates and mortality causes, including those that take biomedical improvements into account, have consistently underestimated longevity.

Oeppen and Vaupel (2002) published the graph shown in Figure 1.15, indicating that the highest female life expectancy in the world appears to follow a straight line, which is called the "best practice" line (shown in light grey), and that the United Nations consistently underestimated such longevity in 1980, 1990 and 2000.

Later, Vallin and Meslé (2010) reported that the best practice line could also be viewed as a succession of different lines, each

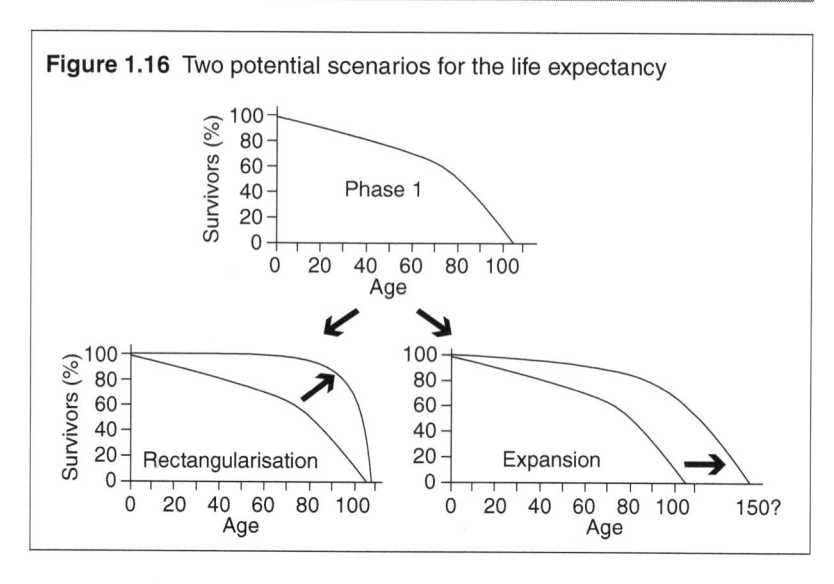

Figure 1.16 Two potential scenarios for the life expectancy

[Phase 1 survival curve, with arrows leading to two scenarios: Rectangularisation and Expansion (extending toward age 150?)]

corresponding to major social and biomedical changes. The question remains whether or not such changes will continue in the future.

Two potential scenarios for the limit to life expectancy

Projections of life expectancy can be guided by the extrapolation of past life expectancies and the experience of the most elderly of the population. Figure 1.16 illustrates two possibilities in the evolution of life expectancy. The first is a squaring-off (also known as rectangularisation) of the distribution of survivors by age: a trajectory corresponding to a population that nearly reaches the maximum age possible, an age which remains constant. The second is an increase in the maximum duration of life (also known as expansion), which appears to be less probable unless major medical advances occur.

Further specific examples related to country examples of rectangularisation and expansion are provided in Chapter 4.

Challenges

Environmental and social changes

One of the reasons why projecting longevity is so difficult is that projection of the main causes of death into the future is an extremely difficult task. As mortality from the current leading causes of death decreases, other causes become more significant and then subsequently reduce. This phenomenon, at least, has been the pattern observed thus far. Furthermore, it is extremely difficult to estimate

Figure 1.17 Body mass index

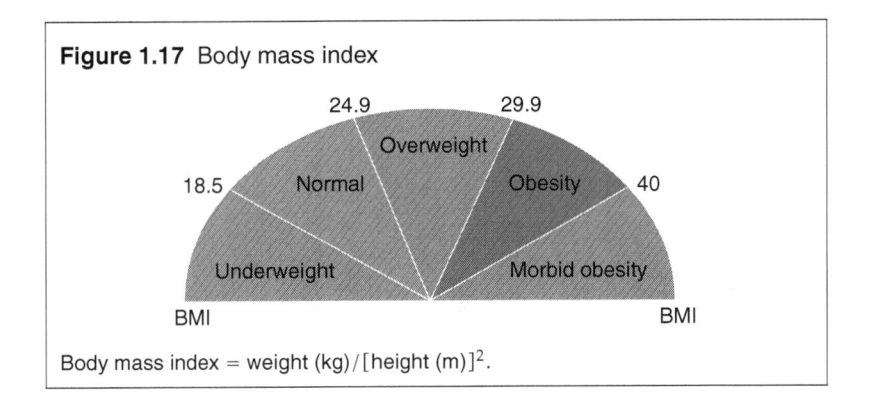

Body mass index = weight (kg)/[height (m)]^2.

what the new leading causes of death will be. Fifty years ago it was not foreseen that smoking, cardiovascular diseases and cancers would cause so many problems. Is it any easier now to predict the risks of the future?

There is also a wide range of factors, including environmental, behavioural and social changes that may give rise to increases in mortality. Moreover, they are often unknown or nascent. At one time or another, the dangers posed by smoking or asbestos, for example, were not well understood, as such substances may not lead to cancer until 20 or 30 years after the first exposure. While the part that tobacco and asbestos plays in cancer and other life-threatening diseases is now well recognised, other potential risks are still emerging. A good example is the dilemma that cell phones pose. To try to determine the dangers from mobile telephones, Interphone, an international study of 13 countries, was launched in 1998 but resulted in no conclusive findings regarding potential dangers.[14] Other risks such as pollution, however, seem to be clearly associated with a higher level of mortality. Using data from 51 metropolitan zones in the US from different periods between 1970 and the early 2000s, American researchers (Pope *et al* 2009) were able to estimate that the reduction of air pollution could contribute to an increase of 15% in global life expectancy.

For some researchers such as Olshansky *et al* (2009), the widespread increase in the number of people with obesity and its associated diseases, such as diabetes, calls into question the progression of life expectancy, particularly in developed countries such as the US and some other Western countries.

At a worldwide level, WHO estimates that there are a billion overweight people, of which at least 300 million are clinically obese (Figure 1.17). In the US, one-third of adults are considered obese, another third are overweight, and the prevalence of severe obesity among children between the ages of 2 and 19 jumped from 0.8% in 1976–80 to 3.8% in 1999–2004.

Despite the growing numbers of people suffering from obesity, life expectancy continues to increase and epidemiological studies show the effects of obesity on mortality are limited. In a longitudinal study of middle- and older-aged Americans, the Health Retirement Study[15] (HRS) showed that the negative impact of obesity on life expectancy was as much as that associated with being underweight, and that the link between mortality and obesity seems limited compared with that for tobacco use or a low level of education.

Diet and longevity

While obesity seems to be a risk factor for a number of diseases, some scientists have recognised for quite a while that there appears to be a link between a very low-calorie but well-balanced diet (eg, 60% of the normal calorie amount) and an increase in longevity. However, this increase in the length of life may also come at a cost to fertility. For example, a British team (Flatt 2009) recently published research on the key role that the amino acid methionine plays in longevity and fertility and inferred that it would be possible to live longer by reducing the intake of methionine within a normal diet.

New diseases

Diseases that are currently infrequent might also become leading causes of death in the future. Cardiopulmonary diseases may be expected to increase due to pollution (particularly from diesel emissions), obesity and an increasing elderly population. Also, the rapidly increasing portion of centenarians and supercentenarians highlights the problem of senile systemic amyloidosis (Mimassi *et al* 2002; Ueda *et al* 2006). Some also speculate on the resurgence of infectious diseases in the case that resistance to antibiotics becomes prevalent. The spread of AIDS has slowed, but allergies seem to have become more and more frequent. As it has happened in the past, some unexpected disease could well become the next leading cause of death.

Possible breakthroughs

Medical advances

Over the past decade, medicine has made significant head way in two important areas for confronting and treating disease: prevention and personalised medicine. For example, many governments now use the media to teach prevention measures such as the need for a healthy diet and exercise and the avoidance of tobacco, excessive sun, speeding or the use of unnecessary antibiotics. Early detection of cancers is starting to become a reality, and the study of treatments for dementia could also lead to earlier detection of this illness. Personalised medicine is mostly appearing through the development of cancer treatments geared to a specific type of cancer, as well as with online genetic tests that indicate which treatments would or would not be tolerated, and influence personal lifestyle choices towards healthier lives.

The impact of these advancements in the detection and treatment on longevity is limited, however, because the improvement in mortality from the eradication of a specific disease is likely to be relatively marginal.

Fundamental longevity research

More fundamental research aimed at tackling ageing itself might offer more insights on how longevity could be increased.

Some advancements have emerged from research that focused on the Hayflick limit and the equilibrium between telomerase and cancer. In 2008, biogerontologists reportedly increased the lifespan of mice after making genetic modifications which increased both cancer protection and telomerase activity (Tomás-Loba *et al* 2008). In the following year, researchers found that Ashkenazi Jews who lived particularly long lives naturally inherited a hyperactive version of telomerase. This finding may offer some promise for pharmaceutical companies and continuing research in this area.

Other efforts in the area include the work of Aubrey de Grey, who developed a radical scientific research programme called "strategies for engineered negligible senescence" (SENS)[16], the goal of which is to eliminate seven forms of damage caused by ageing, like removing rust from an old car. Significant effects are predicted by de Grey, but many obstacles remain. Concrete results that would lead to the

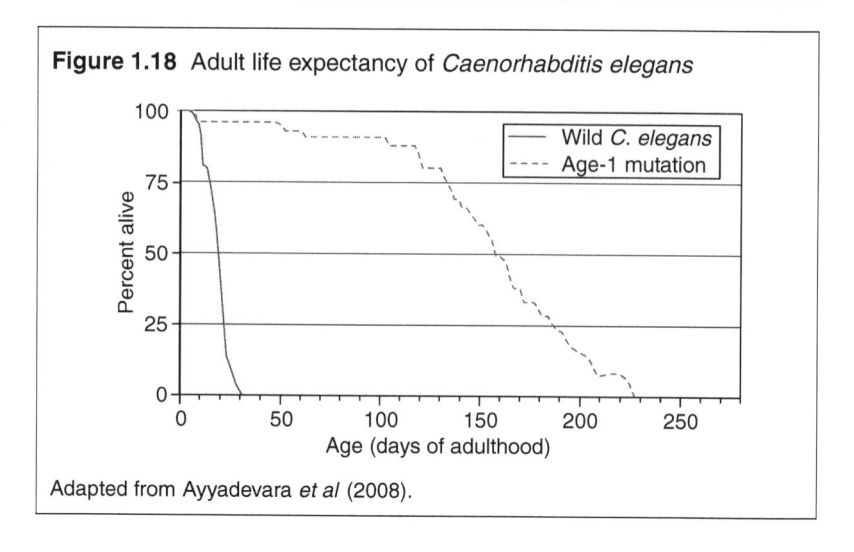

Figure 1.18 Adult life expectancy of *Caenorhabditis elegans*

[Graph showing percent alive vs age (days of adulthood) from 0 to 250, comparing Wild *C. elegans* (solid line) and Age-1 mutation (dashed line).]

Adapted from Ayyadevara *et al* (2008).

extension of the human lifespan are not expected for at least 10 more years and such potential outcomes are also hotly debated.

Other approaches focus on empirical testing of animals and from studying persons who have had remarkably long lives. The past few decades have shown that highly targeted genetic changes can substantially affect the lifespan of animals. For example, a nearly tenfold increase in the adult life expectancy of the tiny worm *Caenorhabditis elegans* followed the genetic suppression of the activity of one gene, called "age-1" (Ayyadevara *et al* 2008). The enormous extension of its lifespan is shown in Figure 1.18 by the survival curve of the worms, with the genetic mutation being significantly longer (grey-dashed line) than the normal survival curve (solid black line).

Much research on worms and other animals with a relatively short lifespan has arrived at similar but less dramatic results, which have been more in the range of a 10–30% increase in lifespan. The increased lifespan, however, comes with some drawbacks. Some, though not all, of these treatments, for example, have resulted in a decrease in fertility. Cynthia Kenyon, a leading scientist in research on longevity, recently reviewed findings in the field (Kenyon 2010). New and even existing drugs and treatments used in humans have been shown to increase survival in mice. Furthermore, genetic mutations found in people that have lived to an old age are very similar to mutations found to extend the lives of mice (Atzmon 2010; Flachsbart *et al* 2009; Willcox *et al* 2008). These promising results in animals may indicate that improvements in human longevity could one day come from similar techniques.

Some species' very long lifespans (Carey and Judge 2002) suggest that there is considerable room for improvement. One Aldabra Tortoise was reported to be 152 years old. Among mammals, fin whales have been reported to live up to 116 years old. A 152-year-old lake sturgeon and a 140-year-old rockfish have been found. One bristlecone pine tree is 4,767 years old, and some Australian trees have been around for 13,000 years (Life Magazine 1956). A bacterium in New Mexico is even 250 million years old.[17] These possibilities, however, pale in comparison to a rollback in time: an ability exhibited by the jellyfish *Turritopsis nutricula*, which was recently found to revert to a young state at adulthood, making it potentially immortal (Piraino 1996; Sun 2009). Yet the ultimate question still remains largely unanswered: how long will humans really live in the future?

> The authors thank Benoit Moreau, Virginie Vasseur and Hans Wagner for their advice in preparing the chapter content and their patient review.

1. See http://www.statistics.gov.uk/cci/nugget.asp?id=2271.
2. Data available at http://www.mortality.org.
3. The EU expanded from UE-25 in 2007 with the entry of Bulgaria and Romania.
4. See http://www.census.gov/ and http://www.ssa.gov/.
5. Such as the Katz Index of Independence in Activities of Daily Living (Katz *et al* 1970).
6. Such as the Lawton IADL scale (Lawton and Brody 1969).
7. See http://www.share-project.org.
8. See http://epp.eurostat.ec.europa.eu.
9. PAQUID: Personnes Agées Quid.
10. National Long Term Care Survey, http://www.nltcs.aas.duke.edu/.
11. See http://www2.lse.ac.uk/LSEHealthAndSocialCare/MAP2030/.
12. The European cancer registry-based study on the survival and care of cancer patients; see http://www.eurocare.it/.
13. See the Gerontology Research Group Table of Worldwide Validated Living Supercentenarians at http://grg.org/ (accessed at the time of writing in 2010).
14. See http://www.ncbi.nlm.nih.gov/pubmed/20483835.
15. See http://hrsonline.isr.umich.edu/.
16. See http://www.sens.org.
17. See http://www.extremescience.com/zoom/index.php/animal-kingdom-records/.

REFERENCES

Atzmon, G., M. Cho, R. M. Cawthon, T. Budagov, M. Katz, X. Yang, G. Siegel, A. Bergman, D. M. Huffman, C. B. Schechter, W. E. Wright, J. W. Shay, N. Barzilai, D. R. Govindaraju and Y. Suh, 2010, "Genetic Variation in Human Telomerase is Associated with Telomere Length in Ashkenazi Centenarians" *Proceedings of the National Academy of Sciences of the United States of America* 107 (Supplement: Evolution in Health and Medicine Sackler Colloquium, Volume 1), pp. 1710–7.

Ayyadevara, S., R. Alla, J. J. Thaden and R. J. Shmookler Reis, 2008, "Remarkable Longevity and Stress Resistance of Nematode PI3K-Null Mutants", *Aging Cell* 7(1), pp. 13–22.

Carey, J. R., and D. S. Judge, 2002, *Longevity Records: Life Spans of Mammals, Birds, Amphibians, Reptiles, and Fish*, Monographs on Population Ageing, Volume 8 (Odense University Press).

Carrel, A., and A. H. Ebeling, 1921, "Age and Multiplication of Fibroblasts", *Journal of Expirmental Medicine* 34, pp. 599–606.

Cheung, S. L. K., and J.-M. Robine, 2007, "Increase in Common Longevity and the Compression of Mortality: The Case of Japan" *Population Studies* 61(1), pp. 85–97.

Christensen, K., M. McGue, I. Petersen, B. Jeune and J. W. Vaupel, 2008 "Exceptional Longevity Does Not Result in Excessive Levels of Disability", *Proceedings of the National Academy of Sciences*, doi:10.1073/pnas.0804931105.

Christensen, K., G. Doblhammer, R. Rau and J. W. Vaupel, 2009, "Ageing Populations: The Challenges Ahead", *The Lancet* 374, pp. 1196–208.

Doblhammer, G., and R. Hoffmann, 2010, "Gender Differences in Trajectories of Health Limitations and Subsequent Mortality: A Study Based on the German Socioeconomic Panel 1995–2001 with a Mortality Follow-Up 2002–2005", *Journal of Gerontology* B 65(4), pp. 482–91.

Dublin, L. I., 1928, "Vital Statistics", *American Journal of Public Health and the Nation's Health* 18(3), pp. 359–62.

The EHEMU/EHLEIS Team, "Trends in Disability-free Life Expectancy at Age 65 in the European Union 1995–2001: A Comparison of 13 EU countries", Technical Report, June 2009, URL: http://www.ehemu.eu/pdf/Reports_2009/2009TR5_1_Trends_13EUMS.pdf.

Flachsbart, F., A. Caliebe, R. Kleindorp, H. Blanché, H. von Eller-Eberstein, S. Nikolaus, S. Schreiber and A. Nebel, 2009, "Association of FOXO3A Variation with Human Longevity Confirmed in German Centenarians" *Proceedings of the National Academy of Sciences of the United States of America* 24, 106(8), pp. 2700–5.

Flatt, T. 2009, "Ageing: Diet and Longevity in the Balance", *Nature* 462, pp. 989–90.

Flourens, P. 1850 *Histoire des Travaux et des Idées de Buffon*, Second Edition (Paris: L. Hachette). (First published in 1844.)

Greider, C. W., and E. H. Blackburn, 1985, "Identification of a Specific Telomere Terminal Transferase Activity in Tetrahymena Extracts", *Cell* 43, pp. 405–413.

Hayflick, L., and P. S. Moorhead, 1961, "The Serial Cultivation of Human Diploid Cell Strains" *Experimental Cell Research* 25, pp. 585–621.

Jagger, C., C. Gillies, F. Moscone, E. Cambois, H. Van Hoven, W. Nusselder and J.-M. Robine, 2008, "Inequalities in Healthy Life Years in the 25 Countries of the European Union in 2005: A Cross-National Meta-Regression Analysis", *The Lancet* 372, pp. 2124–131.

Jeune, B., J.-M. Robine, R. Young, B. Desjardins, A. Skytthe and J. W. Vaupel, 2010, "Jeanne Calment and Her Successors: Biographical Notes on the Longest Living Humans", in H. Maier *et al* (eds), *Supercentenarians*, Demographic Research Monographs (Springer).

Katz, S., T. D. Down, H. R. Cash and R. C. Grotz, 1970, "Progress in the Development of the Index of ADL", *The Gerontologist*, 10(1), p. 20–30.

Kenyon, C. J., 2010, "The Genetics of Ageing", *Nature* 464, pp. 504–12.

Kinsella, K., and W. He, 2009, "An Aging World: 2008", US Census Bureau, International Population Reports, P95/09-1, US Government Printing Office, Washington, DC, URL: http://www.census.gov/prod/2009pubs/p95-09-1.pdf.

Lawton, M. P., and E. M. Brody, 1969, "Assessment of Older People: Self-Maintaining and Instrumental Activities of Daily Living', *The Gerontologist* 9, pp. 179–86.

Life Magazine, 1956, "The Oldest Thing Alive", *Life Magazine* 41(21), pp. 69–70.

Matthews, R., C. Jagger and the MRC CFAS Team, 2009, "Trends in Disease and How They Will Impact on Disability in the Older Population", Proceedings of 21st REVES Conference, p. 36ff, URL: http://www.si-folkesundhed.dk/upload/telechargement_fichier_en_conference.book.11.05.09.pdf.

Mimassi, N., P. Youinou and Y. L. Pennec, 2002, "Amyloidosis and Ageing", *Annales de Médecine Interne (Paris)* 153(6), pp. 383–8.

Oeppen, J., and J. W. Vaupel, 2002, "Broken Limits to Life Expectancy", *Science* 296, pp. 1029–31.

Office for National Statistics, 2009, *Health Quarterly*, Summer.

Office for National Statistics, 2010, "Inequalities in Disability-Free Life Expectancy by Social Class and Area Type: England, 2001–03", Report, URL: http://www.statistics.gov.uk/.

Oksuzyan, A., K. Juel, J. W. Vaupel and K. Christensen, 2008, "Men: Good Health and High Mortality. Sex Differences in Health and Aging", *Aging Clinical and Experimental Research* 20(2), pp. 91–102.

Olovnikov, A. M., 1971, "Principles of Marginotomy in Template Synthesis of Polynucleotides", *Doklady Akademii Nauk SSSR* 201, pp. 1496–9.

Olshansky, S. J., D. P. Goldman, Y. Zheng and J. W. Rowe, 2009, "Aging in America in the Twenty-First Century: Demographic Forecasts from the MacArthur Foundation Research Network on an Aging Society", *The Milbank Quarterly*, 87(4), pp. 842–62.

Organisation for Economic Co-operation and Development, 2007, "Trends in Severe Disability Among Elderly People: Assessing the Evidence in 12 OECD Countries and the Future Implications", Report, URL: http://www.oecd.org/dataoecd/13/8/38343783.pdf.

Park, Y., M. F.Leitzmann, A. F. Subar, A. Hollenbeck and A. Schatzkin, 2009, "Dairy Food, Calcium, and Risk of Cancer in the NIH–AARP Diet and Health Study", *Archives of Internal Medicine* 169(4), pp. 391–401.

Pérès, K., C. Jagger, A. Lièvre and P. Barberger-Gateau, 2005, "Disability-Free Life Expectancy of Older French People: Gender and Education Differentials from the PAQUID Cohort", *European Journal of Ageing* 2(3), pp. 225–33.

Piraino, S., F. Boero, B. Aeschbach and V. Schmid, 1996, "Reversing the Life Cycle: Medusae Transforming into Polyps and Cell Differentiation in *Turritopsis nutricula* (Cnidaria, Hydrozoa)", *Biological Bulletin* 190(3), pp. 302–12.

Pope, C. A. III, M. Ezzati and D. W. Dockery, 2009, "Fine-Particulate Air Pollution and Life Expectancy in the United States", *New England Journal of Medicine* 360, pp. 376–86.

Quinn, M., P. Babb, A. Brock, E. Kirby and J. Jones, 2001, *Cancer Trends in England and Wales 1950–1999*, Studies on Medical and Population Subjects, No. 66 (Basingstoke/London: Palgrave Macmillan/Office for National Statistics).

Rau, R., E. Soroko, D. Jasilionis and J. W. Vaupel, 2006, "10 Years after Kannisto: Further Evidence for Mortality Decline at Advanced Ages in Developed Countries", MPIDR Working Paper, URL: http://www.demogr.mpg.de/papers/working/wp-2006-033.pdf.

Rau, R., E. Soroko, J. Domantas and J. W. Vaupel, 2008, "Continued Reductions in Mortality at Advanced Ages", *Population and Development Review* 34, pp. 747–68.

Robine, J.-M., S. Le Roy, C. Jagger and the EHEMU Team, 2005, "Changes in Life Expectancy in the European Union since 1995: Similarities and Differences between the 25 EU countries", Report, November, URL http://www.ehemu.eu/pdf/JM_Budapest.pdf.

Robine, J.-M., F. Paccaud and L. Seematter-Bagnoud, 2009, "Le Futur de la Longévité en Suisse", URL: http://www.bfs.admin.ch/bfs/portal/fr/index/news/publikationen.document.119758.pdf.

Scholz, R. D., and A. Schulz, 2010, "Assessing Old-Age Long-Term Care Using the Concepts of Healthy Life Expectancy and Care Duration: The New Parameter Long-Term Care-Free Life-Expectancy (LTCF)", URL: http://www.demogr.mpg.de/papers/working/wp-2010-001.pdf.

Stallard, E., "Estimates of the Incidence, Prevalence, Duration, Intensity and Cost of Chronic Disability among the US Elderly", Presented at the "Living to 100 and Beyond" Symposium, January 7–9, 2008, URL: http://www.soa.org/library/monographs/retirement-systems/living-to-100-and-beyond/2008/january/mono-li08-3b-stallard.pdf.

Sun, L., A. A. Sadighi Akha, R. A. Miller and J. M. Harper, 2009, "Life-Span Extension in Mice by Preweaning Food Restriction and by Methionine Restriction in Middle Age", *The Journals of Gerontology* A 64(7), pp. 711–22.

Thatcher, A. R., 2010, "The Growth of High Ages in England and Wales, 1635-2106", in H. Maier et al (eds), *Supercentenarians*, Demographic Research Monographs, (Springer).

Tomás-Loba, A., I. Flores, P. J. Fernández-Marcos, M. L. Cayuela, A. Maraver, A. Tejera, C. Borrás, A. Matheu, P. Klatt, J. M. Flores, J. Viña, M. Serrano and M. A. Blasco, 2008, "Telomerase Reverse Transcriptase Delays Ageing in Cancer-Resistant Mice", *Cell* 135(4), pp. 609–22.

Ueda, M., Y. Ando, K. Haraoka, S. Katsuragi, Y. Terasaki, M. Sugimoto, X. Sun and M. Uchino, 2006, "Ageing and Transthyretin-Related Amyloidosis: Pathologic Examinations in Pulmonary Amyloidosis", *Amyloid* 13(1), pp. 24–30.

Vallin, J., and F. Meslé, 2010, "The Segmented Trend Line of Highest Life Expectancies", *Population and Development Review* 35(1), pp. 159–87.

Velkoff, V. A., and P. R. Kowal, 2007, "Population Aging in Sub-Saharan Africa: Demographic Dimensions 2006", US Census Bureau, Current Population Reports, P95/07-1, US Government Printing Office, Washington, DC.

Vollset, S. E., 2008, "Baisse Générale de la Mortalité adulte en Europe de l'Ouest: Les Espagnoles et les Suédois Tiennent la Tête", *Population & Sociétés*, Volume 450, URL: http://www.ined.fr/fichier/t_publication/1375/publi_pdf1_pop_soc450.pdf.

Willcox, B. J., T. A. Donlon, Q. He, R. Chen, J. S. Grove, K. Yano, K. H. Masaki, D. C. Willcox, B. Rodriguez and J. D. Curb, 2008, "FOXO3A Genotype Is Strongly Associated with Human Longevity", *Proceedings of the National Academy of Sciences of the United States of America* 105(37), pp. 13987–92.

Willets, R., 2003, "The Cohort Effect: Insights and Explanations", Report, Willets Consulting Limited.

World Cancer Research Fund and American Institute for Cancer Research, 2007, "Food, Nutrition, Physical Activity, and the Prevention of Cancer: A Global Perspective", Report, American Institute for Cancer Research, Washington, DC, URL: http://www.dietand cancerreport.org/. (Retrieved February 20, 2009.)

World Health Organization, 2008, "Closing the Gap in a Generation (Part 1)", Report, URL: http://whqlibdoc.who.int/publications/2008/9789241563703_eng.pdf.

Yang, Z., E. C. Norton and S. C. Stearns, 2003, "Longevity and Health Care Expenditures: The Real Reasons Older People Spend More", *Journal of Gerontology* B 59(3), S197.

2
Magnitude of the Longevity Issue: The Market Opportunity and Capacity

Ed Collinge, Joseph Lu
Legal & General

The populations of many industrialised countries, such as the UK, are ageing and living longer. These trends affect the economy, health care and provisions for retirement. However, we still have much to learn about the drivers of human longevity and the uncertainty surrounding future longevity trends in populations.

This chapter provides an overview of the key sources of longevity risk as well as the pension schemes and types of insurance products that have longevity risk. In addition, we consider the size of the longevity issue and provide thoughts on how longevity risk may be managed and mitigated going forward. Several of the themes covered in this chapter are covered in greater detail later in this book.

FINANCIAL IMPACT OF LONGEVITY

A variety of now indisputable demographic trends are unfolding in many countries, but the one development which is likely to have dramatic social, cultural and economic consequences that are germane to our discussion is the fact that people in developed countries are having fewer children and are living longer. As the working population shrinks relative to that of retirees, governments will struggle to provide future pension benefits from future tax revenues. Projections from the UK Office for National Statistics shown in Figures 2.1 and 2.2, for example, show that the proportion of workers versus retirees will shift drastically over the next few decades. Over the next five decades the number of people over the age of 65 in the UK

Figure 2.1 Projection of UK population

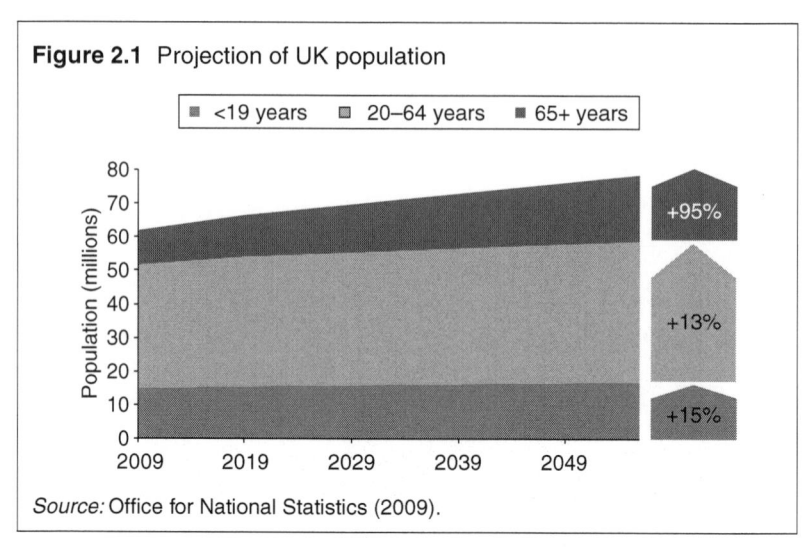

[Legend: <19 years, 20–64 years, 65+ years]

Changes shown: 65+ years +95%; 20–64 years +13%; <19 years +15%.

X-axis: 2009, 2019, 2029, 2039, 2049. Y-axis: Population (millions), 0–80.

Source: Office for National Statistics (2009).

Figure 2.2 Projection of UK dependency ratios

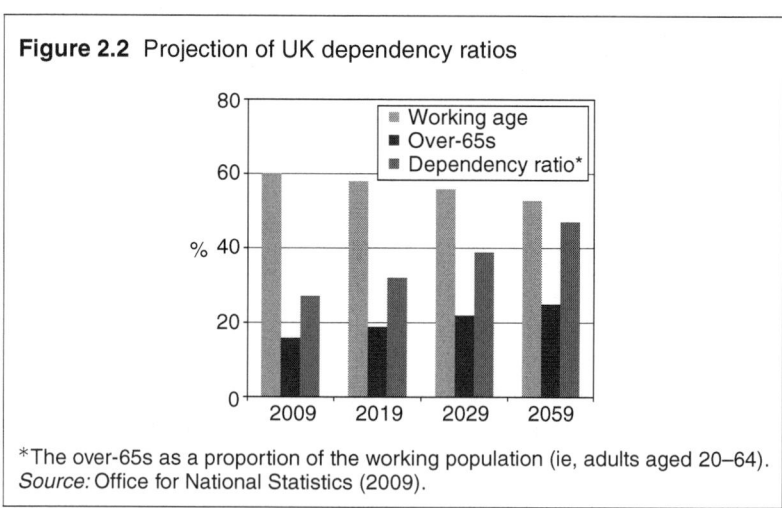

[Legend: Working age, Over-65s, Dependency ratio*]

X-axis: 2009, 2019, 2029, 2059. Y-axis: %, 0–80.

*The over-65s as a proportion of the working population (ie, adults aged 20–64).
Source: Office for National Statistics (2009).

is expected to increase by 9% of the total population, whereas the ranks of the working population will fall by 7%. The shift will cause the projected old-age dependency ratio to climb substantially.

The total pensions market is huge. UK pension liabilities alone are estimated to be in excess of £3 trillion,[1] of which around £2.1 trillion are UK government, £1 trillion are defined-benefit occupational pension plans and £125 billion are life insurers.

As staggering as these amounts are, an increase in life expectancy would cause liabilities to grow significantly. Roughly, a one-year

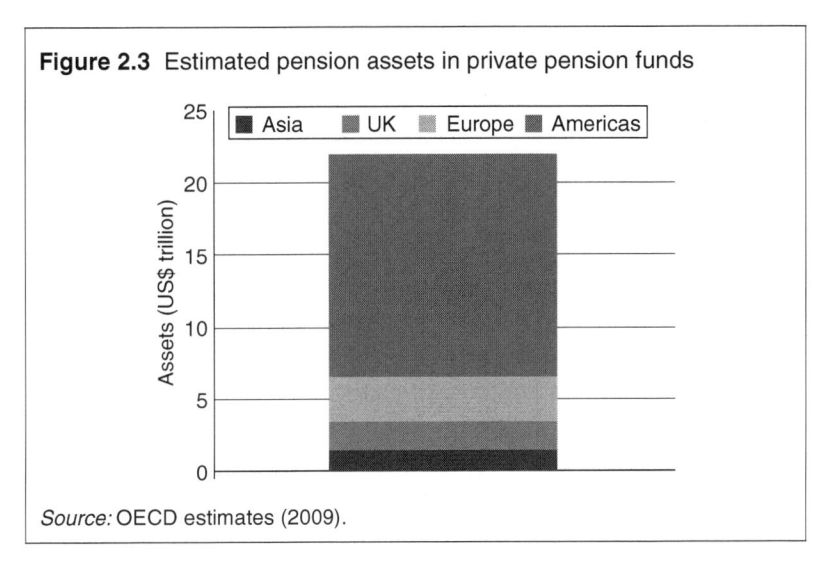

Figure 2.3 Estimated pension assets in private pension funds

Source: OECD estimates (2009).

extension in life expectancy is likely to increase pensioner liabilities between 3 and 5%.

Worldwide, it is estimated that private pension funds hold in excess of US$22 trillion of assets. Figure 2.3 shows an approximate breakdown of these assets by major region.

A relatively small number of markets dominate the market for private pension provision. The majority of assets are held in US, UK, Dutch and Swiss markets. Taking into account liabilities from state provision would significantly increase the amount of the total pensioner liabilities.

Longevity trends and the changing demographic of populations bestow on governments a crucial responsibility for creating an environment that aids the development of strong, stable and well-funded private market solutions to longevity risk, for, without a vibrant marketplace, governments may be unable to provide state pension benefits at the levels needed in the future.

Creating a stable environment for the private market can be achieved through the following.

- **Education and increasing financial awareness:** studies have shown that most people underestimate how long they can live. This miscalculation has important implications for pensioners planning for their retirement who could outlive their savings, or receive a lower pension amount that could lower their expected standard of living.

- **Providing tax incentives to support self-provision:** an example of this type of incentive is an arrangement in the UK where payments into an authorised pension plan are taken from gross of tax salary and individuals are allowed to take 25% of their benefit on retirement as a tax-free lump sum.
- **Compulsion:** in some countries, such as Australia, individuals are required to place a proportion of their salary into a private pension plan. This ensures that at retirement they are less likely to require support from the state.
- **Sponsoring the issuance of/creation of financial instruments that hedge longevity risk:** longevity linked bonds and other instruments that mitigate longevity risk will increase the potential capacity of the private sector to write longevity risk and drive down costs for pensioners.

Longevity risk provides both a potential challenge and a huge opportunity for investors that may want to participate in longevity-related asset returns. These investors may include reinsurers that want to diversify their exposure to mortality risks (the risk of policyholders dying more quickly than expected), or, for example, hedge funds which seek to identify a new asset class that provides scope for improved strategies for diversifying risk and optimising investor returns.

SOURCES OF LONGEVITY RISK

The main product type containing longevity risk is an annuity or pension, which pays an income during retirement to an individual for the remainder of their life. Sometimes these products also have secondary features, such as guarantees and spouse's pensions that are covered later. Three main types of institutions provide annuities or pensions.

- Government/state provisions provide a pension that may be based around a guaranteed minimum standard of living for pensioners. Pension amounts will typically increase with reference to an inflation measure. Existing taxpayers usually pay for state pension benefits. Government pensions are often unfunded and rely on the ability of taxpayers, primarily those in the workforce, to afford pension payments as they become due.

- Corporate/occupational pension schemes provide pension benefits sponsored by companies, as part of their staff remuneration policy. These benefits typically fall into two categories: a defined-benefit plan and a defined-contribution policy. A defined-benefit plan makes payments to pensioners based on, for example, their final salary and the number of years they worked for the company. Under a defined-contribution policy, however, the company pays fixed amounts into an investment account, which will be available at the time of retirement for the member to purchase an annuity product from a life insurance company.

  In contrast to government plans, corporate pension schemes are in the most part funded, but schemes still rely on the sponsoring parent company to make up any shortfall in the funding required.

- Insurance companies guarantee to make pension payments to the annuitant until their death in return for receiving a premium up front. Unlike state and occupational pension schemes, annuity policies issued by life insurance companies must be fully funded and insurance companies must hold significant additional regulatory capital to ensure that policyholders continue to receive their benefits under extreme stress scenarios.

Insurance companies write annuity policies directly with individuals, but also provide insurance policies (a market known as bulk annuities) directly to corporate pension schemes to cover their underlying members' benefits. The bulk annuity market is significant in size. For example, around £15 billion of premium was written in the UK between 2007 and 2009.

The basic annuity product type can vary in a number of ways, but annuities typically fall into two categories: immediate annuities (annuities or pensions in payment) and deferred annuities, which guarantee an income to the policyholder from their future retirement date. The main types of annuities are outlined in Figure 2.4.

An illustration of an annuity cashflow profile is summarised in Figure 2.5, which provides projections on both an expected and stressed longevity basis. The impact of lower mortality on the potential annuity payments is assumed in the stressed cashflow scenario.

> **Figure 2.4** Basic annuity product types (Telford *et al* 2010)
>
> **Level, or escalating (increasing).** A level annuity pays a fixed income, usually monthly, for an individual's lifetime. Because the income is fixed, its real value will decline over time as a result of inflation. Escalating annuities increase each year by either a fixed amount, typically 3 or 5% per annum, or a figure indexed to an inflation index. For a given premium, the starting income on an escalating annuity will be less than that for a level annuity.
>
> **Investment linked.** The amount of annuity payments will reference the asset returns achieved on the assets backing the annuity policy. These assets may either be linked to an insurer's with-profits fund whereby the annuity increases as bonuses are declared in line with the smoothed asset performance of the with-profits fund or, alternatively, linked to the performance in underlying unit funds. A selection of unit funds will usually be available based on risk appetite.
>
> **Variable.** A type of unit-linked annuity that incorporates some kind of additional guaranteed benefit. These may include a guaranteed minimum income or a guaranteed minimum withdrawal amount from the unit funds the policy is invested in even when the policyholder's funds have been exhausted. They aim to provide security in retirement while providing potential upside through a linkage to stock market returns. Variable annuities have been successful in the US and Japanese markets and are emerging across the European market.
>
> **Single or joint life.** Single life annuities will only provide an income during the life of the annuitant and will not pay any benefits to an annuitant's spouse or other financial dependants. A joint life annuity will pay an income to a surviving spouse, or other financial dependant, for the rest of their lives (although in the case of children's benefits these will typically cease at a predetermined age such as on the 18th or 21st birthday). The annuity amount typically will be reduced on the death of the primary annuitant.

Nascent market

In addition to annuity products, a nascent market has surfaced in "longevity-only risk" insurance products and "longevity swaps". These products have been employed by insurance companies to manage their longevity risk and also actively marketed to occupational pension schemes in the UK. The first significant occupational pension scheme public transaction closed in 2009.

Under a longevity swap, a pension scheme agrees to pay a fixed premium profile (the expected pension cashflows plus the providers

Figure 2.4 Continued

Guaranteed.   Some annuity products guarantee to make payments for a minimum number of years (usually for the first five or ten years) after the policy is taken out even if the annuitant dies during this period. This benefit is seen to be particularly attractive to annuitants who have saved throughout their whole life to fund their pension benefit and wish their dependents to still benefit should they die soon after taking out the policy.

Underwritten/enhanced/impaired life.   Similar in nature to conventional annuities, these products allow an annuitant who is in poor health to be able to achieve improved benefits to reflect their shorter life expectancy. To receive an enhanced annuity an annuitant's health will need to be assessed or underwritten by the life insurance company. Underwritten annuities are discussed further in Chapter 5.

Immediate needs.   These annuities provide an income to pay the costs of long-term care should an individual need to move into residential care or a nursing home. They are typically paid for with a single premium and often have an element of capital protection for the estate of the policyholder on their early death.

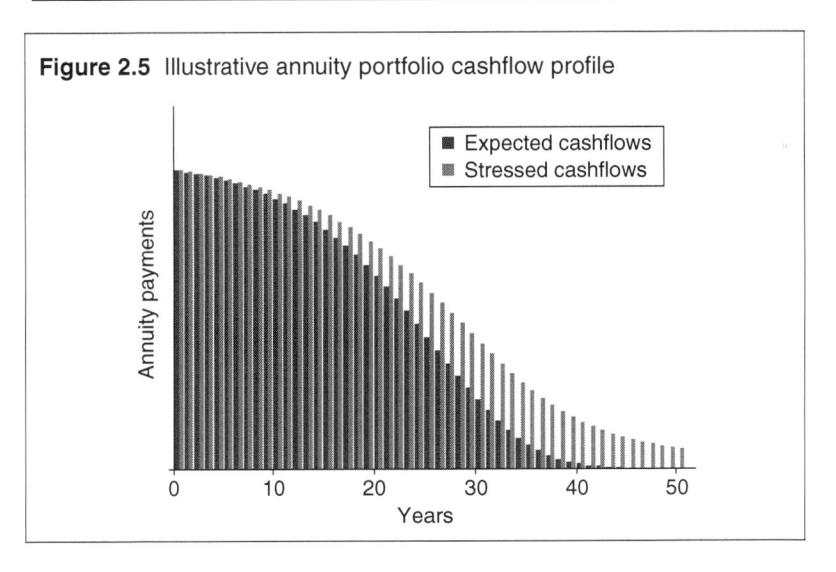

Figure 2.5 Illustrative annuity portfolio cashflow profile

risk and profit loading) to the longevity-swap provider in return for which the longevity-swap provider will pay actual annuity payments as they fall due. Under a longevity swap, the pension scheme retains the underlying asset risk and this product can also be thought of as a regular premium annuity.

LONGEVITY RISK TRANSFER

Occupational pension schemes are able to pass both their underlying longevity and asset risk to an insurer by purchasing an annuity policy. These policies may be in the form of a buy-out, whereby the pension scheme extinguishes its liability to its members and the insurer issues individual polices to the scheme members, or in the form of a buy-in, which is a contract between a pension scheme's trustees and the insurer, under which the buy-in insurance policy acts as a perfectly matching asset against the pension scheme liabilities covered by the buy-in policy. Pension schemes are also able to access capital market solutions to longevity risk where available.

Insurers have in a limited capacity used the reinsurance market to reduce their exposure to longevity or annuity risk. Much of the reinsurance in the annuity market has been designed and placed on a fairly simple basis, eg, a quota share basis. This approach contrasts with the frequently sophisticated financial designs in the protection market, where an insurer has often used multiple reinsurers: one reinsurer to provide reinsurance cover on term assurances for smokers; another for non-smokers. For this reason, it is likely that the reinsurance market for annuities will likewise become more sophisticated, with different reinsurers specialising in different risks. Our estimate of reinsurance capacity for longevity-only solutions in the UK at the time of writing is between £10 billion and £15 billion per annum.

In the past, insurance writers of annuity business have had only a limited number of risk-transfer options available. They have typically involved

- removing the risk entirely by selling a block of annuities to another insurer (also known as a full portfolio transfer),
- entering into a quota-share arrangement in which a tranche of the underlying risks are passed to a reinsurer or
- passing only the mortality/longevity risk to a reinsurer through longevity reinsurance.

More recently, capital market solutions have also emerged, but they do not yet provide a well-established common method for transferring significant amounts of risk to the capital markets, especially in cases in which smaller or medium sized portfolios are involved. Capital market solutions are also often based on an index

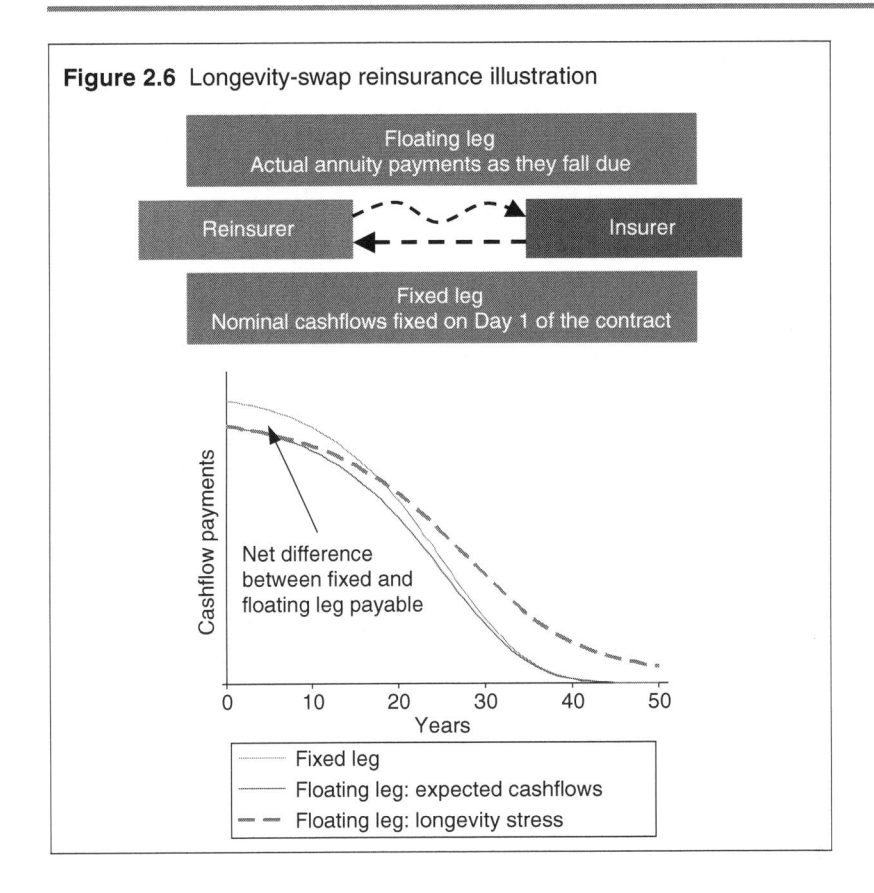

Figure 2.6 Longevity-swap reinsurance illustration

- Floating leg: Actual annuity payments as they fall due
- Reinsurer ← → Insurer
- Fixed leg: Nominal cashflows fixed on Day 1 of the contract

Net difference between fixed and floating leg payable

Cashflow payments vs Years (0, 10, 20, 30, 40, 50)

- Fixed leg
- Floating leg: expected cashflows
- Floating leg: longevity stress

or a formulaic definition of longevity improvements, which creates potential basis risk for insurers.

The majority of investors sponsoring these early capital markets transactions have also been reinsurers or hedge fund investors who have followed the reinsurers' assessment of the risk. Significant interest from capital markets investors beyond these groups has yet to be seen and the solutions so far represent a small proportion of the capacity provided by more traditional reinsurance solutions.

As mentioned previously, a significant new market in longevity-only risk insurance, or "longevity swaps", has emerged. Under these contracts, the annuity provider retains the underlying asset risks while passing the longevity risk to a third party.

Most of these contracts have been backed by reinsurance. A simple form of a longevity-swap/reinsurance arrangement typically has the following features.

LONGEVITY RISK

- The insurer agrees to pay the reinsurer a fixed set of monthly cashflows (the fixed leg), which are equal to the expected annuity payments on day 1 plus the reinsurer's risk and profit margin.
- The reinsurer agrees to make actual monthly annuity payments (the floating leg) to the insurer over the duration of the contract.
- If the underlying annuities are index-linked, typically both the fixed leg and floating leg will increase with actual inflation experience.
- Current swap/reinsurance products mainly target annuities in payment, and may be offered on an indemnity basis that references the experience of the annuitised lives or a parametric basis that references an index based on some other data such as population statistics. (Capital market solutions often reference an index.) In the parametric design, the ceding insurer faces the risk that the longevity trends of the annuitised lives do not move in line with those of the population referenced by the index and hence introducing some basis risk.
- Counterparty risk is often reduced or mitigated through collateral arrangements which usually reference a negotiated view of best-estimate future mortality used to determine the relative value of the swap. The rate and frequency with which this best-estimate view changes will have a significant impact on how effective the collateral arrangements are in minimising counterparty exposure.

Figure 2.6 provides an overview of longevity reinsurance together with the projected cashflows for the fixed and floating legs on an expected basis and a stressed longevity basis.

Longevity de-risking options available to annuity writers and pension schemes are discussed further in Chapters 8 and 9, respectively. In addition, reinsurance solutions are explored in further detail in Chapter 10. Further discussions of capital market solutions for longevity risk are given in Chapter 12.

Sources of future capacity for transferring longevity risk

Future efforts to build market capacity could turn to developing existing capital market solutions or creating new ones which would also allow the transfer of some or all of the risks underlying an annuity. Alternatives that may help to bring further capacity to the market include the following.

- Annuity securitisation: the issuance of notes whose repayments reference surplus arising from an underlying annuity portfolio. Typically, these notes would be split into different seniority tranches to maximise the potential investor base and obtain maximum price efficiency for the annuity provider.
- Longevity bonds: the issuance of bonds whose repayments reference an underlying mortality/longevity index. The first attempted launch of such a longevity bond was by the European Investment Bank in 2004, but the bond was not issued because this initiative did not receive sufficient interest from investors.
- Mortality or survival longevity forwards: an arrangement in which future payments are referenced to the movements in an underlying mortality/longevity index. Such indices have already been created by investment banks and can be traded against.
- Longevity linked convertible bonds: the issuance of bonds whose repayments reference an underlying mortality/longevity index. Should the expected capital repayment at maturity be impaired, the bondholder would have the option to convert the bond into equity. This structure provides the insurer with a higher quality of capital, but also increases the probability that the investors would be able to recover some or all of their investment in extreme scenarios.

Currently, the reinsurance market in longevity-only risk can be characterised as active. Several reinsurers are expected to enter the market alongside the existing providers, and growth of this market is being nurtured by an interest from pension scheme trustees, which like insurers are keen to look at ways to mitigate their exposure to longevity. While earlier longevity-swap transactions occurred between insurers and reinsurers, in 2009 we saw the first longevity-swap transactions between pension scheme trustees and insurers, under which the risk was in the most part directly passed on to reinsurers.

Our expectation is that this reinsurance market will continue to grow. However, insurers and reinsurers are unlikely to have the capacity to support more than a small proportion of the total longevity exposure in the UK and an even smaller proportion globally. For example, the current combined annuitant liabilities for insurers and pension schemes in the UK is estimated to be well in excess of £1 trillion. For significant amounts of the risk to be passed to third parties, large-scale capital market solutions would need to be developed. Due to the size of the longevity opportunity, a 1% transfer of UK longevity risk to the capital markets in a year would equate to in excess of £10 billion notional of transactions.

Some have suggested that governments should issue longevity bonds to facilitate the retirement product market and management of longevity risk. In doing so, governments would need to balance the policy perspectives of assisting the annuity market with their already significant exposure to longevity risk through state benefits and public sector pension schemes. In funding cost terms, the benefits of receiving a premium for longevity risk would need to be weighed against the likely lower liquidity of such bonds. For insurers, these bonds may not necessarily be attractive instruments in their own right, since they would combine government bond exposure with the longevity hedge. However, they would create additional longevity supply which insurers could access via the capital markets, in the same way that government issuance of index-linked gilts supports capacity in the inflation swap markets.

Large-scale capital market solutions may emerge in the short to medium term. Evidence of this possibility can be seen in the activity of the insurance and pensions sectors and several investment banks that are currently investigating this area.

In late 2009, the (non-profit organisation) Life and Longevity Markets Association (LLMA) was formed with the aim of promoting the development of a liquid traded market in longevity- and mortality-related risk. The LLMA brings together several market participants from the insurance, reinsurance and investment banking communities and demonstrates the strength of desire for a viable liquid secondary market in longevity risk transfer to be created. A few bespoke longevity-related transactions have also been completed, although often reinsurers rather than capital markets investors have been actively involved in the pricing and warehousing of the risk.

The potential benefits of a significant capital market solution are substantial and could one day provide

- an effective longevity risk mitigation tool to insurers and pension schemes, which could create significant capital benefits,
- a market price for longevity risk, which should allow shareholders to better assess the risks held within, and the value of, annuity providers' portfolios,
- a new asset class that provides investors scope for improved strategies for diversifying risk and optimising investor returns.

Managing longevity risk

Holders of longevity risk need to ensure that they actively manage the underlying risk and ensure that their longevity exposure remains within acceptable risk tolerances. In particular, occupational pension schemes and insurers will need to hold sufficient assets and capital against the longevity risk they hold to ensure that annuitants receive payments as they fall due.

Whilst market and credit risk remain the largest risks in an annuity contract, longevity risk is still significant. For example, a typical UK insurer may hold between 6% and 8% of capital against annuity contract longevity risk on an economic capital basis (pre-diversification), according to Milliman estimates (Milliman 2009). A discussion of reserving and capital requirements are covered in greater detail in Chapters 6 and 7 of this volume.

Longevity risk poses a unique problem due to the long duration of the underlying transactions. A typical duration is approximately 15 years for an immediate annuity and in excess of 25 years for a deferred annuity.

There is also inherent uncertainty in projecting the rate at which longevity improvements will occur. A small mis-estimation in expected longevity could easily result in an insurer writing a product on unprofitable terms, or in a pension scheme having insufficient assets to cover its liabilities.

Mis-estimation in expected longevity could be due to issues relating to modelling, judgement and random variation in results and data. Longevity products are also exposed to future changes that stem from higher life expectancy due to improvements in healthcare provision, healthier life styles and advancements in medicine, among other factors.

An annuity can be seen as an insurance product in which the annuitant insures against the event of living longer than expected: a possibility that the annuitant wishes to occur. This situation is in sharp contrast with life assurance, which insures a person against their (unwanted) death or the death of another. In this respect, the annuity is a relatively unique insurance product because it sets up a clear conflict of interest in which the annuitant effectively desires the insured event (longevity) to happen.

The long time frame over which the outcome of longevity risk needs to be measured makes it impossible to know today whether a contract will be profitable or whether sufficient capital has been held against the risk. For this reason, risk mitigation techniques and capital requirements tend to be prudent. However, companies can reduce their exposure to longevity risk by

- altering the nature of the underlying policy by, for example, paying for a maximum term,
- selectively underwriting business which only provides cover to lives that are expected to have less longevity risk,
- actively researching trends in longevity and creating more refined and sophisticated longevity prediction models,
- making use of reinsurance or capital markets longevity solutions (although previously this has been a relatively small market, it is growing),
- investing in assets, which arguably provide a hedge against longevity risk.[2]

CONCLUSION

The global longevity risk market is enormous, and its underlying risk is hard to quantify in practice. Longer life spans are creating a significant burden on state provision, particularly in developed countries, where falling birth rates are funnelling fewer and fewer people into the ranks of the working population, which is reducing in size relative to the pensioner population.

Existing systems of unfunded state provisions that rely on current tax payers to pay for the current pensioners' benefits will therefore need to consider moving to a model which encourages individuals to save appropriately for their retirement within the private market.

One area where developments are likely is in the area of longevity risk transfer to third parties. Until the 2000s, holders of longevity risk have had relatively limited opportunity to mitigate their exposure and pass it on to third parties through either reinsurance or capital markets transactions. Largely untapped, the longevity risk transfer market is therefore poised for growth and is an area that is already gaining significant exposure through the creation of trade organisations such as the LLMA.

1   Life & Longevity Markets Association estimates.
2   For example, home equity release (lifetime mortgage) providers and health-care providers are likely to benefit with increased longevity.

REFERENCES

LLMA, 2010, "The Development of a Longevity and Mortality Trading Market", Presented at Sixth International Longevity Risk and Capital Markets Solutions Conference, June.

Milliman, 2009, "Longevity Risk Capital under Solvency II: Internal Models versus the Standard Formula Approach", in *Issues in Brief,* Autumn.

OECD, 2009, Global Pension Statistics Database, URL: http://www.oecd.org/daf/pensions/gps.

Office for National Statistics, 2009, "2008-Based National Population Projections", Statistical Bulletin, October 21, URL: http://www.statistics.gov.uk/.

Telford, P. G., B. A. Browne, E. J. Collinge, P. Fulcher, B. E. Johnson, W. Little, J. L. C. Lu, J. M. Nurse, D. W. Smith and F. Zhang, 2010, "Developments in the Management of Annuity Business", Presented to the Institute of Actuaries, March 22.

Part II

Pricing Longevity Risk

3

Pricing Longevity Risk: Establishing Base Mortality Level

Eli Friedwald
RGA UK Services Ltd

This chapter aims to set out the key considerations needed to estimate the base mortality for a portfolio of vested pensions, or annuity in-payment policies. For purposes of discussion, base mortality means the mortality rates that are applied as at a designated point in time, for example, the date of the intended transaction or valuation, for males and females over the complete range of ages in the underlying annuity portfolio.

We first introduce the main risk factors which influence the level of mortality. This discussion is followed by a description of a number of methodologies used for pricing portfolios of business for which mortality experience is available. But, as many in the pension and annuity field know, mortality experience is not always available. We then explore how to develop predictive pricing for portfolios without experience, which poses some distinct challenges. Lastly, we take up the issue of timing adjustments and conclude with a discussion of some possible complications.

Although the process described in this chapter is essentially scientific, it is very much a practical science and considerable judgement needs to be exercised along the way. There is no doubt that two actuaries working separately on the same pricing exercise would arrive at different sets of base pricing levels.

While the examples used throughout the chapter primarily relate to the pricing of UK annuity portfolios, the general principles and methods presented may also have a much broader application to the pricing of portfolios in other territories.

But before we embark on a discussion of specific pricing methodologies, let us briefly turn to the major factors which influence mortality levels.

Table 3.1 The main risk factors influencing mortality

Factor	Direct influence on mortality rates	Usefulness as a proxy factor in pricing
Age	Very high	Very high
Sex	Very high	Very high
Medical history	Very high	Very low
Genetics	High	Very low
Smoking status	High	Very low
Diet	High	Very low
Obesity	High	Very low
Occupation/socioeconomic class	High	Moderate
Alcohol consumption	Moderate	Very low
Regular exercise	Moderate	Very low
Exposure to stress	Moderate	Very low
Wealth	Moderate	Very low
Marital status	Moderate	Moderate
Education	Moderate	Low
Degree and method of medical underwriting	Low	Very low
Family medical history	Low	Very low
Geographical location	Low	Low
Postcode	Low	High
Annuity amount	Low	High

Source: Board for Actuarial Standards (2008).

FACTORS INFLUENCING MORTALITY

The mortality level of an annuitant population is affected by a variety of risk factors.

The influence of a particular factor and its usefulness as a proxy predictor for estimating base mortality is shown in Table 3.1. Some, such as age and sex, strongly influence mortality and are most useful in pricing. Medical history is also strongly influential on mortality but is considerably less useful in pricing, because for most annuity portfolios other than underwritten/enhanced annuities the medical status of the annuitants is not known. Other risk factors such as postcode and annuity amount have only a weak influence on mortality, but they are often readily available and are strongly correlated with socio-economic class, which itself is correlated with mortality levels, ie, higher economic classes tend to experience lower mortality. For this reason, the distribution of postcodes or annuity amounts in a portfolio can be used to estimate the portfolio's base mortality.

When credible experience is available, the most relevant starting point for pricing is the portfolio's past experience. This is usually measured against age and sex (see the next section), but may also be measured against other risk factors such as annuity amount bandings.

Credible mortality experience for a portfolio, however, may be unavailable. In this case, it may be possible to use knowledge of the influence of the rating factors as indicated in Table 3.1 to predict a base mortality, a topic that is discussed in further detail in the section on "predictive pricing".

PRICING FROM EXPERIENCE
Pricing fully credible populations

For large annuity portfolios with a reliable past history encompassing thousands of deaths, the historical mortality experience is the best starting point to set the base mortality level for a transaction. The challenge is to determine the historical mortality experience for key risk factors such as age and sex over a recent investigation period and then to adjust this experience for assumed further improvements between the investigation period and the date of the transaction.

The data provided by the scheme actuary or the insurer will include a detailed listing of all annuitants who were drawing annuities over the investigation period, their sex, dates of birth and the corresponding details of dependant spouses. The data should also include the amounts of annuity, escalation rates, guaranteed periods applicable to each annuitant and a list of deaths and their dates. Once the data is reviewed for consistency and completeness, the actuary can then undertake any further analysis required, such as calculating crude mortality rates from the experience.

Crude mortality rates

Crude mortality rates are calculated separately for males and females, at each age, using the standard actuarial formulae in which D_x is the number of annuitant deaths aged between x and $x + 1$ in the period, E_x is the number of life-years exposed to risk of death for

LONGEVITY RISK

Figure 3.1 Ungraduated mortality rates: crude μ_x

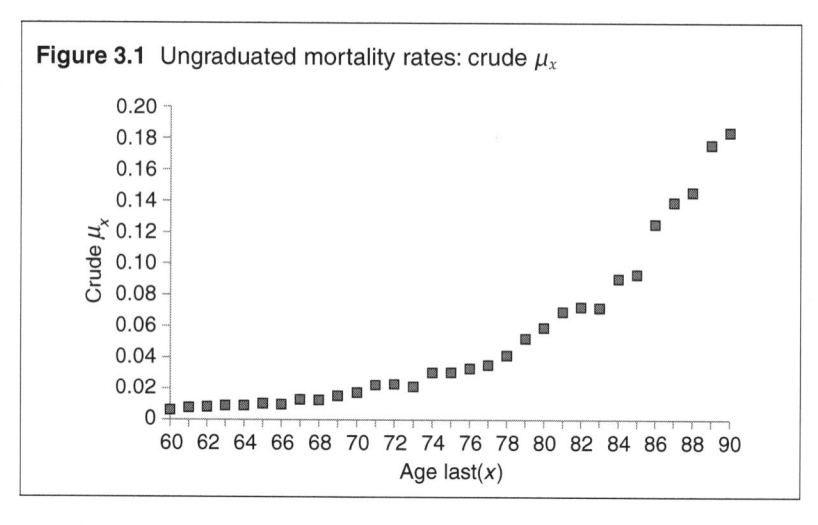

ages between x and $x + 1$ in the period and the standard formula is stated as

$$\mu_{x+1/2} = \frac{D_x}{E_x}$$

where μ_x represents the crude mortality rate at exact age x. At this point, the μ_x are known as "crude", because they have not been graduated or smoothed.

The above formula is stated in terms of the numbers of lives. But an analogous method can be used to determine μ_x for amounts of annuity, by replacing the number of deaths with the annual annuity amounts ceasing on death and life-years' exposure with the annual annuity amounts exposed. The μ_x for amounts is the key mortality rate for pricing purposes, since it is the annuity cost which needs to be priced. In general, μ_x (amounts) is less than μ_x (lives), because the former is more heavily weighted by larger annuity sizes in which the annuitant is likely to derive from a higher socio-economic class and hence experience lower mortality.

Calculating a set of crude μ_x (an example of which is shown in Figure 3.1 for an illustrative annuity portfolio) is only the first step in the pricing process. The next challenge is to graduate the crude μ_x in order to develop a smooth and continuous series.

Graduation methods

Graduation involves fitting a smooth curve through the crude μ_x series. A number of approaches can be used, but our discussion is confined to the Gompertz–Makeham (GM) method and the method

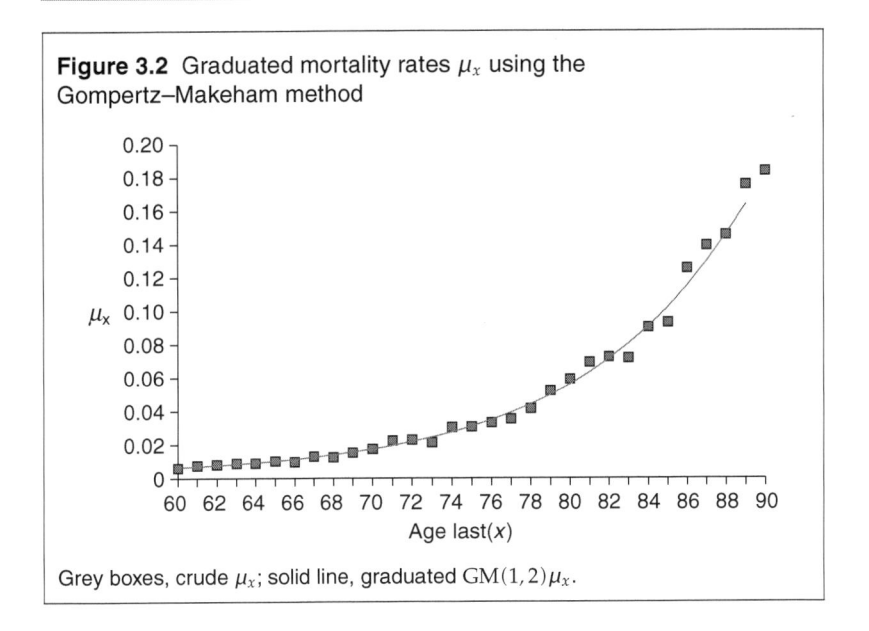

Figure 3.2 Graduated mortality rates μ_x using the Gompertz–Makeham method

[Chart showing μ_x on the y-axis (0 to 0.20) versus Age last(x) from 60 to 90, with grey boxes representing crude μ_x and a solid line representing graduated $GM(1,2)\mu_x$.]

Grey boxes, crude μ_x; solid line, graduated $GM(1,2)\mu_x$.

of P-splines, two of the most popular techniques used by actuaries in the field.

Gompertz–Makeham method

This technique assumes an *a priori* formulaic relationship between mortality rate and age, based on observations of human and animal mortality over a long period. Associated with the GM formula is a class of curves commonly used for graduations. (The formula for a particular case from this class, GM(1, 2), is given by $\mu_x = \alpha_1 + \exp(\alpha_2 + \alpha_3 x)$, where α_i are parameters whose values determine the shape of the curve. Standard mathematical techniques are available to determine optimal values for the parameters α_i, which best fit the crude μ_x series calculated earlier. These can be used to solve for α_i to generate a graduated set of μ_x.)

An example of the smoothing effect of the GM graduation process is illustrated in Figure 3.2.

A GM-type curve-fitting technique has the advantage of automatically shaping the mortality at young and old age ranges, where the data may be sparse, according to a pattern typical of mortality distributions. This feature may be somewhat of a drawback, however, if the older ages at which data is typically scanty are important to the pricing exercise. Under these circumstances, it may be necessary to test a number of parameterisations to assess which one is the most appropriate to the portfolio being priced.

Other regressive curve-fitting techniques however make no *a priori* assumptions as to the relationship between mortality and age, but seek only to determine the best fit to the data. The method of P-splines discussed next is an example of a non-parametric regression model that is frequently used and turned to today for smoothing series of data.

P-spline method

The P-spline method seeks to balance goodness of fit with smoothness by fitting a surface over historical data, using an appropriate choice of parameter values as discussed in further detail in the next subsection.

An application of the P-spline graduation using the data set shown above appears in Figure 3.3. The crude and GM(1,2) graduated values for μ_x are also shown below for comparison.

How P-spline fitting works. Splines are piecewise polynomials which can be fitted through a series of points.

The objective of regression by splines is to fit the piecewise surface function $S(x)$ through a series of data points, $x_1, x_2, \ldots, x_n$, in a smooth fashion.

In the case of cubic splines, the function $S(x)$ is of the form

$$S(x) = \begin{cases} s_1(x) & \text{if } x_1 \leqslant x < x_2 \\ s_2(x) & \text{if } x_2 \leqslant x < x_3 \\ \vdots \\ s_{n-1}(x) & \text{if } x_{n-1} \leqslant x < x_n \end{cases}$$

where s_i is a third-degree polynomial defined by

$$s_i(x) = a_i(x - x_i)^3 + b_i(x - x_i)^2 + c_i(x - x_i) + d_i$$

for $i = 1, 2, \ldots, n - 1$.

For a continuous function to be fitted, the $n - 1$ equations above need to satisfy a number of conditions in respect to their first and second differentials. Standard statistical packages are available to solve the differential equations, determining the coefficients a_i, b_i and c_i, and hence to fit the regression curve.

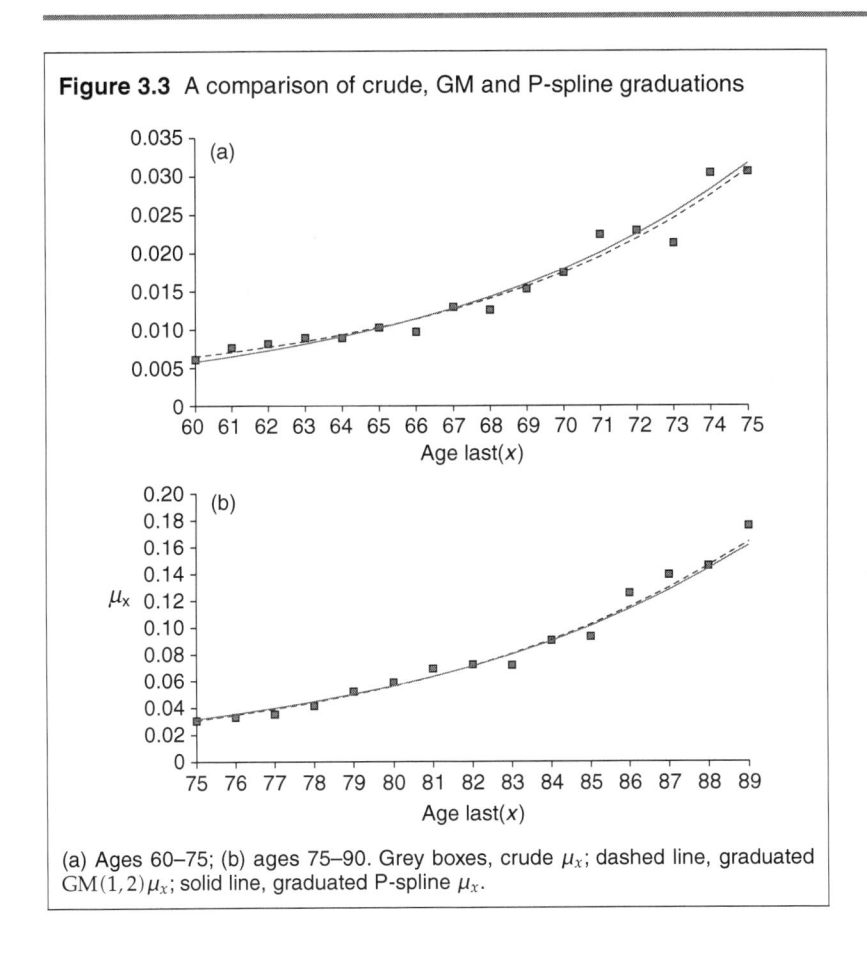

Figure 3.3 A comparison of crude, GM and P-spline graduations

(a) Ages 60–75; (b) ages 75–90. Grey boxes, crude μ_x; dashed line, graduated $GM(1,2)\mu_x$; solid line, graduated P-spline μ_x.

In the method of P-splines, a further smoothing parameter λ is introduced, which can be chosen to optimise a certain penalty function which trades off smoothness against goodness of fit. The choice of a higher value for λ will lead to a smoother curve through the data points, but will follow the data less faithfully. How to balance smoothness and the goodness of fit required in the curve-fitting is a decision the user must make.

Figure 3.3 shows the similarity between the two graduations over the majority of the full age range, but the two graduations are certainly not identical. This is particularly apparent for graph (a), where the graduations can differ by up to 5% at the youngest ages.

Two other graduation methods in common use are Whittaker–Henderson and survival models.

The Whittaker–Henderson method is a non-parametric approach, which graduates by minimising a difference equation. The method allows for an explicit balance between smoothness and goodness of fit. It is commonly used in North America.

Survival model methods differ from all the graduation methods previously described in that they model the time till death, rather than the number of deaths.

Calculating q_x from μ_x

In the graduations used in Figures 3.2 and 3.3, μ_x represents the force of mortality at exact age x. For most pricing purposes the mortality rates are more commonly quoted as initial rates of mortality, q_x, where q_x is the mortality rate between exact age x and exact age $x + 1$. The values of q_x can be calculated from those of μ_x using the approximation formula

$$q_x = 1 - \exp\left(-\frac{\mu_x + \mu_{x+1}}{2}\right)$$

Goodness-of-fit testing

The results of a graduation need to be formally tested for goodness of fit to the underlying data. A number of tests are traditionally employed to measure goodness of fit. These include

- χ^2 tests, which compare actual numbers of deaths with deaths expected on the graduated basis, to confirm or reject the graduation hypothesis,
- signs tests, which count the number of positive and negative deviations between the crude and graduated mortality rates and tests whether these deviations conform to a binomial distribution as they should be if the deviations were random,
- runs tests, which measure the number of successive deviations with the same sign as a way of determining whether they are consistent with a random distribution.

Other goodness-of-fit tests include serial correlation, standardised deviation and Kolmogorov–Smirnov.

The goodness-of-fit tests can be used to hone in on the best graduation method for the annuity portfolio, or decide between alternative parameter or curve choices within a method. A number of factors will influence the final decision, one of the most important being the range of ages that are most significant to the pricing of the specific portfolio, which may vary from transaction to transaction.

Because mortality tables typically employ a terminal age (usually age 120), the goodness-of-fit process also calls for the graduated rates at very high ages to be blended in towards the terminal age, when it is assumed that all survivors will die.

Standard graduated tables

Graduated tables have been prepared by government, academic or actuarial bodies in many countries in respect of population, assured lives and annuitant mortality experience. These tables are often used as the starting points for mortality pricing and are useful for comparison purposes. Examples of international standard tables can be found in Chapter 4.

In the UK, the Continuous Mortality Investigation (CMI) is a research undertaking of the Actuarial Profession which performs graduations, on a regular basis, of industry-supplied data on pre-defined business types. Details of some sets of UK annuitant tables graduated by the CMI are given in Figures 3.4 and 3.5.

Companies that write a significant volume of annuity business may also prepare their own internal graduated mortality tables for incorporation into their terms of trade, but standard graduated tables play a key role in pricing portfolios for those companies with little experience, as we shall see in the following section.

Pricing medium and smaller populations

While graduating an individual base mortality table (as discussed above) may be appropriate for annuity portfolios with fully credible experience, in practice, such large volumes of experience data may not be available and alternative pricing methods must be sought. The common methodology used in these situations is to express the mortality experience of the portfolio to be priced in terms of a base graduated table, usually a standard mortality table or one derived from their aggregate internal experience analysis for large annuity writers. The experience is then expressed as $X\%$ of the selected table.

Expressing experience in this way, however, may be somewhat complicated by the fact that a number of standard tables with different shapes often exist. The potential variation in shapes of mortality by age is shown in Figure 3.6, which provides a comparison of levels

Figure 3.4 The UK CMI "00" Series annuitant and pensioner tables are graduated from pension data provided by life offices for the period 1999–2002

The table description shows the business type covered by each table (Life Office Pensioners, Retirement Annuitants etc). These types are differentiated by the legislation under which the business was written. The retirement type shows the variant sub-categories graduated for each table (early retirement, etc) and the basis indicates whether "amounts" as well as "lives" graduations are available. An initialism is used to denote a particular table description, retirement type, sex and basis. For example, "PCMA00" is used to designate the table for life office pensioners, combined, male amounts mortality basis.

Sex	Table description	Retirement type	Basis
Male (M) Female (F)	Life Office Pensioners (P)	Early (E) Normal (N) Combined (C)	Lives (L) Amounts (A)
Female (F)	Retirement Annuitants (R)	Vested (V) Deferred (D) Combined (C)	Lives only (L)
	Personal Pensioners (PP)		
	Immediate Annuitants (I)	Not Applicable	
	Widows (W)	Not Applicable	Lives (L) Amounts (A)

and shapes of UK standard mortality tables for the "00" and "S1" Series tables with an England and Wales population table, English Life Table 16 (ELT16) for males. The challenge becomes to select the most appropriate table and to determine the multiplier X%.

When compared with a population table, standard annuitant and pensioner mortality tables can be shown to have considerably different shapes as shown in Figure 3.6. For this reason, the selection of a population table in the absence of annuitant or pensioner tables may not be the most appropriate approach, because the population table can have a materially different shape.

The standard annuitant and pensioner tables share a broadly similar shape across most ages but at different levels. As might be expected, the amounts tables generally have lower mortality rates than the lives tables, because the amounts rates are weighted more to the experience of larger annuities, where those annuitants are generally from a higher socio-economic class.

Figure 3.5 The UK CMI "S1" Series self-administered pension scheme tables are graduated from pension scheme data provided by consulting actuaries for the period 2000–2006

The classification of these tables differs from that of the "00" Series as indicated by the different headings used for these tables. The "S1" Series tables include separate graduations for light and heavy mortality categories, corresponding to larger and smaller annuity sizes. As an example, "S1NMAL" is used to designate the table for normal health, males, amounts, light mortality basis.

Sex	Retirement type	Basis	Pension amount band
Male (M) Female (F)	All pensioners (excl dependants)	Lives (L)	All
		Amounts (A)	Light
			Heavy
			All
	Normal-health pensioners	Lives (L)	All
		Amounts (A)	Light
			Heavy
			All
	Ill-health pensioners	Amounts (A)	All
Female (F)	Dependants	Lives (L)	All
		Amounts (A)	Light
			Heavy
			All

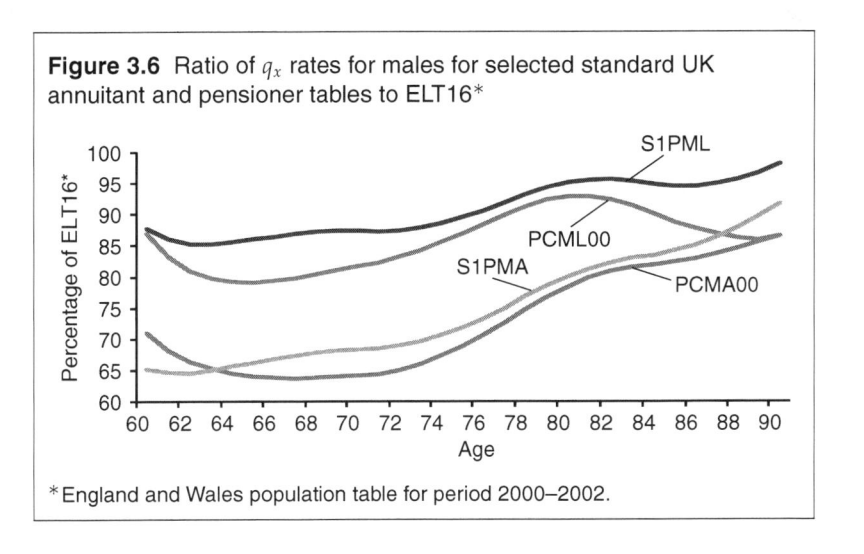

Figure 3.6 Ratio of q_x rates for males for selected standard UK annuitant and pensioner tables to ELT16*

*England and Wales population table for period 2000–2002.

A knowledge of the type of annuitants in a portfolio may point to the use of an appropriate standard table in pricing. For example, the "00" Series would be the obvious candidate tables to be used for an insured UK annuity portfolio; on the other hand, a self-administered UK pension scheme portfolio is likely to call for the use of a table from the "S1" Series. No matter what the characteristics of the underlying annuitant portfolio are, it is advisable to compare the shape of the portfolio's experience by age with a number of the standard tables before making a choice. This is done by calculating the expected deaths (E) (for both lives and amounts) for the portfolio by age on each of the standard table mortality bases and comparing these results with the actual deaths (A). The A/E ratios for each age, or age band, can then be plotted for each standard table. The standard table for which the A/E ratios are flattest across the range of ages, is the most appropriate base table for comparison purposes, adjusted by the appropriate multiplier ($X\%$).

More formally, the standard deviation of A/E ratios across all age bands can be calculated for the different standard tables in order to determine the table providing the lowest standard deviation. However, before the portfolio's experience can be compared against the standard tables, an intermediate step is required to "synchronise" the standard table with that of the portfolio.

Synchronising the standard table with the annuity portfolio

A simple example can demonstrate the method of synchronising a standard table with the annuity portfolio. To carry out the example, it is assumed that

- the annuity portfolio's experience is measured over the four-year period 2003–6,
- the standard tables for comparison are from the "00" Series (Figure 3.4), which are based on industry experience over the four-year period 1999–2002.

We can then determine mid-points of the portfolio's experience and the standard table's experience simplistically as January 1, 2005 for the portfolio and January 1, 2001 for the standard table. For synchronicity and consistency between the annuity portfolio experience and the comparison standard tables, we need to apply notional mortality improvements to the standard tables in respect of the four-year period from January 1, 2001 to January 1, 2005.

Figure 3.7 Illustrative annuity portfolio A/E for annuity amounts, with 95% CI, against standard table after synchronising. Male experience

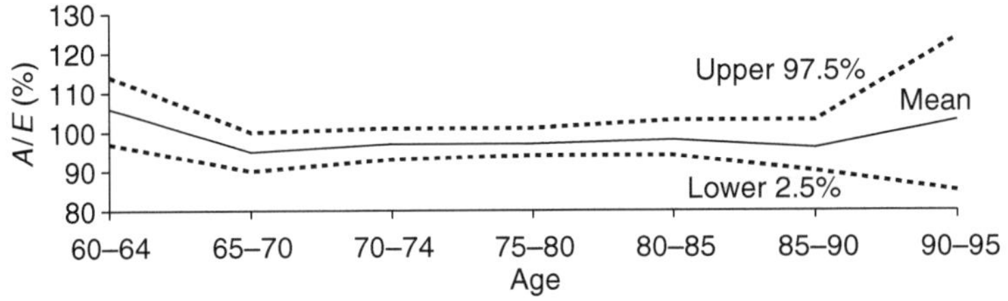

[Chart showing A/E (%) on y-axis ranging from 80 to 130, and Age bands on x-axis: 60–64, 65–70, 70–74, 75–80, 80–85, 85–90, 90–95. Three lines plotted: Upper 97.5%, Mean, Lower 2.5%.]

For simplicity, the CI bands have been calculated using a "lives analysis" formula. See the text for why this is not strictly valid for an amounts analysis.

A number of assumption tables and mortality sources are available for setting the necessary improvement adjustments for each age to synchronise the tables. One approach is to use the published cumulative historic population mortality improvements for the period. Another is to use a projected improvements table, produced internally or widely adopted in the industry. The standard table mortality rates can then be reduced by the smoothed cumulative improvements for the relevant period.

As an example of a base table selection, Figure 3.7 shows A/E ratios for an annuity portfolio along with lower and upper 95% confidence intervals (CIs), which are plotted against a standard table after synchronising.

The chart produces a relatively flat A/E ratio over the majority of age bands, indicating that the selected standard table is appropriate to use as a base for measuring the level of experience of this annuity portfolio for most ages. Once the appropriate base table to use as a starting point has been selected, the overall A/E result determines the level of the experience against that table.

If none of the standard tables appear to provide a good fit to the portfolio's experience across the full range of ages, then manual adjustments to a table's shape may be necessary, based on judgement.

Confidence intervals

Once the level of the experience of the portfolio has been estimated against the base mortality table, a measure of the uncertainty of the experience result should be determined.

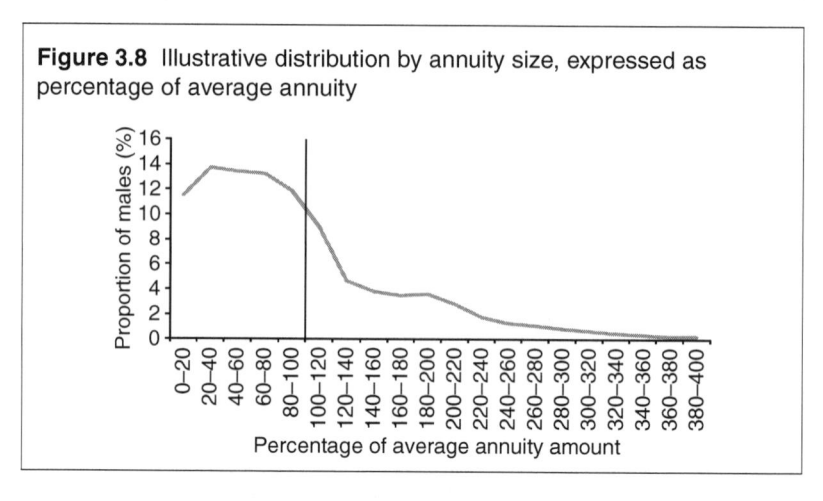

Figure 3.8 Illustrative distribution by annuity size, expressed as percentage of average annuity

[Chart: x-axis "Percentage of average annuity amount" with bins 0–20, 20–40, ..., 380–400; y-axis "Proportion of males (%)" from 0 to 16]

For a lives analysis, the expected statistical fluctuation may be determined directly from the claims data, using a simple formula. The formula is typically based on the assumption that claims events are independent and occur at a known average rate, these being properties of a binomial distribution.

Assuming a binomial distribution, the 95% confidence intervals around the lives A/E result can be calculated as

$$CI_{95\%}(\text{lives basis}) = \frac{\text{actual number of deaths}}{\text{expected number of deaths}} \pm 1.96 \frac{\sqrt{\text{actual number of deaths}}}{\text{expected number of deaths}}$$

For an amounts analysis, however, there is also an additional stochastic fluctuation in annuity amount for deaths which creates more uncertainty and increases the width of the confidence intervals. The uncertainty will depend on both the numbers of lives in the annuity portfolio and the distribution of annuity amounts by size.

The confidence intervals of an amounts A/E analysis may be calculated using Monte Carlo simulations, although there are also approximate numerical solutions available.

We illustrate the wider confidence intervals associated with an amounts analysis in Figures 3.8 and 3.9. Figure 3.8 shows the distribution of annuity amount sizes for a specimen annuity portfolio, as a percentage of the average annuity in the portfolio. Figure 3.9 indicates the spread of A/E simulated scenarios, for portfolios of 10,000 and 50,000 annuitants respectively, for the amount distribution given

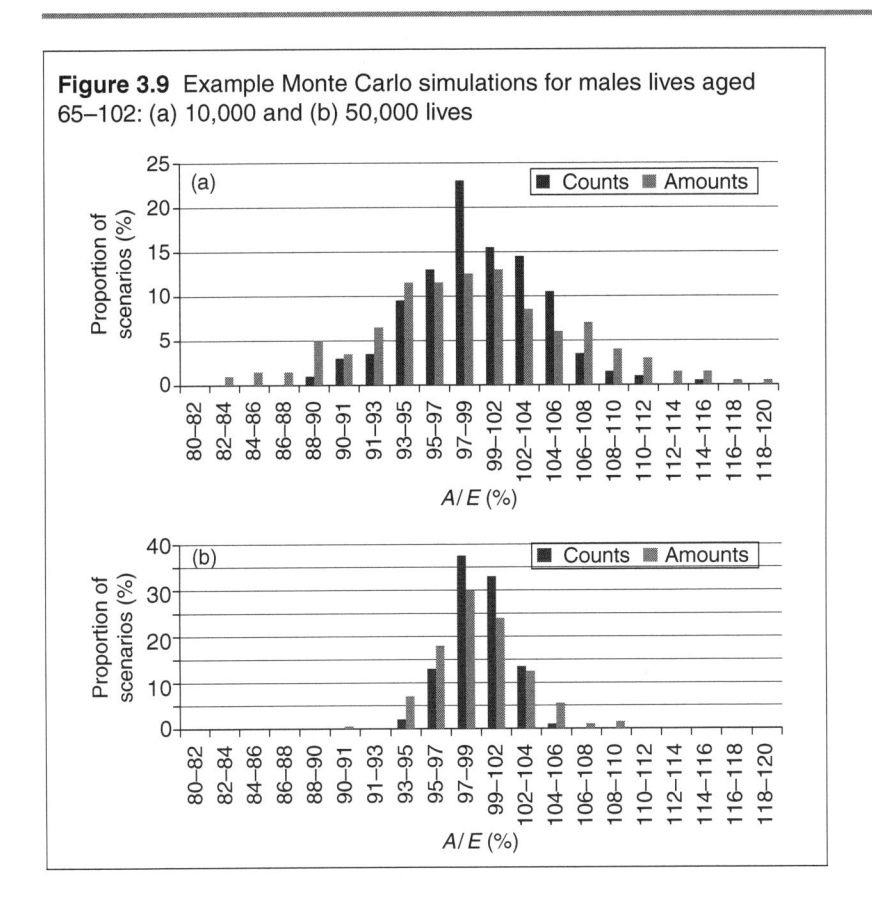

Figure 3.9 Example Monte Carlo simulations for males lives aged 65–102: (a) 10,000 and (b) 50,000 lives

Table 3.2 Illustrative 95% confidence interval limits for three population sizes (annuity size distribution)

	A/E (%) for 95% CI limits for		
	1,000 lives	10,000 lives	50,000 lives
Lives	77–138	92–108	96–104
Amounts	63–154	85–114	95–106

in Figure 3.8. These have been calculated for a single year of investigation using Monte Carlo simulations on an assumed base mortality and show the proportion of simulations which produced A/E ratios in the specified ranges compared with an average 100% result.

Figure 3.9 indicates the wider spread of amounts A/E ratios compared with lives A/E ratios, particularly with the smaller portfolio size. These results correspond to 95% confidence intervals as given in Table 3.2 (with 1,000 lives added).

The results shown in Table 3.2 provide insight into the uncertainty of the A/E derived from an experience analysis, particularly for annuity amounts and for smaller populations. The size distribution as shown in Figure 3.8 is not particularly skewed. In instances where the annuity sizes are more right-skewed than those in this example, the uncertainties of the experience result will be higher and the "amounts" confidence intervals will be even wider than those illustrated.

This possibility introduces a potential mispricing risk which can, to some extent, be mitigated by transacting a large number of annuity portfolios, on the assumption that no bias is introduced in the experience analyses and that pricing errors can therefore be assumed to cancel out across portfolios. Such diversification of risk may not be achievable in practice, so it is usual to introduce a credibility adjustment before the result of an experience analysis is used in pricing.

Adjusting for credibility of portfolio's experience

In situations in which it is fair to assume that the annuity portfolio being priced is similar to another for which credible mortality rates (the "book" basis) exists, it is reasonable to blend the experience rates of the portfolio with the book rates, using credibility factors as weights.

The choice of an appropriate book basis can itself be quite problematic. Where the particular portfolio is made up of annuity policies similar in characteristics to those for which a set of mortality rates has already been adopted into terms of trade, these rates can form the book basis. Otherwise a standard table, such as the base table used in the A/E analysis, could be used, adjusted for an appropriate multiplier.

One way to check the reasonableness of a book basis is to determine whether the book experience falls within the confidence intervals that were calculated for the annuity portfolio. If the annuity portfolio has unusual characteristics, in terms of any of the factors listed in Table 3.1, then it may be necessary to devise adjustments to a current book basis or standard table to generate a customised book basis.

Table 3.3 Number of deaths required for P% confidence within range ±K% (binomial)

Probability (P%)	Range parameters (K)				
	5%	4%	3%	2%	1%
90	1,083	1,691	3,007	6,764	27,056
95	1,537	2,401	4,269	9,604	38,415
99	2,654	4,147	7,373	16,588	66,350
99.5	4,332	6,768	12,031	27,070	108,278

A general formula may then be applied to determine a credibility-adjusted blended experience rate as follows

adjusted experience = Z × portfolio experience
$$+ (1 - Z) \times \text{book experience}$$

where Z is the credibility factor assigned to the portfolio and obeys $0 < Z < 1$.

There are various theoretical approaches to determining Z, but in practice a simplified procedure to credibility adjustments, known as the limited fluctuation approach, is adopted by a number of market participants. Originally used in Canada, the approach assigns 100% credibility to an experience size that meets a predefined standard for confidence. For smaller experience sizes, the credibility percentage is reduced.

A popular formula used in mortality analyses for Z is

$$Z = \min\left\{\sqrt{\frac{\text{actual number of deaths}}{\text{number of deaths required for full credibility}}}, 1\right\}$$

Alternative formulae based on numbers of life years exposed are also in general use.

The denominator (number of deaths required for full credibility) is customarily set in relation to chosen probability and error-range parameters, relating to a binomial distribution. Table 3.3 shows the numbers of deaths required to provide accuracy at probability P within error range ±K%.

The Canadian practice for valuation purposes has been to adopt $P = 90\%$, $K = 3\%$ as the basis for assigning 100% credibility, according to the Committee on Life Insurance Reporting (Canadian Institute of Actuaries 2002). This practice means that $Z = 1$ for 3,000 death claims (3,007 to be precise in this example), a criterion for full credibility that is in quite common usage. But it should be pointed out that this number has been derived in the above example from a straight binomial distribution of deaths, which is appropriate to a lives A/E, but not to an amounts A/E, where the confidence intervals are wider. In theory, when we are adjusting an amounts A/E, the number of deaths for $Z = 1$ should be greater than 3,000.

A simplified example of the application of credibility adjustments is shown below.

A simple example of credibility adjustment.

- Assume portfolio experience is $A/E = 88\%$ standard table.
- Assume book pricing is equal to 92% standard table.
- Assume that the portfolio has 1,000 deaths.
- Assume that we set $z = 1$ at 3,000 deaths.

Then, the credibility of portfolio experience is equal to

$$z = \sqrt{\frac{1{,}000}{3{,}000}} = 0.577$$

Therefore, the credibility-adjusted portfolio experience is equal to

$$0.577 \times 88\% + (1 - 0.577) \times 92\% = 89.7\% \text{ (of standard table)}$$

Adjusting for heavy or light years

In the real world, there are additional external inputs to mortality levels, over and above the purely statistical fluctuations, which can be measured by binomial or Monte Carlo techniques. Mortality levels are subject to seasonal variations (summer/winter), influenza and other epidemics or pandemics and exceptional heat or cold, among other factors.

As a consequence, some years or groups of years may have higher mortality or lower mortality than the general background level due to such factors.

To what extent can mortality be affected by one of these factors? A prime example is shown in Figure 3.10, which is based on data for excess winter mortality deaths (Office for National Statistics 2009) that occurred in England and Wales over three consecutive years. The spike in mortality for year 2008–9 has been attributed to the exceptionally cold temperatures in this year.

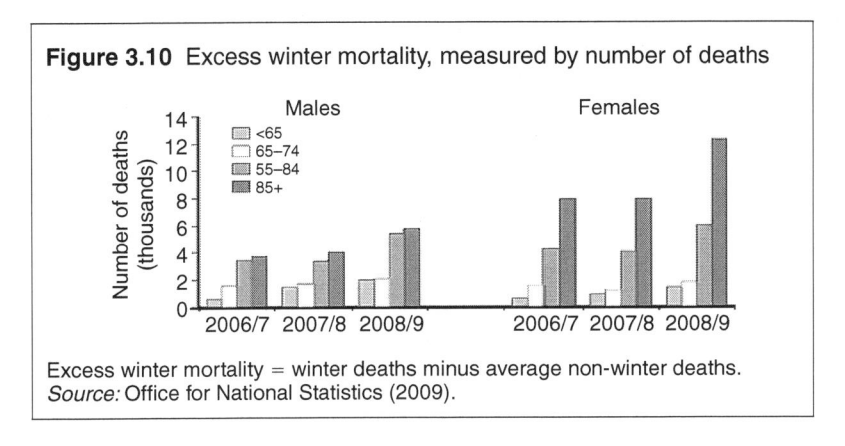

Figure 3.10 Excess winter mortality, measured by number of deaths

Males / Females, categories <65, 65–74, 55–84, 85+, years 2006/7, 2007/8, 2008/9. Number of deaths (thousands).

Excess winter mortality = winter deaths minus average non-winter deaths.
Source: Office for National Statistics (2009).

In theory, it is possible to adjust the portfolio's experience for the year(s) in which mortality was affected by external drivers compared with the background level. In practice, it is exceptionally difficult to achieve. One reason is that frequently the genuine "background" level is unknown. Under these circumstances, the use of a longer experience period may average out annual fluctuations stemming from external drivers of the kind described in this section. In general, an experience period of at least three years is normally used and ideally the yearly A/E experience should be charted along with confidence intervals to determine whether any adjustments can be justified.

PREDICTIVE PRICING AND VALIDATION OF EXPERIENCE RESULTS

In some situations, a mortality price is needed for a portfolio for which past experience is unavailable or the portfolio is very small. Even when experience is available and measures up to the rigours discussed above, it may still be desirable to assess the reasonableness of the result against external criteria.

In these situations, benchmarking methods may be used to develop mortality rates, although the margin for pricing error will be quite wide. This concept is referred to below as "predictive" pricing.

The following paragraphs examine the predictive use of data as they related to selected risk factors taken from Table 3.1. They include

- annuity amount,
- geographical spread,

- socio-economic class,
- postcode.

An especially close focus will be on the predictive nature of these factors when determining mortality for an annuity portfolio and the reliability of these results relative to other credibly priced risk factors.

Predicting by annuity amount (size)
The size of an annuity is typically correlated to the wealth of the annuitant. This relationship is important because, as measured in a number of ways, financially secure individuals generally live longer than their less well-off counterparts. For this reason, we should expect the mortality of annuitants with large annuities to be lower than those with smaller annuities and Figure 3.11, which plots the variation of mortality experience by annuity size for the standard table S1PMA, clearly demonstrates this relationship. While the data for Figure 3.11 only reflects mortality experience of pensioners within self-administered schemes in the UK, other similar studies are available for different annuity types and for different territories.

From the figure it is evident that mortality experience by annuity size varies considerably for this standard table during the majority of key annuitant ages but then converges at older annuitant ages.

The data underlying this type of chart can be used to determine a predicted mortality price for a portfolio, providing the portfolio's specific distribution of annuities by size is taken into account. At any age band define P_s as the proportional exposure of annuity amounts for the sth size band for the portfolio to be priced. Then, if $(A/E)_s$ is the A/E value for the sth size band in the standard table (relative to 100% overall), the predicted price for the portfolio, relative to the standard table is $\sum (P_s \times (A/E)_s)$, where the summation is across all s size bands. However, this methodology makes many implicit assumptions about the congruence of mortality drivers between the standard table (eg, S1PMA above) and the particular annuity portfolio. As a result, the predicted result should be treated with caution. Nevertheless the method can be refined over time, with the experience gained from repeated usage.

Predicting by geographical spread
It is well established that there are large differences in mortality across regions of countries, such as observed in the UK.

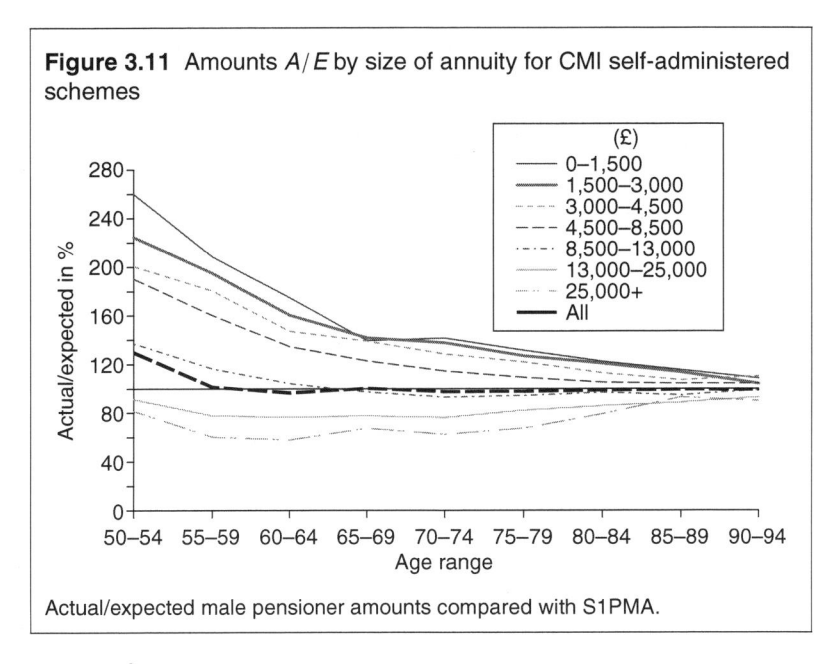

Figure 3.11 Amounts A/E by size of annuity for CMI self-administered schemes

[Figure: Actual/expected in % vs Age range (50-54 to 90-94) for annuity size bands (£): 0–1,500; 1,500–3,000; 3,000–4,500; 4,500–8,500; 8,500–13,000; 13,000–25,000; 25,000+; All. Actual/expected male pensioner amounts compared with S1PMA.]

An illustration of regional mortality variation is given in Figure 3.12, which is based on England and Wales population data published by the ONS for 2008. In this graph, the regional mortality levels are expressed as a proportion of total England and Wales mortality. Similar studies of regional mortality variation are available for many other countries.

As with mortality variations due to annuity size shown in Figure 3.11, regional mortality differentials also narrow at older ages. Likewise the data underlying this type of chart can be used to determine a predicted mortality price for a portfolio relative to other credibly priced portfolios, if the portfolio's specific distribution of annuities by region is considered in the analysis.

An illustrative calculation of the predicted price is shown in the next paragraph. However, the methodology implicitly assumes that the underlying characteristics in terms of regional socio-economic mix are comparable for the annuity portfolios being compared and across the full population. When these assumptions are not met, adjustments will be necessary.

Calculation of predicted mortality price from geographical distribution. Using the data underlying Figure 3.12 or similar, we can determine the ratio "regional mortality rate/national mortality rate" for

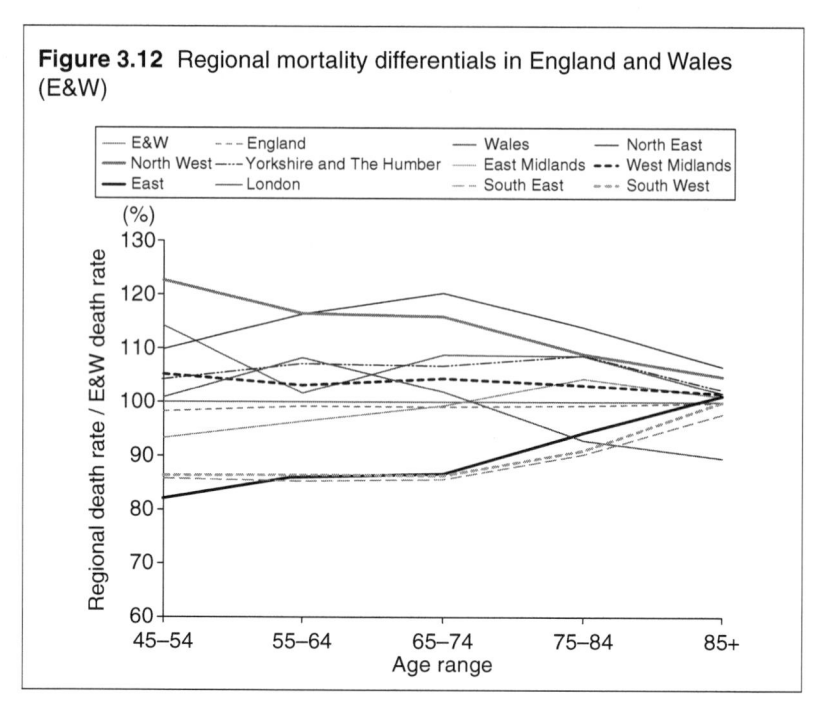

Figure 3.12 Regional mortality differentials in England and Wales (E&W)

[Legend: E&W, England, Wales, North East, North West, Yorkshire and The Humber, East Midlands, West Midlands, East, London, South East, South West]

[Chart: Regional death rate / E&W death rate (%) vs Age range (45-54, 55-64, 65-74, 75-84, 85+)]

each region at any age band when R_r is the ratio for the rth region. "A" denotes a portfolio whose price has been previously established from a credible experience analysis; "B" denotes the portfolio to be priced. P_r^A is the proportional annuity amount exposure for the rth region in portfolio A; P_r^B is the proportional annuity amount exposure for the rth region in portfolio B.

Then the predicted price for portfolio B, relative to that of portfolio A, can be calculated as

$$\frac{\sum(P_r^B \times R_r)}{\sum(P_r^A \times R_r)}$$

where the summation is across all regions.

Predicting by socio-economic class

Studies across the globe have also convincingly established that mortality rates tend to be correlated with socio-economic class; the higher or wealthier classes generally enjoying lower mortality. In the UK, this phenomenon has been well documented by the ONS in studies that measured socio-economic mortality differentials over a long period. Significant differences in mortality relative to socio-economic class occur across many key annuitant ages, as shown in

Figure 3.13 Socio-economic mortality differentials in UK (males)

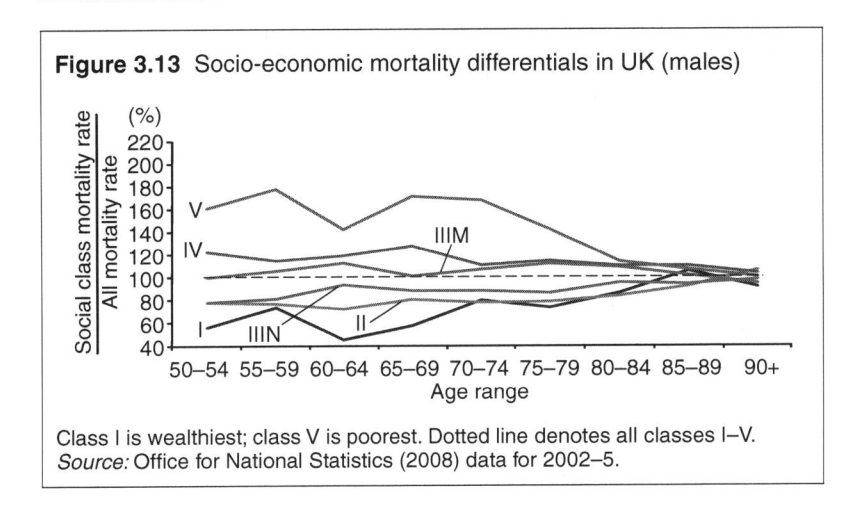

[Chart: Social class mortality rate / All mortality rate (%) plotted against Age range 50–54 to 90+, with curves labelled I, II, IIIN, IIIM, IV, V]

Class I is wealthiest; class V is poorest. Dotted line denotes all classes I–V.
Source: Office for National Statistics (2008) data for 2002–5.

Figure 3.13, which plots the mortality relativities between the different socio-economic classes for males in the UK over the period 2002–5. But at older ages, these differentials are reduced.

A similar observation is also made for improvement differentials in Chapter 4, which examines levels of mortality improvements relative to higher socio-economic classes.

As is the case with geographical spread and annuity size, the data underlying this type of chart can be used to determine a predicted mortality price for a portfolio relative to other credibly priced portfolios; the portfolio's specific distribution of annuities by socio-economic class is taken into account. The methodology will be analogous to that illustrated above for geographical distribution.

Predicting through postcode analysis

Mortality differentiation for annuity portfolios by postcode classes has existed in various forms for a number of years.

In the UK there are in excess of 1.5 million individual postcodes, each of which identifies only a handful of homes. Postcode mortality differentiation relies on segmentation of postcodes by profiling agencies such as Experian and ACORN in the UK, which collect wide-ranging census and survey data to group the postcodes into a few dozen relatively homogeneous socio-economic types. The postcodes in each type are not contiguous by geography but rather are linked only by the similarity of the householders resident in

Table 3.4 Illustrative mortality relativities by postcode level

Postcode level	Relative mortality (%)
Low	85
Medium	100
High	120

The relative mortality percentages for the three postcode levels should converge at old ages. Average relative mortality = 100%.

those postcodes. In a sense, the postcode type is a factor which contains combined geographical and socio-economic information on the annuitant, making the "whole" better than the "sum of the parts".

For the purposes of mortality pricing, the few dozen postcode types are usually collected into a far smaller number of postcode levels, typically between three and six. The objective is for each postcode level to contain postcode types of roughly similar mortality, with a significant differential between the mortality for each postcode level.

To determine the mortality relativities for the postcode levels, generalised linear models (GLMs) or survival models, can be used on large portfolios of experience data, rather than simple one-way experience analyses. These techniques allow interactions with other factors, such as age and annuity size, to be taken into account.

Table 3.4 shows a sample set of mortality relativities on the basis of three postcode levels for a typical annuity portfolio.

Postcode pricing models often incorporate relativity adjustments for annuity size and other characteristics, which improve the accuracy of the result. Predictive pricing on an annuity portfolio requires the postcode for each record to be translated into a postcode level (in our example: low, medium or high), with a relative mortality like those shown in Table 3.4 assigned to each annuitant. The relative mortality for each annuity is weighted by the actuarial reserve and the product is summed across all annuitants in the portfolio to produce the relative mortality for the portfolio. The result can then be compared with the results for portfolios which have been previously priced on experience analyses, allowing the predicted price for the new portfolio to be assessed relative to those previously priced portfolios.

The preceding example illustrates postcode pricing using just three postcode mortality levels. But the methodology can be expanded to accommodate many more levels.

FINAL ADJUSTMENT FOR TIMING

At this stage, the pricing basis will relate to mortality levels at a date which is earlier than the date at which the proposed transaction is to be effective. For example, if the price has been determined by an experience analysis, then the basis may be assumed to relate to the mid-point of the experience period. A final adjustment is needed to incorporate notional mortality improvements to the mortality rates from that mid-point up to the intended date of the transaction. As described earlier, such adjustment can be made using historical population improvements or some standard projected improvements table. Methods for projecting mortality improvements are covered in Chapter 4.

COMPLICATIONS

There are many complications which can arise in relation to experience analysis and predictive pricing for annuity portfolios. Some have been raised in previous sections but the following two examples may shed light on other complications.

Heterogeneity

In the preceding discussion, it has been assumed that a portfolio of annuities, for which a pricing basis is needed is homogeneous and can be analysed and priced as a single entity. This may not be the case. The portfolio may contain a number of tranches which differ by product type, company of origin, scheme membership type or in some of the risk factors set out in Table 3.1. In theory, each tranche's experience should be analysed and priced as a separate entity and then the cashflows or reserves should be recombined. No single-entity basis will accurately reflect the features of the underlying tranches, as the tranches will each display differing mortality levels and shapes. However, a tranche-by-tranche analysis may be problematic because of lower data volumes, which will widen the confidence intervals and therefore increase uncertainty in the individual tranche pricing. It is a matter of judgement whether individual tranche pricing can be justified in these circumstances.

Underwritten annuities

In recent years, the introduction of underwritten or enhanced pension annuity products into the UK pension vesting market has posed an additional pricing challenge. These products offer enhanced terms to annuitants who have health problems or raised risk factors, which reduce their life expectancy but they have made it much more difficult to set a predictive pricing basis for recent business cohorts, or to price with only limited experience. The pricing difficulties posed by these products vary according to the circumstances of the portfolio to be priced, as discussed below.

- The portfolio to be priced consists entirely of underwritten annuities and the policies carry individualised mortality loadings, which need to be carried into the pricing exercise.

- A portfolio consists only of standard annuities, but prospective annuitants with medical conditions did have an enhanced option at commencement through another provider. In this case, the pricing needs to assume some level of anti-selection in the standard portfolio, ie, to reflect that these annuitants were generally a healthy group at commencement with lower than average mortality due to the impaired lives seeking enhanced terms no longer forming part of the standard portfolio.

- A portfolio is made up of both underwritten and standard annuities because an originating insurer marketed both products simultaneously. It may then be possible to ignore the product differentiation and to assume that the portfolio's overall experience will be in line with usual book pricing. This is justifiable provided that, over the two products, the usual mix of vesting pensioners has been attracted by the insurer; ie, that the enhanced terms being offered are relatively as attractive to unhealthy applicants, as the standard terms are to healthy applicants. Otherwise, some allowance for anti-selection may be necessary.

For a more detailed discussion of market background and pricing of underwritten annuities, see Chapter 5.

CONCLUDING REMARKS

In this chapter, we have examined the theoretical considerations and a methodology for setting the base mortality for both large and small annuity portfolios.

The process of estimating base mortality clearly involves many judgements, interpretations and adjustments that keep certainty at arms length. In a competitive market, annuity portfolios will be priced differently by the bidders to a tender and competitive pressure will often influence them to review their judgements and to make further adjustments in the quest to win business. Caution and discipline need to be exercised such that judgements and adjustments can be sensibly supported by the available data and are not overly optimistic across all portfolios priced.

REFERENCES

Board for Actuarial Standards, 2008, "Actuarial Mortality Assumptions", Discussion Paper, March.

Canadian Institute of Actuaries, 2002, "Expected Mortality: Fully Underwritten Canadian Individual Life Insurance Policies", Educational Note, Document 202037, July, Canadian Institute of Actuaries Committee on Life Insurance Financial Reporting.

Office for National Statistics, 2009, "Excess Winter Mortality in England and Wales", *ONS Statistical Bulletin*, November, URL: http://www.statistics.gov.uk/pdfdir/ewm1109.pdf.

Office for National Statistics, 2008, "Trends in ONS Longitudinal Study Estimates of Life Expectancy, By Social Class 1972–2005", URL: http://www.statistics.gov.uk/statbase/Product.asp?vlnk=8460.

4
Projecting Future Mortality

Bridget Browne
Partner Reinsurance Europe Ltd

Chapter 1 discussed the notion that mortality is continuously evolving. Over time the origins of these changes have come to be better understood. This chapter now turns to the challenge of predicting the future evolution of mortality rates.

The task effectively moves from establishing the best possible picture of mortality as it stands at a given point in time into predicting the future. But it does not stop there. Special care must be taken to explain to an intended audience the associated uncertainty of any future projections in the context of their end use.

The lack of a recommended common view on future mortality projections subjects the projection of future changes to much debate and a divergence of opinions. The difficulty in making projections is furthermore muddied by substantial changes in past mortality rates and challenges also arising from changes in the recording of data (such as exactly which companies have contributed to industry mortality experience data over time), in underwriting practices, in the pace and type of medical developments and of course in diseases themselves, such as AIDS and influenza.

Extensive groundwork enabling practitioners to meet the challenge of projecting future mortality has been laid by other bodies such as the Continuous Mortality Investigation (CMI) bureau of the Actuarial Profession in the UK along with several research efforts aimed at facilitating access to global mortality data (an example of which is the Human Mortality Database) and at improving and disseminating knowledge about possible models for projecting future mortality, such as those provided by JP Morgan's LifeMetrics (JP Morgan 2007).

We examine briefly how practitioners have allowed for changes in mortality rates in the past and show how traditional approaches have required a major overhaul in the light of rapidly emerging experience and analysis capability.

We then touch on some of the ways to make the communication of potential changes in future mortality rates accessible to all concerned audiences. Next we turn to the sources of data available and the techniques in use to analyse this data and produce projections of the possible future changes.

We conclude the chapter with a brief discussion of some of the key issues arising in projecting mortality at older age ranges and an outlook on likely future areas of improvement in our capacity to predict future mortality.

HOW HAVE MORTALITY AND THE CAUSES OF DEATH EVOLVED IN THE PAST?

The major contributors to decreasing mortality and associated increasing life expectancy by each major cause of death were introduced in Chapter 1. These are considered in further detail in this section. The trends that have generally been experienced in Western countries, particularly over the 20th Century, are presented for the UK as an example (Figure 4.1). The graph shown is for males, but females have experienced similar overall patterns.

Finally conquered after World War II with the widespread use of antibiotics, infectious diseases were largely eliminated as one of the major potential killers in the 20th Century. However, the appearance of new infectious diseases such as HIV continues to be a concern. Furthermore, concerns also exist around the re-emergence of old diseases, such as tuberculosis, that could be resistant to current drugs. Declines in child immunisation rates in certain developed countries also raise fears that diseases such as measles may become more prevalent and threats of bio-weapons have sparked unease about the re-emergence of diseases such as smallpox.

Respiratory diseases have followed a similar path of reduction to infectious diseases, and their effect was significantly reduced by the beginning of the 21st Century. The spike in deaths due to the pandemic influenza of 1918 is hard to miss. Pandemic flu is an excellent example of a disease that can have a strong seasonal pattern but may also have a variety of different patterns by age. In general, influenza causes most extra deaths in the very young and the very old, but some of the worst pandemic influenzas, including the Spanish flu

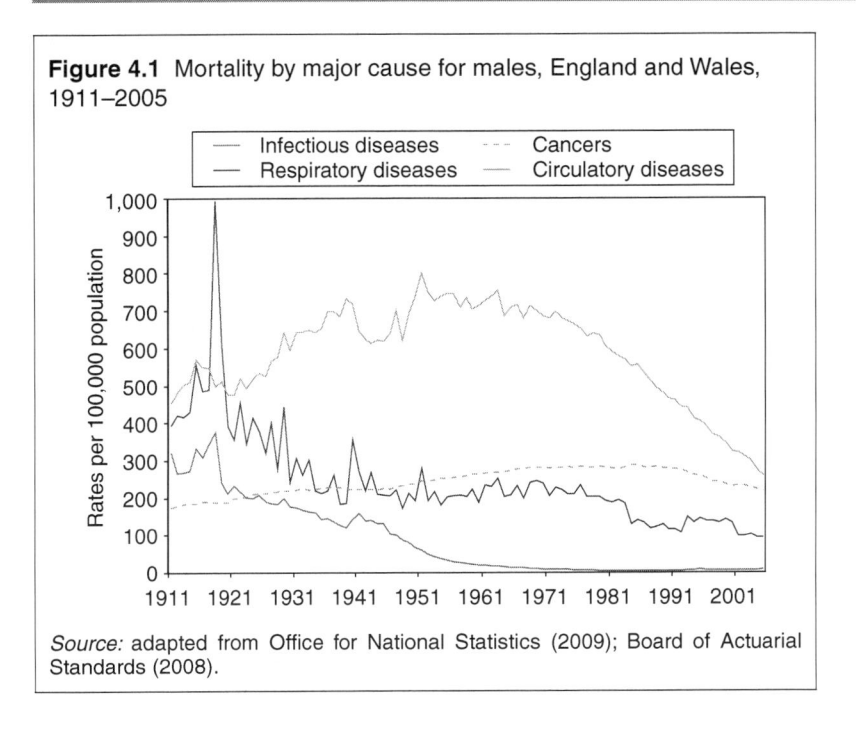

Figure 4.1 Mortality by major cause for males, England and Wales, 1911–2005

[Figure: Line graph showing rates per 100,000 population from 1911 to 2001 for Infectious diseases, Cancers, Respiratory diseases, and Circulatory diseases. Y-axis ranges from 0 to 1,000.]

Source: adapted from Office for National Statistics (2009); Board of Actuarial Standards (2008).

of 1918, have had a disproportionate effect on the working-age population. It is uncertain how a temporary mortality event such as a pandemic may have ripple effects on future mortality rates over time, especially for the populations that have survived the event. Further discussion on pandemic risk is covered in Chapter 11.

Circulatory diseases such as heart disease and stroke have experienced a different pattern, which highlights the inter-related nature of different causes of death, ie, "if x doesn't get you, y will, at least sooner or later". This concept will also be touched on later in the chapter. On the one hand, decreases in certain causes of death "allowed" individuals to survive and hence be susceptible to other causes. On the other hand, the rising impact of smoking as well as general lifestyle and dietary changes (including reduced activity levels) led to increased rates of mortality due to circulatory diseases. Mortality rates fell dramatically over the last 30 years of the 20th Century due to the benefits of reduction in smoking prevalence and major medical advances in treating and preventing circulatory diseases, which include angioplasty, heart bypass surgery, statins and beta blockers.

Smoking bans in certain public places in some countries (eg, Ireland, Australia, South Africa and Mexico, which were among the first and strictest in their respective continents to introduce wide bans) will most likely help to further reduce mortality although these restrictions are likely to be more effective among younger populations that have the most years to gain from abstinence. In general, reduced smoking prevalence should reduce a range of diseases such as cancers (lung and mouth), respiratory diseases (bronchitis) and cardiovascular disease (high blood pressure and heart attack). However, smoking prevalence and its evolution vary by many factors including sex, age and socio-economic class. These variations serve to demonstrate the multi-factor nature of the modelling required to develop predictions.

Cancers have followed yet another track. While improvements have unquestionably been made in treatment, these have effectively been counteracted by the increasing part of the population succumbing to cancer rather than, say, circulatory diseases. The major breakthrough in treating or preventing cancers, especially treatments that avoid severe side effects, remains to be found. It is perhaps more likely that early detection of cancers due to screening programmes or the development of future vaccinations may be more successful at improving mortality outcomes for the wider population. Genetic cures may also be developed, but their impact could vary by the particular type of cancer. The obvious relationship between research and development, the amount of funding available for research and the role of government intervention via budgets and targets, for example, only serves to underscore the reasons why future mortality evolution can be considered so uncertain.

Other lifestyle factors also drive mortality trends. Obesity prevalence is rising in some countries, especially among the younger populations, and those overweight individuals are at higher risk of certain diseases such as diabetes. In addition, diabetes has co-morbidity with other diseases including heart disease, strokes and renal failure. Conditions that combine multiple risk factors such as abdominal obesity, hypertension and high cholesterol may also lead to increases in mortality.

As previously discussed, female mortality is generally lower than male mortality at all ages and throughout all developed countries. The relationship between female and male mortality has not remained constant over time, however. Over some periods UK females have experienced faster rates of mortality improvement than males, whereas, for example, UK males aged older than 40 experienced exceptionally rapid rates of mortality improvement in the last three decades of the 20th Century. This spurt in improvement has led to a narrowing of the gap between male and female mortality rates. In other countries, for example, France, the gap is widening.

Patterns of mortality change often vary quite significantly between countries. For example, in the late 20th Century mortality increased in Russia, leading to reduced life expectancies, owing to a mixture of effects following the collapse of the Soviet Union. On the other hand, in the UK, commentators have often spoken of the "cohort effect" and the "Golden Cohort" in referring to the very significant mortality improvements experienced by the generations born between approximately 1925 and 1945, which are greater than those experienced by the generations born either before or after the cohort. In Spain, where no such cohort effect is apparent, mortality improvements have been closely tied to specific periods in the country's history with large improvements for all during the 1950s and stabilisation post the Spanish Civil War.

The level of awareness of practitioners, from actuaries to demographers, about the pattern, pace and impact of changes in mortality grew significantly in the first decade of the 21st Century. Before the late 20th Century mortality changed more slowly and the computing power was not available to manipulate the large volumes of data required to clearly identify the patterns. At the same time the impact of changes in mortality and the associated cost for annuity and pension products was strongly mitigated by the masking effect of relatively high interest rates. This dynamic made the financial impact of future changes less significant than in a low interest rate environment.

HOW TO COMMUNICATE ABOUT PROJECTED FUTURE MORTALITY

In general, changes in annual mortality rates are expressed in terms of annual improvement rates (eg, as a percentage improvement per year). A $y\%$ improvement rate over a given year simply means that the mortality rate for a person in that year will be $(1 - y\%)$ times the

Table 4.1 Reaction of key indicators to direction of changes in mortality rates

Rates of change in mortality are either	negative	or	positive
This is described as mortality	improvement		deterioration
	which translates into		
mortality rates (q_x) are	decreasing		increasing
life expectancies (e_x) are	increasing		decreasing
annuity values (a_x) are	increasing		decreasing
annuity benefits received are	decreasing		increasing

mortality rate in the year before. The mortality rates themselves are usually denoted using "q".

Changes in mortality rates are often specific to a given age and calendar year. For example, the mortality rate of a 65-year-old in 2012 may be compared with that of a 65-year-old in 2011.

To illustrate, if the mortality rates are assumed as follows

mortality rate for a 65-year-old in 2011 $q(65,2011) = 0.10\%$

mortality rate for a 65-year-old in 2012 $q(65,2012) = 0.09\%$

then the rate of change in mortality is equal to

$$\frac{q(x,t)}{q(x,(t-1))} - 1 = \frac{0.09\%}{0.10\%} - 1$$

$$= -10\% \text{ per annum}$$

where x represents age and t represents the calendar year.

This rate of change in mortality is also described as an annual mortality improvement of 10%.

Table 4.1 summarises the terms used and the way in which changes in mortality rates have an impact on other measures used in longevity.

Heat maps of mortality changes

Because of the two-dimensional aspect to describing changes in mortality rates in terms of age and calendar year, it is common in some countries to use colour "heat maps" to illustrate the underlying patterns of improvement. These tools map the changes in mortality rates by attained age and calendar year (Figure 4.2) and can be read much like a topographical map, where high rates of improvement can be seen as peaks and deteriorating mortality rates can be seen as troughs.

PROJECTING FUTURE MORTALITY

Figure 4.2 Illustrative projected rates of mortality improvement (% pa)

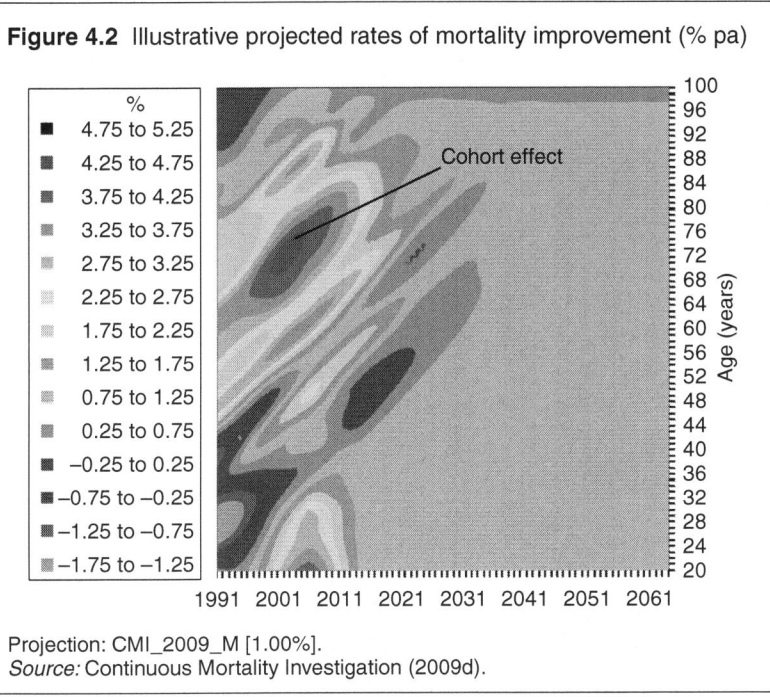

%
4.75 to 5.25
4.25 to 4.75
3.75 to 4.25
3.25 to 3.75
2.75 to 3.25
2.25 to 2.75
1.75 to 2.25
1.25 to 1.75
0.75 to 1.25
0.25 to 0.75
−0.25 to 0.25
−0.75 to −0.25
−1.25 to −0.75
−1.75 to −1.25

Projection: CMI_2009_M [1.00%].
Source: Continuous Mortality Investigation (2009d).

Table 4.2 Example prospective (or two-dimensional) mortality tables in use in 2010 by country

Country	Prospective mortality table
France	TGF/H05
Germany	DAV 2004 R
Spain	PERM/F 2000 P/C
Italy	IPS55

Many countries use two-dimensional mortality tables (also called prospective or generational tables) to estimate the future mortality of populations exposed to longevity risk. Some examples are shown in Table 4.2.

An important point to remember as we look at any heat map is that a lower rate of improvement than that of previous years is still an improvement.

The power of communicating with a heat map is shown in Figure 4.2 by the ridge running diagonally up the top left-hand corner of the graph, which in fact is the "cohort" effect. In narrative terms, a person who is aged 76 in 2001 would have been born in 1925 and be 86 years old in 2011: diagonal effects follow the lifetimes of a specific generation.

Period and projected life expectancy

While heat maps are perhaps the most comprehensive way to communicate many of the main features of change in mortality rates, it is often helpful to summarise the impact of alternative improvement projections into single key figures. The most commonly used include life expectancies (LEs) and annuity values. Expectations of life can be calculated in two ways: "period life expectancy" or "cohort life expectancy". The Government Actuary's Department (GAD)[1] in the UK provides a straightforward explanation of the difference between the two.

- **Period life expectancy** at a given age is the average number of years a person would continue to live if they experienced the age-specific mortality rates for that time period throughout their remaining lifetime. It makes no allowance for any later actual or projected changes in mortality. In practice, death rates are likely to change in the future, so period life expectancy does not give the number of years any one person could actually expect to live.

- **Cohort life expectancy** is calculated using age-specific mortality rates which allow for known or projected changes in mortality in later years and is thus often regarded as a more appropriate measure than period life expectancy in determining how long a person of a given age would be expected to live on average.

In most Western countries, the life expectancy that is often reported in the press as a way of updating the public on the ongoing gains in lifetime is nearly always the "period life expectancy at birth", which effectively provides a snapshot of the observed mortality rates for the entire population concerned in a given calendar year. Examples of period life expectancies at birth by country were also provided in Chapter 1.

For most insurance practitioners specialising in the area of longevity risk it is the remaining life expectancy after retirement age that is of particular interest. Figure 4.3 shows the evolution of

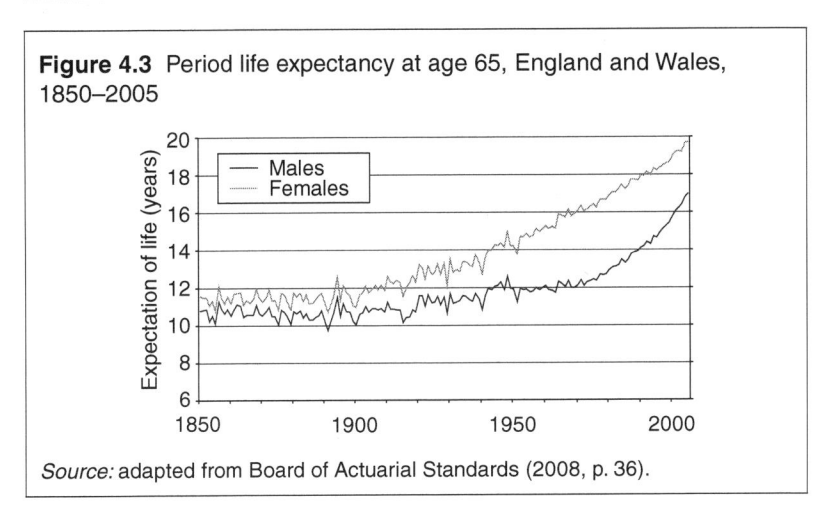

Figure 4.3 Period life expectancy at age 65, England and Wales, 1850–2005

Source: adapted from Board of Actuarial Standards (2008, p. 36).

period life expectancy at age 65 for males and females in England and Wales. The pattern is similar for most of the Western world. The rapid increases in life expectancies over the 20th Century, particularly for males from 1970, when life expectancies increased by more than 25% over the period, encapsulates the reason why changes in mortality rates have attracted so much attention.

For example, period life expectancy at age 65 in 2000 is worked out using the mortality rate for age 65 in 2000, for age 66 in 2000, for age 67 in 2000, and so on. On the other hand cohort life expectancy at age 65 in 2000 is worked out using the mortality rate for age 65 in 2000, for age 66 in 2001, for age 67 in 2002, and so on. In the latter approach the cohort life expectancy is that of a cohort of individuals aged 65 in 2000, effectively relating to the generation or cohort born in 1935, hence the descriptor "cohort".

Period life expectancy has the advantage of being observable once the time period is over and the data has been collected. Projected life expectancy, by comparison, requires estimations of future mortality rates for its calculation, so cannot be directly observed and its value only becomes known once all lives in the given generation have died (ie, the generation is extinct), which, at the time of writing, means for generations born through to, say, 1915.

KEY TYPES OF DATA AVAILABLE

The first type of data required for projecting future mortality is past experience, either expressed as mortality rates by sex, age, calendar year and possibly other factors or broken down further into exposures and deaths (since the mortality rate, at its most basic level, is the number of deaths divided by the number of individuals exposed to the risk of dying).

In some respects the data sources are the same as those for determining base mortality. However, because the objective is different, there are important differences in the usability and appropriateness of the different data sources when they are to be used for estimating future mortality improvements.

As previously outlined there typically are three major types of data source:

- national or population level for a given country;
- industry level, eg, insured people such as those individuals in occupational pension schemes;
- portfolio specific, eg, the portfolio of a particular insurance company, pension scheme or other grouping of lives.

National data is usually made available by the national statistical organisation of each country, and will be published with a certain delay after the end of the observation period. The data may vary in the level of detail available, but in general sex, age and calendar period are nearly universally provided. Cause of death or geographical information may also be made available, but usually on a less frequent basis.

The national statistics organisation will always have to respect specific requirements pertaining to data protection, which may limit the level of detail made public.

To illustrate the types of mortality data available, Table 4.3 lists a small sample of the countries whose populations are currently included in the Human Mortality Database, and the range of years covered by the period life tables.

National statistical organisations or other entities such as research foundations may also be a source of data for items such as specific longitudinal studies in which a given population is followed for part or all of its lifetime. These sources often have the advantage of providing much more information, such as socio-economic, behavioural or lifestyle information, about the group that is followed, although they are almost universally only conducted on a small subset of the total population of the country concerned.

Table 4.3 Selected sample of data sets available in the Human Mortality Database

Country and data series	Period life tables
Australia	1921–2007
Canada	1921–2006
Chile	1992–2005
Germany	
Total population[1]	1990–2008
West Germany	1956–2008
East Germany	1956–2008
Hungary	1950–2006
Italy	1872–2006
Japan[2]	1947–2008
New Zealand	
Total population[3]	1948–2003
Maori	1937–2003
Non-Maori	1876–2003
Sweden[4]	1751–2007
Taiwan	1970–2008
UK	
Total population	1922–2006
England & Wales (total)	1841–2006
England & Wales (civilian)	1841–2006
Scotland	1855–2006
Northern Ireland	1922–2006
US	1933–2006

[1] Note impact of separation and reunification on times series. [2] Available post World War II only. [3] Note historical influences on data availability: sub-populations with distinct mortality characteristics should ideally be studied separately. [4] The longest continuous time series available.
Source: www.mortality.org (data downloaded on July 4, 2010).

Some countries, such as the US, Canada, Australia and the UK, have established entities to collect and analyse data on insured lives: clients of insurance companies or members of pension funds. Examples of such organisations include the non-commercial Continuous Mortality Investigation (CMI), whereas Club Vita, established by Hymans Robertson, a pension consulting firm, is a commercial initiative. One of the advantages of such data sets is that they have often been constructed in a way that is mindful of the issues faced by longevity practitioners. In particular, they are specific to the populations that directly contribute to pension schemes' or insurance companies' longevity risk exposure, whereas the general population data covers everyone.

For practitioners, an understanding of the specific experience of the annuity or pension-in-payment portfolio is fundamental, especially in determining base mortality, but it is quite unlikely to be of any meaningful value when establishing a view on the future evolution of mortality rates.

This is because the data used for estimating future mortality must be available over a reasonably long time period and must be available in much more significant volumes than that needed for establishing base mortality in order to produce credible and stable results.

In fact, for base mortality it is the level of mortality that is determined, whereas for future mortality it is a rate of change. In a sense, the difference between the two can be compared with observing the speed of a car at a given point in time versus its acceleration.

A simple measure used to indicate the value of a data source for analysis is the number of deaths contained in the data.

For example, in England and Wales there are around 500,000 deaths per year. In the relevant CMI studies[2] that attempt to collect information from the entire UK life insurance industry, there were a total of 380,000 deaths for the 16 years of the study from 1990 to 2006; that is less than 5% of the population death count. An individual portfolio might contain anything from 5 to 500,000 lives, but even the largest portfolio might only produce 5,000–10,000 deaths per year, or around 1–2% of the national data volume.

This relationship applies to all countries and is further complicated by the fact that many countries do not collect industry-level information in a structured manner, which results in the absence of an interim exploitable data set between national and portfolio-specific levels.

Other data inputs for projecting future mortality should include mortality rates by specific cause of death, when available, and expert opinion about the future development in either incidence or prognosis for specific diseases or disease groups (eg, cancer or cardiovascular).

OVERVIEW OF THE MAIN METHODOLOGIES AND TECHNIQUES AVAILABLE

Extensive educational and research literature exists on alternative improvement projection methodologies and examples are listed in the "References" section for the interested reader. In this section we outline briefly the different approaches that are currently used to project future mortality and the main differences between them.

One approach to considering the types of methods available to project future mortality is to group them into expectation, extrapolative and explanatory models as identified in Booth and Tickle (2008). A useful summary of the main features of each of these methods is provided in Telford *et al* (2010).

- **The expectation approach.** This involves expert opinion, specification of a forecast scenario and usually comes with alternative high or low scenarios. Certain national statistical organisations as well as industry bodies often make use of the expectation approach in projecting future mortality. This approach has the advantage of drawing on expert opinion using a wide range of knowledge in the fields of demography, public health, medicine and other relevant disciplines. However, it also has the disadvantage that expert opinion may be biased, subjective or difficult to numerically justify. In the UK, the Office for National Statistics and the Continuous Mortality Investigation both provide examples of the application of this approach.

- **The extrapolative approach.** This essentially assumes that historical trends will continue into the future. Examples of this approach include the families of P-spline, Lee–Carter and Cairns–Blake–Dowd (CBD) models described later. This approach has the advantage that most historical trends do continue in the short and medium term (say, 5–15 years) and that many of the examples are stochastic models. The explanatory power of the model regarding the past (ie, how well the model fits to the actual historical changes) becomes key to its value in projecting the near term future. However, it is unclear that historical trends will continue in the longer term and these models are also incapable of explicitly anticipating exogenous future changes.

- **The explanatory approach.** This seeks to predict mortality based on relationships between mortality and disease processes or risk factors. Examples of this approach include smoking- and disease-based mortality models.[3] Epidemiologists have also used various explanatory models to assess the impact of future changes in patterns of risk factors or treatments on mortality.[4] Such an approach has the advantage of using medical, epidemiological and other relevant data to inform future outcomes. It could be used in a complementary manner to help experts form their opinion under the expectation approach. However, the causal relationships between risk factors, morbidity and mortality are complex and not well understood at the time of writing, hampering the use of the explanatory models. A complete and fully predictive model based on the explanatory approach is no doubt the most satisfactory and complete and potentially the least uncertain method to apply.

Deterministic versus stochastic projection models

The approach used to project future mortality typically falls into one of two categories: deterministic or stochastic.

Deterministic models imply a fixed set of assumptions that produce one single result for the projected future mortality rates. While they are reassuring and perhaps easier to manipulate, they have a major disadvantage in that the models say nothing about the uncertainty associated with the future mortality projection (often called the "expanding funnel of doubt"), which, as the term implies, tends to increase over the duration of the projection.

Deterministic models can be run using a variety of different assumptions, producing scenarios which may be more or less arbitrarily assigned to a certain percentile or likelihood of occurrence. An example of such a scenario is the base-level longevity-stress scenario under the QIS5 study for Solvency II,[5] which requires an instantaneous and permanent reduction in mortality rates by 20% (equivalent to multiplying the entire rectangle of mortality rates by age and calendar years by 80%). This stress was intended at the time of the study to be broadly calibrated to the 99.5th percentile (ie, a 1-in-200 chance of outcome) over a one-year time horizon.

Stochastic models have the ability to generate a range of results, which not only allows the user to produce both a best-estimate view (the "mean" outcome) but also coherently quantify the various percentiles implied by the model. While any model output should be used with caution, and users should assess the raw results and adjust as appropriate to their needs, the production of percentiles is extremely useful in a variety of settings such as

- internal capital modelling, including easier explicit manipulation with other result distributions (assuming an assumption about correlation can be reasonably set),
- risk assessment, that is, examination of a range of potential outcomes (eg, 1 in 10, 1 in 50 as well as 1 in 200) in an internally consistent manner,
- communication of uncertainty, especially to stakeholders, in an effective and comparable manner.

The use of such models for setting reserving and capital requirements is covered in further detail in Chapters 6 and 7.

In the past, practitioners have primarily relied on deterministic models but now both stochastic and deterministic models are in use. A simple stochastic model has also been proposed that can be applied to any deterministic set of assumptions and which may be of use when one of the standard stochastic models has not been used or exclusively used to set the best estimate (Browne *et al* 2009).

Solvency II provides an excellent example of the way in which simple deterministic and more complex stochastic models may coexist. For example, the "Solvency Capital Requirement" calculation under the "Standard Formula" is based on a single deterministic scenario, whereas most internal models are likely to use a stochastic model. The use of stochastic modelling for the calculation or adjustment of technical provisions, given that this value should be the probability-weighted (ie, mean) result of the possible outcomes, rather than a deterministic "median" calculation is also a consideration. Further discussion and examples of the application of Solvency II are also provided in Chapters 6 and 7.

All of the models outlined below start with an imposed structure or "view" of the parameters that can be used to "describe" mathematically the evolution of mortality rates. They then effectively examine the past and try to "smooth" or "fit" it by determining different sets of parameters in order to have the best possible representation of the past changes. Having performed this step, the model uses this set of parameters as well as other assumptions imposed by the chosen models to make a projection into the future. In all cases, the precise choice of parameters for the projection always remains with the user, and the range of outcomes will usually be heavily influenced by the parameterisation process and the historical data period/range used in the process.

Deterministic models

To illustrate how deterministic models have evolved over time, Table 4.4 briefly summarises the development of deterministic models used for UK annuitants and pensioners over the second half of the 20th Century.

The evolution in complexity of the models is mirrored in many other countries, including France, Germany, Spain and Italy, as insurance practitioners have recognised the importance of explicitly allowing for the evolution of future mortality rates in their pricing, reserving and reporting.

Two major deterministic approaches in use in the UK at the beginning of the 21st Century are described in the following.

National population: ONS/GAD

The ONS publishes mortality projections for the UK population every two years, using a methodology that draws on consultation with an external expert panel, the offices of the three Registrars General and users of the projections. Often described as a "target" method, the expectation approach used sets a long-term rate of mortality improvement and then trends towards that point from current levels. It is a deterministic method, although the ONS provides three scenarios (the principal projection as well as the high and low life expectancy projections), without assigning a probability of realisation to any of them.

Insured population: CMI model

The CMI model (Continuous Mortality Investigation 2009a,b,c) is effectively a tool that supports users in setting their own deterministic expectation-based approach. It also allows the user to take current levels of mortality improvement and make various assumptions about the duration and form of convergence towards a long-term rate of mortality improvement. This type of model was proposed to make it widely accessible to the greatest number of users. In addition,

Table 4.4 Summary of past methods used to project future mortality for UK insured lives

Year	Mortality table	Improvements
1955	a(55)	First formal use of improvements
1980	PA(90), a(90)	Linear reduction of mortality rates (1 year of age per 20 years)
1990	"80" Series	Mortality rates assumed to decrease exponentially to a limiting value
1999	"92" Series	As per "80" Series, but slower convergence ⟹ faster mortality improvements
2002	CMI Working Paper 1*	"Cohort effect" included; mortality improvements linked to year of birth, whereby "extra" mortality improvements for the relevant cohort are run off over a certain period towards a long-term underlying trend, with the following run-off time period • short: cohort period of 10 years ie, excess run-off by 2010 • medium: cohort period of 20 years ie, excess run-off by 2020 • long: cohort period of 40 years ie, excess run-off by 2040
2007	Various	The CMI Library of mortality projections (Version 1.1 issued 2009); since the "00" Series contained no projections, this resource allowed users to use and communicate a variety of frequently used mortality projection bases
2009	User choice, a selection of current tables is provided in tool	CMI Mortality Projections Model: a deterministic expectations-based model combining current levels of mortality change and assumptions about the form and duration of convergence towards a long-term rate of change

* Adjustments to "92" Series for cohort effects.
Source: adapted from internal presentation, RBS Global Banking and Markets and updated.

none of the stochastic models described in the following paragraphs can yet be said to be the "definitive" method, not least because they are all extrapolative models with the drawbacks that this implies.

Stochastic models

Stochastic models are usually, by their nature, extrapolative: they examine the historical data to fit a surface of past trends and then, based on defined parameters, project these trends into the future.

It is difficult to have a discussion about stochastic models without first describing the different sorts of characteristics that are used in these models. The naming conventions for the component parts of such models are summarised below.

In multi-factor modelling using age, period and cohort, for example, mortality is often expressed using α_i (alpha) to represent a parameter related to age, β_j (beta) to represent a parameter related to time/calendar year/period and γ_k (gamma) to represent a parameter related to cohort/year of birth, where $k = j - i$.

A summary of the characteristics of the major models that have been used in the recent past to project future mortality changes is given in Table 4.5.

With all models, external adjustments may be made for items such as minimum levels of improvements and older age adjustments which are discussed later.

OTHER INFLUENCING FACTORS

Most projection models consider the major factors that influence mortality. These factors can include sex, age and calendar year; the latter two can then also be combined in a "year of birth" or "cohort" effect.

However, as the discussion on base mortality in Chapter 3 pointed out, there are many other influences on mortality that are likely to have some influence on future mortality rates also.

The essential question to be answered is whether the changes in future mortality rates are likely to be different between different sub-groups of the population such as

- smokers and non-smokers,
- different socio-economic groups,
- groups with different health status.

Table 4.5 Summary of major models used to project future mortality

Model family	Model	Summary
Lee–Carter	Lee–Carter Age-Period Model	Approach developed in 1992 models mortality as a function of age (bringing in the effect of mortality increasing with age) and time (bringing in the effect that as time passes mortality changes). This model is one of the most widely used in analysing and projecting changes in mortality rates, although most users find it is not a good fit with UK mortality data because it does not allow for a cohort effect.
	Renshaw–Haberman Model	Extension/generalisation of the Lee–Carter Model by adding a cohort effect (so that the year of birth, or cohort, is included as a factor together with age and time in projecting mortality). This model is able to pick up idiosyncrasies by age, cohort, and time, but can be challenging to fit.
	Simplified Renshaw–Haberman Model	Simplification of Renshaw–Haberman that requires fewer parameters to be fitted but still maintains the same functional form. This model is able to pick up idiosyncrasies by age, cohort, and time and can be fitted more easily.
	B- and P-Spline Models	Assume that mortality is a smooth surface rather than having idiosyncrasies for individual ages, periods, and cohorts. B-splines: can be parameterised to provide a near perfect fit to historical data the more the specification is manipulated. P-splines: a form of B-spline that introduces penalties to adjust for the above "overfitting" problem. These models are extremely helpful for describing the past, but of limited use for projecting the future.

Source: adapted from internal presentation, RBS Global Banking and Markets, and JP Morgan (2007).

Table 4.5 Continued

Model family	Model	Summary
Cairns, Blake and Dowd	CBD Age-Period Model	Similar to the Lee–Carter Model in terms of functional form, the approach models mortality as a function of age and period only. Uses the logit transform of mortality rates, rather than natural log of death rates as the other models.
	CBD Cohort Model	Same as above but includes a cohort effect. All the CBD models imply randomness between cohorts, which can seem intuitively unlikely.
	CBD Cohort and Curvature Model	Same as above except that it adds a quadratic term into the age effect to pick up on curvature observed in other countries (ie, that the age effect increases with time when we look at logit transforms of death rates). A quadratic effect has been observed, eg, in US data but is not necessarily the case for other countries.
	CBD Diminishing Cohort Model	Same as the CBD Cohort model except that the cohort effect for any given generation is modelled as diminishing as the individual ages. A diminishing cohort effect is not unreasonable for "younger old", and for the "older old" this is not necessarily an important issue.
	Koller Ct Model	A natural approach to modelling uncertainty in variation around mortality rates that can generate stochastic output independently of the underlying approach used to create the deterministic best estimate (Browne *et al* 2009). Simple to parameterise and to run, not dependent on choice of approach in establishing deterministic best estimate.

Table 4.6 Illustrative example of interaction between smoking prevalence and apparent changes in mortality rates

---

Smoker mortality rate: 15‰, assume constant from 1980 to 2005
Non-smoker mortality rate: 10‰, assume constant from 1980 to 2005
Smoker prevalence in 1980: 40%
Smoker prevalence in 2005: 25%
Population mortality rate in 1980: 12‰*
Population mortality rate in 2005: 11.25‰**
Apparent annual rate of mortality improvement: 0.26%***

---

*12‰ = 40% × 15‰ + 60% × 10‰. **11.25‰ = 25% × 15‰ + 75% × 10‰. ***0.26%, since 11.25% = 12% × $(1-0.26\%)^{25}$.

But before we continue, it is important to point out the need to fully understand apparent changes in mortality rates. For example, changes in smoking prevalence in a population can produce apparent mortality improvements at a population level even when the mortality of the two sub-groups is unchanged as shown in Table 4.6.

This "apparent" improvement is in fact a real improvement in the total mortality rate for this population, and should be taken into account when making future projections regarding populations in which specific separate assumptions for smokers and non-smokers have typically not been made in the past, for example, in traditional annuity insurance portfolios.

However, when separate assumptions for smokers and non-smokers are made (for example, in a term-assurance product, or in an enhanced or underwritten annuity offering), in the case of the example above, rates for each sub-group could assume zero future changes in their own mortality rates.

This phenomenon highlights the importance of considering the characteristics of the population for which projections of future mortality are required and the appropriateness of a given projection for its purpose.

When considering socio-economic influences, the situation is the same. To illustrate this, the ONS Longitudinal Study[6] shows that there appear to be clear differences in the rate of change in mortality between different social classes as illustrated in Figure 4.4.

According to the studies, differentials are lower over the second half of the study period, possibly due to the fact that individuals may

Figure 4.4 Average annual rate of mortality improvement by social class for males in England and Wales, 1972–76 to 2002–5, by age group and social class

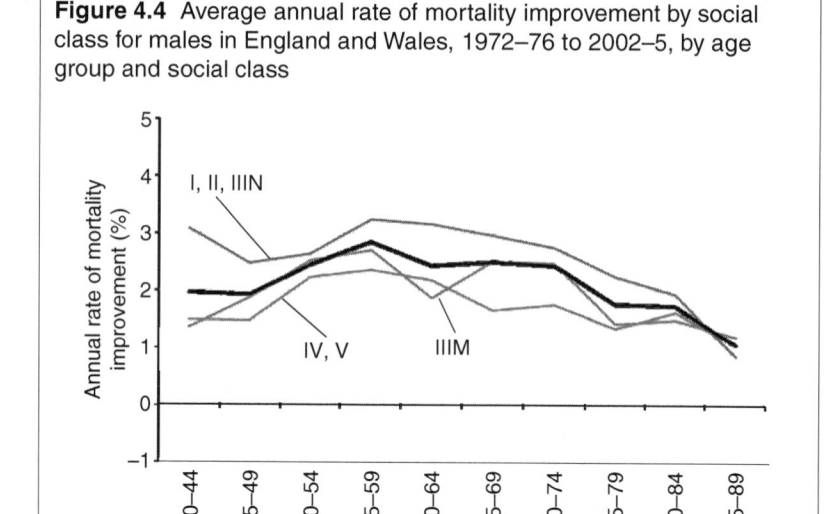

The thick black line denotes the rate for the sum of all classes.
Source: Continuous Mortality Investigation (2009b) and ONS Longitudinal Study.

Figure 4.5 Average annualised rates of mortality improvement, 1965–2004

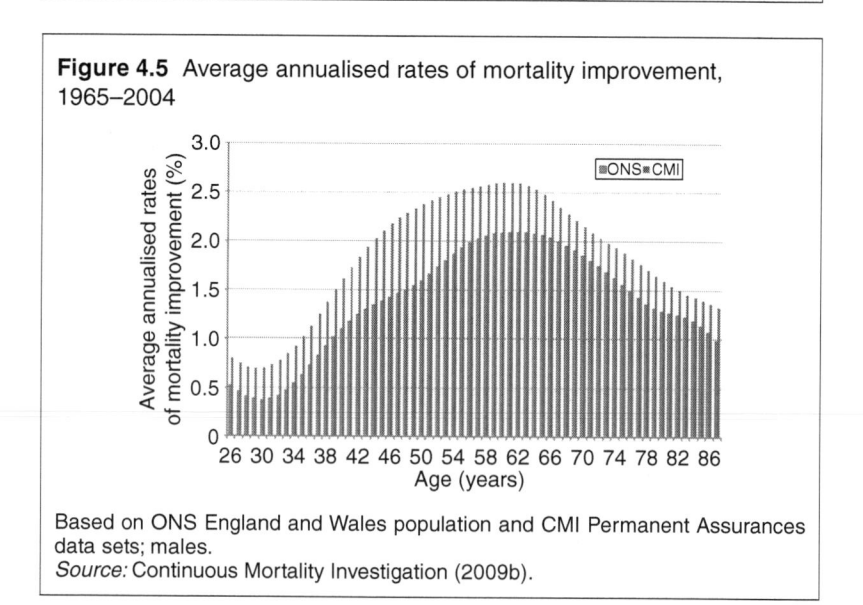

Based on ONS England and Wales population and CMI Permanent Assurances data sets; males.
Source: Continuous Mortality Investigation (2009b).

have changed class over time, moving from the social class assigned at the start of the study to another. For example, if an individual dropped to a lower socio-economic class because of ill-health, this change would not have been detected in the study. The situation is analogous to the diminishing effect of the underwriting selection process over time.

Another explanation could be the impact of government policies with respect to the National Health Service and targeted spending on particular regions or medical conditions and treatments. These efforts may have more impact on the lower socio-economic groups, in which the potential for improvement was greater. The plausibility of any of these explanations demonstrates the difficulty of using only historical data to make predictions, as the future may be influenced by medical developments and directions in health-care funding that cannot be directly extrapolated from past experience.

This effect is also observed in the historical differences observed between the 1965–2004 ONS England and Wales population and CMI Permanent Assurances data sets shown in Figure 4.5 which, while hampered by relative data volumes and corresponding lack of credibility in the smaller data set, reinforces the importance of making due allowance for the appropriate level of mortality improvement for the specific population under study.

Returning to Figure 4.4, the differences between the rates of change also appear to converge to a similar level for the older age groups. In this case the level is not zero, indicating an example of data supporting the imposition of a particular minimum level of mortality improvement in a chosen projection model. Also it can reasonably be expected that most mortality differentials between sub-groups, whatever the original cause, weaken with increasing age and this observation most likely applies equally to the rate of change.

CONSIDERATIONS AT OLDER AGES

One of the major issues in determining the rate of change in mortality at older ages is the relative sparsity of data. Although the mortality rate itself is quite high at older ages, the improvement rates can be highly volatile from year to year and age to age, often even at a national population level. For this reason studies are often performed at supranational level, ie, across several countries, and using grouped data to improve the stability of the observations.

Indeed, at the extreme older ages, say, above 100 years old, most countries have little data to credibly support a view on how mortality rates are changing.

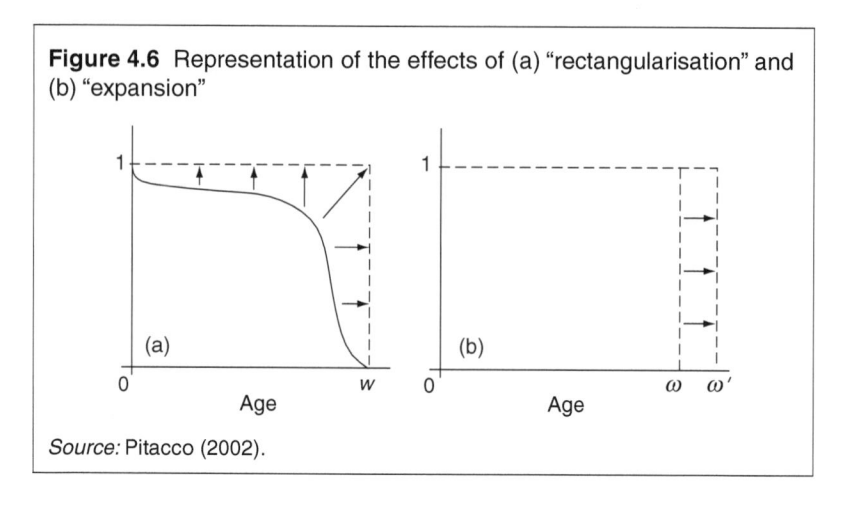

Figure 4.6 Representation of the effects of (a) "rectangularisation" and (b) "expansion"

[Figure 4.6: Two graphs showing survival curves. (a) shows a rectangularising curve with arrows indicating deaths concentrating at older ages, with maximum age w. (b) shows an expanding curve where the maximum age shifts from ω to ω'.]

Source: Pitacco (2002).

Thatcher et al (1998) studied the mortality rates of 13 European countries over the period 1980–90 and estimated the mortality rates at age 120 (q_{120}) as between 0.528 and 0.649 for males and between 0.512 and 0.639 for females.

Statistically, somewhat surprising is the fact that mortality rates do not reach 100% even though of course everyone in a given "extinct" generation has died. Despite this, many mortality tables are assumed to have a cut-off age of around, say, 120, a point at which the mortality rate is assumed to be 1.

In fact, the major contributing factor to an increase in life expectancy is the decrease in mortality rates in the age range of 65 to the late 80s rather than decreases beyond this age or indeed a dramatic extension in the oldest age to which people are surviving.

These two effects, known as rectangularisation and expansion, can be visualised quite simply, as shown in Figure 4.6.

As explained in Chapter 1, rectangularisation of the survival curve as shown in Figure 4.6(a) is the result of the increasing concentration of deaths at an old age. At the same time, the modal age of death (the age at which most people of a given generation die) moves to the right, closer to the maximum possible age (often denoted by ω or "omega").

These effects can be observed in actual data, as illustrated in Figures 4.7 and 4.8, which show survival curves and death counts by age at death, developed from the Italian national mortality tables (SIM) for given calendar years.

PROJECTING FUTURE MORTALITY

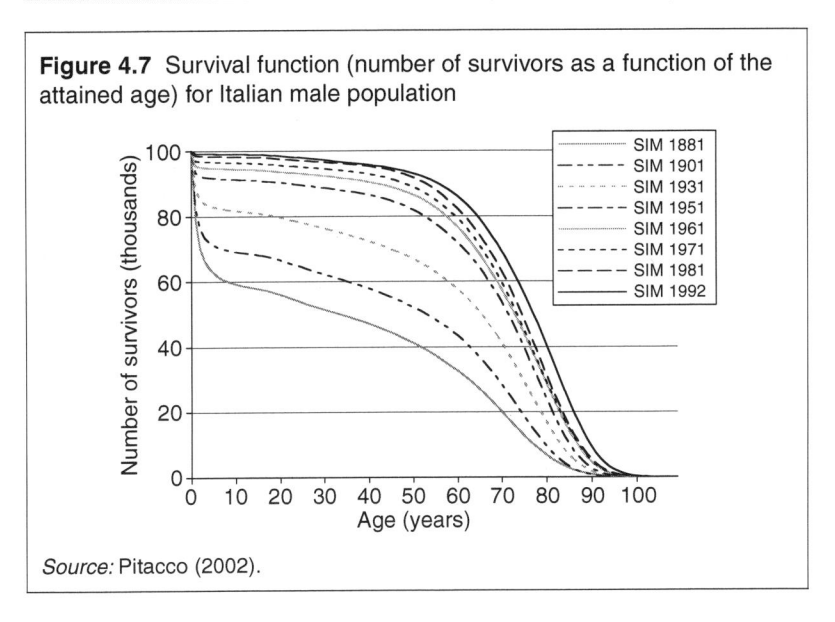

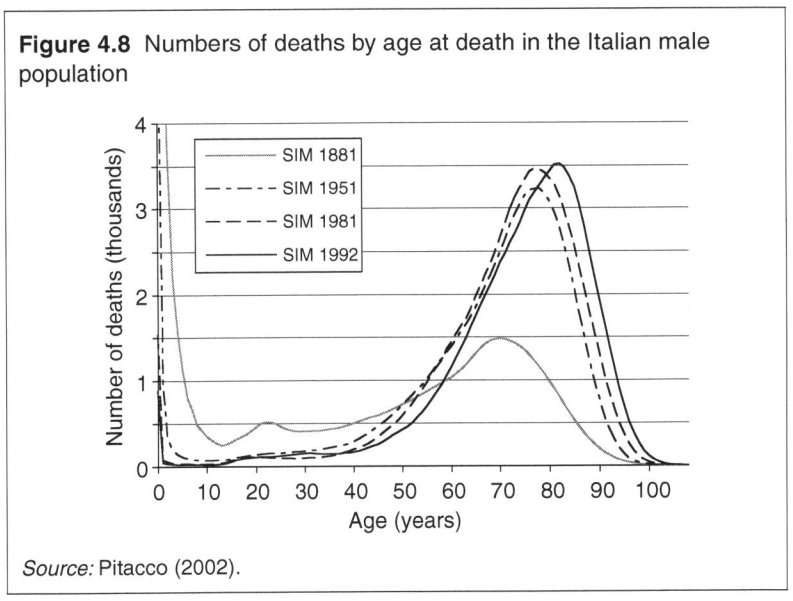

Figure 4.7 Survival function (number of survivors as a function of the attained age) for Italian male population

Source: Pitacco (2002).

Figure 4.8 Numbers of deaths by age at death in the Italian male population

Source: Pitacco (2002).

As Figure 4.7 indicates, rectangularisation of the survival curve clearly develops over time. In Figure 4.8 the expansion effect can be seen as more and more people begin to die at a specific advanced age. What is not clearly observable in the figures is a significant increase in the maximum age attainable (omega) in these data.

115

LONGEVITY RISK

Figure 4.9 Female life expectancy in Chile, Japan, New Zealand (non-Maori), Norway and the US compared with the trend in record life expectancy

Source: Oeppen and Vaupel (2002).

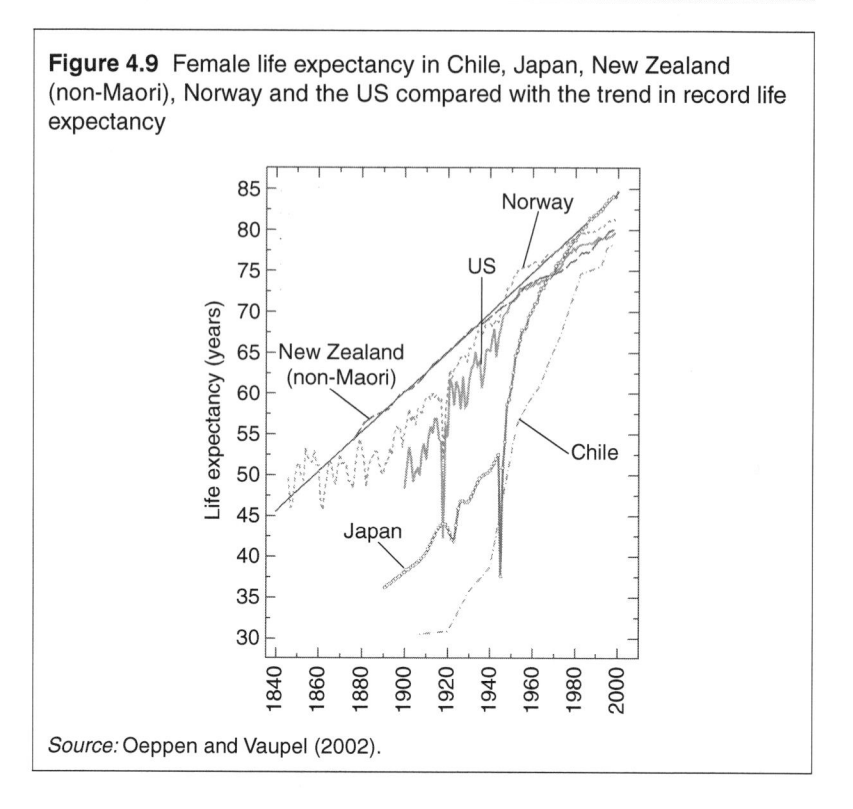

However, this fact does not contradict the observation by Oeppen and Vaupel (2002) that life expectancy is continuously rising, as shown in Figure 4.9.

Many believe there is some underlying rate of improvement that can be expected up to a certain advanced age, which holds for the duration of the projection (effectively the target rate in the expectation approach), but may then trend down to zero after this age.

FUTURE DEVELOPMENTS

Examination of changes in the cause of death and their incorporation into future projections has become an important area of study. In particular, there have been concerns about "correctly" allowing for the impact that a reduction in one cause of death would have on others. Most current models are fairly simplistic in that they assume each cause is independent of the others.

However, there are a number of well-documented issues with projecting mortality by cause (Continuous Mortality Investigation 2004).

1. Deaths from specific causes are not always independent and the complex inter-relationships are not always well understood.
2. There is limited understanding of how various risk factors (eg, smoking) affect different causes of death.
3. It is not possible to identify a unique solution for the relationship between "competing" risks by analysis of past data.
4. Medical resources will shift between causes over time as their relative importance changes.
5. Specific problems may exist with respect to the accuracy of cause of death as recorded on death certificates, eg, changing methods of diagnosis and classification over time and the difficulty of establishing a single cause, particularly at very advanced ages.
6. At extreme old ages, there may be causes of mortality that have not yet been identified as other, known, causes have resulted in deaths at earlier ages.

These have essentially remained valid in spite of efforts to investigate methods built around projecting the evolution of specific causes of death. Scenario testing can help to put the rate of future reductions in mortality by cause into context by showing for example the "equivalent" minimum annual rate of improvement implied by different hypotheses. Practitioners can then appreciate the assumptions of different scenarios in terms that are "easy" to communicate. An example might be to assume that rates of improvement for each major cause-of-death grouping remain at the same level in the first 10 years of the projection as for the last 10 years of observation. They could then slow down or, alternatively, remain at the same level throughout the next several decades of the projection, given a much stronger and long-lasting trend in the rate of reduction. These two scenarios produce outcomes in line with an expectation model with quite different minimum annual rates of improvement. These rates can then be compared with past observations over extended periods and age ranges or with expert opinions regarding the future, which may support the practitioner in coming to a view for their purpose. Refinements that use more complex multivariate models, such as generalised linear models, are being applied to changes in mortality in much the same way they have been used to determine base level mortality, introducing more sophisticated relationships between the evolution of different subgroups such as male and female or different socio-economic groups. What has become clear is that multidisciplinary efforts are required if practitioners are to have the most complete understanding possible of the evolution of mortality rates. Conferences and joint research projects that bring together practitioners and researchers from the actuarial, medical and public health areas are essential in order to arrive at a holistic picture of the likely future developments in mortality rates. The biennial "Living to 100 Symposium" stands out as a striking example of an international forum to serve this purpose, and these types of gatherings are becoming more widespread as users recognise the need to work across disciplines.

SENSE CHECKS ON PROJECTIONS

Once the quantitative and qualitative steps required to produce the projection have been performed, the reasonableness of a projection needs to be reviewed. Are the results in line with *a priori* expectations, if any? If not, efforts should be devoted to understanding the reasons for the discrepancies. For example, the German table DAV 2004 R originally produced future rates of mortality for males lower than those of females. This finding was considered to be incompatible with the developers' views on likely outcomes and so was rejected, and the model was adapted to eliminate this result.

Projecting mortality is a complex process with many nuances. Some of the most important aspects of the process can easily get lost in the detail but they should never be overlooked.

A projection model should give results that seem sensible to the creators and the users based on their wider understanding and knowledge of longevity developed from both their own analyses and that of experts.

The results should fit reasonably well to the past and flow smoothly into a projection of the future, unless some form of discontinuity or jump from the recent past to the near future can be explained according to the views of the group producing or using the projection.

The chosen method should be robust, that is it should be applicable over various time and age ranges and possibly over a range of populations (depending on how specific it is to the characteristics of the population under study). Robustness can be demonstrated by a variety of standard statistical tests, but one of the more powerful is the process of back-testing. Simply speaking, the data can be split into two halves, usually a first and second time period. The projection method is applied to the data in the first time period as a way of developing a projection that serves as a basis for performing a projection for the remaining time period. The projection is then compared with what actually occurred. In addition, the likelihood of the actual observation is calculated, where a method has been used, say, that calculates percentiles.

It is preferable if the method used is well described in the available literature: there is so much research available and, clearly, as in most fields of scientific endeavour, researchers are building on one another's work in a very interdependent manner. The benefit of taking advantage of others' work is far outweighed by the potential risk of "group-think", provided that users also establish their own view of the wide variety of sometimes contradictory approaches available.

It is desirable that the method is only as complex as necessary for the purpose. Taking an extreme example, there is no value in developing a method that requires the establishment of parameters to determine the rate of mortality change by eye colour if the data does not exist or the users know this factor is unlikely to influence the result.

It should be possible to introduce judgement into the process, as a purely mathematical model is unlikely to capture completely the complexity of mortality changes.

It is useful if the parameters can be "explained". For example, parameters relating to sex, age, time period and cohort may all have a natural sense to them: medical advances may be of specific benefit to a certain age group or may come into generalised and widespread use over a specific time period. Parameters that are difficult to explain in a narrative fashion may leave users concerned that they cannot understand the basis or the behaviour of the projection model over time.

Comparison to market practice when possible is a useful further validation of the approach and projection retained. This step can be performed by reference to other available projections from national statistical bodies or, say, financial or regulatory reports describing the longevity bases used by comparable competitors on similar annuity or pension-in-payment portfolios. The purpose of the projection (for example, estimating the need for senior health services or setting aside prudent reserves), however, needs to be compared with the practitioner's objectives.

Lastly, there is great value in a projection that can provide insight around the potential level of uncertainty associated with it.

CONCLUSION

Longevity risk is a field where a definitive insight, allowing development of a generally accepted and complete view on modelling this risk, remained largely undiscovered at the beginning of the 21st Century. Its continuing development is one of the reasons that the uncertainty around this risk must be communicated effectively and fully appreciated by all stakeholders.

The development of techniques for modelling mortality improvements at older ages beyond retirement has had a paradoxical result. As we have learnt more and developed much more powerful insight into the diversity of the current level of mortality and the complexity of the structure of changes in mortality rates, interested practitioners have increasingly realised how much more remains to be understood.

Given the uncertainty that will most likely remain around possible future outcomes, it is clear that some level of prudence or allowance for risk in reserving and setting capital levels is required. Any entity that assumes longevity risk must ensure it has sufficient capital resources available to be able to meet its obligations in the event that financially extreme longevity shocks develop for the risk assumer. Reserving and capital requirements will be examined in Chapters 6 and 7.

1 See http://www.gad.gov.uk/.

2 Investigations 31 and 33, covering insured pensioners.

3 For example, those presented to the Staple Inn Actuarial Society (Humble and Wilson 2008; Love and Ryan 2007).

4   Examples include Aslan *et al* (2005) and McPherson *et al* (2007).

5   For more details see http://www.fsa.gov.uk/pages/about/what/international/solvency/qis/qis5/technical/index.shtml.

6   See http://www.ons.gov.uk.

REFERENCES

Aslan, B. U., J. A. Critchley and S. Caperwell, 2005, "Small Changes in UK Cardiovascular Risk Factors Could Halve Coronary Heart Disease Mortality", *Journal of Clinical Epidemiology* 58, pp. 733–40.

Board of Actuarial Standards, 2008, "Mortality Research Working Group Report", March, URL: http://www.frc.org.uk/bas/publications/pub1698.html.

Booth, H., and L. Tickle, 2008, "Mortality Modelling and Forecasting: A Review of Methods", *Annals of Actuarial Science* 3, pp. 3–44.

Browne, B., J. Duchassaing and F. Suter, 2009, "Longevity: A 'Simple' Stochastic Modelling of Mortality", *British Actuarial Journal* 15, Supplement, pp. 249–65.

Cairns, A. J. G., D. Blake, K. Dowd, G. D. Coughlan, D. Epstein, A. Ong and I. Balevich, 2009, "A Quantitative Comparison of Stochastic Mortality Models Using Data from England and Wales and the United States", *North American Actuarial Journal* 13(1), pp. 1–35.

Continuous Mortality Investigation, 2004, "Projecting Future Mortality", Working Paper 3, URL: http://www.actuaries.org.uk/sites/all/files/documents/pdf/cmi-wp3.pdf

Continuous Mortality Investigation, 2009a, "A Prototype Mortality Projections Model: Part One", Working Paper 38, URL: http://www.actuaries.org.uk/sites/all/files/documents/pdf/mpmwp-workingpaper38final.pdf

Continuous Mortality Investigation, 2009b, "A Prototype Mortality Projections Model: Part Two", Working Paper 39, URL: http://www.actuaries.org.uk/sites/all/files/documents/pdf/mpmwp-workingpaper39-final.pdf

Continuous Mortality Investigation, 2009c, "CMI Mortality Projections Model", Working Paper 41, URL: http://www.actuaries.org.uk/research-and-resources/pages/cmi-working-paper-41.

Continuous Mortality Investigation, 2009d, "CMI Mortality Projections Model: 'CMI_2009'", URL: http://www.actuaries.org.uk/sites/all/files/documents/xls/cmi2009.xls.

Humble, R., and B. Wilson, 2008, "Drivers of Longevity Projection with Particular Reference to Smoking", Paper Presented to the Staple Inn Actuarial Society on April 22, URL: http://www.sias.org.uk/data/papers/DriversofLongevitySmoking/DownloadPDF.

JP Morgan, 2007, "LifeMetrics: A Toolkit for Measuring and Managing Longevity and Mortality Risks", Technical Document, URL: http://www.jpmorgan.com/directdoc/lifemetrics_technical.pdf.

Love, H., and D. Ryan, 2007, "Disease and Death: Improving Our Knowledge of the Future", Paper Presented to the Staple Inn Actuarial Society on July 17, URL: http://www.sias.org.uk/data/papers/DiseaseandDeath/DownloadPDF.

McPherson, K., T. Marsh and M. Brown, 2007, *Tackling Obesities: Future Choices – Modelling Future Trends in Obesity and Their Impact on Health*, Second Edition, Foresight Programme Publication (London: Government Office for Science).

Oeppen, J., and J. W. Vaupel, 2002, "Broken Limits to Life Expectancy", *Science* 296, pp. 1029–31.

Pitacco, E., 2002, "Longevity Risk in Living Benefits", Center for Research on Pensions and Welfare Policies, Working Paper 23/02.

Telford, P. G., B. A. Browne, E. J. Collinge, P. Fulcher, B. E. Johnson, W. Little, J. L. C. Lu, J. M. Nurse, D. W. Smith and F. Zhang, 2010, "Developments in the Management of Annuity Business", Paper Presented to the Institute of Actuaries Sessional Meeting, March 22.

Thatcher, A. R., V. Kannisto and J. W. Vaupel, 1998, "The Force of Mortality at Ages 80 to 120", Monographs on Population Aging, Volume 5 (Odense University Press).

Vaupel, J. W., 1997, "Trajectory of Mortality at Advanced Ages", in K. W. Wachter and C. E. Finch (eds), *Between Zeus and the Salomon: The Biodemography of Longevity*, pp. 17–37 (Washington, DC: National Academy Press).

5

Underwritten Annuities: The Market and Pricing of Longevity Risk

Jason Hurley, Greg Becker
RGA UK Services Ltd

Underwritten annuities are annuities that take medical and lifestyle evidence into consideration at the time the annuity is purchased. These products aim to target insured lives which have a below-average life expectancy, and to use this shortened life expectancy to offer a higher annuity payment.

Products issued as underwritten annuities run the gamut from the impaired annuity market to the enhanced annuity market. For our purposes, the term "underwritten annuities" covers both impaired and enhanced products.

In the case of the impaired annuity market, qualification for an underwritten product is contingent on the customer suffering from, or undergoing treatment for, a particular medical condition (such as cancer) which can be shown to have a proven link with increased mortality. Under these circumstances, the mortality loadings are significant.

In the case of enhanced annuities, the mortality rating can be based on lifestyle factors, such as smoking or obesity, rather than a life-threatening condition. For this reason, the mortality loadings – and thus annuity enhancements – are smaller than those used for impaired annuities. Due to the differences in the uplift, the amount that can be invested in underwriting the case varies, and many enhanced annuities rely on standard loadings if simple quantitative criteria are met.

In the following sections we consider underwritten annuities from a market perspective, including topics such as attitudes towards saving, regulation, commission and the impact of compulsion on underwritten annuity sales, as well as the size of the market and future prospects such as the move to commoditisation. With this as background, we then move on to a discussion of the pricing of longevity risk, including various approaches that can be used to assess the longevity risk component, the link between the sales and underwriting process, the question of over-disclosure and an overall approach to pricing. As part of the discussion of an overall approach to pricing, we cover the issues related to estimating base mortality, approaches to adding mortality loadings and allowances for mortality improvements, and then conclude by considering the impact of the underwriting philosophy, and several potential adjustments that may be needed for mixed blocks of business.

MARKET BACKGROUND

In order to understand the underwritten annuity market, it is important to first look at various regional differences that have affected the funds available to purchase these products and the regulations that encourage or discourage their purchase. This discussion is therefore our starting point.

International differences in pension saving practices

Underwritten annuities are purchased at an individual level by people who have made private provision for their pension or retirement income needs. Regulatory, cultural and historical factors have led to different pension provision "solutions" evolving in different markets. In some countries, such as France and Italy, pension provision is largely the responsibility of the state, while in South Africa and many developing countries it is largely left to the private sector.

Private pension provision can take many forms, but the most common schemes are defined-benefit and defined-contribution pension plans.

Funds in defined-benefit pension schemes do not create a demand for underwritten annuities. The scheme liabilities associated with defined-benefit plans are based on a group of lives, and mortality risk is not managed at an individual level.

In many markets where pension saving does not attract tax advantages, private pension provision may be through asset accumulation or an informal social system of inter-generational assistance.

This possibility should be kept in mind when comparing pension statistics across markets.

While underwritten annuities need not be purchased using pension funds, the vast majority of underwritten annuities in the UK show that this is likely to be the case.

Country differences in tax structures and public policy can muddy the pension waters, but estimating the amount of pension savings in a particular market can act as an important guide to the potential for underwritten annuities in a region.

One source of information is an analysis of international pension saving schemes that was conducted by Towers Watson (Towers Watson 2010). As the study points out, huge differences exist among countries. For example, defined-contribution funds account for only 1% of private pension savings funds in Japan, and even through France's GDP per capita is more than three times the size of South Africa's, the country has a lower level of private pension provision per capita.

Regulation of annuities

Local regulations affect an underwritten annuity market in two important ways: pricing and demand.

A prime example is regulatory reserving requirements, which effectively define the capital required by these products; these can have a significant impact on the price. For instance, reserving is required to follow a standard table in France. Thus, if an annuity writer is paying an enhanced annuity benefit to an underwritten life which is expected to have increased mortality, it will have a funding shortfall in all years prior to the insured's death. The availability of substitute pension-related products (most importantly variable annuities) also affects demand, although "compulsory annuitisation" regulations can compel people to purchase annuities and ensure demand.

Solvency II, which is discussed in more detail in Chapters 6 and 7, is likely to lead to higher capital requirements for writers of annuities than Solvency I. The higher capital requirement may have profound implications for the market as a whole but especially for the specialist players who concentrate on underwritten annuities, and who, for example, write about 70% of the UK underwritten annuities. Specialist annuity companies may be at a material disadvantage over those that write both longevity and mortality business, which would affect the price that they can offer to the customer.

Regulation is increasingly influencing the sales process and commission that can be charged on products. For example, the Retail Distribution Review in the UK, which will require advisers to take professional exams and to adhere to a higher professional standard, will promote a move to a fee for advice rather than a commission arrangement. These requirements could have a number of consequences.

Customers who are unwilling or unable to pay for advice may refrain from shopping around. By not making use of their open market option and staying with their pension plan provider, they are unlikely to obtain the best deal.

If advice becomes fee based, the adage "time is money" takes on new significance for brokers who are likely to demand an efficient service. While this greater efficiency is possible, as outlined above, it may not be in the customer's interest to accept the first quote: fastest is not necessarily best. There are also concerns relating to changes in customer behaviour that may lead to increased over-disclosure, which we address below.

New regulations relating to commission may also prompt more companies to sell directly to the public, for example, via their websites. This change in marketing would circumvent the need for broking fees, and would be a logical step for companies with strong brands. If customers are able to repeatedly amend their details and medical history to improve the price offered to them by obtaining multiple quotes, issues relating to over-disclosure will increase. These new challenges would force insurers to develop new techniques to combat over-disclosure.

Compulsory annuitisation

Prior to "annuitisation", pensioners are effectively bearing their longevity risk personally. Private pension solutions exist in many markets. These products have different names and include income drawdown in the UK, living annuities in South Africa and term allocated pensions (TAPs) in Australia, where the majority of pensioners bear the market and longevity risk. These products have proven to be very popular due to a combination of factors, and some would argue that increasing longevity, falling bond yields and (until the financial crisis) a rising stock market have collectively encouraged individuals to delay or avoid annuitisation.

In some markets, however, a compulsory annuitisation requirement forces people to purchase an annuity. For individuals with substandard health, the purchase of an impaired annuity can create value, although the age at which people are able to annuitise varies considerably. For example, in Mexico the compulsory annuitisation age is 65. In other markets, the questions of compulsory annuitisation and the age of adoption are under review. For example, the 2010 manifesto for the UK coalition government stated that they will review the need for compulsory annuitisation at age 75. At the time of writing, this requirement was under consultation, which leaves the matter of its long-term effects open to discussion. Looking at UK-based 2009–10 sales, 16% of new business was sold to people over age 70, who have a much higher than average purchase price. It is believed that these are often customers who have had a drawdown pension, and who are switching to an annuity as they approach the mandatory age as stipulated in the regulations.

Annuity buyers at even younger ages might migrate to other products, for example, drawdown or variable annuities. In practice, it could be argued that changes to the compulsory annuitisation age are unlikely to affect the annuity buyer's primary decision to purchase a certain product.

Underwritten annuity sales

The global market for underwritten annuities is relatively small compared with the market for standard annuities. In new markets where this product has been launched, it has typically been initially dominated by niche market players. Over time, more mainstream insurers have entered the market. Using the UK as an example, the first company offered smoker annuities in 1995. Since then a number of companies have entered the underwritten annuity market, and at the time of writing there are now some 8–10 companies in the market. Underwritten annuity sales in 2010 approached £2.5 billion per annum (Figure 5.1).

Despite differences in the retirement markets around the globe, underwritten annuities have been sold in markets outside of the UK. In South Africa, Metropolitan Life launched an enhanced annuity, but the product was unsuccessful as it was launched at the same time

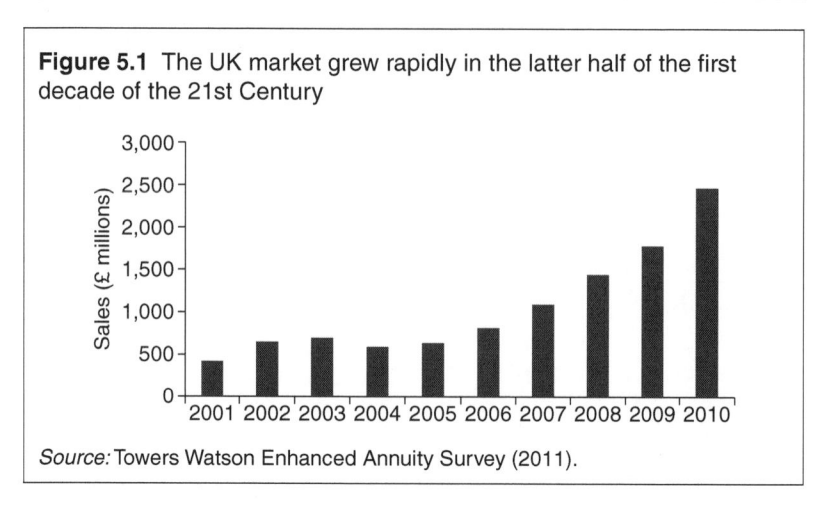

Figure 5.1 The UK market grew rapidly in the latter half of the first decade of the 21st Century

Source: Towers Watson Enhanced Annuity Survey (2011).

as living annuities and a rising stock market. As such, it appeared poor value for money against the competing products.

In the US, underwritten or "substandard" annuities, as they are known, are sold by many providers. For the 11 providers that sold underwritten annuities in 2004, substandard lifetime payout annuities accounted for more than a quarter of their standard and substandard single premium immediate annuity sales: a figure that is still a small percentage (less than 5% for the period 2000–2004) of total contracts sold by providers of both underwritten and non-unwritten annuities (Drinkwater *et al* 2006). The average size of substandard annuity purchases, however, has risen rapidly, a trend that is thought to stem from increased "mortality arbitrage".

Future market prospects

Market prospects for underwritten annuities are generally good for a number of reasons.

- In many countries, increasing numbers of people are in defined-contribution as opposed to defined-benefit pension schemes. Upon retirement they will receive a lump sum payment which can be used to buy an annuity.
- In countries where individuals can make use of an open market option, they should be advised to consider an underwritten annuity product if they are in poor health. Regulatory initiatives have begun to ensure that this option is communicated more clearly to the customer. These efforts have prompted

insurers to advertise impaired annuities, pointing out that these alternatives may represent a better deal for customers in poor health.

- In many markets, brokers have been under pressure to increase their professionalism, which has been followed up by improved policing efforts to ensure that they are acting in their clients' best interests. In combination, this has led to more brokers considering underwritten annuities for more of their clients.
- The development and continuous improvement of electronic tools and portal systems enable brokers to get quotes for underwritten annuities without doing any additional work.
- There are increasing levels of broker and customer awareness of underwritten annuity products, partly as a result of regular articles being featured in the media.

On the other hand, the impact of changing regulations related to capital requirements and reserving, commission and compulsory annuitisation needs to be watched closely.

Product standardisation and strategies to deal with the resulting commoditisation

Over time, a more commoditised structure will be a natural outcome in many markets. This development has already happened in the UK underwritten annuity market.

Product commoditisation stems from a desire by customers, regulators and insurance sellers for simple, straightforward products. The forces driving product and process standardisation, or commoditisation, has led to the development of many similar and comparable offerings. With companies offering comparable levels of service and having similar levels of financial strength, the main way for buyers and brokers to differentiate between companies is to compare the amount of pension benefit provided for a given purchase price. There are a number of strategies that insurers can follow to compete effectively.

1. **Find a new product:** companies can offer substitute products, like income drawdown or variable annuity contracts, as alternatives.

2. **Compete on service and brand:** as a market becomes more competitive, with similar products and service levels among competitors, customers will find it harder to discern between any two companies. A more effective strategy might be for the better quality company to offer to "price match" the rates of a weaker competitor.

3. **Find ways to differentiate your product:** companies could be more lenient with their underwriting and take on riskier lives, or offer quotes with long guarantee periods. These strategies are ways to compete, but in essentially offering something more generous than the market, are these strategies sustainable? It may be possible to develop a low-cost product feature, which is viewed as valuable to the customer. Ultimately, such features are hard to find and are generally quickly copied by competitors.

4. **Look to grow market share and achieve economies of scale:** if a company operates under the premise that the market will be big and priced competitively with thin margins, then efficiency will be critical and scale paramount. Under these circumstances, a company could aim to grab market share by using its distribution, looking for new ways to sell the product, shutting out competitors, investing in systems to analyse data and/or leveraging its buying power with external suppliers such as reinsurers and IT suppliers. Mergers and acquisitions, an alternative to organic growth, is another route to increasing market share.

5. **Enhance investment risk management practices:** the annuity rates charged to the customer reflect a combination of investment and mortality projections. Therefore, when looking at the customer proposition, companies should be looking for advantage in both the investment and mortality dimensions. In the investment area, this could be achieved through either research or quality investment risk management practices. Another possibility is a review of administration capability, although this area is generally a small factor when compared with the impact of either investment or mortality.

6. **Invest in mortality pricing and risk management practices:** for a large, competitively priced market with thin margins,

some may argue that the first priority is not efficiency, but rather the identification of substandard lives and accurate pricing: ie, the ability to underwrite carefully and price appropriately. In this case, the only sustainable long-term strategy to keep ahead of the competition is to make better use of data. This can be achieved by having more and better quality data and/or a stronger research team. Moreover, this strategy could work in tandem with the fourth strategy outlined above.

These strategies are not mutually exclusive: one strategy does not preclude another, and a variety of strategies could be implemented in tandem.

PRICING OF LONGEVITY RISK

Armed with a broad knowledge of the market for underwritten annuities, we can now consider the pricing of the longevity risk embedded in such products.

Assessing longevity risk for an underwritten annuity

When assessing the annuity rate to offer a customer, some companies will underwrite the individual life, the aim being to take account of the expected mortality of the individual analysed on a client-by-client basis. The more accurately a company can assess the individual's mortality, the more accurately it can set the premium for the risk.

An assessment of a buyer's health can take a number of different forms, but most focus on lifestyle factors, medical factors or a combination of both.

Lifestyle factors

Assessments that use lifestyle factors are typically based on objective factors, such as postal code, smoker status and policy size. Key advantages in using this type of information are its ease of collection and objectivity. Its use also leaves less room for over-disclosure, especially because the insurer or pension scheme should know the information without needing to contact the customer. It also avoids the need for a customer to complete a more detailed medical questionnaire. This lifestyle method is used within the individual market and when setting rates for group scheme transfers. Annuities underwritten in the individual market using these types of underwriting factors are known as "lifestyle annuities".

This approach to pricing annuities individually started in the UK in 1995 when Stalwart Life offered enhanced annuity terms for smokers.

Medical factors

As well as using the lifestyle factors, some companies ask for medical information. Forms may involve simple yes/no questions or more detailed medical questions and, in general, applications ask a few simple yes/no questions before drilling down into more detail on an individual's specific conditions.

For example,

> Have you ever been diagnosed with high blood pressure (hypertension)?
>
> If you answer "no", then move to the next question. If you answer "yes", please provide the following information:
>
> (i) specify readings, both dates and level;
>
> (ii) specify the treatments, amounts and names of medication.

The first annuity to take into account medical factors was launched in the UK by The Pension Annuity Friendly Society (PAFS), which extended the smoker annuity to take into account medical factors in 1995, and was joined by Stalwart in 1996. The Simplified Medical Underwriting System (2000) further increased annuity underwriting sophistication with a points-based system: the more medical conditions a customer had, the more points they scored, and the higher the enhanced annuity payment.

The link between the sales and underwriting processes

In order to assess longevity risk for underwritten annuities, the sales and underwriting process is the key stage at which valuable medical and lifestyle information is sought to appropriately price the risk.

There are two routes that insurance brokers may use to submit applications to the insurance companies: electronic portals or a paper-based application form. In the UK, a common quote request form has been drawn up by the leading companies to reduce the burden on the broker during the application process.[1] Instead of completing many varied forms (one for each underwritten annuity provider following their bespoke question set), the broker completes a single form and then submits it to a number of insurers, based upon which insurers will make their underwriting decision. This decision may be automated (made by an electronic rules-based system) or manual (made by an underwriter who reads and interprets the medical information provided on the form).

Some insurers offer rates based upon the information on the form, and some may ask for further medical evidence. Companies generally have an underwriting limit based on policy size. Above that limit, they ask for medical evidence.

There are a number of portals that allow electronic submission, which aim to give an instant quotation. The advantage of the portal is that the questions are simpler and easier to answer than a paper-based application. However, a more detailed application form allows for greater disclosure, and the opportunity for underwriters to apply their skill and judgement when assessing the risk and making their underwriting decision. For example, a portal may ask an applicant "how many tablets do you take?", while the paper-based form will allow the applicant to specify the medication they take by name. With this information, the underwriter can more accurately assess the severity of the applicant's medical condition(s) and hence more accurately price the longevity risk. The downside is that the decision-making process may be slower and more expensive than an automated computerised decision.

Checking for over-disclosure

Over-disclosure is encountered in many areas of insurance. In the case of life insurance, it could be the mysterious phenomenon in which smokers "forget" that they smoke cigarettes. In the case of enhanced annuities, applicants may be encouraged to give information that will suggest that their mortality risk is higher than it actually is: in the case of underwritten annuities, applicants have an incentive to make themselves seem as sickly as possible. Non-smokers who claim to be smokers are an example. Given that material underwriting decisions regarding mortality assumptions and other issues are based upon the information disclosed by the applicant, incorrect information will clearly lead to mis-estimation of the longevity risk.

Therefore, one question that is constantly asked is: "How can we check that the customer has told the truth?" There are a number of ways to achieve this. Examples of techniques that may be used to ensure appropriate disclosure include the following.

- The customers are encouraged to send in hospital letters or other medical information with their application.

- Doctor's reports can either be collected on a case-by-case or a random sample can be drawn. The delay between an insurer offering a quotation and receiving money from the pension provider usually gives the insurer an opportunity to collect the necessary medical evidence. If there is evidence of over-disclosure, the policy can be rewritten on standard terms, giving a lower benefit amount to the customer.

- Tele-underwriting allows the insurer to speak to the customer and record the conversation; the recording can be used as evidence if a dispute arises.

- Checks are made to ensure that the treatment and medication is appropriate for the disclosed medical condition(s).

As useful as these techniques are, it is important to keep in mind that, based on past experience, applicants have been surprisingly honest when completing the form.

Some of the issues arising from over-disclosure can be avoided, or at least minimised, by ensuring that the sales literature, application forms and other parts of the sales process are clear. Such a sales process will enable the insurer to change the terms in cases of over-disclosure without legally or morally breaching their contractual agreement with the customer. The insurer should also consider the reputational damage associated with an unwanted change.

Will customer honesty deteriorate over time, making it harder to assess longevity risk? While the market is gradually moving from one in which the broker speaks to the customer and completes a paper-based application form to one in which an electronic application has largely eliminated the need for broker involvement, there is a fear that some of the existing checks and balances may not be as effective, and that the integrity and honesty of both the advisers and the applicants will decline. This could lead to mis-estimation of the mortality risk, and a potential reduction in the insurer's future profitability.

Pricing: overall approach

The traditional approach to pricing has been to use a number of mortality tables for people with similar characteristics, for example, a different table for smokers, diabetics and so on. For each disease group (eg, cancers, cardiovascular risks), the mortality tables will have been derived by determining appropriate survivorship curves, driven by shaping parameters such as the "expected life expectancy" (ELE) and "maximum life expectancy" (MLE), defined as follows.

Expected life expectancy: for a cohort of lives, the ELE is the number of years before 50% of the cohort is expected to be dead.

Maximum life expectancy: the MLE is the age at which, say, 5% of the population is expected to survive.

Medical research is used to develop appropriate values for the ELE and MLE for each disease group.

The survivorship curve, which reflects the number of lives still alive at each future point in time, can then be plotted using a survival function. One of the most common is the Weibull distribution, which uses the ELE and MLE as parameters. From this distribution, we can work backwards to estimate the probability of an individual surviving to a particular age, and thus the probability that the insurer will need to make the annuity payment. This information can be used to determine the appropriate annuity rate to quote.

As the market has become more competitive, companies have become more sophisticated in terms of how they price these risks. One method has been to increase the number of mortality tables used to reflect the different disease groups. Another extension has been to increase the number of points that are used to define the survivorship function. This could be done by including estimates of the time it takes before 25% and 75% of the population have died, as well as the time it takes before 50% (ELE) and 95% (MLE).

While this "multiple table" approach served the UK market well for a number of years, more sophisticated approaches for more accurately estimating the risk have since been developed. These techniques are particularly well suited to situations in which candidates with multiple risk factors have more than one reason for an enhancement. For example, how should the "multiple table" approach be applied to a diabetic who smokes? Some may argue that we should use the diabetic table, while others that we should use the smoker table, while most would agree that the mortality for this individual is likely to be higher than that of a non-smoking diabetic or a non-diabetic smoker. The "multiple table" approach does not allow for this.

Approaches that take into account multiple factors are closer to the traditional approach that insurers and reinsurers use for underwriting term-assurance risk, where individual loadings are applied to a "healthy" mortality table.

Estimating the base mortality

Pricing the mortality element typically begins with the construction of a mortality base table for healthy annuitant lives. The base table can then be adjusted for each life, with different mortality loadings applied to reflect each of the different diseases that the individual suffers from. These extra loadings may be modelled as

- a mortality loading,
- an age rating or
- a mortality loading for a finite term.

To derive an appropriate base mortality table for healthy lives, alternative approaches such as graduation techniques or the adoption of appropriate standard tables and experience analyses can be used. These techniques are described in Chapter 3.

Before adding a loading to a healthy annuitant mortality table, a critical step in this approach is to strip out all unhealthy lives from the healthy lives experience when estimating it. Adding the mortality loading to a base table that includes some sick lives would lead to future longevity being underestimated. This needs to be remembered when using published standard tables and data which includes a mixture of healthy, unhealthy and very unhealthy lives.

The process of "stripping" could be approached in a number of ways, for example, by taking published pensioner mortality and stripping out the impact of those in poor health. (This can be a big issue when developing a base table for people in their fifties, when many of those that have retired will have retired early due to poor health.) Another approach could be to use life insurance experience to build the mortality table. Furthermore, when using published standard mortality tables or data, it is important to consider whether

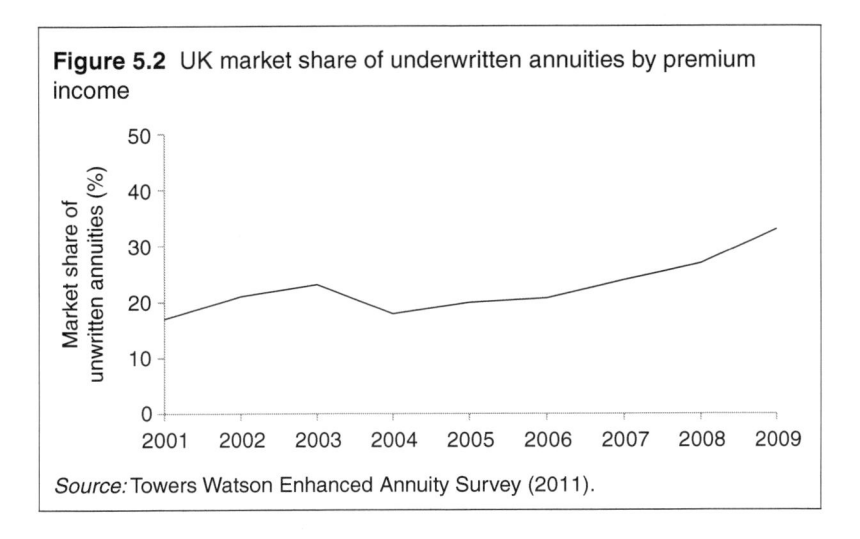

Figure 5.2 UK market share of underwritten annuities by premium income

Source: Towers Watson Enhanced Annuity Survey (2011).

there has been a change in the underlying mix of lives over time. For example, in the UK, where the underwritten annuity market continues to grow, the growth has had a knock-on effect, constantly changing the underlying proportions of healthy and unhealthy lives buying annuities at standard rates.

As the underwritten annuity market grows (relative to the standard annuity market), less healthy lives increasingly drop out of the "average" portfolio, causing the mortality of the remaining average annuitants to fall. Over time the "average" pool of lives that is reflected in the standard mortality tables will tend to reflect the experience of healthier and healthier lives. This phenomenon is likely to be an issue as more lives are underwritten, which will mis-estimate the difference between "healthy" and "average" lives.

Using the UK as an example, Figure 5.2 illustrates that enhanced annuities are a significant and growing share of external annuities.

Adjusting base mortality to reflect impairment

A range of loadings may be applied when underwriting annuities. The most common risks and medical conditions for which a loading is applied relate to either cardiovascular conditions or cancers. Due to the different patterns of mortality, these two classes of risk should be treated separately when assessing the appropriate loadings to apply on top of base mortality, and each are considered further in the following sections.

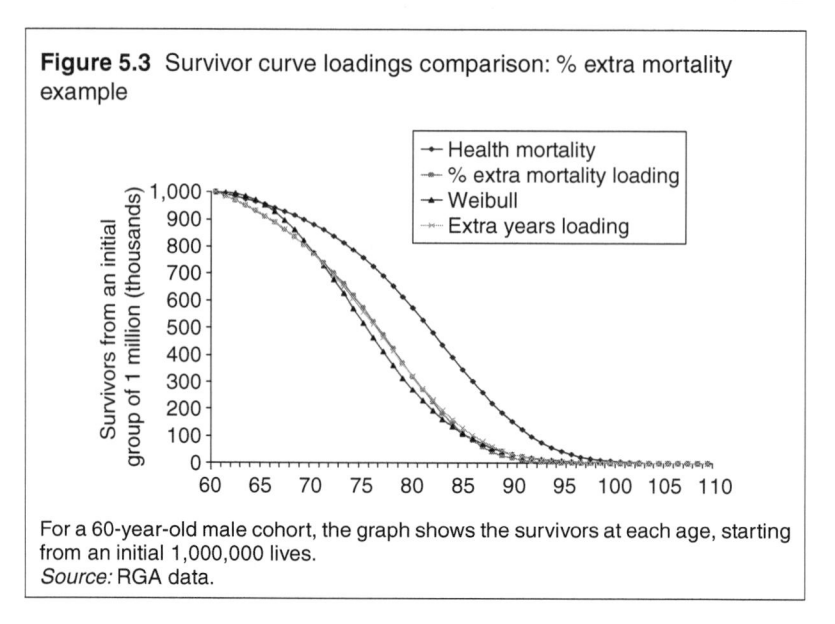

Figure 5.3 Survivor curve loadings comparison: % extra mortality example

- Health mortality
- % extra mortality loading
- Weibull
- Extra years loading

Survivors from an initial group of 1 million (thousands) vs age (60–110)

For a 60-year-old male cohort, the graph shows the survivors at each age, starting from an initial 1,000,000 lives.
Source: RGA data.

Cardiovascular conditions

Common examples of cardiovascular risks include smoking and obesity, and related medical conditions include

- diabetes,
- hypertension,
- hypercholesterolemia,
- angina,
- coronary artery bypass graft.

For these medical conditions some companies assume that there is a smooth and steady increase in mortality. In this case, the loadings for these risks are typically described as a fixed percentage addition to mortality. For example, smokers can be modelled as having a mortality loading of 50% in each future year.

Some companies allow for such risk factors cumulatively: the more conditions an applicant has, the greater the addition to their mortality. This approach may not be applied on a simple cumulative basis: the impact of some conditions may negate or compound each other. Moreover, the actual percentage applied may vary by other factors such as age and sex.

By combining the mortality base table with the extra loadings for risk, we can develop survival curves, as shown in Figure 5.3. For

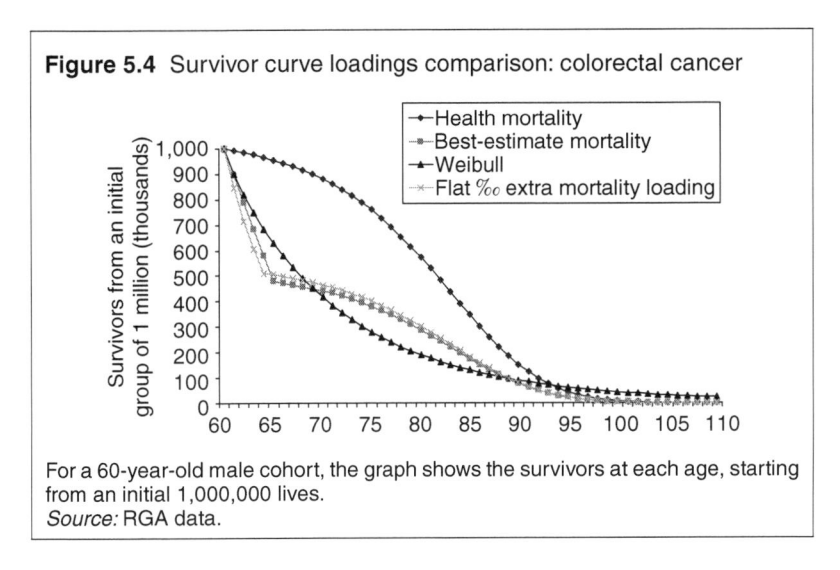

Figure 5.4 Survivor curve loadings comparison: colorectal cancer

[Chart showing survivors from an initial group of 1 million (thousands) vs age from 60 to 110, with four lines: Health mortality, Best-estimate mortality, Weibull, and Flat ‰ extra mortality loading]

For a 60-year-old male cohort, the graph shows the survivors at each age, starting from an initial 1,000,000 lives.
Source: RGA data.

an initial cohort of 1 million lives, the graph shows the number of people who are expected to survive to each year in the future. The top line (black diamonds) shows the number of survivors if they are all healthy at age 60. The other lines illustrate the assumed survival distribution for unhealthy lives modelled in different ways, which includes applying a fixed percentage extra mortality (grey squares), adding years to age (grey crosses), or by using the ELE/MLE Weibull methodology described above (black triangles). In this chart, all three approaches have been set so that they are actuarially equal in terms of the present value of future annuity payments.

Cancer risks

Intuitively, the additional loadings to mortality for cancer risks are not uniform. Cancer may lead to a relatively higher chance of death in the near future, but the longer an individual survives, possibly due to effective treatment that sends the cancer into remission, the smaller the extra mortality loading needs to be (ie, after an initial period of higher mortality, mortality rates will converge to those of standard lives). This logical development is supported by the data.

Cancer risk factors are complex and tend to be classified based on the different forms and stages of the cancer disease's development. A more accurate approach ideally considers the shape of the appropriate cancer survival curve for each life, reflecting the lives' specific cancer and their most recent staging diagnosis, but this would be immensely complex and very difficult to administer. Due to practical pressures, some companies have made use of a simplified approximation, and load for specific cancer risks using, say, a mortality loading for a limited term (similar to the standard approach for term assurance).

Figure 5.4 shows four curves: one for "cancer free" healthy lives (black diamonds) and three others generated by using the ELE/MLE Weibull approach (black triangles), a survival function reflecting a fixed flat per mille addition (grey crosses) and a "more accurate" approach based upon the actual U-shaped cancer survival curve (grey squares). It is important to note that the flat per mille loading is a better match to the actual cancer survival curve than the ELE/MLE Weibull approach.

As in Figure 5.3, the three cancer curves are each equivalent in terms of expected future outgo.

Allowing for mortality improvements

The techniques used to assess future mortality improvement for standard annuities were examined in detail in the previous chapter. One important difference for underwritten annuities is the knowledge that the lives are, by definition, already substandard. This information raises many questions relating to the future mortality improvement of lives, such as

- to what extent are mortality improvements in the general population due to improved screening and improved public education which help people to delay the onset of poor health until later in life?
- are people receiving better treatment that allows them to live for longer even after being diagnosed?

The latter question is more relevant for pricing underwritten annuities, because the lives are, by definition, substandard.

The contribution of improved treatments to mortality improvement is difficult to assess, and expert judgement is vital. Clues as to the direction of future trends can be derived from analysis of historical improvements categorised by cause of death, which then need to be integrated with expert advice from the medical profession on the prospects for future improvement on a condition-by-condition basis. Pricing the benefits for substandard lives should also consider shocks, such as one-off improvements in treatment, or new drugs that may prolong the period between detection and death.

The traditional pricing methodology has been to classify lives into different buckets based on the underlying disease, and then to apply a particular mortality table to each bucket which has a shape that reflects the disease in question. In the past, the underwriting objective has been to select the tables which have the most appropriate shape for the risk.

With increased sales, and as the quality of information systems continues to improve, mortality experience data for underwritten annuitants has become more abundant. In an increasingly competitive market where insurance companies seek to use ever more accurate measures, experience data is a competitive advantage.

Adjustments to longevity assumptions for "mixed blocks"

As more underwritten annuities are sold, the mix of an individual company's experience will vary, and the underlying mixture of annuitants in their underwritten and non-underwritten cohorts will change. Using past claim experience is problematic due to changes in the mix of business which can overwhelm more subtle changes. There are two possible outcomes that need to be considered when performing any analysis.

Where a block consists of standard annuities, but where the prospective annuitants with medical conditions had an enhanced option, it can be assumed that the block's annuitants at vesting would be a select group, and in good health. Many of the unhealthier lives, it could be assumed, would have accepted improved annuity terms with another provider. Predictions of the mortality pricing of annuitants can only be made after following a complex and subjective modelling exercise, disaggregating the total annuitant population into groups differentiated by their health status. Such a model requires assumptions regarding

- the proportions of the annuitant population at each level of enhanced risk factor or medical condition (and their associated additional mortality rates) and
- the underwritten annuity penetration rates for each enhancement level, when the annuities vested.

A model reflecting these factors is capable of estimating the lower select base mortality that could have been assumed to apply at the time of vesting to those choosing standard annuities. This initial level of selection will gradually be eroded as these lives develop medical conditions. The predictive pricing model should therefore incorporate an annual increase in the mortality rate, up to an "ultimate" rate, to be achieved after a number of years.

If the block is made up of both underwritten and standard annuities, then it may be possible to ignore the product classification and to assume that the block's overall experience will be in line with the usual "book price". This assumption is justifiable provided that, over the two products, the usual mix of vesting pensioners has been attracted by the insurer.

Unfortunately, in practice this is often not the case, and modelling adjustments, of the type described in this section, may be necessary.

CONCLUSIONS

The underwritten annuity market has healthy prospects for growth. This outlook is driven by global pressures on insurers to be fair to their customers, pressures on financial advisors to do the best job for their clients and by the increasing numbers of people in defined-contribution or money-purchase schemes. These developments are compounded by the annuity customers' increasing propensity to make use of their open market options, and the increasing numbers of people that are soon to reach retirement age. This trend has already been borne out in the UK, and could take shape in other markets.

Given the size and price competitiveness of the underwritten annuity market, it is hardly surprising that insurance companies are looking at this market closely, and considering all opportunities to try to gain a pricing advantage by assessing the mortality risk as accurately as possible.

There are many techniques used across the market to price underwritten annuities. The tools involved in the pricing are often held back by both data constraints and the actuarial judgement that is required to reflect the changing landscape, most notably with regard to the continuous introduction of improvements in medical technology that have a knock-on effect on diagnosis, treatment and mortality rates.

Regulatory changes and product commoditisation have added to insurers' challenges. Long-term success can be achieved by an effective investment in market-leading pricing and risk-management practices that leverage an insurers' data and mortality experience. A strategy that combines quality product development and risk management with a proactive investment in the latest research will inevitably be the way to remain on top of developments.

1 See http://www.commonquotation.co.uk/.

REFERENCES

Drinkwater, M., J. E. Montminy, E. T. Sondergeld, C. G. Raham and C. R. Runchey, 2006, "Substandard Annuities", Report, LIMRA International, Inc, and the Society of Actuaries in collaboration with Ernst & Young LLP.

Towers Watson, 2010, "2010 Global Pension Asset Study", January, URL: http://www.towerswatson.com/assets/pdf/966/GPAS2010.pdf.

Towers Watson, 2011, "Enhanced Annuity Survey", February, URL: http://www.towerswatson.com/press/3783.

Part III

Reserving and Capital Requirements

6

Reserving and Regulatory Requirements

Stephen Makin
Stephen Makin Consulting Ltd

In this chapter we provide an overview and discussion of the reserving and regulatory requirements for insured annuity and pension scheme liabilities. On an economic basis, these liabilities are very similar, yet the annuity liabilities written by insurers and the benefit obligations of pension schemes are governed under very different regulatory regimes. However, a discussion of the many different national regulations by country is beyond the scope of this chapter. For the purpose of examining reserving and regulatory requirements, we therefore focus on Europe, especially the UK, where the majority of longevity risk transactions have occurred and where these transactions seem poised to continue to increase.

The first part of the chapter therefore outlines the regulatory regimes for European insurance companies and pension schemes. Particular emphasis is given to economic-based regimes for insurers which are of increasing importance because of Solvency II legislation. The second part of the chapter discusses the principles of setting longevity assumptions in each of the different regulatory contexts.

REGULATORY REGIMES
Solvency I regime for life insurers

Historically, Solvency I, as it pertains to European insurers and reinsurers, has been a predominantly "rules-based" framework, centred on a requirement to hold assets in excess of the sum of a prudent value of liabilities (or technical provisions) and a prescribed solvency margin. With the establishment of the European Union, rules became more harmonised, and the current regulatory regime is set by the Consolidated Life Directive.[1] This is primary European legislation that consolidates three previous Life Directives. The Consolidated Life Directive is ultimately codified, via legislation, into rules and guidance issued by the local regulator in each member state of the European Union. In the UK, for example, the rules are implemented by powers given to the Financial Services Authority, and a similar approach is taken in other member states.

Rules relating to the valuation of assets have focused on how to value them in a regulatory context and the extent to which a particular type of asset can be taken into account. Rules relating to the valuation of liabilities require that they are valued using actuarial principles, making proper provision for all liabilities (including expenses), policyholder options and guarantees. The underlying valuation basis should be based on prudent assumptions which have due regard to policyholders' reasonable expectations and include appropriate margins for adverse deviation of the relevant factors. The solvency margin requirements are calculated using a simplistic, non-risk-based approach.

Economic capital regimes for life insurers

Recent years have seen a move towards new regulatory standards, increasingly based on economic principles. Such regimes are typically "principles based" rather than rules based, but do prescribe a probability with which insurers should remain solvent over a prescribed time period. With the introduction of the Individual Capital Adequacy Standard regime on December 31, 2004, the UK was a forerunner in adopting principles-based standards. Other countries in the European Economic Area have also adopted an economic approach, including Switzerland in January 2008 (Swiss Solvency Test) and Germany in January 2009 (Minimum Requirements for Risk Management). Each of these is discussed briefly below.

- **UK: Individual Capital Adequacy Standard (ICAS).** ICAS is a one-year value-at-risk framework calibrated to a 99.5% confidence level, often referred to as a 1-in-200 confidence level. Supplementing the previous Solvency I regime, ICAS requires an economic valuation of assets and liabilities. Under the standard, firms are also required to hold sufficient capital in excess of a market-consistent value of liabilities to enable them to withstand with 99.5% certainty all risks which might materialise over one year from the valuation date. The centrepiece of this principles-based framework for a firm is its view of the particular risks which it faces, taking account of its specific circumstances and operating models. The ICAS regime is similar in many regards to the quantitative solvency pillar of Solvency II (often referred to as Pillar I, which is discussed in more detail later), this being a clear advantage to many UK firms implementing Solvency II.

- **Switzerland: Swiss Solvency Test (SST).** In November 2007, the Swiss Financial Market Authority issued a circular, known as the SST.[2] This required that, from January 1, 2008, the solvency of insurance companies be measured by applying the SST as well as the existing Solvency I rules. SST requires an economic valuation of assets and liabilities. It is structurally and conceptually similar to Solvency II, including both a risk margin and a one-year value-at-risk capital requirement (see more later) albeit to a 99% confidence level. This requirement gives a clear advantage to Swiss insurers in respect of Solvency II implementations.

- **Germany: Minimum Requirements for Risk Management (MaRisk VA).** In January 2009, the German regulator issued the MaRisk VA directive[3] to its insurance industry. The directive's aim was to improve risk management standards in preparation for Solvency II. MaRisk VA also has elements of economic valuation in that it requires an economic valuation of assets and liabilities for the purpose of risk quantification, expected to accelerate the modelling changes required for Solvency II. However, MaRisk VA is more than a set of economic valuation rules. It also contains a set of principles for a coherent risk management system. In many ways, MaRisk VA is taking a lead on the risk management pillar of Solvency II (often referred to as "Pillar II", which is discussed later), leaving German insurers well placed too in their implementation of Solvency II.

An approach to calculating capital requirements

Table 6.1 sets out an approach commonly taken in the calculation of capital requirements under an economic valuation framework. The application of the framework in Table 6.1 to the derivation of

Table 6.1 Calculating capital in an economic valuation–correlation matrix

Identify all risks	First, identify all risks to which the business is exposed. For a block of with-profits business the principal risks might be market prices (eg, equity, property, bonds, etc) as well as persistency, mortality, expenses and so on. For a block of annuity business, the principal risks would relate to interest rates, credit spreads, longevity and expenses.
Define the 1-in-200 event for each risk	Define the 1-in-200 (99.5%) one-year event for each risk. Analytical techniques would ideally be used at this point, eg, in quantifying the statistical uncertainty surrounding recently observed annuitant mortality experience, but expert judgement often plays a part. It is not uncommon for firms simply to define the 1-in-200 event, as opposed to the full probability distribution.
Determine capital requirements for each risk	Separately for each risk, determine the capital required to cover the 1-in-200 one-year event for that risk. Denote by $C = (C_j), j = 1, 2, \ldots, n$, the corresponding n-vector of marginal 1-in-200 capital requirements.
Allow for diversification among risks	This step allows credit to be taken for the fact that not all risks will occur simultaneously. A number of approaches can be used, and this is extended in Chapter 7. The approach outlined here uses a correlation matrix. Specifically, if $D = (\rho_{i,j})$, $i, j = 1, 2, \ldots, n$, is the $n \times n$ matrix of correlation assumptions between risks i and j (eg, between longevity risk and interest rates), then the diversified capital requirement is given by $\sqrt{C^T D C}$, where C^T is the vector transpose of C. Noting that $\rho_{i,j} = \rho_{j,i}$ and that $\rho_{i,i} = 1$, this can be expressed as $\sqrt{\sum_{i=1}^{n} C_i^2 + 2 \sum_{i=1}^{n} \sum_{j=i+1}^{n} \rho_{i,j} C_i C_j}$. From a technical perspective, the matrix D needs to be positive semi-definite, so that $C^T D C$ is non-negative for any vector C.

diversification benefits requires firms to make some strong technical assumptions, outlined in Figure 6.1. These assumptions may or may not be valid, a point which requires careful consideration when applying this approach and which is discussed later in this chapter.

> **Figure 6.1** Technical requirements of applying correlation matrices
>
> In applying correlation matrices to the calculation of diversification benefits, firms are required to make some strong technical assumptions. However, because they are implicit in applying the methodology, firms may not always be fully aware of them. Specifically, it is assumed that
>
> - the joint distribution of the risk factors is multivariate elliptical (McNeil *et al* 2005) (note that the normal distribution belongs to the elliptical family),
> - this distribution is centred on the best-estimate assumptions and
> - the balance sheet response to changes in risk factors is linear in all variables.
>
> It is common for firms to allow for any expected non-linearity of balance sheet response, as described in this chapter. The first two assumptions are revisited in Chapter 7.

Tables 6.2 give an example of applying the framework in a relatively general situation, namely the application of correlation matrices for a portfolio of five risks to calculate the diversified capital requirement. The example is extended in Chapter 7.

Longevity and credit risk: process correlation versus capital correlation

The framework outlined in Table 6.1 is based on considering the correlation among different risks. The nature of the correlation between longevity and credit risk is a particularly interesting and thought-provoking topic. It can be argued that there is a positive correlation between the underlying processes in companies with final salary pension schemes that may be less able to service corporate debt if longevity, and hence pension costs, were to increase. On the other hand, companies now actively manage risks from their pension scheme obligations (for example, by raising the retirement age, by increasing employee contributions or by reshaping scheme benefits), so any positive correlation ought to be weak. In addition, increasing longevity will directly benefit certain companies and sectors, for example, health care and pharmaceuticals, and so there are clearly arguments for negative correlation too.

It is relatively common for firms to assume that longevity and credit risk are independent of each other. However, it can also be argued that the capital requirements for longevity and for credit risk are negatively correlated, with the link coming via interest rates.

Table 6.2 Applying correlation matrices

By way of example, consider a portfolio with five risks, as follows.

(a) Risks, 1-in-200 stresses and capital requirements

Risk	1-in-200 stress	Capital for stress (€ million)
Equity	40% fall in prices	1,000
Property	30% fall in prices	250
Interest rates	2% fall in yield curve	500
Persistency	20% pa rise in lapse rates	250
Longevity	20% pa fall in mortality rates	1,000
Undiversified capital requirement		3,000

Suppose also that the following matrix describes the correlation among the risks. So, for example, property prices are 75% correlated with equity prices, and longevity is independent of all other risks.

(b) Example correlation matrix

Risk	Equity	Property	Interest rates	Persistency	Longevity
Equity	1	0.75	0.25	0.25	0.00
Property	0.75	1	0.25	0.25	0.00
Interest rates	0.25	0.25	1	0.25	0.00
Persistency	0.25	0.25	0.25	1	0.00
Longevity	0.00	0.00	0.00	0.00	1

The undiversified capital requirement is

$$€(1{,}000 + 250 + 500 + 250 + 1{,}000)m = €3{,}000m$$

Applying the approach outlined in Table 6.1, the capital requirement after allowing for diversification is €1,811m. This is often expressed as saying that the diversification benefit is €1,189m, or that diversification has reduced the required capital by 39.6%.

Higher interest rates will normally lead to poorer credit experience from firms servicing floating-rate debt, and so will also act to dilute longevity capital requirements through the discounting mechanism. The capital processes, as distinct from the underlying risk processes, are therefore negatively correlated, although by how much is difficult to quantify. As a result, an assumption of independence of longevity risk and credit risk is considered by some to be prudent.

The diversification framework: validating the assumptions

When making any assumptions, it is important to consider just how valid those assumptions are. Of the assumptions in Figure 6.1, the one most commonly felt to be invalid is that the balance sheet reacts linearly to changes in the underlying risk factors. A fundamental consideration in assessing the appropriateness of this assumption is the extent to which risks interact with, and potentially even reinforce, each other.

By way of explanation, consider a portfolio of non-profit annuities. It is natural to expect a non-linear interaction to exist between, for example, longevity risk and interest rate risk. A longevity event, after which people are expected to live longer, will lengthen the portfolio's cashflows. A longer cashflow stream will in turn change the asset–liability cashflow matching position, which will then alter the exposure to changes in interest rates. By assumption, the methodology developed so far does not allow for the effects of non-linear interactions.

Allowing for non-linearity

There are many ways in which non-linear effects might be allowed for. A common approach is to identify an equivalent 1-in-200 scenario, namely the combination of events which gives rise to the 1-in-200 capital requirement after the effects of diversification, and to explicitly recalculate the balance sheet in that overall scenario. If the risks have a non-linear interaction, this result is likely to lead to a larger capital requirement than from simply applying the correlation matrix approach on its own. This larger value is then taken to be the 1-in-200 capital requirement, allowing for both diversification and non-linearity.

The approach poses two key challenges, however. The first is in developing a methodology which will identify the equivalent 1-in-200 scenario. The second is in determining with some degree of certainty that the correct 1-in-200 scenario has been identified and that there are no other scenarios which would generate the 1-in-200 capital requirement (after the effects of diversification) but which have larger non-linear effects. So-called "risk geography" techniques exist to assist in overcoming these challenges, although Chapter 7 demonstrates that this possibility can be dealt with automatically through the application of other modelling techniques.

Pension scheme financial and regulatory regimes

As mentioned previously, the annuity liabilities written by insurers and the defined-benefit obligations of defined-benefit pension schemes are economically very similar, but are typically governed under considerably different regulatory regimes. A number of different valuations may be applied in a pension scheme context, depending on the country and the purpose of the valuation. These can include, for example, valuations for financial reporting purposes under International Accounting Standards, valuations for funding and valuations for securing the liabilities with an insurance company (buy-out). A brief discussion of each of the three valuations is provided below.

- **International Accounting Standard 19 (IAS19).** IAS19 prescribes the accounting and disclosure framework of employee benefits for companies, including pension schemes. IAS19 aims to ensure comparability among companies. Under the standard, liabilities are calculated using market yields on high-quality corporate bonds (usually "AA" rated bonds, albeit with no allowance for expected levels of default), regardless of the assets actually held by the pension scheme. In practice, a number of schemes invest a large proportion of their assets in equity-type investments, leading to an asset–liability mismatch and a consequent volatility in the IAS19 position.

- **Funding basis.** An important measure of liability is the one which the sponsor and the scheme's trustees (or equivalent) agree to use for the purposes of ongoing funding. Funding strategies will often take account of the sponsor's covenant, anticipating that the ultimate cost of pension provision will be met through a combination of sponsor contributions and income and capital proceeds from existing assets. Margins in the assumptions for setting technical provisions for funding purposes should take account of the extent to which the sponsor's covenant can support them. When the employer covenant is strong, valuation yields are typically larger than those under IAS19, perhaps by 1–2%, and the funding position is correspondingly improved as a result. The funding position is usually more stable than the IAS19 position, as market movements will tend to cause a re-assessment of the valuation yield, leading to asset and liability values moving in concert.

- **Buy-out.** A measure gaining increasing currency in pension scheme management in the UK is the buy-out deficit, being the additional funds needed if accrued liabilities were to be secured by the purchase of annuities from an insurance company. Buy-out liabilities are generally larger than those on both the IAS19 and the funding measures owing to the pricing assumptions typically made by insurance companies. For example, pricing yields will tend to be risk-adjusted and reflect the assets actually held to back the liabilities. Additionally, there will perhaps be a more cautious (although some would argue more realistic) view on longevity, and insurers will include loadings for profit and for the costs of covering their own regulatory capital requirements.

The new regime for European insurers: Solvency II

Representing a fundamental overhaul of the solvency and risk management regime, Solvency II has unquestionably been one of the most topical issues in the European insurance sector. Solvency II aims, for the first time, to introduce risk-based solvency requirements across all European Union member states in a consistent manner.

The four principal objectives (Van Hulle 2008) of Solvency II are to

(i) deepen the European single market,

(ii) enhance policyholder protection,

(iii) improve the international competitiveness of European insurers and

(iv) promote better regulation.

Only time will tell whether Solvency II will ultimately fulfil its aims. This forum is indeed not the place to debate these points.

Although it applies to most European insurance and reinsurance firms, there is disappointment in some quarters that the Solvency II Directive[4] does not apply at its outset to the vast wealth accumulated in pension funds covered by the Occupational Pension Funds Directive.[5] Many have viewed the lack of attention to this matter as a significant omission in the prudential supervision of financial provision in the wider sense and therefore as an issue for urgent attention. On the other hand, occupational pension schemes unquestionably benefit from sponsor covenants, and others would argue that a solvency regime as onerous as Solvency II is unnecessary in this context, especially when the covenant is strong.

Before discussing longevity assumptions in the second part of this chapter, it is worthwhile giving an overview of Solvency II. While the broad structure of the regime, which passed into European law November 2009, is stable, the underlying details have changed frequently in recent times and may see future changes. The description that follows was current as of September 2010.

Structural overview of Solvency II

Solvency II is often called "Basel for insurers", although this has no legislative basis. Like Basel II, it is often described in terms of three regulatory themes (or "pillars"), as shown in Figure 6.2. Pillar I focuses on quantitative solvency requirements, including the rules relating to the calculation of technical provisions and the quantification of solvency capital. Pillar II addresses controls, governance and risk management processes, as well the supervision of insurers. Pillar III is concerned with regulatory reporting and disclosure.

Solvency II, Pillar I (quantitative)

Pillar I is based on a market-consistent valuation of assets and liabilities with economic risk-based capital requirements. The main elements of the Pillar I balance sheet are simplistically illustrated in Figure 6.3 and consist of the assets (on one side) and best-estimate liabilities, risk margin and the Solvency Capital Requirement (on the other). The sum of best-estimate liabilities and the risk margin is referred to as the technical provisions. A description of the terms used follows.

Assets and liabilities. Assets are typically valued at market value. Best-estimate liabilities are valued using market-consistent principles.[6] It is expected that the valuation yield curve will include an allowance for an illiquidity premium (according to product characteristics), with pure longevity business attracting the full illiquidity premium because of its comparatively predictable cashflow profile. Liabilities are to be calculated gross of reinsurance, with the effect of reinsurance to be quantified and shown as an asset on the balance sheet,[7] reduced to allow for expected levels of defaults. This presentation is different from Solvency I.

Figure 6.2 Overview of the three pillars of Solvency II

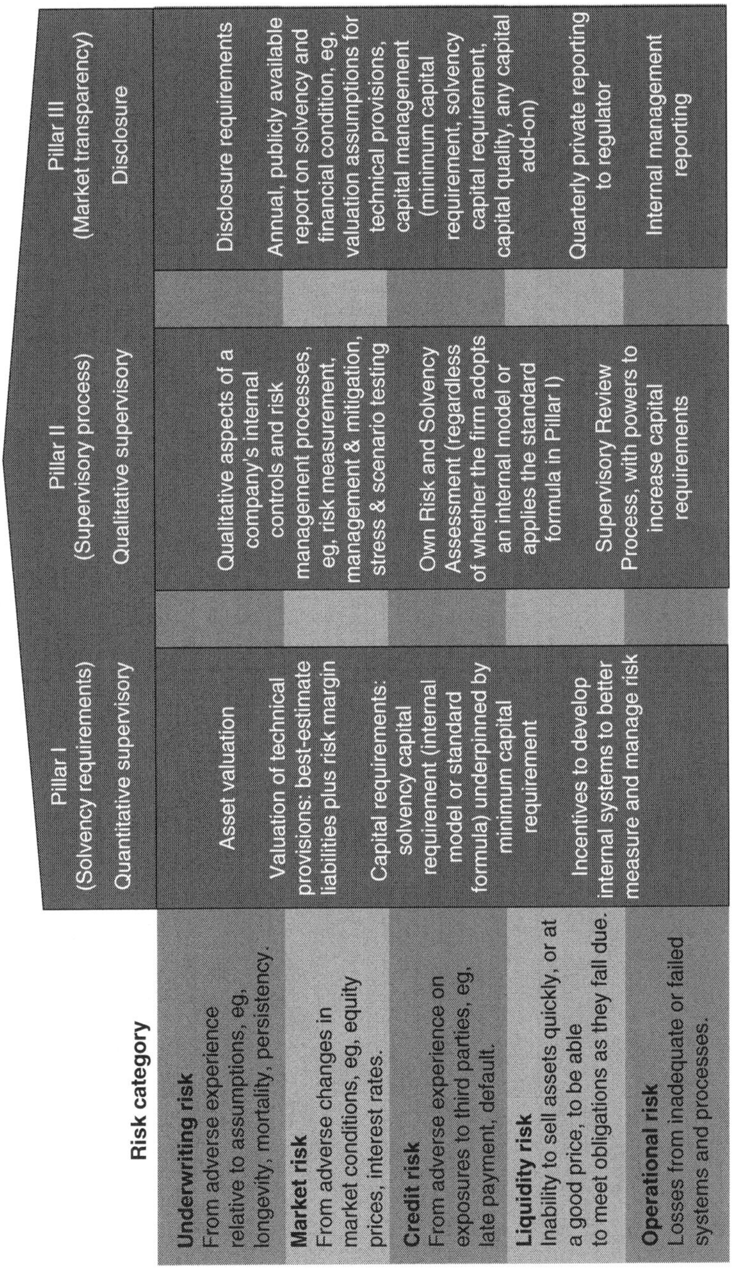

Risk category	Pillar I (Solvency requirements) Quantitative supervisory	Pillar II (Supervisory process) Qualitative supervisory	Pillar III (Market transparency) Disclosure
Underwriting risk From adverse experience relative to assumptions, eg, longevity, mortality, persistency.	Asset valuation	Qualitative aspects of a company's internal controls and risk management processes, eg, risk measurement, management & mitigation, stress & scenario testing	Disclosure requirements
Market risk From adverse changes in market conditions, eg, equity prices, interest rates.	Valuation of technical provisions: best-estimate liabilities plus risk margin		Annual, publicly available report on solvency and financial condition, eg, valuation assumptions for technical provisions, capital management (minimum capital requirement, solvency capital requirement, capital quality, any capital add-on)
Credit risk From adverse experience on exposures to third parties, eg, late payment, default.	Capital requirements: solvency capital requirement (internal model or standard formula) underpinned by minimum capital requirement	Own Risk and Solvency Assessment (regardless of whether the firm adopts an internal model or applies the standard formula in Pillar I)	
Liquidity risk Inability to sell assets quickly, or at a good price, to be able to meet obligations as they fall due.	Incentives to develop internal systems to better measure and manage risk	Supervisory Review Process, with powers to increase capital requirements	Quarterly private reporting to regulator
Operational risk Losses from inadequate or failed systems and processes.			Internal management reporting

Figure 6.3 Pillar I, the solvency pillar

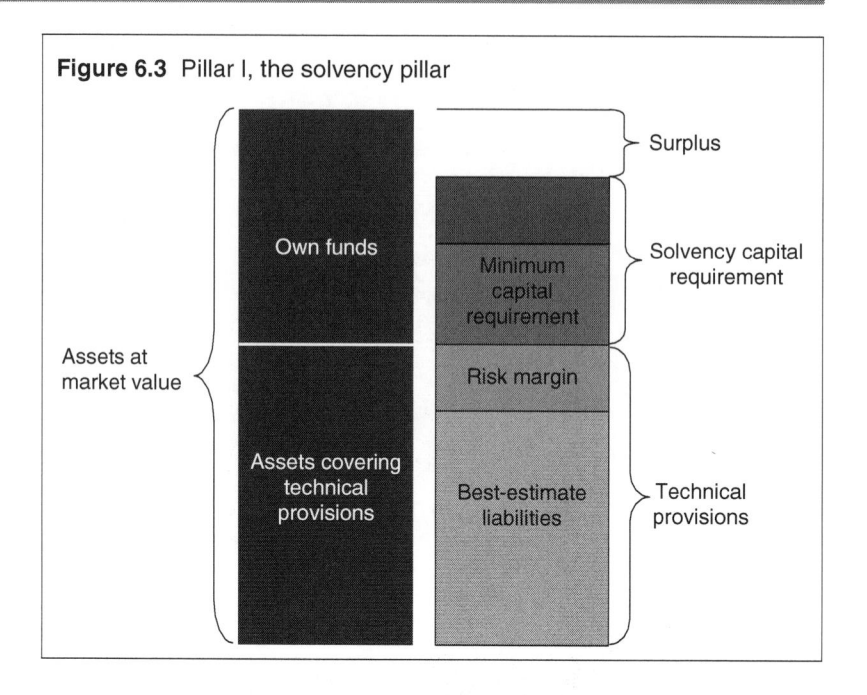

Risk margin. Technical provisions are intended to be adequate for a third party to take over the liabilities. For this reason, technical provisions equal to best-estimate liabilities alone would not sufficiently satisfy a rational third party which requires explicit compensation for risks that cannot be hedged. A risk margin serves this purpose. Its calculation is discussed in detail in Chapter 7.

The risk margin constitutes the single biggest difference between Solvency II and the UK's ICAS framework, especially in the context of longevity risk. Its underlying philosophy is the notion that resources should be adequate to transfer liabilities to a third party after an equivalent 1-in-200 scenario, not just to pay claims at that time.

Under Solvency II, the risk margin for annuity business is of a similar order of magnitude to the undiversified longevity risk capital itself. This will naturally change the economics of writing or retaining longevity risk. In respect of current generations of annuitants, firms are likely to seek ways to reduce or mitigate this additional requirement, some of which are discussed in the next chapter. For future generations of annuitants, this additional requirement will most likely increase the price of securing an annuity, either reducing income in retirement or forcing individuals to fund their retirement in different and potentially less secure ways.

Solvency Capital Requirement. In addition to covering technical provisions, insurers are also required to hold capital against the risks which they face. There are two levels of capital:

- the Minimum Capital Requirement (MCR), which is the absolute minimum level of capital which an insurer must cover;
- the Solvency Capital Requirement (SCR), which is based on a one-year value-at-risk measure calibrated to a 99.5% confidence level and should take full account of any risk mitigating actions adopted by the insurer such as reinsurance.

While the SCR is designed to provide a 1-in-200 one-year level of protection, the MCR is intended to provide an approximate 1-in-7 level of protection,[8] although there is debate as to whether or not this will be the case in practice.

Calculating the Solvency Capital Requirement: standard formula or internal model. The SCR may be calculated using either the so-called "standard formula", a generic formula specified by the European Commission or, if approved by local supervisors, by an insurer's own "internal model". The standard formula approach, if not the calibration of its stresses and correlations, is similar the UK ICAS regime.

Risks, which are considered in modules (eg, market risk, life underwriting risk), are first aggregated within each module, across various defined sub-modules. For example, market risk is subdivided into equity risk, property risk, interest rate risk and spread risk (among others), which are aggregated to give the overall market risk capital requirement. Risks are then aggregated across the modules, ie, market risk, life underwriting risk and so on, as shown in Figure 6.4. Each stage of aggregation allows for diversification through the application of correlation matrices, as described earlier.

The standard formula makes no explicit allowance for non-linearity. However, its correlation assumptions are felt by many to incorporate a level of prudence in certain areas, and this may be viewed as providing a non-linearity adjustment, if rather bluntly and indirectly. Indeed, one of the stated considerations in the choice of correlation coefficients was to adequately reflect potential dependencies in the tail of the distributions.

Figure 6.4 Modular risk structure

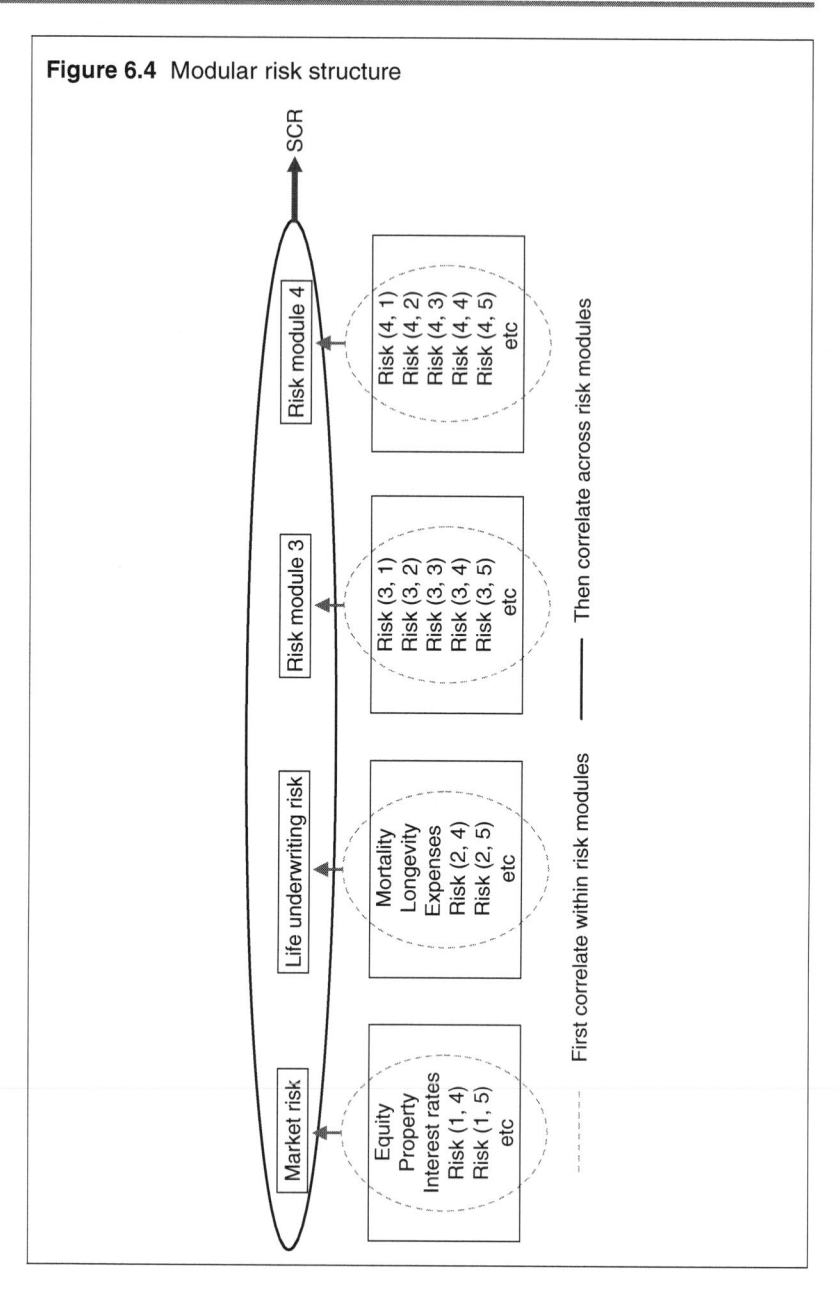

Module contents (left to right):

Market risk:
- Equity
- Property
- Interest rates
- Risk (1, 4)
- Risk (1, 5)
- etc

Life underwriting risk:
- Mortality
- Longevity
- Expenses
- Risk (2, 4)
- Risk (2, 5)
- etc

Risk module 3:
- Risk (3, 1)
- Risk (3, 2)
- Risk (3, 3)
- Risk (3, 4)
- Risk (3, 5)
- etc

Risk module 4:
- Risk (4, 1)
- Risk (4, 2)
- Risk (4, 3)
- Risk (4, 4)
- Risk (4, 5)
- etc

First correlate within risk modules — Then correlate across risk modules → SCR

Solvency II, Pillar II (qualitative risk management)

The introduction of qualitative risk management standards (covering all risks, not only those captured by the quantitative requirements of Pillar I) requires insurers to place risk assessment and risk

RESERVING AND REGULATORY REQUIREMENTS

management at the heart of their governance system. As part of their overall risk management framework, firms must

(i) identify, assess, monitor, manage and report the risks which they face now or may face in the future,

(ii) determine the capital needed to ensure that their overall solvency requirements are met at all times and

(iii) understand the link between (i) and (ii) and explain it to their regulator.

This whole process is covered by the Own Risk and Solvency Assessment (ORSA).

The ORSA has a dual nature. On the one hand, it is very much an ethos to be embedded within a firm and its decision-making processes. For well-run firms this way of working will become a natural part of its culture. However, in line with (iii) it is also very much a supervisory tool, designed to allow supervisors to develop a detailed understanding of individual firms' risks and controls. The ORSA is not intended to create an additional solvency hurdle, and differences in the SCR and the own-risk capital assessment will not necessarily lead to a capital add-on. Although the ORSA is specific to each firm's own risk profile, it does not require firms to develop or apply an internal model. However, firms with internal models are required to use them for the ORSA.

Solvency II, Pillar III (disclosure)

Under Pillar III, the disclosure pillar, insurers are required to provide both public and private disclosure reports. The principal ones include the following.

- **The Solvency and Financial Condition Report:** the public annual disclosure report to be produced and published by all firms. This report will contain both quantitative and qualitative disclosures ranging from valuation assumptions for technical provisions to required and available capital.

- **The Report to Supervisors:** a report submitted solely to the supervisor, containing more sensitive information which is considered to be necessary for the purposes of effective supervision.

Comparing Solvency II to previous economic capital regimes

In order to compare Solvency II to previous regulatory economic capital regimes for life insurers, we will use the UK regulatory regime as an example. Its local implementation of Solvency I is supplemented by the ICAS regime, a risk-based economic capital regime.

In the UK, Solvency II is generally viewed as an evolution of the ICAS regime. To compare it to Solvency II, it is therefore useful to step back and first consider the requirements of ICAS, which are broadly that firm must hold sufficient capital to cover the one-year value-at-risk with 99.5% probability. However, FSA guidance[9] explicitly recognises the possibility of choosing a longer time horizon over which to assess capital requirements, albeit with a lower confidence level, when it is appropriate. This possibility is also recognised in formal guidance from the UK's Board for Actuarial Standards,[10] which specifically points to the use of assessing capital requirements in run-off as being most appropriate for annuities. The Solvency II Directive[11] is framed in terms of a 99.5% one-year value-at-risk approach and alternative approaches (eg, different time periods or different risk measures) are permitted in firms' internal models[12] provided that they are equivalent to a 99.5% one-year value-at-risk. It is therefore convenient to think of Solvency II as a pure one-year value-at-risk framework, regardless of the modelling approach that firms might adopt. This raises the question of how to reconcile ICAS in run-off with a one-year value-at-risk Solvency II measure, which is discussed in the context of longevity risk below.

In ICAS, risk capital is added to a best-estimate liability, and, as discussed above, firms are directed towards calculating the capital required for longevity risk in run-off. This typically leads to a larger capital requirement than would be the case for a 99.5% event strictly viewed over one year, although naturally this depends on the confidence interval considered in run-off. The run-off approach can therefore be considered to represent a strict one-year event plus a residual risk margin. Pillar I of Solvency II, on the other hand, requires capital to be added to technical provisions which comprise best-estimate liabilities and an explicit risk margin. The two frameworks are therefore entirely comparable, except that the risk margin is an explicit requirement of Solvency II Pillar I. Finally, the presence of a Solvency II risk margin, which acts as a proxy for the market price for taking on the (non-hedgeable) risks in a year's time, makes it entirely appropriate to look at the 99.5% longevity stress strictly over one year.

SETTING LONGEVITY ASSUMPTIONS

This section examines the principles of setting of longevity assumptions in a number of different regulatory contexts. Before discussing this topic, it is worth first establishing some concepts related to opening (or base) mortality and mortality improvement assumptions in the context of setting longevity assumptions for regulatory purposes. A detailed discussion of establishing assumptions relating to both opening mortality and projecting improvement was covered in Chapters 3 and 4, respectively.

Opening (or base) mortality assumptions

Whether they are needed for pricing purposes and are derived from the application of a geo-demographic model, or are needed for financial reporting purposes and are derived from more general experience data, opening mortality assumptions should fundamentally be driven by recently observed mortality experience.

There are of course exceptions. A lack of credible or relevant data would seriously hamper the process. Adhering to this practice would also prove to be problematic in situations in which current mortality experience is expected to be select (Benjamin and Pollard 1980) in some way, ie, temporarily atypical of the average population as a result of "passing" some form of qualification criterion. One example of select mortality is in the context of medically underwritten term-assurance policies, where a group of lives have recently purchased policies. These lives are known to be healthy (they have just been underwritten) and are therefore expected to have lighter mortality than the average population. Another example is on a portfolio of underwritten annuities,[13] where mortality experience will be temporarily heavy relative to an average group of annuitants. In both examples, it is imprudent to set assumptions based on observed experience.

As covered in Chapter 5, selection could significantly affect standard annuities too. If, as is the case in the UK, for example, a market exists for underwritten annuities, it will be the healthiest lives that remain to buy standard annuities. The effect of this "impaired life" selective dynamic is to significantly lighten the observed levels of mortality for the standard annuitant population. However, this is expected to be a temporary effect. Modelling assumptions need to be made about how the select mortality rates will change over time and converge upwards towards ultimate long-term rates. The topic of impaired life anti-selection is also explored in more detail in Makin (2009) in a longevity-focused edition of *The Actuary* magazine.

Mortality improvement assumptions

Mortality improvement assumptions are of course rather more difficult to set, and there is a wide range of views on the appropriate assumptions to apply. For reporting purposes, most firms tend to adopt a variant of a published improvement table. This practice, of course, is perfectly respectable, provided that the firm has sound reasoning underlying its calibration of the published table. In arriving at this view, firms employ a number of different approaches including (but not exclusively)

- the application of extrapolative models, such as the P-Spline Model,[14] or the Lee–Carter Model and its numerous variants[15]
- cause-of-death projections (an increasing number of firms now have an understanding of this approach and its limitations),
- expert opinion, benchmarking and, importantly, reasonableness checking.

The working premise is therefore that best-estimate assumptions (ie, assumptions which are as likely to be wrong in one direction as they are in the other) are available and are the starting point for determining bases for all other purposes.

Insurance company valuations: Solvency I regulatory regime

A liability valuation carried out under the Solvency I regime should include an appropriate margin for adverse deviation in the assumptions such that the best-estimate plus the margin is expected to be adequate in all reasonably foreseeable circumstances. In terms of opening mortality risk, the prudent margin will likely be proportionately smaller for larger portfolios. This result is a direct and natural consequence of scale. A doubling of a firm's portfolio is roughly expected to lead to the ability to hold margins which are proportionately smaller, perhaps by about 30% $(1 - 1/\sqrt{2})$.

The same cannot be said of mortality improvement assumptions. Longevity trend risk is systemic and does not diversify through increased scale. Proportionately, and all else being equal, large and small firms are likely to be justified in having the same size margins. The composition of margins between opening mortality and mortality improvement is a matter for individual firms. Overall, the margin for deviation should be smaller than a 1-in-200 longevity stress. For example, if a 1-in-200 stress is set to be at the lower end of the two-sided 99% confidence interval, a prudent margin might be expected to be at or around the lower end of the two-sided 95% confidence interval. Such statements, however, should not be viewed as absolute, and firms will be more concerned with the adequacy of the overall basis for a number of reasons, not least because mortality (longevity) is but one assumption among many.

Longevity stresses in economic capital regimes

Under economic capital regimes for life insurers, practices and approaches to setting the 1-in-200 one-year stress for longevity risk vary across the industry. There are undoubtedly two main underlying risks:

- current mortality risk, which is the risk of mis-estimating (overstating) opening levels of annuitant mortality, despite the estimates being prepared without error;
- longevity trend risk, which is the risk that an incorrect (inadequate) allowance is made for the rate of improvement in annuitant mortality.

While best practice is to consider these risks separately, not all firms do so within their economic capital models. Furthermore, of those firms that do, not all actually apply them separately. For example, some firms apply both as a single, combined stress to opening mortality rates. In the context of longevity trend risk, practice is further divided in that some firms set their 1-in-200 stresses based on a combination of expert judgement and scenario testing that, for example, takes into consideration what a 1-in-200 one-year cause-of-death elimination might be, based on expert medical and gerontological input. Other firms apply a stochastic mortality model.

A further risk exists in relation to volatility of mortality experience over the one-year period. However, for most portfolios it is small when compared with current mortality and longevity trend risks, and therefore it is often allowed for approximately or implicitly within other stress assumptions.

Longevity assumptions in pension scheme valuations

The concepts and considerations in setting longevity assumptions for pension schemes are similar to those for insurance companies, and assumptions are required for opening levels of mortality and for rates of improvement. Scheme funding requirements typically centre on technical provisions, the assumptions for which should be chosen prudently. However, the exact meaning of "prudent" in relation to mortality assumptions is a matter for the scheme trustees (or equivalent), on the advice on the scheme's actuary, and will be subject to a number of considerations including

- the purpose of the valuation,
- the strength of the sponsor's covenant and
- any margins in the other elements of the assumption set.

An appropriate overall level of prudence in the technical provisions should be the paramount objective.

In some countries, it has been relatively common practice to adjust the discount rate as a proxy for future improvements in mortality, although this approach is somewhat crude. Indeed, The Pensions Regulator in the UK would not typically consider this practice to be consistent with the requirement to adopt a prudent mortality assumption, or indeed to achieve clarity of assumptions (The Pensions Regulator 2008).

Longevity within the new Solvency II regime for European insurers

In contrast to the ICAS regime within the UK, the calculation of Solvency II capital using an internal model requires the specification of the full probability distribution, albeit it is expected that the supervisory authorities may allow the use of certain approximations.[16] Such approximations aside, this requirement will tend to lead to a greater use of stochastic modelling, especially for the trend element of longevity risk. In line with current (base level) mortality risk and longevity trend risk noted above, two longevity risk distributions will be needed for Solvency II.

Under the Solvency II Pillar I framework, distributions are required on a pure one-year value-at-risk basis, and in particular it is necessary only to measure uncertainty in longevity over one year. In the Pillar II framework, on the other hand, firms may take a different approach and, indeed, some consider it appropriate to look at longevity risk in run-off. In doing so, however, firms should revisit the calibration of and need for an explicit risk margin within technical provisions, with specific consideration given to longevity risk capital in the context of the risk margin and vice versa.

Current mortality risk

Uncertainty in opening levels of mortality will depend on a number of features of the portfolio in question: its size, the observed variability in death claim amounts and the levels of anti-selection. Portfolio size will directly affect observed variability in death claims, and, from the Central Limit Theorem (Grimmett and Stirzaker 1992), the distribution of this element of the risk can be assumed to be normal for all but the smallest portfolios, with a standard deviation which may be derived using standard statistical techniques.

More challenging are the effects of anti-selection. As previously discussed, for blocks of business exposed to the selection effects from the underwritten annuity market, currently observed levels of mortality will be temporarily light. Because this is expected to be a temporary effect, modelling assumptions can be made about how the select mortality rates will change over time and converge upwards towards long-term ultimate rates. However, the use of a model to inform assumptions increases the risk that the assumptions are ultimately inadequate. This in turn leads to a requirement to hold capital against this risk, to allow for the additional uncertainty within the current mortality risk distribution. There are many ways to achieve this end, but a powerful technique is to develop and use a stochastic model of selection effects.

The overall current mortality risk distribution can then be simulated empirically, although this step requires an assumption about the correlation between uncertainty from base experience data and the additional uncertainty from selection. Depending on the firm's modelling framework and strategy, the overall distribution could be left in empirical form, although it is desirable, even if only for presentation and communication, to express the results in terms of a closed-form distribution. It is likely that a skewed distribution will be needed to adequately fit the selection effects, but in any case the distribution should be subjected to a series of goodness-of-fit tests.

Longevity trend risk

The direct modelling of longevity trend risk requires the use of a projection model which could be a parametric statistical model or a stochastic model. By requiring a one-year 1-in-200 value-at-risk approach, Pillar I of Solvency II is effectively asking "to what extent could mortality be lighter (ie, there be fewer deaths) over the year ahead such that only 0.5% of outcomes correspond to lighter mortality still?" If a parametric model is used, it will be possible to derive the answer through application of its parametric form, and perhaps even in closed form. On the other hand, if a stochastic model is used, it will be necessary to simulate changes in mortality over the next year and to choose the appropriate percentile.

In practice, applying a stochastic model is often simpler than applying a parametric one, and the production of sufficiently many simulations will lead directly to an empirical probability distribution. As with current mortality risk, this result could be left in empirical form or it could be expressed in terms of a good-fitting closed-form distribution.

For other purposes, such as for the ORSA under the Pillar II framework, it may be more appropriate to consider trend risk in run-off as previously mentioned, and again a statistical or stochastic approach may be used. A stochastic model will lead directly to simulated mortality paths that can readily be applied to analysing mortality risk in run-off, although somewhat more effort is needed to apply a statistical model in this context. In either case, the distribution of outcomes will change with each year of the projection. Depending on the capital modelling framework, it may be possible to use each year's projected distribution directly, although clearly it will be simpler to apply a single distribution. The main conceptual challenge is then how to derive a single distribution which represents longevity risk in run-off. There are different ways to accomplish this, including

(i) choosing a single year's distribution, perhaps at or around the average term of the projection and

> **Figure 6.5** Annuity equivalence techniques
>
> "Annuity equivalence" refers to the process of equating the present value of one set of annuity cashflows (the "object" annuity) to the value of another set of annuity cashflows (the "target" annuity). This is done by solving for a parameter value in the calculation of the object annuity value so that it equals the target annuity value.
>
> The power of this technique is that it can be used readily to express quite disparate mortality assumptions in terms of, say, a percentage ℘ (the parameter being solved) of a standardised assumption, ie, by solving for ℘ in the equation of value
>
> $$\sum_{t=1}^{t}\left(\prod_{j=1}^{t}(1-\wp q_{x+j-1}^{\text{standard}})\right)v^{t} = \text{target annuity value}$$
>
> where $\{q^{\text{standard}}\}$ represents a standard mortality table and v^t is the discount factor applying to cashflows at time t.
>
> It is most common for the same discount rate assumptions to be used in both annuity calculations, and to vary a mortality-related parameter in the calculation of the object annuity, but this need not be the case.

(ii) applying annuity equivalence techniques (see Figure 6.5) to express the full projection along a given sample path in terms of a single figure, and deriving an empirical distribution by repeating the equivalence calculation for each simulation.

Option (i) can be applied in the context of both statistical and stochastic projections, while option (ii) does not apply in the context of the statistical approach because such an approach does not produce sample paths. Once again, the resulting distributions could be left in empirical form or they could be expressed as a closed-form distribution.

Choosing the probability level is the final consideration in run-off. The choice will depend on the application.

Combining current mortality and longevity trend risks

With perfect information, the underlying processes for current mortality risk and longevity trend risk would naturally be assumed to be independent of one another. In practice, however, it is difficult to untangle current mortality risk from longevity trend risk, particularly over one year. For this reason, a small positive correlation might be assumed to guard against longevity trend risk being mistaken for current mortality risk. The current mortality and longevity trend distributions would then be simulated with the chosen correlation structure. Depending on the modelling framework, these correlated stochastic processes might be combined or they might be left separate, as is discussed further in the next chapter.

The need to project longevity distributions

Projected combined longevity distributions are needed for different purposes. The most obvious example in Solvency II is the risk margin. Consideration is therefore required as to how to project current mortality and longevity trend distributions through time. For business exposed to select effects, the mean of the distribution will change, and the additional uncertainty will reduce, as the select effect runs off. These points need to be addressed in the projection of current mortality risk through time.

Different considerations apply to projecting longevity trend distributions for one-year value-at-risk purposes compared with projecting longevity trend distributions for run-off. In the former case, the distributions might be expected to stay relatively stable over time, although their stability does depend on the precise approach taken. In the latter case, the distributions will become less variable over time as the outstanding term of the remaining payment obligations reduces.

Calibration of the standard formula longevity stress in Solvency II

The purpose of the "quantitative impact study" (QIS) exercises was to allow the European Commission to shape the design of the overall Solvency II framework. The proposed calibration of the standard formula longevity stress in QIS5, the fifth exercise, was a permanent 20% reduction in mortality rates. Viewed from first principles, the reduction in mortality rates highlights some interesting areas for consideration.

As has been established, a technically sound calibration of a longevity stress should at least take into consideration the following areas:

(i) a quantification of the uncertainty in opening mortality;

(ii) a quantification of longevity trend risk strictly over one year rather than in run-off;

(iii) a correlation between (i) and (ii).

An appropriate allowance for the first consideration can be based on standard statistical confidence interval techniques. In theory, the statistical uncertainty should depend on the size of the insurer's portfolio. A value in the range 5–10% may be appropriate to many insurers. Allowing for the second consideration requires the implementation of a statistical or stochastic approach. Analysis (Nielson 2010) indicates a value of typically slightly less than 10% in major European countries, which is not inconsistent with what may be gleaned from other analysis[17] by the Committee of European Insurance and Occupational Pensions Supervisors. As above, the first and second areas would most naturally be assumed to be independent of one another, but a small positive correlation might be assumed. On this basis, some may consider a 20% longevity stress for Solvency II, when taken alongside a risk margin, to be overly prudent.

It is also instructive to think of the 20% longevity stress in real-world terms and what it means from a medical and epidemiological perspective. Mortality improvements can be considered to have three components (Richards *et al* 2008) by cause of death:

- delay in onset by cause;
- reduction in incidence by cause;
- a genuine elimination of that cause.

The format of the QIS5 standard formula longevity stress is equivalent to assuming that either the second or third of the above possibilities occurs for some causes of death. But what would a 20% permanent reduction in mortality rates mean in practice in a particular territory? Figure 6.6 shows a recent breakdown of causes of death in England and Wales for lives aged 60 and older.

Assuming that deaths from each cause are entirely independent, a 20% fall in mortality would result from the following scenarios which are given by way of example: for men, some 60% of circulatory deaths are eradicated (equivalent to eliminating all deaths from ischaemic heart disease); for women, virtually all cancer deaths are eradicated. These would seem to be rather extreme scenarios, and in practice they would have to be still more extreme because the eradication of these diseases ignores the competing nature of the underlying processes whereby the reduction or elimination of one

Figure 6.6 Death by cause (England and Wales) for lives aged 60 and older

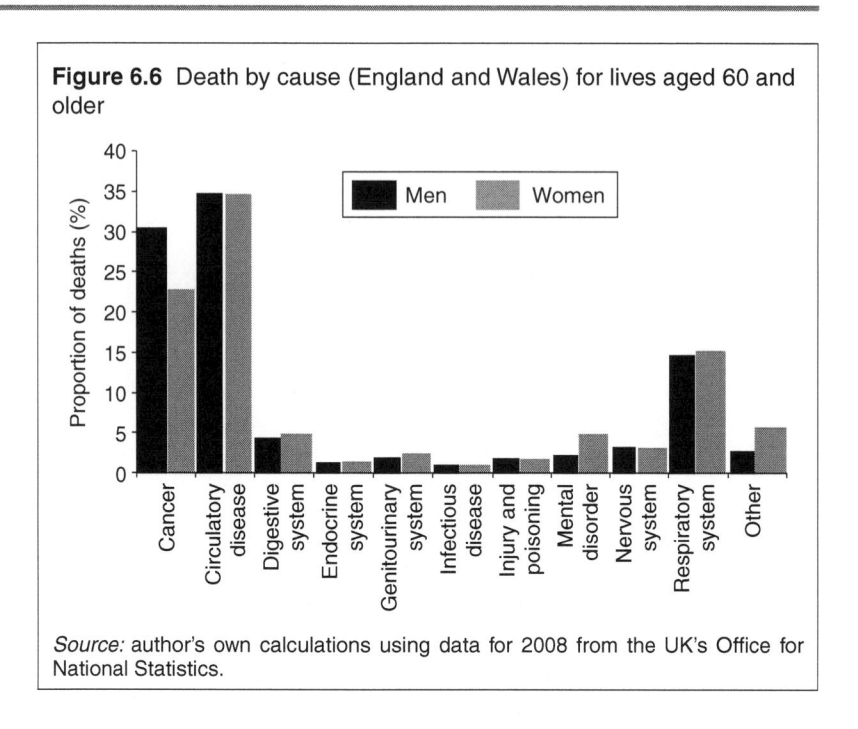

Source: author's own calculations using data for 2008 from the UK's Office for National Statistics.

cause of death is expected to result in other causes becoming more prevalent.

Summary

We began this chapter by outlining the quite different regulatory regimes for European insurance companies and pension schemes, giving particular emphasis to economic-based regimes for insurers. These economic regimes are based on market-consistent valuations of assets and liabilities, with an economic quantification of capital, typically related to 1-in-200 one-year value-at-risk. The concepts of diversification and non-linearity were introduced as being of particular importance in calculating economic capital, and are discussed in more detail in Chapter 7. In addition, we outlined the Solvency II framework for European insurers. A number of different valuations were also discussed for pension schemes, which depend on the country and the purpose of the valuation. We discussed three possible approaches. Finally, we discussed the principles of setting longevity assumptions in both insurance and pension regulatory contexts. These principles were then extended to considerations relating to deriving and projecting distributions of longevity risk for use in an economic valuation and under Solvency II.

> The views and opinions expressed in this chapter are those of the author, as at the date of writing. They may not accord with those of any past or current employer. They do not constitute advice, and nor may they be construed as such. The author thanks Guy Barton, Debbie Laird, David Shaffer, Esther Strickland and Paul Teggin for their helpful suggestions and comments. Any remaining errors are entirely those of the author.

1 European Directive 2002/83/EC.
2 FINMA Circ. 08/44 – SST.
3 Directive 3/2009 Regulatory "Minimum Requirements for Risk Management (MaRisk VA)".
4 European Directive 2009/138/EC.
5 European Directive 2003/41/EC.
6 See Article 77 of the Solvency II Directive.
7 In accordance with Article 77(2) of the Solvency II Directive.
8 See Article 129(1)(c) of the Solvency II Directive. The MCR is calculated using a much simpler method than the SCR, and its currently proposed calibration is crude, deriving the MCR by applying a factor, depending on the line of business, to the best-estimate liabilities. The overall result has to lie within a "corridor" of 25–45% of the SCR.
9 Prudential Sourcebook for Insurers: INSPRU 7.1.42R and INSPRU 7.1.45G.
10 Sections 6.6, 10.2.3 and 10.2.4 of Guidance Note GN46: Individual Capital Assessment.
11 Article 101(3) of the Solvency II Directive.
12 Article 122(1) of the Solvency II Directive.
13 Often referred to as enhanced or impaired annuities, these annuities pay larger pensions to those medically assessed as being in poor health, reflecting the associated shorter life expectancy. (See Chapter 5 for more details.)
14 This is a parametric "penalty" model applied to forecasting by utilising the regulating properties of the penalised basis functions used in fitting the model in the area of the data.
15 These are examples of time series stochastic forecasting models.
16 Article 122(3) of the Solvency II Directive.
17 QIS5 Calibration Paper (CEIOPS-SEC-40-10), April 15, 2010.

REFERENCES

Benjamin, B., and J. H. Pollard, 1980, *The Analysis of Mortality and Other Actuarial Statistics*, Second Edition (Portsmouth, NH: Heinemann).

Grimmett G., and D. Stirzaker, 1992, *Probability and Random Processes*, Second Edition (Oxford University Press).

Makin, S. J., 2009, "Standard Deviation", *The Actuary*, May, URL: http://www.the-actuary.org.uk/853810.

McNeil, A., R. Frey and P. Embrechts, 2005, *Quantitative Risk Management: Concepts, Techniques and Tools* (Princeton University Press).

Nielson, L. H., 2010, "Assessment of the VaR(99.5%) for Longevity Risk: Implementing Measures on Solvency II", Report, Sampension, Hellerup, Denmark.

The Pensions Regulator, 2008, "Regulatory Guidance on Mortality Assumptions", URL: http://www.thepensionsregulator.gov.uk/guidance/guidance-mortality-assumptions.aspx

Richards, S. J., J. R. Ellam, J. Hubbard, J. L. C. Lu, S. J. Makin and K. A. Miller, 2008, "Two-Dimensional Mortality Data: Patterns and Projections", *British Actuarial Journal* 13(III), pp. 479–555.

Van Hulle, K., 2008, "The Challenge of Solvency II: A Lecture to the Faculty of Actuaries in Scotland", *British Actuarial Journal* 14(I), pp. 19–39.

7

Economic Capital, Modelling and Longevity Risk

Stephen Makin
Stephen Makin Consulting Ltd

Building on the reserving and regulatory concepts discussed in Chapter 6, in this chapter we focus on a framework for modelling economic capital with an emphasis on the risks posed by longevity. We begin by outlining a generic economic capital framework, using Solvency II as a specific example. Potential Solvency II modelling approaches are then discussed in general terms and more specifically in the context of calculating and projecting capital requirements in respect of longevity risk. A case study of a firm entering into a longevity swap is used to show how the modelling techniques developed in this chapter can be applied practically to risk management. We conclude the chapter with other considerations in terms of a wider approach to modelling and enterprise risk management.

MODELLING FRAMEWORK

Economic capital frameworks aim to quantify capital requirements according to a preconceived degree of numerical confidence. Rooted in probability theory, such frameworks seek to model the probability distribution of the balance sheet over a specified time horizon, as a function of a range of underlying risk factors. The output often expresses the distribution in a single measure, which is intended to communicate complex phenomena in such a way that senior management can understand the risks faced by their business and hence manage capital more effectively.

A general approach to economic capital can be broken down into five major components, as shown in Figure 7.1. This generic framework can be applied in nearly any context, including regulatory capital (eg, the calculation of capital for a Solvency II balance sheet)

> **Figure 7.1** Economic capital in five simple steps
>
> 1. **Time horizon:** select the time horizon over which economic capital is to be measured, eg, one day, one year or over the full term of the liabilities.
> 2. **Risk factors:** identify the risk factors that drive the balance sheet (both assets and liabilities) and their joint probability distributions.
> 3. **Construct loss functions:** establish the response of the balance sheet to each risk factor via so-called "loss functions". These functions are not probabilistic in themselves, but the combination of loss functions with risk factor distributions gives the probability distribution of losses.
> 4. **Aggregate the results:** establish the multivariate loss distribution of the balance sheet allowing for the interaction of the risk factors.
> 5. **Choose the risk metric and calculate its value:** convert the loss distribution into a single number quantifying the overall risk to the balance sheet in line with a preconceived degree of numerical confidence.

or internal economic purposes (eg, in determining adherence with risk appetite).

Solvency II is an example of such a regime and in it the first and fifth steps shown in Figure 7.1 are specified[1] – the time horizon (step 1) is one year, while the risk metric (step 5) is the 99.5th percentile value-at-risk as defined by the change in net asset value – whereas the approach to be taken in the other steps is for each company to decide. Other time periods are possible in economic capital frameworks. Banks, for example, will be interested in intra-day quantities. It is possible to use other risk metrics such as standard deviation, as used in mean-variance portfolio theory, or conditional tail expectation, which is based on expected losses given that an event of a specified severity has occurred.

More specific insights into economic capital frameworks can be gained by reconsidering Solvency II in terms of a firm's use of the approach as detailed in Figure 7.2.

The term "aggregator" in part (e) of Figure 7.2 refers to the overarching platform which produces the asset and liability values in each of the simulations. This is not to be confused with the meaning it is sometimes given in the context of techniques used to construct joint risk factor probability distributions from marginal ones.[2] It is expected that the structure outlined in Figure 7.2 will be used by many firms developing internal models for Solvency II, where the internal model Solvency Capital Requirement (see Chapter 6) is the 99.5th percentile from the distribution of rank-ordered changes in net asset value.

This approach, however, is not the only feasible option available to firms, and some firms may make greater use of approximations.[3]

Adopting the approach in Figure 7.2, the capital for each risk on its own can be derived by using a similar process, but holding constant, at best-estimate, the value of each risk not being considered, ie, by sampling only from the marginal distribution of a particular risk factor. In the final stage in the process, capital requirements are allocated back to each individual risk, allowing for diversification. This allocation can be done in many different ways. Ensuring consistency with the capital allocation process is important because crediting a particular risk with a different amount of diversification benefit can directly influence business decisions. The topic of allocating diversification benefit is theoretically complicated, and the subject of much academic study.

THE NEED FOR SPEED

To ensure that the tail of the distribution of net asset values is well defined, stable and not overly susceptible to simulation error, a relatively large number of simulations is needed. The precise number is debatable, and will depend on the percentile being examined. For example, 10,000 may be appropriate for a 99.5% value-at-risk measure but inadequate for a 99.9% value-at-risk measure. In any case, the need for many asset and liability calculations requires either great speed or extreme patience and fortitude. In practice, patience and fortitude will make way for mathematical formulae in the form of loss functions, which serve as an efficient way of describing the value of assets and liabilities as a function of the chosen risk factors. The formulae and their parameters are chosen to give a good fit of the modelled values of assets and liabilities to the actual values across appropriate combinations of realised values of the risk factors. By enabling the rapid recalculation of asset and liability values in any particular scenario, such formulae lend themselves well to simulation-based techniques.

Figure 7.2 Calculating Solvency II capital requirements

(a) Identify risk factors

Identify the risk factors, ie, the principal factors which materially influence asset and liability values, eg, equity prices, interest rates, longevity, credit, etc.

(b) Risk distributions

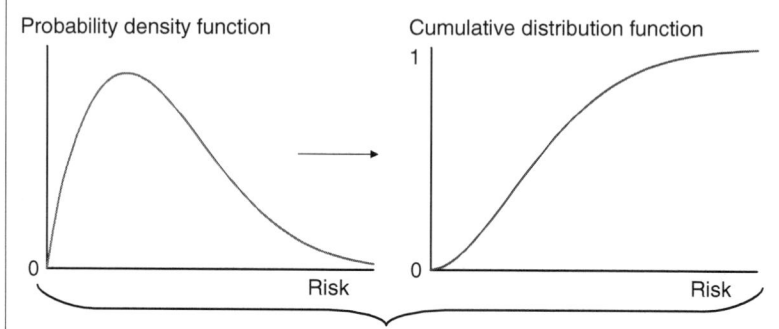

Probability density function

Cumulative distribution function

Risk

Risk

Empirical distributions, parametric distributions

Derive or define full probability distributions for each risk factor on its own, known as the marginal distribution, as well as a means of combining the marginal distributions into a joint distribution where the risks have an appropriate dependency structure (which might be expressed through correlations or copulas). There is no need for firms to make the same strong assumptions as underlie the correlation-matrix approach, as discussed in Chapter 6.

(c) Loss functions

Asset models

$$A = \sum_{t=1}^{T} a_t (1 + r_t)^{-t}$$

Liability models

$$L = \sum_{t=1}^{T} {}_t p_x (1 + r_t)^{-t}$$

Interest rate models

$$dr_t = a(b - r_t)\, dt + \sigma\, dW_t$$

Curve fitting, cashflow modelling, replicating portfolios

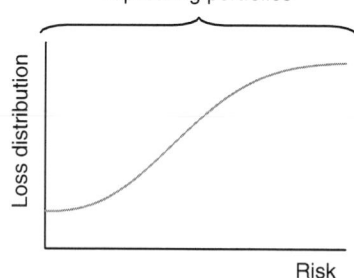

Loss distribution

Risk

Develop mathematical formulae (loss functions) which accurately reflect the values of assets and liabilities as the firm's risk factors change, ie, real-valued response functions of several variables, namely the risk factors.

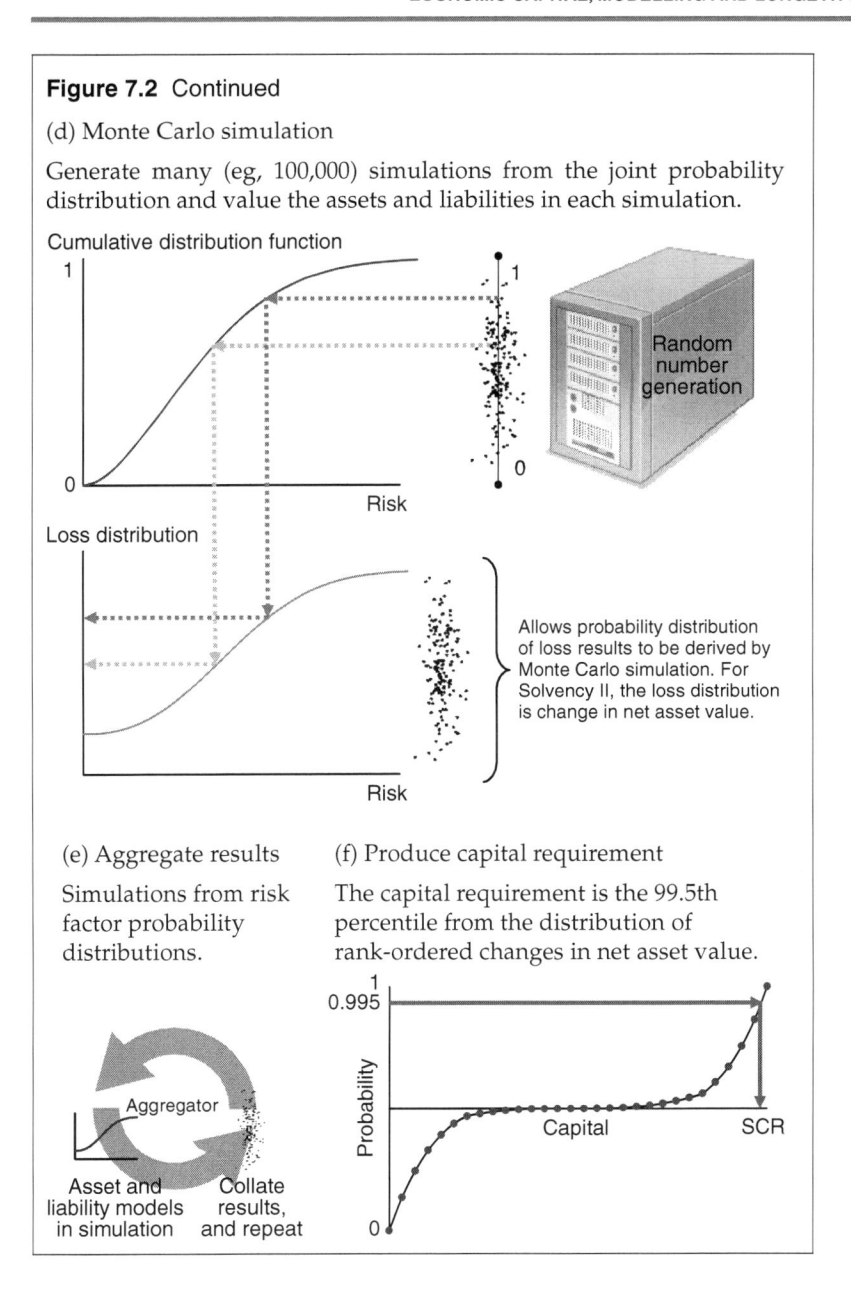

Figure 7.2 Continued

(d) Monte Carlo simulation

Generate many (eg, 100,000) simulations from the joint probability distribution and value the assets and liabilities in each simulation.

Cumulative distribution function

Loss distribution

Allows probability distribution of loss results to be derived by Monte Carlo simulation. For Solvency II, the loss distribution is change in net asset value.

Random number generation

(e) Aggregate results

Simulations from risk factor probability distributions.

Asset and liability models in simulation — Aggregator — Collate results, and repeat

(f) Produce capital requirement

The capital requirement is the 99.5th percentile from the distribution of rank-ordered changes in net asset value.

However, the results of stochastic simulation should not be taken at face value. Insight into whether the resulting capital requirement is sensible can be gained by considering specific stochastic scenarios particularly those at or around the desired level of confidence, as well as the "biting scenario" itself. This rationalisation has a number of uses.

First, it allows consideration of whether the scenarios are plausible, ie, do they have meaningful, real-world interpretations? This line of questioning can also usefully feed back into the approach used to construct the probability distributions and their dependency structure. Second, specifically identified scenarios of interest can be fed back into the models which were used to initially calibrate the formulae, providing a further test on the accuracy of the approach used. Moreover, the inputs to and outputs from these models can be a rich source of scenario tests which should provide valuable insight into the dynamics of the firm's business.

NON-LINEARITY AND DIVERSIFICATION

As discussed in Chapter 6, firms commonly need to make explicit non-linearity adjustments in their economic capital calculations. Other than often being burdensome, the main difficulty with approaches typically taken to non-linearity is in ensuring that the appropriate 1-in-200 scenario has been identified. However, with the mathematical modelling approach described above, such explicit adjustment is unnecessary because the calibrations of the formulae are performed in such a way that they accurately represent the values of assets and liabilities in all scenarios, and so automatically allow for any non-linearity of balance-sheet response. In addition, the empirically correct 1-in-200 scenario is immediately and automatically identified through the rank-ordering process.

It is also worth commenting on diversification. Under the approach described, capital is dictated by the balance-sheet responses to the underlying correlated stochastic processes. This approach is quite different to one in which the capital requirements are generated by each marginal risk and the overall capital requirement is determined by the application of correlation matrices to the marginal requirements. On one level the approach described is not a theoretical breakthrough, but in terms of a modelling mindset it represents a great step forward in carrying out capital assessments. The philosophy "the processes lead and the balance sheet follows" reflects reality.

Such cutting-edge techniques can be invaluable not only in freeing up firms to consider what really matters, namely the underlying risks and how they behave together, but also in actually forcing them to do so.

WHICH TYPE OF MATHEMATICAL MODEL SHOULD BE APPLIED?

The mathematical models underlying the loss functions can be constructed in different ways, some of which include curve fitting, cashflow modelling, and replicating portfolios, as described below. The appropriate approach will depend on a number of factors. Proportionality is one consideration, especially in terms of the materiality and importance of the business line being modelled. The firm's technical capabilities, infrastructure and long-term model strategy will also influence the modelling decision.

Curve fitting

"Curve fitting" is a common approach which involves finding a formula that accurately describes the value of the assets, liabilities, surplus assets or other quantities that are being modelled, in a wide range of scenarios. These scenarios would include individual risks, as well as appropriate combinations. A number of scenarios are used to fit the model, a process referred to as in-sample fitting, calibration or model training. A number of different scenarios are then used to test the model, a process referred to as out-of-sample testing, validation or model testing.

Cashflow modelling

"Cashflow modelling" is another common approach, well suited to annuity and unit-linked business. The approach is similar to curve fitting, except that formulae are fitted to each year's cashflows. Yield curves are applied separately to bring these cashflows to a present value. The cashflow approach involves fitting many more formulae, especially for long-tailed business, but its power is in its flexibility.

For interest-rate-sensitive business such as annuities, this approach decouples the effect of insurance risk factors (eg, longevity) and market risk factors (eg, interest rates). A cashflow approach neatly sidesteps the problem of curve fitting in situations in which it can be challenging to find curves that are practical to fit and that accurately allow for the interactions of changes in these risk factors, particularly yield curve movements (shape, level, twist, etc).

Index-linked benefit cashflows are often best calibrated in "real" (as opposed to "nominal") terms. This calibration allows the impact of inflation to be included explicitly as a risk factor by the application of an inflation yield curve. Such an approach will allow insurers to better understand their exposure to inflation risks, including the effect of capped and floored asset proceeds and/or annuity benefit payments.

Replicating portfolio

A replicating portfolio is most usually considered to be a portfolio of assets which is chosen to match the cashflows on a specific portfolio. In this context, the portfolio of interest could relate to assets, liabilities or both. The basic premise holds that if robust replication can be achieved then the specific portfolio can be re-valued much more quickly by re-valuing its replicating portfolio.

This approach is not always straightforward, especially in the context of complex insurance funds with embedded options and guarantees. Nevertheless, portfolio replication can be powerful because it can provide insight into the investment characteristics of the portfolio.

The replicating portfolio concept can be extended to constructing a replicating portfolio of liabilities (as opposed to assets). The idea is to define a set of standard liability cashflows, each derived from "standard policies". The total liability profile can then be constructed from an appropriately weighted combination of the standard liabilities, with the weights derived to give a good fit across a range of stressed assumptions. In the case of annuities, for example, the total portfolio could be replicated by taking an appropriate combination of cashflows for single life men and women aged 60, 65,..., 95. Revaluing a collection of standard liabilities will be much quicker than revaluing the whole portfolio directly. Conceptually similar to choosing model points, this particular replicating technique might be referred to as "replicating model points".

CALIBRATION AND VALIDATION PROCESS

Calibration is the process used to define the functional form of the asset or liability model and to estimate its parameters. Validation refers to the process used to test that the model is both robust and accurate. The main steps in these processes are described in Figure 7.3.

While model parsimony is always desirable, it is much more important that the models fit well in the areas of most interest and that they accurately capture the interactions of risks. That said, practicality is an important consideration. In Chapter 6 we considered two longevity risk factors in the context of annuities and Solvency II. If having opening (base) mortality risk and longevity trend risk represented as separate risk factors (albeit from correlated stochastic processes) were proving to be a difficult challenge in terms of model calibration, an alternative approach would be to combine them into one factor within the model. This could be achieved by modelling all mortality risks as a scalar multiple of the central mortality assumption, requiring both current mortality risk and longevity trend risk to be expressed in this way. While this approach is the natural way to express current mortality risk, it requires some re-expression of trend risk, for example by using annuity equivalence techniques (see Chapter 6). The separate risk distributions, which will of course still need to be simulated separately with an appropriate dependency structure, can then be combined by multiplication before being entered into the model.

In practice a model will be calibrated in advance of the date at which it is used. For example, a model used for regulatory reporting, which inevitably has tight deadlines, will need to be calibrated ahead of the valuation date. This situation creates three requirements.

Update: a process is needed which can be applied to update the model to the date of its use, adjusting for changes in the composition of the portfolio from the date of the model's calibration among other changes. The exact process will depend on the business line in question, including its materiality.

Validation: users of the model should not only understand the scenarios which could invalidate the model calibration (eg, changes in economic conditions or business mix) but they must also put in place a mechanism to identify whether such scenarios have arisen.

Contingency plan: a contingency plan should be put in place in the event that the model is invalidated.

Taking account of the time needed to calibrate and validate models, the model should be calibrated to give reliable results over an

Figure 7.3 Fitting the model

1. **Define the stresses for model fitting – be sure to capture interactions:** First, define the stresses to be used in the fitting process, ie, the range and combination of risk factor scenarios. The number of stresses, and their values, will naturally depend on the purpose of the model. There should be adequate coverage of each risk that is being stressed to give the model adequate breadth and depth. There should also be adequate coverage of the interaction among the risks so that the model can capture their effects.

   Capturing risk interaction is vital, and judgement will be required as to how to best do this, balanced against the desire to keep the process manageable. An understanding of the risk distributions and their correlations will be helpful here. While it will do no harm in terms of the model and its fit, there is little point in fitting to a scenario which is beyond the realms of probability, either because it is so extreme (eg, a 50% longevity stress in the context of a standard annuity portfolio) or because it is implausible or impossible in the context of the dependency structure (eg, male and female mortality moving in opposite directions in a framework which treats them as being perfectly correlated).

2. **Produce outputs for each scenario:** produce the base and stressed outputs of interest (eg, asset values, liability values, or cashflows) using the main actuarial valuation models. This part of the process may be quite time-consuming, depending on the size of the portfolio and the number of scenarios produced. Scenarios will be required to fit the model and subsequently to validate it.

3. **Find a model which reproduces each scenario:** choose a model form and fit its parameters. This part of the process is inevitably a combination of art and science, with judgement required in choosing a suitable functional form for the model. Once chosen, numerical optimisation techniques can be used to determine the parameter values in such a way that the modelled values closely represent the actual values.

4. **Validate the model:** finally, validate the formulae and parameters by checking how well the fitted model predicts the full model results on a reserve bank of test scenarios.

   Fitting and validation should be carried out against pre-determined acceptance criteria. They will most sensibly have regard to the materiality and importance of the business line under consideration. Stages 3 and 4 of this process may initially be quite iterative, but should eventually hone in on a sufficiently good model.

appropriately wide range of scenarios. Specifically, the calibration scenarios should not be unduly anchored to conditions at the calibration date, so that if conditions change the "depth" of the calibration remains adequate to cope with the implied re-centring of the model.

DELIVERING THE STANDARD FORMULA USING THE INTERNAL MODEL

Under Solvency II, firms with approval to use an internal model may be asked to produce results using the standard formula too (see Chapter 6 for an additional discussion). For this reason, internal models should be developed in a way that would also allow them to produce results on the standard formula basis. Assessing the Solvency Capital Requirement (SCR) in accordance with the standard formula can be achieved by running an internal model a number of times, each with one stress only, based on the standard formula. This process needs to be done for the SCR of each sub-module, which can then be aggregated using the correlation matrices specified by the European Regulator. In practice, this places a number of requirements on firms' internal models, including that the relevant standard formula risks are modelled and that the internal model is able to cope with the standard formula specification of that risk.

PROJECTING LIABILITIES AND CAPITAL

As mentioned above, cashflow models are particularly flexible. In concept, it is therefore straightforward to construct a means of projecting such models. The approach described in Figure 7.4 is largely independent of the type of business modelled, but works particularly well for annuity business.

APPLICATIONS

These projected models have many direct applications, an obvious one being the calculation of the Solvency II risk margin for annuity business. The calculation methodology is specified, and is the present value (at the risk-free rate) of the cost (in excess of risk-free) of holding capital in respect of non-hedgeable risks throughout the lifetime of the business, as summarised in Figure 7.5.

LONGEVITY RISK

> **Figure 7.4** Projecting cashflow models
>
> In the context of liability modelling, a cashflow model is effectively a set of formulae, each representing the cashflow in a particular future time period. Specifically, if $^0\text{CF}_t : \mathbb{R}^n \to \mathbb{R}; x \mapsto {}^0\text{CF}_t(x)$ is a real-valued function representing the liability outgo in time period t ($t = 1, 2, \ldots, \Omega$, where Ω is the final year of the projection) and x represents the n-vector of risk factors on which that outgo depends, then $\{^0\text{CF}_t(x)\}_{t=1}^{\Omega}$ represents the entire model.
>
> The model, referred to as the "time-0 model", is calibrated at time 0, the valuation date, and can be used to project cashflows for business in-force at time 0 on a range of projection assumptions. Moreover, it is possible to construct a whole series of future liability models.
>
> time-0: $^0\text{CF}_1(x)$ $^0\text{CF}_2(x)$ $^0\text{CF}_3(x)$ $\cdots$ $^0\text{CF}_t(x)$ $\cdots$
> time-1: $^1\text{CF}_2(x)$ $^1\text{CF}_3(x)$ $\cdots$ $^1\text{CF}_t(x)$ $\cdots$
> time-2: $^2\text{CF}_3(x)$ $\cdots$ $^2\text{CF}_t(x)$ $\cdots$
> etc
>
> These models can be derived from the time-0 model, which is possible given the cashflow-based nature of the model in question. The time-T model can be constructed first by discarding the first T years' formulae from the time-0 model and then adjusting the remaining cashflow formulae so that they are centred correctly and react appropriately to stress. The time-T model is specifically given by $\{^T\text{CF}_t(x)\}_{t=T+1}^{\Omega}$ where
>
> $$^T\text{CF}_t(x) = {}^0\text{CF}_t(x) \times \frac{^0\text{CF}_T(b)}{^0\text{CF}_T(x)}$$
>
> Note that each $^T\text{CF}_t(x)$ has $(t - T)$ years of sensitivity to changes in risk factors, ensured by the denominator in the ratio applied to $^0\text{CF}_t(x)$. Note also that each $^T\text{CF}_t(x)$ is also scaled appropriately so that it gives the best-estimate outgo $^0\text{CF}_t(b)$ when $x = b$, the best-estimate projection basis, ensured by the numerator in the ratio applied to $^0\text{CF}_t(x)$.

The calculation of risk margin therefore fundamentally requires the projection of future capital requirements for non-hedgeable risks, being risks related to

- underwriting risk in respect of the in-force business,
- counterparty default risk, eg, on reinsurance ceded and other risk mitigation techniques for which credit has been taken in the underwriting risk solvency capital requirement,
- operational risk and
- unavoidable market risk.

> **Figure 7.5** Calculating the risk margin: projected cost of capital
>
> The formula specified for the risk margin calculation is given by
>
> $$y \times \sum_{t=0} \frac{N_t}{(1 + r_{t+1})^{t+1}}$$
>
> where y is the cost-of-capital rate, initially expected to be 6% pa, N_t is the diversified solvency capital requirement at time t in respect of non-hedgeable risks and r_t represents the t-year spot rate from the risk-free yield curve.

How these capital requirements should be projected is not prescribed. Each firm must justify its own choice, and proportionality will play an important part here. A range of methods may be used, from approximate projections in line with simple "proxy" measures at one end of the spectrum to the application of full projected models at the other. Figure 7.6 describes four methods (among many possible others). In increasing order of complexity these are

- projection in line with the run-off of liabilities,
- projection in line with two possible proxy measures and
- the application of projected models.

Comparing the choices

The choice of approach is important. The simplest approach described is clearly overly simplistic. It corresponds to a longevity stress which decreases rapidly with increasing duration. On the other hand, applying the same longevity stress in each year may be considered to be overly prudent: portfolios will progressively converge with increasing age, and any selection effects allowed for in the early years are likely to dissipate. This should be reflected in the risk distributions, and the real answer would therefore seem to lie somewhere in between these two.

Figure 7.7 compares longevity risk capital before diversification for a man aged 65 with what might be considered "average" expected mortality under four approaches:

- a fixed 20% longevity stress (part (a)),
- capital is run off in line with liabilities (part (b)),
- capital is run off in line with two possible proxy measures (parts (c) and (d)).

LONGEVITY RISK

> **Figure 7.6** Projecting capital requirements
>
> 1. **Simplest method:** in line with best-estimate liabilities.
> The simplest proxy approach is to project non-hedgeable capital in line with the expected run-off of best-estimate liabilities.
> For some lines of business this approach may be appropriate, although simple adjustments may improve the accuracy, and indeed different approaches could be taken for the different non-hedgeable risks from a particular line of business.
>
> 2. **Scaling approach 1:** in the context of annuity business, longevity is the material non-hedgeable risk. The following formula was widely used in the QIS4 exercise to project the longevity risk capital L'_t required in year t
>
> $$L'_t = L'_0 \cdot \frac{B_t \cdot T_t}{B_0 \cdot T_0} \cdot 1.1^{t+(T_t-T_0)/2}$$
>
> where L'_0 is the time-0 longevity capital requirement, B_t represents the best-estimate liability at time t and T_t represents a "duration" of the liability cashflows from time t onwards, akin to an expectation of life measure.
> Using this approach, longevity capital reduces in line with both the best-estimate liability and the "duration" of payments, but with an offsetting increase based on the duration of the projection, intended to approximate the effect of the ageing of the underlying portfolio. This approach tends to be too prudent.
>
> 3. **Scaling approach 2:** as part of a suite of "simplification tools" issued for the QIS5 exercise, the following formula was proposed. It calculates directly the longevity risk capital L'_t required in year t
>
> $$L'_t = 20\% \times q_t B_t M_t \times 1.1^{(M_t-1)/2}$$
>
> where 20% is the proposed standard formula longevity stress, q_t represents the average mortality rate in the year ahead from time t, B_t represents the best-estimate liability at time t and M_t represents the modified duration of the liability cashflows from time t onwards.
> A rather crude approach, this methodology calculates the longevity capital requirement as a mortality charge against a duration-based multiple of best-estimate liability. It however does not even produce the same starting risk capital amount as the straightforward application of a 20% longevity stress. It is therefore at best suitable only for those firms which are allowed to adopt a similar approach directly in the Solvency Capital Requirement calculation on grounds of proportionality, although even those firms should be wary of its limitations for projection purposes.

A good "proxy measure" will provide a sensible projection, from both a technical and intuitive perspective, of capital amounts, while at the same time it will have the ability to be applied

Figure 7.6 Continued

4. **Applying projected models:** a robust projection would allow not only for the run-off of the in-force business and the evolution of the mix of lives in the portfolio (eg, progressively more women in the portfolios at longer durations) but also for the evolution of the risk distributions through time. A good approach, which should be well within the technical capability of all insurers, is therefore to derive and use projected liability models as described in Figure 7.4. Specifically, each of the series of liability models $\{\{^T\text{CF}_t(x)\}_{t=T+1}^{\Omega}\}_{T=0}^{\Omega-1}$ may be used, in conjunction with an appropriate number of stochastic non-hedgeable risk scenarios, to determine the capital in respect of non-hedgeable risks at each time $T = 1, 2, \ldots, \Omega$. An implicit but vital requirement here is the use of projected distributions for non-hedgeable risks (ie, x should be written x_T). Some of the considerations in respect of projecting longevity distributions were discussed in Chapter 6.

In applying projected liability models of the form

$$\{\{^T\text{CF}_t(x)\}_{t=T+1}^{\Omega}\}_{T=0}^{\Omega-1}$$

in a general context, care needs to be taken to ensure that the appropriate technical conditions are satisfied, at least materially. In the specific context of annuity business, for example, this approach works well provided that the business modelled within each $^T\text{CF}_t(\cdot)$ is sufficiently homogenous with respect to its sensitivity to changes in mortality (as measured from the calibration date). In this case, each

$$^T\text{CF}_t(x) = {}^0\text{CF}_t(x) \times \frac{{}^0\text{CF}_T(b)}{{}^0\text{CF}_T(x)}$$

represents business which has the same (or similar) $(t - T)$ years of sensitivity to changes in past mortality and which will also react similarly to prospective changes. There are many ways of satisfying this condition, but subdividing the portfolio into broad age categories is both simple and effective.

---

straightforwardly. The proxy approach in part (d) (which is the third option from Figure 7.6) is not particularly well considered. At no point does it produce the same capital requirement as a straightforward application of a fixed 20% longevity stress. It is therefore not discussed further.

On the other hand, the proxy approach in part (c) (the second option from Figure 7.6) is well considered in that it does seem to tread the middle ground between applying the same longevity stress in each year and between projecting longevity capital in line with best-estimate liability. That said, the fact that the stress corresponding

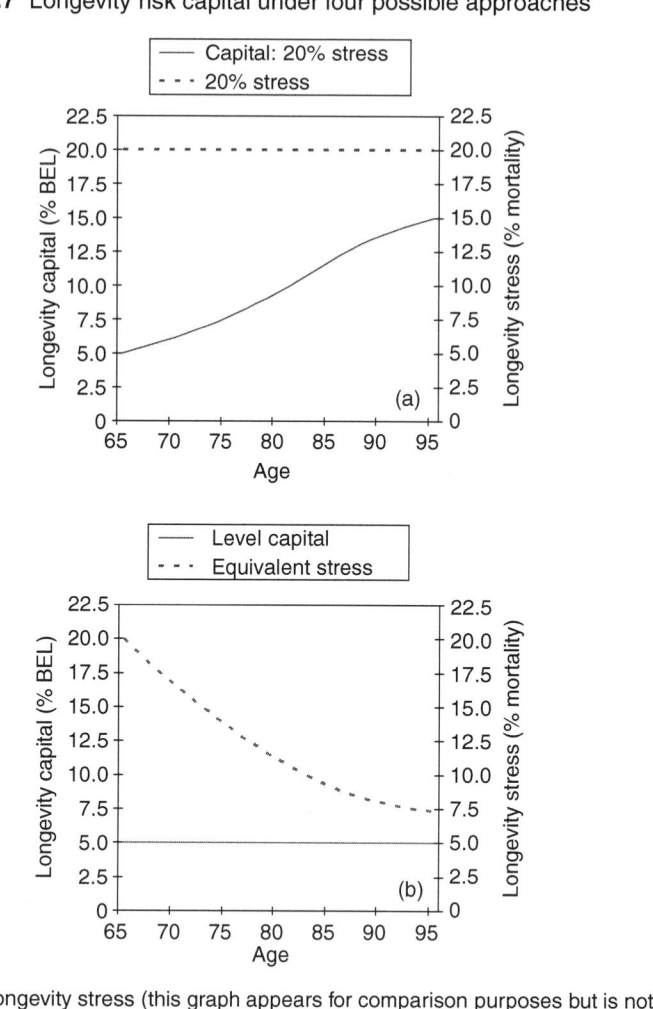

Figure 7.7 Longevity risk capital under four possible approaches

(a) Graph showing Capital: 20% stress (solid line, left axis) and 20% stress (dashed line, right axis) vs Age from 65 to 95.

(b) Graph showing Level capital (solid line, left axis) and Equivalent stress (dashed line, right axis) vs Age from 65 to 95.

(a) Fixed longevity stress (this graph appears for comparison purposes but is not one of the options outlined in Figure 7.6). Solid line (left axis) represents longevity risk capital (as a percentage of liability) with increasing age, based on a fixed 20% longevity stress each year. Dashed line (right axis) represents the longevity stress itself, ie, 20%. (b) Run-off in line with liabilities (a graph of option (1) from Figure 7.6). Solid line (left axis) represents longevity capital which is constant with age, ie, which runs off in line with liabilities. Dashed line (right axis) represents the corresponding longevity stress.

to this approach initially falls before rising again is unappealing. This type of U-shape progression with age might be observed when looking at longevity risk in run-off. In this situation, it is possible that opening mortality may become dominant as trend risk reduces with

Figure 7.7 Continued.

[Graph (c): Capital: proxy (1) and Equivalent stress vs Age 65-95. Longevity capital (% BEL) on left axis, Longevity stress (% mortality) on right axis, both 0 to 22.5.]

[Graph (d): Capital: proxy (2) and Equivalent stress vs Age 65-95. Same axes.]

(c) Run-off using a proxy measure (a graph of option (2) from Figure 7.6). Solid line (left axis) represents longevity capital from applying the first proxy scaling approach. Dashed line (right axis) represents the corresponding longevity stress.
(d) Run-off using a different proxy (a graph of option (3) from Figure 7.6). Solid line (left axis) represents longevity capital from applying a second proxy scaling approach. Dashed line (right axis) represents the corresponding longevity stress.

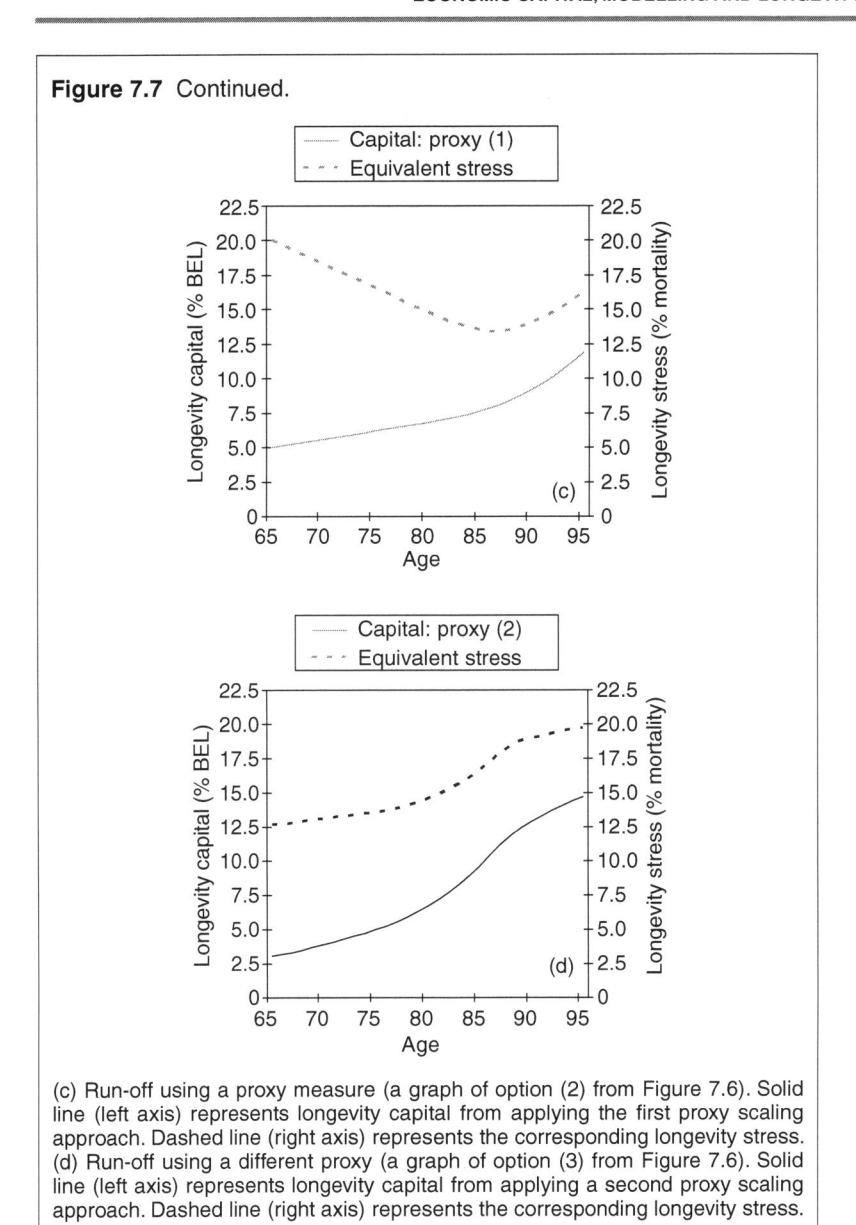

increasing duration, although this possibility depends heavily on the distributions, the method used to project them and the associated dependency structure. However, in the context of a pure one-year approach, it does point to the presence of an excessive "upwards force" on the capital requirements. This comes from the exponential

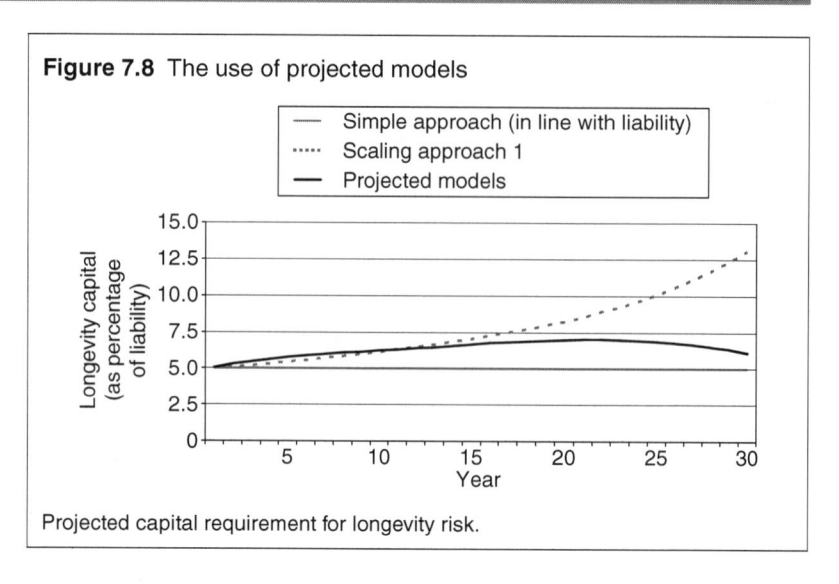

Figure 7.8 The use of projected models

— Simple approach (in line with liability)
····· Scaling approach 1
— Projected models

Projected capital requirement for longevity risk.

term in the formula for L'_t as shown in Figure 7.6, and in fact this approach can quickly become excessive at later durations, leading to nonsensical capital requirements, sometimes larger than 100% of liability. On balance, the proxy approach in part (c) might be expected to contain margins, which indeed is the case.

Figure 7.8 shows how longevity risk capital before diversification might behave based on the use of projected models and projected longevity distributions of the fourth option from Figure 7.6. The underlying analysis has been carried out on a model portfolio constructed to give, among other things, the same starting longevity capital as the simple example in Figure 7.7. However, without developing an approach based on projecting liability models, the proxy methodology in Figure 7.7(c) (the second option from Figure 7.6) may very well be the only option available to firms. Because this possibility could easily lead to the risk margin being overstated by as much as 10%, the incentive to develop and apply projected models is clear.

WIDER APPLICATIONS

Projected liability models may be combined with projected asset models (not discussed here) to project the full regulatory balance sheet through time. Variants of the projections (eg, with the inclusion of new business at varying levels) will be useful for many purposes,

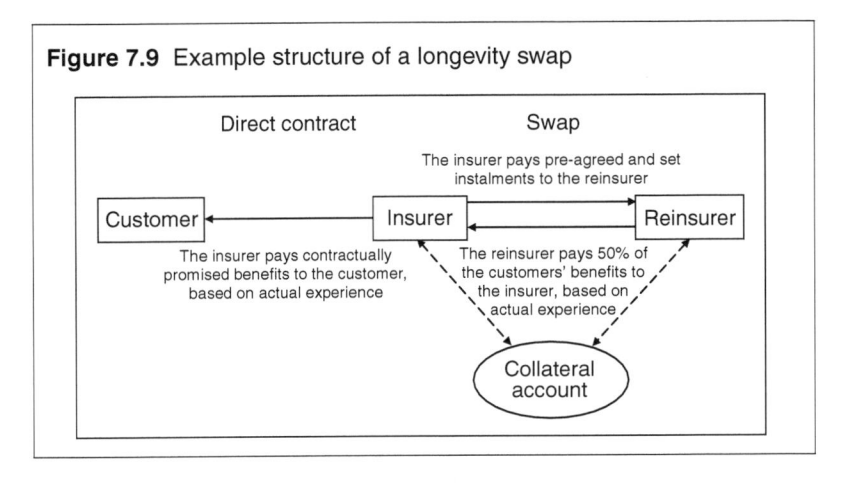

Figure 7.9 Example structure of a longevity swap

```
              Direct contract              Swap
                                    The insurer pays pre-agreed and set
                                       instalments to the reinsurer
  [Customer] ←―――――――――― [Insurer] ―――――――――――→ [Reinsurer]
         The insurer pays contractually   The reinsurer pays 50% of
         promised benefits to the customer,  the customers' benefits to
              based on actual experience    the insurer, based on
                                              actual experience
                                          ( Collateral
                                             account )
```

such as

- product strategy, including product development and pricing,
- underwriting strategy, including developing underwriting policies,
- reinsurance strategy, including choosing reinsurers and designing reinsurance structures,
- asset strategy, including assessing the optimal strategy to manage credit risk on an annuity portfolio,
- capital strategy, including managing capital and its allocation,
- strategic tactical decisions, including assessing business opportunities such as portfolio transfers and merger and acquisition activity,
- Enterprise Risk Management (ERM), including assessing risk appetite and exposure limits and
- Own Risk Solvency Assessment (see Chapter 6) as a specific example of ERM being applied in practice.

A SPECIFIC APPLICATION: REINSURANCE

In this next section we examine how the modelling techniques developed so far (and, specifically, the results of economic capital calculations) can be applied in setting a reinsurance strategy. Let us return to the example of Chapter 6, and suppose that the insurer is considering entering into a longevity swap for 50% of its annuity liabilities. The contractual arrangements might look similar to Figure 7.9.

Reinsuring longevity risk via a longevity swap has the following Solvency II presentation[4]:

(i) liabilities remain shown as gross of reinsurance;

(ii) the risk margin and Solvency Capital Requirement allow for (ie, are net of) the risk-mitigating effects of reinsurance;

(iii) an asset which is equal to the release of best-estimate liabilities as a result of the reinsurance, net of an allowance for expected levels of defaults, is shown.

Perhaps oddly, the asset in (iii) could easily have a negative value, depending on the terms of the transaction (ie, its rationale) or simply because experience has moved adversely relative to original expectations. This asset will be further split into the amount that is expected to be claimed from the reinsurer (the receive leg of the swap, always positive) and the amount that is expected to be paid to the reinsurer (the fixed leg of the swap, always negative).

Suppose that the regulatory balance sheet prior to any transaction looks like the one in "before" column of Table 7.1. The "after" balance sheet in Table 7.1 shows how it might look after a 50% longevity swap.

€X million is the (present) value of payments to the reinsurer. €5,000 million is the value of best-estimate liabilities ceded to the reinsurer (50% of €10,000 million), and €Y million = €(50,000 + 5,000 − X) million is the total asset value allowing for reinsurance. The risk margin before reinsurance is dominated by longevity risk, but allows also for non-hedgeable persistency risk. The risk margin therefore is approximately cut in half, dropping from €1,031 million to €559 million.[5] Somewhat less dominated by longevity risk, the Solvency Capital Requirement (SCR) falls proportionately less, from €1,811 million to €1,591 million.

For insurers with large annuity portfolios, reinsuring longevity risk can help to reduce both the risk margin and the SCR. For reinsurers with large mortality exposures, accepting longevity risk will help to diversify the mortality risk in both the risk margin and the SCR calculation. A corollary of both of these points is that deals involving insurers and reinsurers swapping longevity and mortality risk might be particularly attractive to both parties. Some of the structural solutions available to insurers and pension schemes to transfer longevity risk are discussed further in later chapters.

Table 7.1 Illustrative effect of a longevity swap

Before	(€ million)
Assets	50,000
Claims from reinsurer	—
Payments to reinsurer	(—)
Total	50,000
Best-estimate liabilities	
Annuities	15,000
Other	30,000
Total	45,000
Risk margin	1,031
Solvency Capital Requirement	1,811
Surplus assets	2,158

After	(€ million)	
Assets	50,000	
Claims from reinsurer	5,000	
Payments to reinsurer	(X)	
Total		Y
Best-estimate liabilities		
Annuities	15,000	
Other	30,000	
Total		45,000
Risk margin		559
Solvency Capital Requirement		1,591
Surplus assets		Z

In the example shown here, surplus assets €Z million will increase as a result of the longevity swap if the value of payments to the reinsurer (X in Table 7.1) is less than €5,692 million (€5,000 million plus the sum of the released risk margin and SCR[6]).

Methodologies, models and risk distributions which are appropriate to the total portfolio, to the business to be reinsured and to the residual (retained) portfolio can readily be used to assist in the development of an appropriate reinsurance strategy.

OTHER CONSIDERATIONS

Of course, regulatory capital at the valuation date is far from the only consideration for entering into a reinsurance transaction or managing a portfolio in a wider sense. Economic capital and risk appetite considerations will both play an important part in a firm's decision on whether or not, and on what terms, to enter into a deal. It is indeed highly plausible that a transaction or management approach could be undertaken because it is economically sensible or aligns with the firm's risk appetite, even if it is not optimal from a regulatory perspective.

In the previous example of the longevity swap, the benefit of reinsurance would most naturally be assessed over the run-off of the portfolio. The moneyness of the swap (ie, how in- or out-of-the-money it is) will change depending on observed experience, and firms with risk-averse utility functions will tend to place greater relative value on the increased certainty of outcomes from entering the swap. All else being equal, such firms are more likely to be willing to pay more for the reinsurance.

Different firms will express economic capital requirements and their risk appetite statements in different ways. Internal frameworks are commonly based around regulatory frameworks, usually with modifications to reflect an entity's own views on economic reality and/or to reflect an entity's specific risk appetite. We give some examples below.

- **Failure probability:** firms may view a failure probability of 0.5% as being too large and instead prefer to target capital sufficient for, say, a 1-in-500 or a 1-in-2000 equivalent scenario.

- **Term of projection:** a regulatory one-year value-at-risk measure might be seen to be too short-term for entities with long-term payment obligations such as annuities and pensions in payment. Consequently, it may be more appropriate to consider risks in run-off, especially longevity risk.

- **Reflection of economic reality:** any peculiarities of the regulatory regime would be removed or recalibrated, eg, the calibration of any longevity risk margin should be considered when longevity risk is contemplated in run-off.

It is not uncommon for entities to manage to a collection of requirements. The precise nature will depend on the entity, but some considerations that are important for regulated entities with long-term payment obligations are as follows.

(i) **The ability to meet obligations:** the level of capital required to ensure that payment obligations to policyholders or to pensioners can be met as they fall due should be assessed.

(ii) **Defence of regulatory balance sheet:** the level of capital, in excess of regulatory capital, which is required to ensure that regulatory insolvency does not occur should be assessed.

Typically, firms will look to hold capital to achieve these objectives with a desired level of confidence over a desired time period. This might be linked to internal risk appetite statements or, for entities with financial strength ratings from credit rating agencies, it might be linked to protecting, or improving, their standing. The basis used in assessing the latter type of capital requirements would of course be consistent with any rating agency requirements.

Meeting payment obligations

The models previously described in this chapter may readily be applied in carrying out some of the above analyses. For example, a Solvency II type calculation, but with longevity considered in run-off, would be one way for a pension scheme to investigate its ability to meet its payment obligations. An alternative approach, of course, would be the application of a stochastic asset-liability projection model to project the balance sheet through time allowing for key items such as

- income and outgo, eg, receipt of asset income, payment of benefit obligations and expenses,
- changes in economic conditions, eg, interest rates, credit spreads, equity prices and
- changes in demographic experience, eg, mortality, longevity, transfer rates, etc.

This approach would allow the scheme to investigate its ability to meet benefit obligations in two different ways.

(i) **In-year:** by assessing whether or not the fund has assets sufficient to meet each year's obligations, ie, on a year-by-year basis consider whether there are enough assets to avoid defaulting on payments.

(ii) **All future years:** by assessing whether the fund has assets sufficient to cover its best-estimate liabilities in each future year. This requirement is equivalent to saying that, in each year, all payments from then onwards are expected to be met.

The second of these requirements is more onerous than the first, and in many ways both more sensible and interesting.

Defending regulatory balance sheet

Investigations into entities' abilities to defend their regulatory balance sheet also require the application of stochastic asset-liability projection models. The models already described in this chapter can be extended to do this, or they might be developed so that they can be utilised within an overarching asset-liability projection model.

SUMMARY

Building on the concepts discussed in Chapter 6, we began this chapter by outlining a generic economic capital framework, using Solvency II as a specific example.

Non-linearity and diversification are important in economic frameworks and call for modelling solutions such as curve fitting, cashflow modelling and replicating portfolios. Cashflow modelling is particularly suited to modelling annuities and pension scheme benefit obligations, and we discussed its application in calculating and then projecting capital requirements in respect of longevity risk.

We also introduced and discussed alternative means of projecting longevity capital. A case study of a firm entering into a longevity swap was presented to show how economic capital can influence risk management in a specific context. We concluded with some considerations for a wider approach to modelling and enterprise risk management.

> The views and opinions expressed in this chapter those of the author, as at the date of writing. They may not accord with those of any past or current employer. They do not constitute advice, and nor may they be construed as such. The author thanks Debbie Laird, David Shaffer, Esther Strickland and Paul Teggin for their helpful suggestions and comments. Any remaining errors are entirely those of the author.

1. Actually, firms are permitted to use a different time period or risk measure in their internal model (see Chapter 6) so long as the outputs from it can be used in a manner that provides policyholders and beneficiaries with a level of protection equivalent to a one-year 1-in-200 value-at-risk approach; see Article 122(1) of the Solvency II Directive (European Directive 2009/138/EC).

2. The phrase "joint distribution" is used to refer to the probabilistic relationship of a number of random variables, or how they behave together. The phrase "marginal distribution" usually refers to the way in which just one of these random variables is distributed. For a rigorous exposition of these concepts, see Grimmett and Stirzaker (1992). Joint distributions can be constructed from marginal ones by defining a dependency structure (McNeil *et al* 2005).

3. Article 122(2) of the Solvency II Directive requires this where practicable, but Article 122(3) envisages that some firms may take a more approximate approach.

4. See Articles 77(2) and 81 of the Solvency II Directive.

5. The risk margins before and after reinsurance have been calculated using a correlation-matrix approach. This is deliberately simplistic, and indeed technically incorrect, used only to illustrate the point.

6. This assumes that counterparty risk is zero as a result of an appropriate collateral structure.

REFERENCES

Grimmett, G., and D. Stirzaker, 1992, *Probability and Random Processes*, Second Edition (Oxford University Press).

McNeil, A., R. Frey and P. Embrechts, 2005, *Quantitative Risk Management: Concepts, Techniques and Tools* (Princeton University Press).

Part IV

Risk Management and De-Risking

8

De-Risking Insured Annuity Portfolios

Robert Bugg, Farzana Ismail, Philip Simpson, Nick Dumbreck

Milliman

In this chapter we focus on the avenues that life insurance companies can pursue in managing the longevity risk arising from their annuity and pension-in-payment portfolios. Given an ever-increasing ageing population worldwide, the global market for insurance products exposed to significant longevity risk is huge. In the UK alone, life insurers held around £200 billion in reserves (gross of reinsurance) at the end of 2009 for their in-payment annuity liabilities. This figure seems poised to rise in future years as a result of an ageing population and a relentless trend towards defined-contribution pension provision.

However, there is legislation in some territories which could have a major impact on annuity sales figures. For example, in 2010, the UK government began to consider options on compulsory annuitisation. If the rules, which require an individual to purchase an annuity from the proceeds of their pension by the age of 77, were to be scrapped, annuity sales could fall sharply even as new post-retirement products are developed. By comparison, at the time of writing, the US places limited legal requirements on policyholders to annuitise their pension savings. For the majority of developing countries, there is little or no requirement for pensioners to purchase annuities at retirement, which limits the growth of annuity business in these regions.

As covered in Chapters 6 and 7, the upcoming Solvency II regime will bring significant changes to the European insurance regulatory landscape and uncertainty over future regulatory capital requirements for annuity business. This uncertainty and concerns over the rate of increase of life expectancy have prompted many insurers, particularly those in the UK with a large volume of annuity business, to look at ways to manage their exposure to this business.

For insurance capacity to keep pace with the potential future demand for annuity products, it is essential that methods for life insurers to off-load some or all of the risk associated with their annuity books continue to be available.

Some of the de-risking solutions described in this chapter are well established and have been used effectively for many years by life insurers, particularly in the UK. Others are relatively recent innovations which are gaining traction in the industry and are expected to become more prevalent in the future as insurance companies manage their risk exposures ever more closely. Some of the arrangements used in the largest UK insured-annuity portfolio transactions in recent years are summarised in case studies in this chapter.

As the UK is one of the more developed markets in longevity risk transfer transactions, most of the examples and concepts discussed in this chapter are based on this market.

BACKGROUND TO THE UK ANNUITY MARKET

There is a diverse range of products available in the UK branded as "annuities", many of which relate to the pre-retirement period during which funds are accumulated to provide for the policyholder's retirement. However, for the purposes of longevity risk, "insured annuities" in the UK are generally defined as post-retirement products and are categorised below.

- **Life office pensioners:** members of occupational pension schemes for which the benefits are insured by a life insurance company.
- **Widows:** female spouses granted pensions on the death of life office pension scheme members either in service or after retirement.
- **Retirement annuitants:** individuals who were self-employed or not in pensionable employment (eg, because their employer did not offer an occupational pension scheme) that elected to take out a pension policy with a life insurance company before 1988.

- **Personal pensioners:** individuals who elected to set up a personal pension policy from 1988 onwards when personal pensions replaced retirement annuities.
- **Immediate annuitants:** individuals who elected to purchase an annuity from their own funds. The money used to purchase the annuity is not necessarily related to pension savings. These products are also known as purchased life annuities and may be subject to significant anti-selection effects as opposed to compulsory purchase annuities.

The majority of de-risking transactions which have taken place in the UK have been in respect of products purchased using the proceeds of a pension fund. These products provide a regular prescribed income in retirement to the annuitant until their death (or until the death of a surviving spouse). The level of income may be constant, or may increase at a fixed percentage rate or in line with an agreed inflation index. The inflationary increases are sometimes capped at a prescribed annual percentage.

UK insurers are regulated by the Financial Services Authority (FSA), and UK annuity benefits are at least partially protected by the Financial Services Compensation Scheme (FSCS), which would generally cover 90% of an insured's benefits if the insurer failed.

The size of post-retirement annuity liabilities is shown in Figure 8.1. The chart is based on data obtained from the annual returns submitted to the FSA by UK life insurance companies, for which the companies are required to calculate their liabilities on a prudent basis for each major product group.

Since 2006 the aggregate annuity liabilities have steadily increased and, with the exception of 2009, the proportion of liabilities reinsured to other insurers or reinsurers has also risen.

The majority of annuity business is concentrated among a relatively small number of providers as indicated by the market shares, shown in Figure 8.2, of the top 10 insurance companies for in-force insured annuities in payment in 2009. Collectively, the 10 largest providers accounted for approximately 90% of the total market on this basis, with Prudential and Aviva being the two largest annuity players.

Prudential, Legal & General and Pension Insurance Corporation accounted for around 50% of the market for new annuity business in 2009.

LONGEVITY RISK

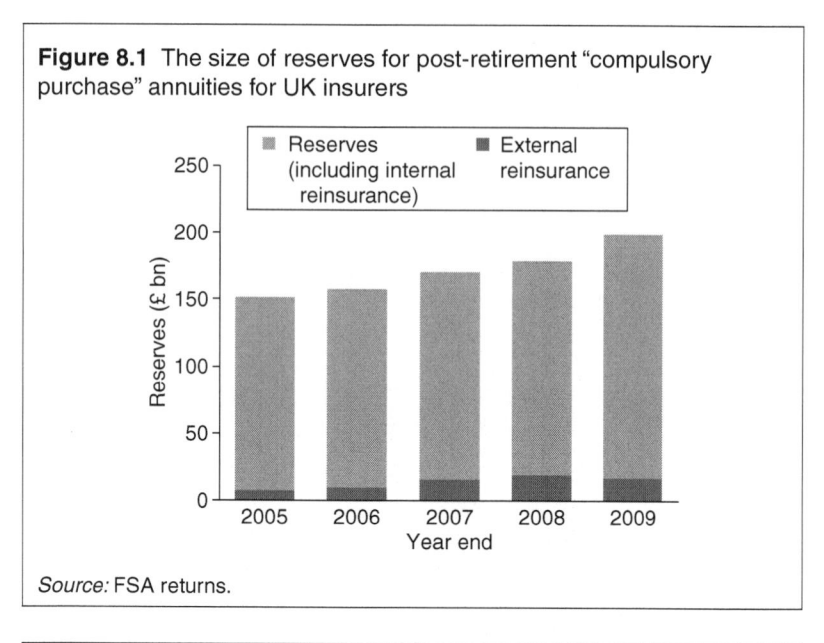

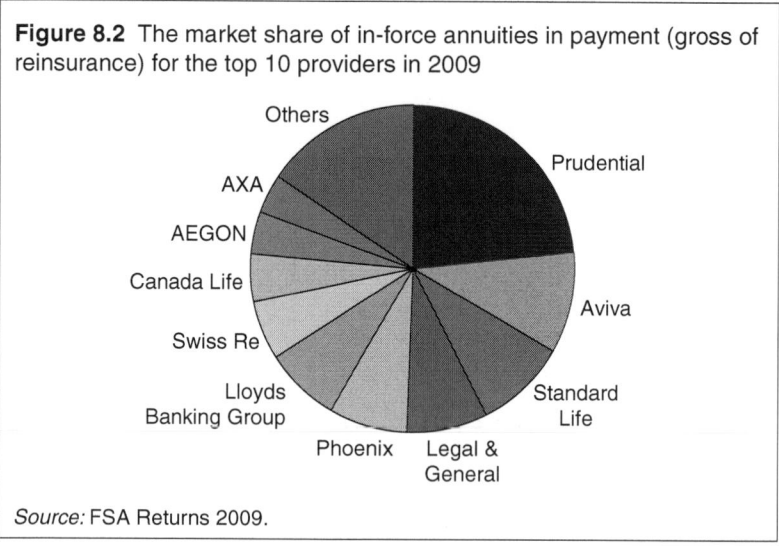

Figure 8.1 The size of reserves for post-retirement "compulsory purchase" annuities for UK insurers

[Bar chart showing Reserves (£ bn) by Year end from 2005 to 2009, with legend: Reserves (including internal reinsurance) and External reinsurance. Values approximately 150, 155, 170, 180, 200.]

Source: FSA returns.

Figure 8.2 The market share of in-force annuities in payment (gross of reinsurance) for the top 10 providers in 2009

[Pie chart with segments: Others, AXA, AEGON, Canada Life, Swiss Re, Lloyds Banking Group, Phoenix, Legal & General, Standard Life, Aviva, Prudential.]

Source: FSA Returns 2009.

The 2009 market shares for the top 10 UK insurance companies for new annuity business are shown in Figure 8.3. The new annuity business includes the corporate pension bulk market (ie, where the corporate pension scheme liabilities are transferred to the insurance company through a pension buy-out or buy-in transaction as described in the next chapter).

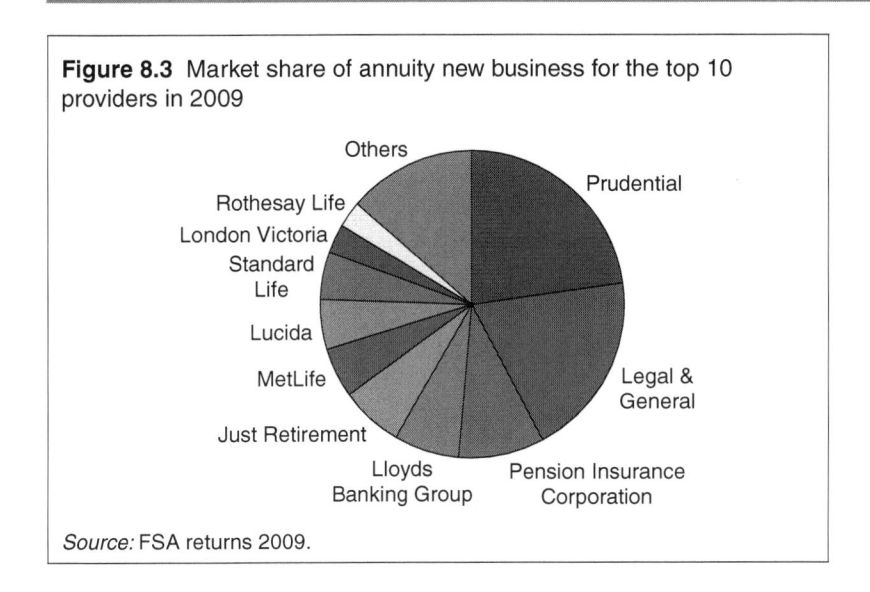

Figure 8.3 Market share of annuity new business for the top 10 providers in 2009

Source: FSA returns 2009.

In recent years, new companies specialising in acquiring some or all of the risk associated with existing annuity portfolios have entered the UK market. Some of these companies, such as Lucida, Paternoster and Pension Insurance Corporation, are regulated insurance companies and others are non-insurance entities, such as investment banks, that typically pass on the risk to capital market investors. Several investment banks have set up insurance divisions focusing on transfers of longevity risk via the capital markets.

An overview of some of the principal players in the bulk annuity risk-transfer market in the UK at the time of writing, divided by category, is given in Table 8.1.

DRIVERS FOR MANAGING LONGEVITY RISK

In this section we summarise the key drivers for managing longevity risk. Longevity risk is systemic, and consequently there is a limit to how much a single entity can, or should, retain, given its capital base and risk appetite. However, the more immediate concerns related to market risk and regulatory compliance have, at times, sidelined insurers' more active management of longevity risk. Nevertheless, concerns over the consequences of rapid improvements in life expectancy exhibited by annuitants in recent years have put longevity risk management firmly on the agenda.

Table 8.1 Illustrative list of key players in the bulk annuity risk-transfer market in the UK

Insurers	Reinsurers	Investment banks
Abbey Life*	Hannover Life Re	Credit Suisse
AEGON	Munich Re	Citibank
Aviva	PartnerRe	Commerzbank
AXA	Pacific Life Re	Deutsche Bank
Canada Life	RGA	JP Morgan
Legal & General	Swiss Re	Morgan Stanley
Lloyds Banking Group	XL Re	Royal Bank of Scotland
Lucida	UBS	
MetLife		
Paternoster†		
Pension Insurance Corporation***		
Phoenix Group		
Prudential		
Rothesay Life**		

*Owned by Deutsche Bank.
**Established by Goldman Sachs.
***Established by Pension Corporation.
†Acquired by Rothesay Life in January 2011.

In the past, insurers' general desire to retain control of assets backing their annuity portfolios has sometimes made it unattractive for them to initiate certain types of risk-transfer transactions. However, out of difficulty comes innovation, and consequently attention has turned to the development of more focused methods of longevity risk transfer, such as the longevity swap.

Other major drivers of the longevity risk-transfer market, especially in Europe, have been Solvency II and the steady decline in the popularity of participating (with-profits) policies, particularly in the UK market. In the UK, with-profits companies typically have a large volume of in-force pension savings policies, the proceeds of which are converted to a non-profit annuity at retirement. The rate of conversion to annuity contracts has been high, as some of the older with-profits policies have included the option to convert to a non-profit annuity at a guaranteed annuity rate, which is often favourable relative to current market rates. Following the closure to new with-profits business by a large number of providers, many with-profits funds have a declining base of with-profits policies and a steady flow of new pension annuities in payment. This situation has led to an increase in the proportion of with-profits funds that are taken up by non-profit annuities, which exposes the remaining with-profits policyholders to a high level of longevity risk. A mismatching issue also occurs because the profits from the annuity business may not emerge until most of the with-profits policies have matured. Reducing or eliminating this risk has therefore become a top priority for some with-profits funds, and prompted several large transactions in the UK market in recent years.

However, as described earlier, any changes to the rules on compulsory annuitisation could result in a big change to the dynamics of the market. Figures 8.5 and 8.12 provide examples of some of the largest UK insured-annuity portfolio transactions in relation to annuity business in participating funds that have taken place in recent years.

TYPES OF DE-RISKING SOLUTIONS FOR INSURED ANNUITIES

A life insurer that wishes to off-load some or all of its longevity risk has a number of options. The solutions include

- full annuity portfolio transfer, which involves a complete risk-transfer solution for the annuity portfolio,
- reinsurance,
- capital markets transaction.

We will address each of these options in turn, highlighting the key features, similarities, differences and relative merits. Some of the solutions are not currently available to pension schemes and, therefore, solutions available to de-risk pension schemes are specifically covered in the next chapter.

Full annuity portfolio transfer

An insurer can remove all the risks relating to the annuity portfolio by selling the block of annuities to another insurer. When a full portfolio transfer takes place, it effectively moves all obligations related to the policies in question to the receiving company.

Local regulation may place restrictions or conditions on the way in which a portfolio is transferred from one company to another. For example, under Part VII of the Financial Services and Markets

Act 2000 (FSMA 2000) UK insurers are permitted to transfer policies to another regulated entity with the agreement of the Court (ie, a Part VII transfer). The Court will require a report from an independent expert, who will consider whether any policyholders involved either directly or indirectly will be adversely affected by the proposed transfer. UK transfers also require the tacit approval of the FSA.

Under a full annuity portfolio transfer, assets which represent the realistic liabilities of the transferred business will usually be transferred to the receiving entity. Additional capital may be required by the receiving company to ensure that appropriate regulatory, accounting and solvency requirements are met and to ensure that the benefit security of policyholders involved is not materially affected.

This approach to de-risking may be preferred if the transferring company does not want to retain any risk posed by the annuity portfolio. Since all liability-related obligations are transferred, it also has no counterparty risk. However, the process of setting up a full annuity portfolio transfer (an example of which is given in Figure 8.4 and a case study in Figure 8.5) is relatively complicated and costly and it may take around 9–12 months, depending on local regulatory requirements, the complexity of the insurer's business and its fund structure. For example, a transfer involving with-profits business will typically be more complex and will, in some territories, require greater scrutiny than a transfer involving a straightforward non-profit fund.

Reinsurance

Reinsurance is perhaps the most familiar option available to a life insurer wishing to transfer some of its longevity risk to another party. In the past this approach has been commonly adopted when the insurer wished to retain only some of the risks and potential profit of the block of annuities and share the remaining risks with the reinsurer. In this context, reinsurance was used to manage capital or reduce the insurer's risk exposures. In addition, reinsurance is often used as an interim step to a full portfolio transfer, as described earlier. It may also be used as part of a capital markets solution.

In a reinsurance arrangement, the life insurer pays the reinsurer a premium in return for the reinsurer paying some or all of the claims arising from the risk transferred by the insurer (known as the

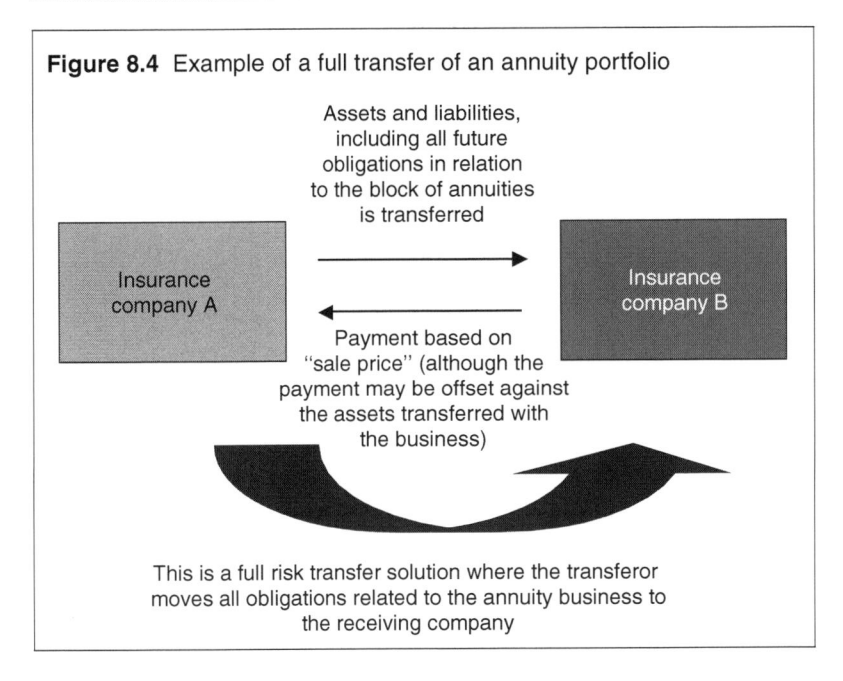

Figure 8.4 Example of a full transfer of an annuity portfolio

Insurance company A → Assets and liabilities, including all future obligations in relation to the block of annuities is transferred → Insurance company B

← Payment based on "sale price" (although the payment may be offset against the assets transferred with the business)

This is a full risk transfer solution where the transferor moves all obligations related to the annuity business to the receiving company

"cedant"). Such arrangements are well established in the insurance industry for annuities and other types of business.

However, a reinsurance arrangement is only a partial risk-transfer solution for the annuity provider. The cedant remains ultimately responsible for any liabilities transferred to a reinsurer in the event the reinsurer defaults on its obligations. For this reason, an appropriate amount of risk capital should be held by the cedant in respect of the counterparty risk related to the reinsurance arrangement.

In some cases reinsurance can also improve capital efficiency. This efficiency, however, should not be viewed in isolation. For example, local regulations need to be well understood in terms of the overall impact of the transaction on the entire capital required for the company rather than just the impact on the annuity portfolio, as the benefits available may not always be as large as anticipated. Under UK FSA rules at the time of writing, there is a limit on the reduction to a cedant's required solvency margin that can be achieved via all reinsurance arrangements. It is based on the long-term insurance capital requirement (LTICR) for annuities that is calculated as 4% of the net mathematical reserves, subject to a minimum of 4% of 85% of the gross mathematical reserves. This means that if more than 15% of the firm's total gross reserves are already reinsured, then no credit

> **Figure 8.5** Case study of a full Part VII annuity portfolio transfer in the UK
>
> During 2007, Equitable Life transferred £4.6 billion of annuity liabilities to Canada Life in a full annuity portfolio transfer. As a mutual with-profits insurer, Equitable Life has no shareholders, but rather its with-profits policyholders bear all the risks the company faces. As such, the company has a duty to manage its operation in the best interests of its policyholders, because its sole source of capital is the free assets which have been built up over time from retained surplus.
>
> Equitable Life experienced well-publicised difficulties caused by onerous guarantees and falling interest rates, forcing the company to close to new business in 2000. Over time, it had built up a large portfolio of non-profit pension annuities from retiring with-profits policyholders who purchased annuities using the proceeds of their with-profits policies, many of which were converted at favourable guaranteed rates. However, Equitable Life's closure to new business meant that the number of with-profits policyholders was gradually decreasing relative to the size of the annuity portfolio, so that the level of longevity and investment risk to which those policyholders were exposed grew to an undesirable level.
>
> Pending the approval of a transfer under Part VII of FSMA 2000 of its non-profit annuity pension liabilities, Equitable Life decided in 2006 to reinsure these liabilities to Canada Life. The transfer involved around 130,000 policies and final approval for the transfer was granted by the High Court in February 2007.
>
> The Equitable Life transfer is the biggest Part VII transfer of annuity business between insurers to date. As a result of the transfer, Equitable Life's required capital under Pillar 1 of FSA rules reduced from £1 billion at the end of 2006 to £0.7 billion at the end of 2007. The effect of the transfer on Equitable Life's Individual Capital Assessment Pillar 2 capital requirement, which is a more risk-based measure, has not been made public.

will be given for part of the reinsurance in the solvency margin calculation. Therefore, it is important to consider the way in which a reinsurance transaction can be set up to optimise capital efficiency relative to the amount of risk to be transferred.

Reinsurance is also a relatively flexible mechanism to use in order to transfer different risks. Treaties can be structured to remove the longevity risk as well as the asset risk from the cedant's annuity portfolio, or to remove only the longevity risk portion while retaining risk relating to interest rate movements and inflation. Currently, there are two major types of reinsurance arrangements commonly used for insured annuity business: the single premium annuity reinsurance and the longevity swap, which are introduced below and are considered in further detail in Chapter 10.

Single premium annuity reinsurance

Historically, most of the reinsurance arrangements on insured annuities have involved the cedant paying a single premium to the reinsurer upfront. These transactions, which are typically known as "single premium annuity reinsurance", are usually structured based on a "quota-share" arrangement, in which the cedant passes an agreed proportion of the underlying asset and longevity risks from the block of annuity business to the reinsurer.

Under this reinsurance arrangement, both longevity risk and asset risk are typically transferred to the reinsurer. To achieve this, the insurer or cedant pays an agreed single premium to the reinsurer at outset. In exchange, the reinsurer agrees to pay the insurer nearly all, or an agreed percentage, of future annuity payments associated with the block of annuities.

Such transactions expose the cedant to credit risk or counterparty risk in the event of reinsurer default. To reduce this exposure, a collateral structure can be set up as part of the reinsurance treaty. Two of the most common collateral structures are "deposit back of premium" and the use of a "trust-like" security account, which is established independently of the insurer and reinsurer. However, both methods only partially eliminate the counterparty risk and the insurer will ultimately remain responsible for the annuity payments to its policyholders. In addition, the reinsurer will usually charge a premium to the cedant for a collateral arrangement, so there is a trade-off between higher reinsurance cost and lower counterparty exposure.

Under a "deposit back of premium" collateral structure, the reinsurer deposits back the single premium with the insurer. The insurer typically has the formal right to offset the amount owed by the reinsurer against the debt represented by the deposit. The "deposit back of premium" amount will be managed in a ring-fenced or segregated fund by the insurer, and the insurer has the additional responsibility to repay the surplus arising from these assets to the reinsurer. The reinsurance treaty will usually dictate the terms for investment of these assets. An example of a quota-share single premium annuity reinsurance arrangement with a "deposit back of premium" collateral structure is illustrated in Figure 8.6.

Figure 8.6 Example of a single premium annuity reinsurance structure with deposit back of premium

- Single premium paid at outset (Insurance company (cedant) → Reinsurance company)
- Collateral arrangement: Reinsurer deposits back the premium to the insurer
- Insurer repays surplus arising from the ring-fenced account to the reinsurer
- Ring-fenced or segregated account
- Reinsurer pays an agreed proportion of future annuity payments
- Cedant shares an agreed proportion of the asset risk and longevity risk with the reinsurer

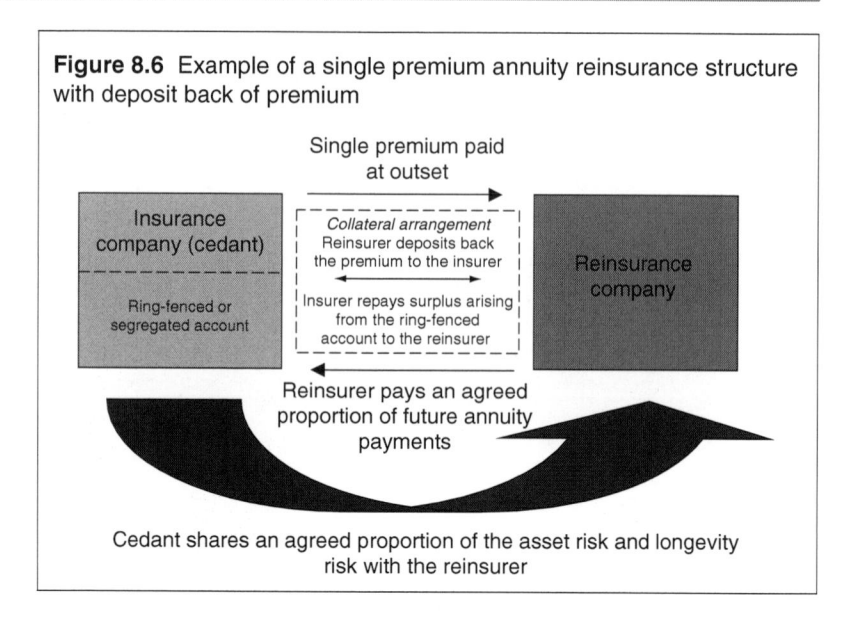

Another collateral arrangement that is commonly used to reduce counterparty risk is a "trust-like" security account which is held separately from the insurer and the reinsurer. The single premium from the insurer is paid into this collateral account and is invested in accordance with the reinsurance treaty to provide some protection to the insurer from counterparty risk. In the event of a reinsurer default, the insurer will have access to assets in the collateral account, thus significantly reducing credit and counterparty risk.

An example of a quota-share "single premium annuity reinsurance" arrangement with a "trust-like" collateral account, separate from the insurer and reinsurer, is illustrated in Figure 8.7.

Longevity swaps

Another common reinsurance structure used for insured annuity business is the longevity swap. This structure is usually a longevity-risk-only transfer solution, although in some cases selected other risks, such as the benefit inflation risk related to the annuity payment, may also be transferred. Under a longevity-swap arrangement, the cedant typically passes the longevity risk to the reinsurer while retaining the underlying asset risks. Longevity swaps have historically also been referred to as "reverse risk premium" reinsurance.

Figure 8.7 Example of a single premium annuity reinsurance structure with a separate collateral account

[Diagram: Insurance company (cedant) pays Single premium at outset → Collateral arrangement "Trust-like" collateral account → Surplus arising from the collateral account → Reinsurance company. Reinsurer pays an agreed proportion of future actual annuity payments back to the cedant. Cedant shares an agreed proportion of the asset risk and longevity risk with the reinsurer.]

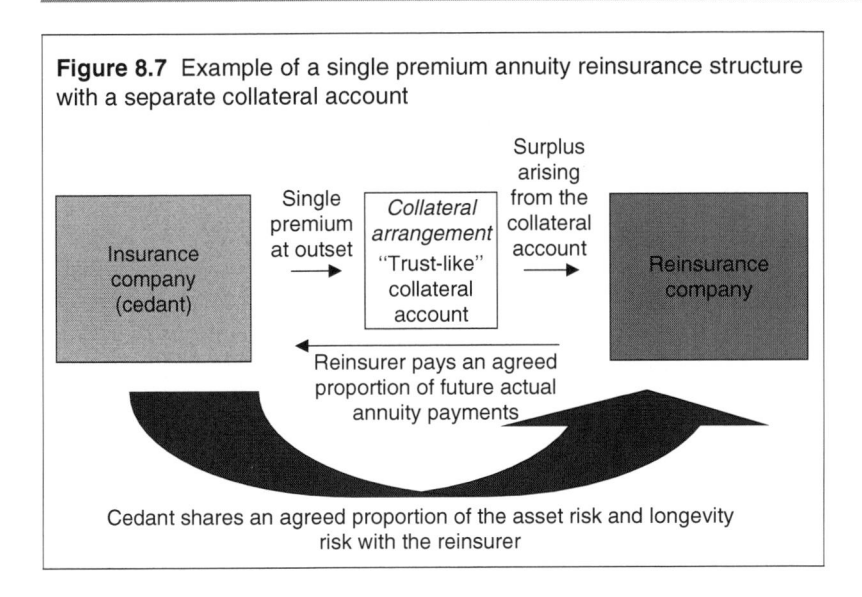

Some of the earliest longevity swaps date back to the 1990s. However, they have gained traction and popularity considerably in recent years as the demand for less asset-intensive risk-transfer solutions rose in the wake of the global financial crisis, and as focus increased on managing longevity risk in light of increasing life expectancies.

Under a longevity swap, the insurer and the reinsurer exchange a series of regular payments, typically on a monthly basis. The reinsurer pays the insurer the annuity payments based on the agreed referenced mortality experience (either the insured annuity lives or some other referenced portfolio such as population lives) over the duration of the longevity-swap contract (the "floating leg"). In contrast, the insurer's payments to the reinsurer are usually prescribed on a fixed basis and agreed at the outset (the "fixed leg"). The fixed leg payments are calculated at the outset of the transaction based on the best estimate of the future annuity payments plus a risk premium to reward the reinsurer for its risk. The term of the longevity swap may be for a fixed term (eg, 10 years), or over the lifetime of the insured annuity contracts.

The reinsurer's floating leg payments can be determined on either an "indemnity" basis or a "parametric" basis. For an indemnity basis transaction, the reinsurer's floating payments are determined by reference to the actual mortality experience of the insured annuity lives in question. In this case, the longevity swap removes all longevity risk from the cedant. For a parametric basis transaction the floating payments are made by reference to some other data such as a population mortality index which reflects the mortality experience of a given population but which is likely to be different from that of the annuity portfolio to be de-risked. Under these circumstances, the cedant retains some residual "basis" risk that the mortality experience of the reference population for the index differs materially from the mortality experience of the insured annuity block. In addition, certain "hybrid" transactions have emerged which apply elements of both an indemnity and parametric basis to specific components of the transactions.

Most of the longevity-swap transactions that have taken place at the time of writing have been on an indemnity basis, which maximises the longevity risk transfer from the cedant's perspective, rather than a parametric solution which presents a residual basis risk. One reason may stem from the existing direction of Solvency II, which suggests that insurers may be able to take little or no credit for reinsurance arrangements or risk mitigation techniques with significant basis risk. For this reason, parametric solutions are likely to be structured in a way that minimises basis risk for cedants in order to maximise the capital relief available.

Longevity-swap transactions do not usually require companies to transfer a significant amount of assets to the risk acquirer at the outset, which may be a more attractive option for companies wishing to retain control of assets used to back their annuity portfolio. The flexibility of the longevity swap also allows for a payment schedule that may take into account a different shape of fixed-leg payments to meet the needs of the cedant.

The widening of credit spreads during the global financial crisis may also have contributed to the affordability of swaps compared with de-risking solutions that require an upfront premium. This may have resulted because of a mismatch in the perception of credit default risk between the risk acquirers and the sellers of the block of business, a situation that possibly caused risk acquirers to be less willing to assume a large allowance for the credit spreads available on corporate bonds when pricing upfront deals. This reservation translated into a reduction in asset values suffered by the transferring company as a result of the widened spreads not being reflected in the price.

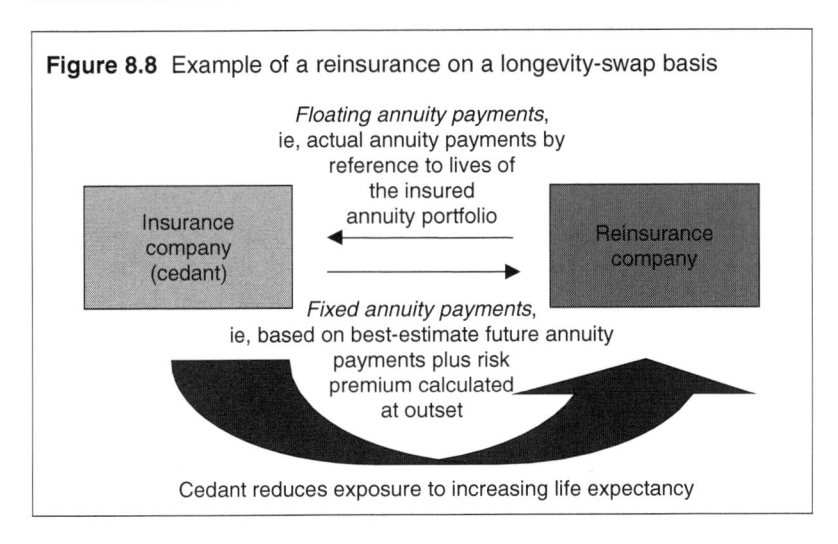

Figure 8.8 Example of a reinsurance on a longevity-swap basis

```
                    Floating annuity payments,
                 ie, actual annuity payments by
                      reference to lives of
                          the insured
   ┌──────────┐        annuity portfolio       ┌──────────┐
   │ Insurance│ ◄─────────────────────────────│Reinsurance│
   │ company  │                                │ company  │
   │ (cedant) │ ─────────────────────────────►│          │
   └──────────┘                                └──────────┘
                   Fixed annuity payments,
              ie, based on best-estimate future
                annuity payments plus risk
                 premium calculated
                       at outset

       Cedant reduces exposure to increasing life expectancy
```

Longevity swaps also have the flexibility to allow the transferring company to retain non-longevity risks such as interest rate and inflation risk and typically companies have retained these risks in longevity-swap transactions seen so far. Conversely, insurers who wish to manage interest rate and inflation risks can also incorporate other financial derivatives such as interest rate swaps within the longevity-swap structure.

Similar to other reinsurance structures, the longevity swap exposes the cedant to counterparty risk in the event that the reinsurer defaults on its obligations, and the cedant is left with the ultimate responsibility for paying the annuities to its policyholders. This risk can be mitigated by collateral arrangements. The amount of collateral can be determined on a number of different bases; one approach is to use a pre-agreed basis to calculate a best estimate of the value of future annuity payments, which is regularly reviewed. An alternative approach is to collateralise the arrangement in line with regulatory requirements, especially where this is needed to achieve capital relief for the cedant (although this is likely to be more expensive).

An example of a longevity swap written on an indemnity basis is shown in Figure 8.8.

Other management solutions

In addition to the solutions described above, there have been various innovative and alternative approaches adopted by insurance companies in their efforts to manage their annuity business.

A solution adopted by one of the largest UK annuity writers is the separation of its annuity business from other business in the fund. The separation was achieved by fully reinsuring the annuity business into a newly established internal reinsurance company. Initially, the internal reinsurance arrangement resulted in a solvency capital requirement that was nearly twice that under the group's original structure. However, the internal reinsurance company was then converted into an Insurance Special Purpose Vehicle (ISPV), which did not have the same capital requirements as a fully authorised insurer and which was only required to be solvent under generally accepted accounting practices. However, it was still required to comply with certain FSA regulations and therefore, in practice, a buffer of assets would typically have been held within the ISPV for regulatory prudence. Nevertheless, the capital requirement of the internal reinsurance company was reduced upon its conversion into an ISPV, and the company achieved its target of separating its annuity business from other business via an internal risk transfer.

Capital markets transactions

If the insurer intends to transfer only the longevity risk to a third party, one of the other key decisions is whether to pass the risk to a reinsurance company or to channel the risk via an investment bank to the capital markets. The credit rating of the reinsurance company or the investment bank will be a key consideration. The reinsurance route is a more tried and tested route and the risk acquirer is subject to the insurance regulatory regime. However, the capacity of reinsurers for longevity risk is finite and the price of off-loading risk to reinsurers will rise as capacity declines.

In a capital markets transaction, risk is not transferred to a regulated entity such as a reinsurance company, but is usually transferred to investors via some form of securitisation or derivative contract. Derivative transactions are usually subject to a different regulatory regime, and are likely to fall under the auspices of the International Swaps and Derivatives Association (ISDA).

Capital market transactions for longevity risk transfers have typically been in the form of longevity swaps, although longevity bonds are also possible. The structure of longevity-swap transactions is similar in many respects to those described above, except the insurer's immediate counterparty in the capital market longevity

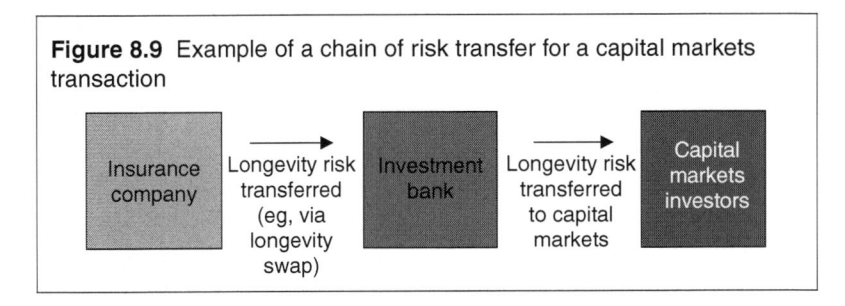

Figure 8.9 Example of a chain of risk transfer for a capital markets transaction

| Insurance company | → Longevity risk transferred (eg, via longevity swap) | Investment bank | → Longevity risk transferred to capital markets | Capital markets investors |

swap is usually an investment bank instead of a reinsurance company. Capital markets transactions are usually arranged through a lead investment bank, which may then redistribute the risk to end investors, as illustrated in Figure 8.9.

Generating enough investor interest is a challenge for the development of capital market solutions. Many of the investors behind capital market transactions have been reinsurers that are already familiar with longevity risk, or specialist hedge fund investors, who have gained comfort through the reinsurer's assessment of the risk or a risk analysis report prepared by a third party independent of the transaction. However, the development of capital markets solutions and the interest of other investors are essential in view of the likely lack of capacity in the insurance and reinsurance market in the future. Further discussion on the role of the capital markets is provided in Chapter 12.

An advantage of passing risk to the capital markets is that investors may not be subject to the capital requirements of (re)-insurance regulated entities. In countries where the insurance regulatory regime is relatively strong, this may allow for a more favourable pricing of risk. In addition, the low level of correlation that is generally believed to exist between longevity risk and market risk could be appealing to investors who want to diversify their portfolio away from volatile equity and bond markets. However, as the market in traded longevity instruments is not yet deep and liquid, the pricing of such deals is still subject to considerable variation, and investors may demand a larger risk premium than a reinsurer.

The main concern of a longevity swap is counterparty default risk, which is usually managed via collateral arrangements, in the same way as for standard financial derivative contracts.

In addition, longevity swaps can also be structured in terms of an exchange of payments based on mortality forward rates, as shown in

Figure 8.10 Example of a capital markets transaction on a mortality forward (*q*-forward) basis

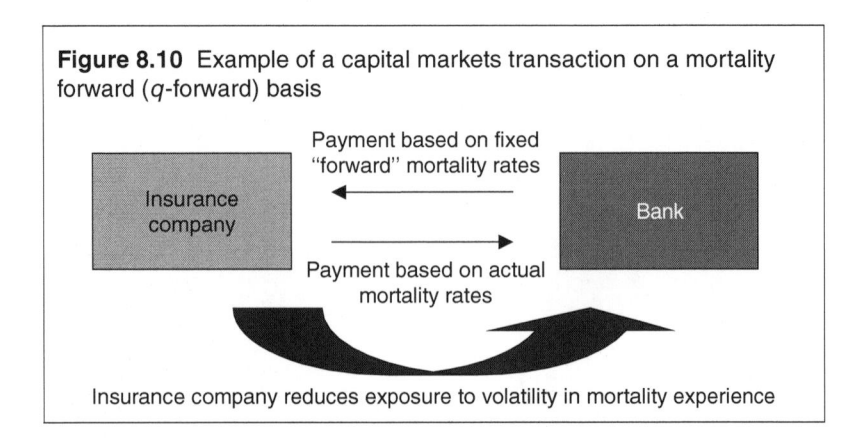

Insurance company ←— Payment based on fixed "forward" mortality rates —— Bank

Payment based on actual mortality rates ——→

Insurance company reduces exposure to volatility in mortality experience

Figure 8.10. These arrangements are also described in further detail in Chapter 12.

Capital market transactions for longevity risk can also be structured in the form of longevity bonds. This structure was first publicly attempted by European Investment Bank, BNP Paribas and PartnerRe in 2004, but no bonds were issued due to the lack of investor interest as well as the perceived high cost and the level of basis risk involved. Moreover, the capital intensive nature of longevity bonds makes it unlikely that they will be well received until stable financial conditions return.

Longevity bonds can be structured such that the bondholder either accepts or transfers the longevity risk. For the purpose of illustration, an example of a potential longevity bond structure in which the bondholder transfers the longevity risk to the capital markets is shown in Figure 8.11.

In the long term, reinsurers' finite capacity for longevity risk makes the development of the capital markets an essential component of a well-functioning insurance and reinsurance environment. Otherwise, the price of off-loading risk to reinsurers is likely to rise as this capacity declines. For this reason, the pricing of capital markets transactions is likely to become more competitive relative to reinsurers, particularly as the capital markets develop further. At the same time, reinsurers will benefit from the development of the capital markets to off-load their risk and free-up capital to write a more diversified portfolio of risks.

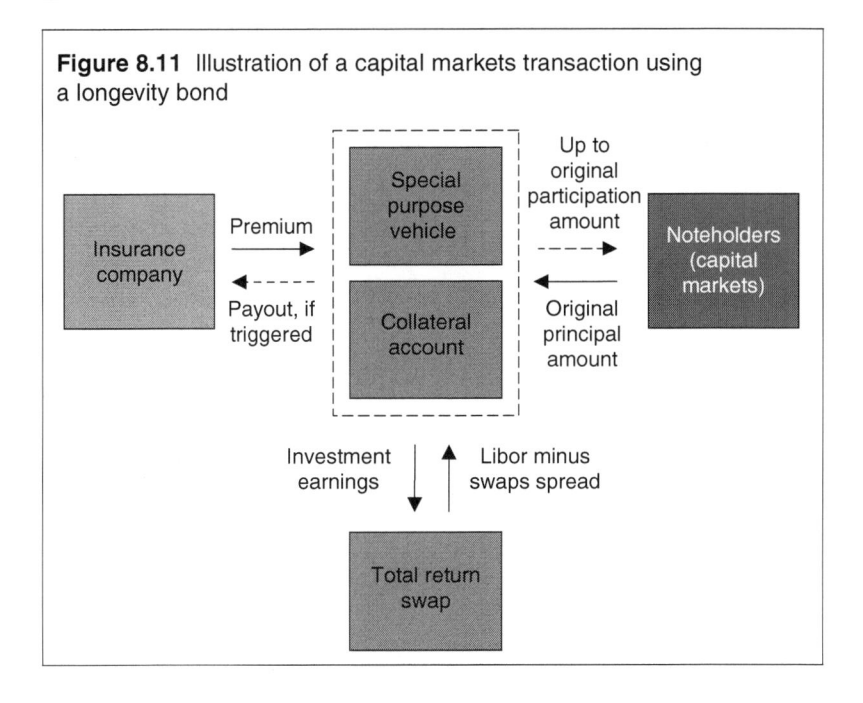

Figure 8.11 Illustration of a capital markets transaction using a longevity bond

[Insurance company] ⟷ [Special purpose vehicle] (Premium →, Payout, if triggered ←)

Special purpose vehicle → Noteholders (capital markets): Up to original participation amount

Noteholders (capital markets) → Special purpose vehicle: Original principal amount

Collateral account: Investment earnings ↓, Libor minus swaps spread ↑

Total return swap

RECENT MARKET ACTIVITY

The UK market has been at the forefront of annuity portfolio and longevity risk transfers and has been perceived to contain some of the first and leading edge examples of such transactions globally. Table 8.2 gives a summary of some of the major UK insured annuity risk transfer transactions which have taken place in recent years.

Most of the earlier de-risking solutions for annuity business were structured as full annuity portfolio transfers or single premium annuity reinsurance on a quota-share basis, both established methods of risk transfer within the insurance industry. Since 2008, longevity swaps, which have been arranged as either reinsurance or capital markets transactions, have gained in popularity as a de-risking solution.

At the time of writing, most of the longevity swaps have been structured on an indemnity basis. The first public deal on a parametric q-forward basis was between JP Morgan and Lucida and took place in February 2008 (an example of a q-forward transaction structure is illustrated in Figure 8.10). The largest public longevity swap between a reinsurer and insurer was the £3.9 billion longevity swap between Swiss Re and Zurich Financial Services in 2007. The largest

Table 8.2 Summary of major annuity risk transfer transactions for insurance and reinsurance companies at time of writing

Date	Risk to	Risk from	Size (£ bn)	Deal type
Reinsurance arrangements and capital market transactions				
2005	XL Re	Cooperative Insurance	1.0	Longevity swap
2007	Swiss Re	Cooperative Insurance	1.8	Single premium annuity reinsurance
2007	Swiss Re	Zurich Financial Services	3.9	Longevity swap (bundled)
2008	Canada Life (International Re)	Standard Life	6.7	Single premium annuity reinsurance
2008	Swiss Re	Friends Provident	1.7	Single premium annuity reinsurance
2008	Pacific Life Re plus others	Abbey Life	1.3	Longevity swap
2008	JP Morgan	Lucida	0.1	10-yr longevity swap (parametric)
2008	JP Morgan	Canada Life	0.5	40-yr longevity swap (indemnity)
2008	Prudential	Rothesay Life	0.3	Single premium annuity reinsurance
2009	RBS / PartnerRe plus others	Aviva	0.5	10-yr longevity swap (indemnity)
2009	Pacific Life Re	Rothesay Life	ca. 0.5	Longevity swap
2009	Pacific Life Re	Credit Suisse	0.3	50-yr longevity swap (indemnity)
2009	Pacific Life Re	Credit Suisse	0.3	50-yr longevity swap (indemnity)
Portfolio (Part VII) transfers				
2005	Canada Life	Resolution	2.2	Full annuity portfolio transfer
2005	Prudential	Royal London	1.7	Full annuity portfolio transfer
2005	Prudential	Resolution	1.5	Full annuity portfolio transfer
2007	Canada Life	Equitable Life	4.6	Full annuity portfolio transfer
2008	Prudential	Equitable Life	1.8	Full annuity portfolio transfer

Source: press releases.

> **Figure 8.12** Overview of large insured bulk annuity transaction
>
> The largest public transaction, shown in Table 8.2, was between Canada Life (International Re) and Standard Life during 2008. It involved a reinsurance transaction in which Standard Life off-loaded the longevity risk of over half of its annuity customers, with total assets of £6.7 billion transferred.
>
> The portfolio primarily consists of existing Standard Life pension customers, who took out an annuity policy on retirement. 90% of Standard Life's annuity sales are conversions from its existing pension policyholders.
>
> The annuity reinsurance transaction was driven by the Standard Life Heritage With-Profits Fund's increasing exposure to longevity risk. The deal provided a significant increase to Standard Life's embedded value operating profit because of a reduction in shareholder burnthrough risk, a release of cash from reserve and a reduction in capital requirements. In addition to the reduced exposure to longevity risk the Standard Life With-Profits Heritage Fund benefited through an enhancement of its residual estate.
>
> Other examples of deals driven by the increasing level of longevity risk in with-profits funds are the Part VII transfers of £1.8 billion of with-profits annuity business from Equitable Life to Prudential in 2007, and £4.6 billion of annuities from Equitable Life to Canada Life in 2008.

bulk annuity public transaction was the reinsurance arrangement between Canada Life (International Re) and Standard Life during 2008. A summary of this transaction is provided in Figure 8.12.

KEY STRUCTURAL DECISIONS FOR LONGEVITY RISK MITIGATION

As described earlier, there are a number of risk transfer options available to a life insurance company that wishes to transfer the underlying risks in a block of annuity business. The choice of structure, however, will typically depend on a number of factors, including the type of risk to be transferred. The flow diagram in Figure 8.13 summarises the key considerations in selecting a longevity risk transfer method. The longevity bond option is not included because of its lack of popularity at the time of writing. In addition to those issues raised in the diagram, there will be further considerations such as the type of counterparty to engage, the detailed features of the structure and the cost implications of each option.

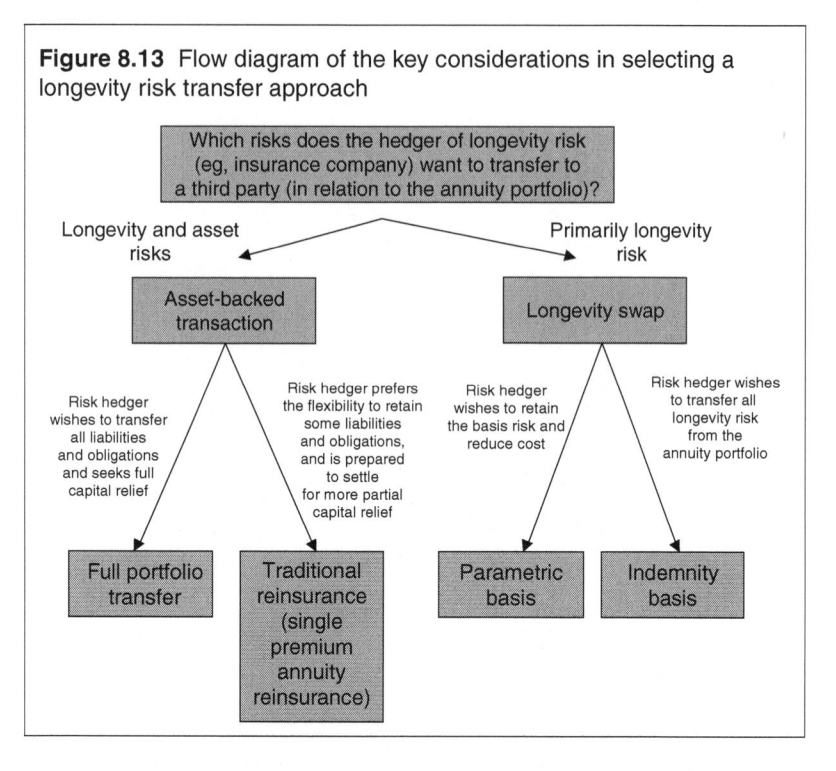

Figure 8.13 Flow diagram of the key considerations in selecting a longevity risk transfer approach

- Which risks does the hedger of longevity risk (eg, insurance company) want to transfer to a third party (in relation to the annuity portfolio)?
  - Longevity and asset risks → **Asset-backed transaction**
    - Risk hedger wishes to transfer all liabilities and obligations and seeks full capital relief → **Full portfolio transfer**
    - Risk hedger prefers the flexibility to retain some liabilities and obligations, and is prepared to settle for more partial capital relief → **Traditional reinsurance (single premium annuity reinsurance)**
  - Primarily longevity risk → **Longevity swap**
    - Risk hedger wishes to retain the basis risk and reduce cost → **Parametric basis**
    - Risk hedger wishes to transfer all longevity risk from the annuity portfolio → **Indemnity basis**

Asset-backed transaction versus longevity swap

An insurer needs to decide if it wants to transfer the longevity risk only and retain the asset risk, or transfer some or all of the asset and longevity risks to a third party. Asset-backed transactions enable the insurer to transfer some or all of the asset and longevity risks. For an insurer that intends to retain the asset risk and is only concerned with transferring longevity risk, a longevity-swap structure is likely to be a more feasible option. Some risk acquirers will actively seek out asset-backed transactions with the aim of managing the assets and credit risk to yield a higher return.

However, asset-backed transactions can be more expensive than longevity risk-only transactions for the risk hedger. For example, in the traditional reinsurance arrangement the risk acquirer may need to post a large amount of upfront collateral, the cost of which is typically charged to the risk hedger. In the case of full annuity portfolio transfers, the transaction is usually time consuming and costly because of the often rigorous regulatory process that needs to be followed. Costs may include legal fees and any outgo required in order to comply with local regulatory requirements. These costs may be shared between the transferring company and the risk acquirer.

Longevity swaps remove the need for an upfront transfer of assets from both parties and allow the transferring company to retain risk-reward potential on its assets, while providing an effective transfer of longevity risk to the risk acquirer.

Asset-backed transaction: traditional reinsurance versus full annuity portfolio transfer

An asset-backed transaction in which there is a full portfolio transfer has no counterparty risk and associated capital requirement because it involves a complete transfer of all liabilities and obligations related to the annuity portfolio to the risk acquirer. It should also allow the insurer full capital relief on the risk that has been transferred, which is not necessarily the case for reinsurance under local regulatory regimes. However, full portfolio transfers do not allow the insurer to retain any of the risk on the transferring policies. Such transfers may also be costly and lengthy processes for the parties involved. There is also a risk that the transfer may not be approved (eg, by the court or the regulator, where applicable) on the proposed terms.

A traditional reinsurance transaction, such as a quota-share reinsurance arrangement, would typically be much quicker to arrange and implement than a full portfolio transfer. It is also likely to allow for more flexibility in the way in which the risks retained by the insurer are structured. However, full capital relief on the risks transferred is not necessarily always available on reinsurance transactions, as discussed earlier, although at the time of writing the position in Europe is likely to improve under Solvency II.

A reinsurance arrangement may also be an interim solution while the full portfolio transfer process is completed.

Longevity swap: indemnity versus parametric

Indemnity basis transactions typically provide a means of achieving a more complete risk transfer, because the risk transferred is based on the actual longevity experience of the annuity portfolio rather than a separate reference portfolio. For this reason, the structure is likely to be more closely aligned to the interests of, say, an insurer wishing to off-load all of its longevity risk. However, the pricing of such deals will generally reflect the increased uncertainty in quantifying longevity risk of the specific annuity portfolio, particularly if it is a small annuitant portfolio with variable mortality experience and the swap is structured over a long duration. Therefore, insurers that wish to enter into such transactions may pay a higher risk premium relative to that charged for a parametric solution based on a larger, more stable block of lives such as the general population. An indemnity structure usually has more rigorous due-diligence and higher monitoring costs due to lack of transparency from the risk acquirer's viewpoint.

Parametric basis transactions pass on the longevity risk with reference to longevity data such as population mortality experience via some form of mortality index that is independent of the underlying portfolio. Therefore, residual "basis" risk between the population and specific annuity portfolio remains with the insurer. In theory, such transactions have the advantage of being priced more competitively due to the increased transparency, and of potentially being simpler to set up. This structure is also more popular with investors because of its greater objectivity and simplicity compared with an indemnity basis structure. Several large investment banks have developed mortality indices, and as the methodology for producing these becomes more standardised, index-based deals could gain wider acceptance among many investment banks and capital market investors that have already shown an interest in them.

In 2010, the Life & Longevity Markets Association (LLMA) was created with the aim to "break down the barriers to market growth by seeking the development of consistent standards, methodologies and benchmarks" (http://www.llma.org). Its work is likely to facilitate the market in parametric as well as other capital markets deals. For example, the LLMA launched a consultation on a longevity index framework in August 2010 (Life & Longevity Markets Association 2010) with a view to developing an industry standard approach to longevity indices. However, it may be difficult for parametric structures to gain popularity with insurers due to the proposed regulatory constraints under Solvency II, which limit the credit that can be taken by insurers for risk mitigation techniques that involve a significant basis risk, although we may see a more capital efficient solution being developed by the capital markets in view of Solvency II regulations.

Other risk transfer considerations include the term of the transaction, the measure of longevity and its exposure and decisions related to whether other risks, such as inflation risk, should be retained or transferred by the insurer.

CONCLUSION

Many factors are driving insurance companies to strategically de-risk their annuity business. However, the choice of de-risking approach will largely be based on the type of risk to be transferred and the resulting amount of capital reduction expected to be achieved under local regulations and under Solvency II.

Asset-backed transactions, such as traditional reinsurance arrangements and full portfolio transfers, are well established in some markets, particularly the UK, and will continue to be used by insurers as both asset risk and longevity risk mitigation solutions. However, longevity swaps, either through a reinsurance company or via the capital markets, will remain a popular solution for those seeking only to de-risk longevity and especially for insurers preferring to retain the assets that back their annuity portfolios. It is likely that innovative solutions, such as longevity bonds, will continue to be developed to de-risk or manage insured annuity business, particularly with the development of a more liquid traded market in longevity-related risk.

REFERENCES

Life & Longevity Markets Association, 2010, "Longevity Index Framework: A Framework for Building Longevity Indices Developed by the LLMA", URL: http://www.llma.org.

9

Longevity De-Risking Solutions for Pension Schemes

Norman Peard, James Morris

Credit Suisse

This chapter sets out to summarise the main methods adopted in de-risking longevity risk within corporate pension schemes such as employer-sponsored defined-benefit pension schemes. Longevity-swap transactions that focus on the transfer of longevity risk have been a major development and the UK has been at the forefront of such transactions globally. Therefore, this chapter focuses primarily on longevity swaps but also touches on some of the wider solutions such as buy-outs and buy-ins that are aimed at de-risking market risk alongside longevity risk.

This chapter includes

- an introductory description of the main tools available to trustees looking to de-risk a pension scheme (buy-outs, buy-ins and longevity swaps),
- a summary of the main categories of membership of such schemes in relation to which each is typically most relevant and the principal market and demographic risks transferred,
- a summary of some of the advantages and drawbacks of each approach, including a discussion of the relative merits of funded and unfunded solutions and the assessment and management of credit risk,
- an outline of a strategy of "progressive de-risking" being adopted by the trustees of many pension schemes,
- a more detailed discussion of longevity swaps,
- an introduction to some of the more sophisticated variations of longevity swaps (longevity swaps with bespoke fixed legs, synthetic buy-ins, insurance-wrapped solutions),

- other features relevant to the implementation of a longevity swap including novation and early termination, administration, overpayments and late notifications, as well as considerations for trustees and for sponsors.

THE MAIN DE-RISKING TOOLS AVAILABLE TO THE TRUSTEES OF A PENSION SCHEME

There are three main tools available to trustees who want to de-risk a pension scheme. Two involve insurers and the third principally involves investment banks and (re)insurers. The three tools are

- buy-outs under which risks are transferred to an insurer,
- buy-ins under which risks are hedged with an insurer and
- longevity swaps under which risks are (typically) hedged with an investment bank and (re)insurers.

Buy-out: de-risking by transferring the risk

In a buy-out, individual members of the pension scheme transfer their rights under the pension scheme to new pension plans operated by an insurance company (Figure 9.1). The new plans may not precisely reflect the terms of the existing arrangement, but the benefits related to annuities in payment should be reproduced by the new insured plan.

Once a full buy-out has been completed, the individual members concerned have a relationship directly with the insurer and cease to have any financial relationship to the pension scheme trustees of the original scheme. Under a partial buy-out only selected members will be affected.

Following the payment of a single premium to the insurer, assets and liabilities are transferred from the pension scheme to the insurer into the new individual pension plans (Table 9.1). Consequently, this transaction removes, or de-risks, the scheme of all risks including both asset risk and longevity risk. Some insurers have also offered experience refunds in relation to the buy-out, for example based around longevity assumptions.

The credit rating of the insurer and regulatory regime under which it operates are key considerations in evaluating buy-outs as an option, especially because, in the unlikely event that the insurer fails to meet its obligations to the individual members, they will

Figure 9.1 Overview of buy-out structure

```
                    Payment of single premium
        ┌──────────────────────────────────────┐
        ▼                                      │
   ┌──────────┐   Transfer    ┌───────────┐   Pay member
   │ Pension  │──liability───▶│ Insurance │──▶   or
   │ scheme   │               │ company   │    scheme
   └──────────┘               └───────────┘
        ▲                           │
        └───────────────────────────┘
           Experience refunds, if applicable
```

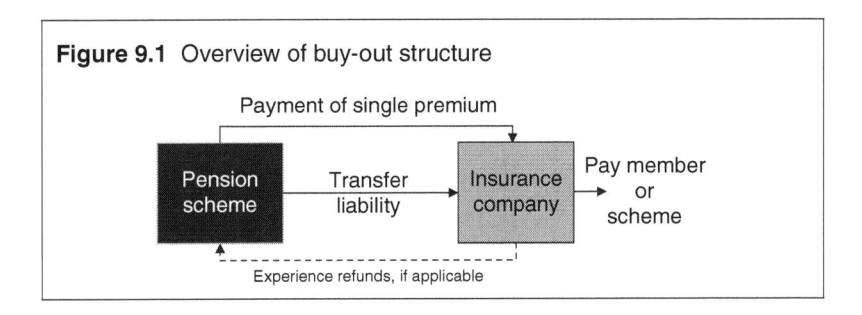

Table 9.1 Overview of buy-out structure

	Full buy-out	Partial buy-out
Assets and liabilities	Full transfer Liabilities discharged	Proportion converted to annuities
Responsibility	Insurer: all liabilities	Insurer: agreed liabilities
Charging structure	Single premium	Single premium

suffer a loss. The financial strength and capital of the insurer will also need to be considered in relation to the strength of any existing employer covenant on the pension scheme and the regulatory regime that applies to the pension scheme. For example, in the UK, the pensions regulatory regime is generally less restrictive regarding the possible investment of assets than the insurance regulatory regime. In addition, the pensions regime allows deficits, whereas UK insurers are subject to additional solvency requirements, including an internal capital assessment on an economic capital basis aimed at limiting the risk of "ruin" to less than 1 in 200 over a 12-month period.

Other key considerations in selecting an insurer for buy-out include price, market reputation and commitment, quality of administration, the ability to split, say, pensioners and individuals with deferred pensions between insurers which offer differential terms, and additional innovative features such as experience refunds.

Buy-in: the "traditional" route to hedging pensioners

In a buy-in, the pension scheme passes assets to an insurance company in exchange for an agreement from the insurance company to assume, by means of an insurance policy issued to the trustees, the liability to pay pensions to the existing pensioners of the scheme. The insurance policy purchased by the pension fund trustees will meet an agreed set of benefits due to an agreed list of members of the pension fund. The purchase of insurance is a hedge in the sense that the pension fund retains the obligations to the scheme members, but the risk is matched by the claims received under the insurance policy. The effectiveness of the hedge, of course, depends on the financial strength of the insurer and the regulatory regime under which it operates. The insurance company must remain solvent and meet all of its obligations for the effective transfer of both asset and longevity risks.

The price of a buy-in depends on insurance company capital requirements, longevity estimates and the current value of the pension scheme assets transferred. The buy-in premium, which needs to be paid to the reinsurer, usually includes an amount in addition to the transfer of pension scheme assets held against the liabilities to the members.

The pension scheme effectively takes long-dated credit risk to the insurance company that has sold the buy-in policy. While the buy-in is often uncollateralised in relation to the specific pension scheme, the insurer should be funded according to the local regulatory requirements under which it operates. However, the pension scheme no longer has control over the underlying pool of assets. In the event of an insurance company becoming insolvent, the pension scheme would typically have only a senior unsecured claim against the insurance company. If the policy is not individually collateralised, the monetary value of this claim could be very large.

Longevity swaps

Traditionally longevity risk could only be hedged with annuities in buy-out/buy-in transactions. This has become onerous in terms of funding requirements, as pension schemes seeking to transfer only longevity risk have also needed to transfer assets. As an alternative, longevity swaps offer a more efficient way to achieve the transfer of longevity risk alone, from a funding perspective, than buy-outs or buy-ins, because assets do not need to be transferred initially. A longevity swap can be transacted to transfer risks in relation to the pensioner category of member.

The basic features of a longevity swap typically include:

- the swap provider, or risk-accepting counterparty to the swap (eg, an investment bank or insurer), pays cash amounts to the

pension scheme trustees equal to the actual pensions payable over the lifetime of the pensioners or for a defined period;
- the pension scheme pays pre-determined monthly amounts over a fixed period of time to the swap provider.

There is usually no upfront funding requirement, ie, no assets need to be transferred from the pension scheme at the outset. Indeed, during the term of the swap, the two sets of cashflows are netted and only the net amount is paid from the pension scheme to the swap provider or vice versa.

Longevity-swap transactions with an investment bank as swap provider are typically fully collateralised (normally in accordance with the terms of an International Swaps and Derivatives Association (ISDA) governed Credit Support Annex (CSA)) and the pension scheme trustees retain legal and physical ownership of the pension scheme assets. The pension fund's credit exposure to the investment bank is thus structured to be minimal. The capital held by an insurer accepting the risk on such transactions typically depends on the local regulatory regime in which the insurer operates. For example, in the UK, a prudent valuation is required as well as an internal capital assessment on an economic capital basis aimed at limiting the risk of "ruin" to less than 1 in 200 over a 12-month period. Some insurers may also be willing to put in place collateral account mechanisms according to a pre-determined basis but will charge accordingly, as this would typically require additional capital to be held over and above the regulatory capital. In assessing the relative merits of various alternative longevity-swap structures, an important factor is the relative likelihood that the counterparty will default on its obligations during the term of the arrangement and the potential loss given default, making allowance for the significant risk-mitigating effect of any collateral arrangements.

THE RELATIONSHIP OF SOLUTIONS TO MEMBERSHIP CATEGORIES AND RISKS TRANSFERRED

A description of the main approaches to pension scheme de-risking is aided by a reference to the following two criteria:
- the categories of membership directly affected;
- the main market and demographic risks transferred.

Principal categories of membership

The membership of a pension scheme can, in general, be divided into the following principal categories:

- pensioners;
- deferred pensioners;
- "actives".

Pensioners have benefits that are generally lifetime annuities or pensions in payment and are fixed in the sense that no further benefits are accruing, since these members have left employment and their benefits are already determined and in payment. For these reasons, pensioners are the easiest category for which longevity risk can be hedged.

Deferred pensioners are those individuals who have left employment but are not yet receiving annuity benefits (for example, because they are still younger than the retirement age at which pensions are payable under the terms of the pension scheme). While the benefits are largely pre-determined and fixed in the sense that no further benefits are accruing, hedging longevity risk that is associated with the benefits of deferred pensioners is typically not as easy as that associated with pensioners because deferred pensioners may opt to take a transfer value and move to alternative pension arrangements.

"Actives" are those members still in active service with the sponsoring employer and thus still accruing benefits in respect of their continuing service. Benefits accrued to date are, in a sense, fixed, but these members, like deferred pensioners, may opt to take a transfer value and move to alternative pension arrangements.

Not only do rights accrue to members of the scheme, but reversionary benefits may also accrue, which are payable to dependants of the member following the member's death. These reversionary benefits are present in respect of members in each of the principal membership categories. Assessing the dependency profile of pensioner members tends to be easiest because precise data pertaining to their dependants tends to have been collected at retirement, which is less likely to be the case for the other categories, and the data for pensioners' dependants also tends to have a lower likelihood of changing.

Main market and demographic risks

Employer-sponsored pension schemes are exposed to a wide range of significant risks. These can usefully be grouped into two broad categories: market (asset) risks and demographic risks.

Market risks include equity, property (real estate), interest rate, inflation and credit risk.

Demographic risks include longevity risk and risks associated with member choice, such as the extent to which members opt to transfer benefits to another scheme or the proportion of members in respect of which reversionary benefits are payable to their dependants.

Market risks can in general be hedged with market instruments, such as interest rate, inflation and credit default swaps. Some are less easily hedged than others; for example, markets for property and inflation hedges tend to be less deep and less liquid than those for interest rate or equity hedges.

Longevity risk can be transferred or hedged using longevity swaps as described above. Both buy-outs and buy-ins achieve longevity risk transfer and hedging at the same time as transferring market risk; consequently, for pension funds seeking to transfer only longevity risk and retain exposure to market risk in anticipation of long-term positive returns, these may not always be desirable.

Longevity risk may be hedged in isolation using longevity swaps. Since assets are not transferred from the pension fund, the trustees retain the potential for upside but also the risk of downside. If it is desired, market risks may be hedged separately, which can improve transparency in the overall management of the pension fund's assets.

The risks associated with member actions are less easily hedged. To some extent the risk associated with lack of precise knowledge about the proportion of members in respect of which reversionary benefits accrue may be transferred in any of the main approaches, but the cost of transferring this risk is high.

Risks associated with members opting to transfer benefits to another pension plan are typically not hedgeable, but they are effectively transferred in a buy-out.

As longevity risk has become the main focus of hedging of demographic risk for pension funds, especially in the UK, it is important to briefly consider the importance of longevity assumptions.

As recently as 2005, many pension schemes paid little attention to their longevity assumptions, partly because valuation interest rates were relatively high, which meant that an extra year of life had little impact on liability values.

More recently a number of factors have led many schemes to focus much more heavily on their longevity assumptions. Often the result has been a significant increase in the assumed life expectancy. The key drivers for this focus have been lower real discount rates, publication of improvement cohorts and intervention of the Pensions Regulator.

The use of more conservative longevity assumptions and the greater sensitivity of funding levels to changes in longevity assumptions in an environment of low (real) interest rate have led many pension schemes to look at ways of hedging their longevity risk. Schemes want to minimise the impact of future potential step changes in longevity assumptions. Importantly, the use of more conservative assumptions by a pension scheme means the views of the longevity market and the assumptions underlying the valuation of the pension scheme are increasingly in line with each other.

Comparison of different solutions' abilities to transfer risk

Buy-outs may be used to transfer all demographic and market risks in relation to "actives", deferred pensioners and pensioners.

Buy-ins are typically used in relation to the risks associated with benefits for pensioners and reversionary benefits due to their dependants. Like buy-outs, they may be used to transfer all demographic and market risks.

Longevity swaps are typically applicable to pensioner members and, while variations which transfer market risk are available, in their basic form they transfer demographic risk in isolation.

SOME ADVANTAGES AND DRAWBACKS OF BUY-OUTS, BUY-INS AND LONGEVITY SWAPS

A buy-out is the only arrangement suitable to achieve a full de-risking of a pension plan, since it is the only format which severs the financial relationship between the members and the plan, and thus from the sponsoring employer. However, its implementation usually requires the acceptance of the arrangement by the plan members affected and requires the pension fund to move to be fully funded on a buy-out basis.

A buy-in is readily amenable to transferring market and longevity risks on schemes with pensioner members. It can be used to de-risk schemes in respect of pensioner members in isolation, or in conjunction with a buy-out in respect of "actives" and deferred pensioners to achieve a near complete de-risking. The use of a buy-in results in incomplete de-risking, because the obligations of the insurer are typically not collateralised in respect of the specific scheme and thus a material credit exposure arises. The level of this risk will depend on the local regulatory regime and credit rating of the insurance company and will be lower for those that are well capitalised. Some insurers may also offer collateral account mechanisms but, as discussed previously, this is likely to come at a higher cost.

Both buy-ins and buy-outs are funded solutions and require the pension fund to pass across ownership of its assets in return for the future protection offered. Future upside potential (as well as downside risk) is therefore lost. When the scheme is insufficiently funded, it is impractical to de-risk using these approaches without a significant capital injection into the scheme first. Consequently, a strategy of "progressive de-risking", which starts with unfunded longevity risk transfer, may be preferred for such schemes and is described below.

Under Solvency II, the capital requirements for insurance companies which offer buy-in solutions to hedging longevity risks are, at the time of writing, expected to increase, leading to considerably higher buy-in costs. This could act as a further driver for longevity hedging using derivative contracts, such as longevity swaps.

Longevity swaps may be used in relation to pensioner members. In their basic form, they transform longevity risk, either in isolation or together with the demographic risk associated with reversionary benefits, but in any event independently of market risk. However, variations may be used to transfer market risk also. They may be used to hedge longevity risk while still taking advantage of market opportunities from which trustees wish potentially to profit. For example, trustees may wish to benefit from the yield on UK government gilts relative to the trustees' assessment of the default risk (see the section on longevity swaps with bespoke fixed legs below). As an unfunded approach, swaps have the major advantage that the scheme can be de-risked even in the absence of sufficient funding to de-risk using a buy-out or buy-in mechanism.

A further differentiator of longevity swaps is the mitigation of credit risk through collateralisation. A full assessment of the relative merits is beyond the scope of this chapter, but the risk associated with the default of the counterparty varies depending on, among other items, whether a buy-out, buy-in or longevity swap has been implemented, the regulatory regime under which the counterparty operates and whether or not a collateral account mechanism has been put in place.

In the case of a buy-out, the credit risk of a default of the insurer rests with the individual member. In the case of a buy-in, the credit risk of a default of the insurer rests with the pension scheme and thus, ultimately, with the sponsoring employer. The insurance-contractual nature of the agreement may give access to the protections offered by local compensation schemes such as the Financial Services Compensation Scheme (FSCS) in the UK, but these protections neither are guaranteed nor provide for the full amount of the obligations of the insurer. In contrast, the collateralisation of the longevity swap is for the full assessed value of the swap, with haircuts reflecting any risks associated with the nature of the collateral posted. Trustees will need to consider the relative merits carefully.

THE STRATEGY OF "PROGRESSIVE DE-RISKING"

A large proportion of employer-sponsored defined-benefit pension schemes (for example, in the UK) are in deficit on a buy-out basis. As discussed above, a buy-out is the only arrangement suitable to achieve a full de-risking of a pension plan because it is the only format which severs the financial relationship between the members and the plan, and thus from the sponsoring employer.

Rather than implementing a full buy-out, for those schemes for which the sponsoring employer cannot currently afford the injection of further contributions into the pension fund, one strategy being adopted is "progressive de-risking". The approach is initially to hedge longevity risk on the basis of an unfunded longevity swap, retaining the exposure to the pension scheme assets and thus to the anticipated long-term investment upside. The intention is to wait until this investment upside is realised and, once the scheme funding improves, to implement a full buy-out. As individual asset classes achieve the objective, a decision may be taken also to hedge individual market risks. Thus, there is a progressive de-risking of the pension fund. As discussed later in this chapter, the longevity swap should be structured so as not to interfere with the eventual implementation of a buy-out and, hence, should include appropriate recapture clauses, novation clauses or the like.

As reinsurance solutions are covered in depth in the next chapter of this book, the following illustrations of longevity swaps focus primarily on longevity de-risking solutions that involve an investment bank or insurer. Many of the design features remain the same for both, except that the collateral account mechanisms tend to be an optional feature of (re)insurance longevity swaps.

LONGEVITY SWAPS IN MORE DETAIL

As noted above, a longevity swap (Figure 9.2) can be transacted to transfer risks in relation to the pensioner category of member. Under the terms of an unfunded longevity swap,

- the swap provider, or risk-accepting counterparty to the swap (eg, the investment bank or insurer) will pay cash amounts to the trustees of the pension scheme equal to the actual pensions payable over the lifetime of the pensioners (the "floating leg"),
- in return for receiving the floating leg, the pension scheme will pay a pre-defined series of cashflows to the swap provider payable for a fixed period of time (the "fixed leg").

The fixed leg payable by the pension scheme typically comprises the best-estimate projection of the pension amounts to be paid plus a longevity risk hedging fee. The fixed leg therefore has a very similar "shape" to the expected pension payments (Figure 9.3).

The swap typically has a term of up to 50 years when the swap is transacted with an investment bank and an unlimited term with an insurer.

The swap provider will usually provide administration of the swap (death tracking, escalations, etc).

The transaction is typically fully collateralised to mitigate credit exposure when the swap provider is an investment bank. The credit exposure will be somewhat mitigated depending on the level of capital held in accordance with local regulatory requirements when the swap provider is an insurer.

Figure 9.2 Longevity-swap structure

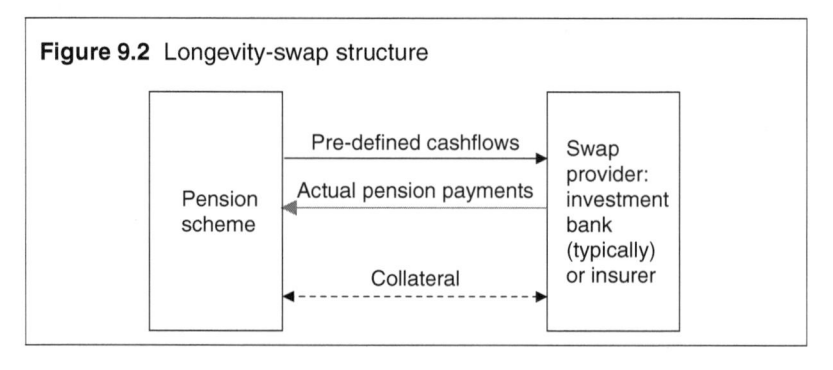

Pension scheme — Pre-defined cashflows → Swap provider: investment bank (typically) or insurer
Swap provider → Actual pension payments → Pension scheme
Collateral ←-------

Figure 9.3 Longevity-swap cashflows

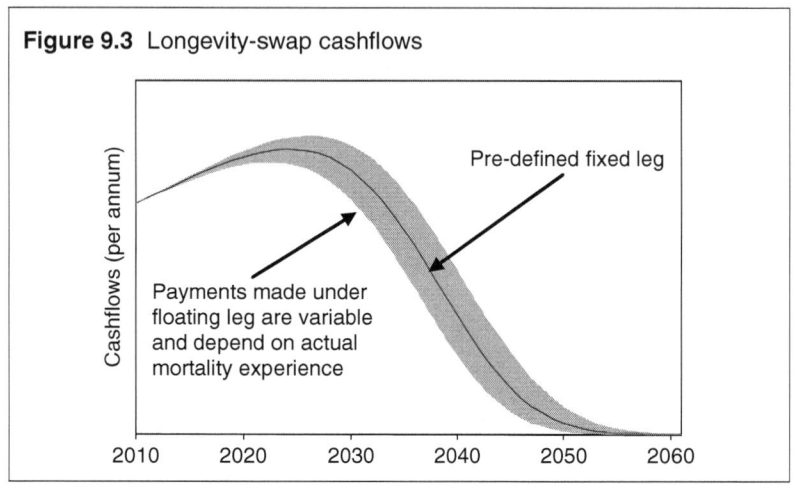

Cashflows (per annum) vs years 2010–2060. Pre-defined fixed leg shown as central curve; shaded band shows that payments made under floating leg are variable and depend on actual mortality experience.

In a subsequent section we consider the impact of restructuring the fixed leg to a "bespoke fixed leg" in a way that makes the fixed leg more consistent with the assets that might actually be held by the pension scheme. At this point it is important to note that, in this structure, the risk associated with the underlying assets is retained by the pension scheme. We also discuss below a structure known as a "synthetic buy-in", under which the asset risk is also passed to an investment bank.

Pricing of a longevity swap

The price of the longevity hedge (or the cost of the fixed leg) can be broken down into the following components (Figure 9.4).

- **Current mortality.** This component will be assessed using past experience data and other economic and demographic information relating to the membership of the pension scheme.

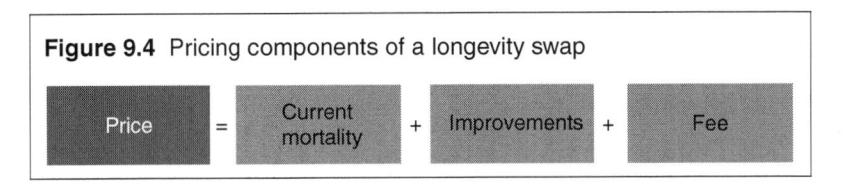

Figure 9.4 Pricing components of a longevity swap

Price = Current mortality + Improvements + Fee

- **Improvements.** The pricing assumptions related to improvements will vary materially from scheme to scheme, depending on economic and demographic factors and are, thus, key.
- **Fee.** The fee charged will reflect a wide range of factors, including capital costs in relation to warehousing of unhedged risks accepted by the swap provider and will include a profit margin.

The data typically required to provide an indicative price for a longevity swap includes, in addition to mortality history data for the pension scheme, the following data for each pensioner member in respect of whom risks are to be transferred:

- a unique identifier which is usually used in place of receiving each pensioner's name, because the latter may have implications under local data protection requirements such as the Data Protection Act (in the UK);
- date of birth;
- sex;
- pension amount;
- (former) occupation;
- postal code;
- contingent dependants' details.

Cashflows payable in a longevity swap

Under the terms of a longevity swap, the pension scheme agrees to pay a pre-defined series of cashflows to the swap provider in return for receiving cash amounts equal to the actual pensions payable over a defined term or the lifetime of the pensioners. Cashflows are typically exchanged on a monthly basis. The fixed- and floating-leg cashflows are netted each period, with only a net amount being payable from one party to the other each month.

The fixed- and floating-leg cashflows of the longevity swap may or may not be linked to inflation in the same way as the actual pensions, depending on the agreed structure of the swap. When the cashflows are linked to the same inflation as the actual pensions, the longevity hedge does not have a material impact on the level of inflation risk within the scheme. There is only a second-order impact, as future longevity experience causes the fixed and floating legs to diverge, because the pension scheme has swapped inflation risk in relation to the underlying pensions for inflation risk in relation to the fixed leg.

Once the longevity swap is in place, the net amount paid out by the pension scheme each month is unaffected by the mortality of the underlying pensioners and is fixed at the level of the pre-agreed fixed leg. The examples in Figure 9.5 show how this works in practice.

Collateral mechanics

When the swap provider is an investment bank, it will offer the pension scheme a full collateral package, which is typically structured using an ISDA governed CSA, assuming the product is a derivative, to reduce the pension scheme's counterparty risk.

Security is provided to ensure that both parties are compensated for the replacement cost of the transaction in the event of early termination or default. Collateral is posted by a party when it is "out-of-the-money", subject to an agreed minimum unsecured threshold.

One of the most efficient collateral mechanisms has been found to be a hybrid between mark-to-model and mark-to-market. An initial mortality basis and spread are agreed on day 1 and are used to value the floating leg; the mortality basis and spread are updated by the parties at regular intervals (eg, every three years to coincide with the latest actuarial valuation of the pension scheme).

Collateral calls are calculated monthly, by valuing the floating leg using these assumptions. If a liquid market for the transfer of longevity risk is deemed to exist at some point in the future, the spread payable in this liquid market will be incorporated into the collateral calculation.

A pension scheme's preference is typically for collateral to be physically transferred under a CSA. Pledges of interests over secured accounts can be considered (ie, floating charges) but offer less security than outright transfer. Counterparty risk is mitigated most fully in situations in which parties have physical possession of collateral.

Figure 9.5 Net cashflows when actual pension differs from fixed leg

(a)

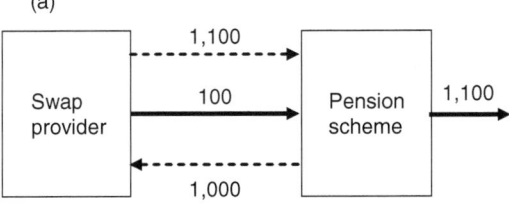

```
              1,100
         ┌ ─ ─ ─ ─ ─ →
┌─────────┐   100      ┌─────────┐  1,100
│  Swap   │ ─────────→ │ Pension │ ───────→
│provider │            │ scheme  │
│         │ ←─ ─ ─ ─ ─ │         │
└─────────┘   1,000    └─────────┘
```

Pension scheme net payment:
= amount paid to pensioners
+ amount received under longevity swap

= (1,100) + 100 = (1,000)

(b)

```
               900
         ┌ ─ ─ ─ ─ ─ →
┌─────────┐   100      ┌─────────┐   900
│  Swap   │ ←───────── │ Pension │ ───────→
│provider │            │ scheme  │
│         │ ←─ ─ ─ ─ ─ │         │
└─────────┘   1,000    └─────────┘
```

Pension scheme net payment:
= amount paid to pensioners
+ amount paid out under longevity swap

= (900) + (100) = (1,000)

Pension scheme net cashflow always equal to fixed leg

(a) Net cashflow when actual pension is above fixed leg; fixed payment = 1,000; actual pension = 1,100. (b) Net cashflow when actual pension is below fixed leg; fixed payment = 1,000 Actual pension = 900.

Eligible collateral is determined by the parties prior to execution. Eligible collateral usually includes cash, gilts and highly rated corporate bonds. Concentration limits for issuers, together with similar limits for sector and geographical regions, also typically apply to ensure that the collateral pool is well diversified.

When the counterparty is an insurer, any collateral account mechanisms are typically negotiated on a scheme-by-scheme basis, which may or may not follow a similar approach to that described above. Any additional associated cost of such collateral account mechanisms will need to be evaluated in terms of the additional security benefit to the scheme.

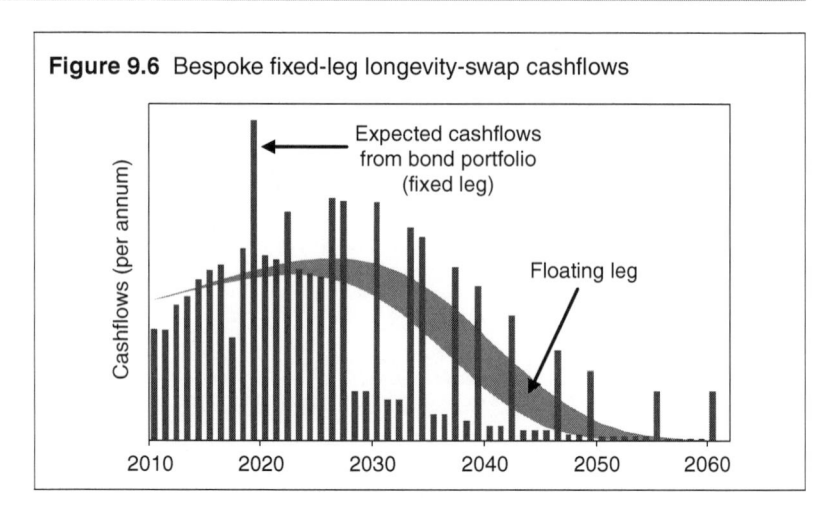

Figure 9.6 Bespoke fixed-leg longevity-swap cashflows

MORE SOPHISTICATED VARIATIONS OF THE MAIN TOOLS
Longevity swap: bespoke fixed leg

A "bespoke fixed-leg" longevity-swap structure is very similar to the unfunded longevity swap in that it transfers only longevity risk to the swap provider. The only difference is that the fixed leg is restructured to be consistent with the cashflows arising from a specified portfolio of assets and, therefore, is typically more likely to be offered by an investment bank, as illustrated in Figure 9.6.

The pension scheme and the swap provider jointly determine the asset portfolio, subject to the pension scheme's investment guidelines. Assuming no default on the underlying assets, the cashflows generated by the portfolio will match precisely those payable by the pension scheme under the longevity swap. Should an asset default, the pension scheme is still liable to pay the cashflow that the asset would otherwise have generated.

This type of approach is likely to appeal to trustees of the pension scheme in situations in which it is perceived that credit spreads are artificially high given underlying fundamentals. Recently, for example, the credit spread available on UK government debt has been much higher than many market participants consider to be justified purely by reference to the perceived low risk of UK government default.

Table 9.2 illustrates how the market value of an underlying UK bond portfolio might vary depending on the credit quality of the bonds.

Table 9.2 Credit quality impact on UK market bond portfolio value

	Market value of assets backing the longevity swap (£ million)	Yield on underlying assets (% pa)
Gilts	500	3.94
AAA corporate	467	4.45
AA corporate	419	5.29
A corporate	396	5.77
BBB corporate	376	6.21

Synthetic buy-in

The synthetic buy-in structure is akin to a traditional buy-in as both asset and longevity risk pass to the swap provider. Like the bespoke fixed-leg longevity swap, it is typically more likely to be offered by an investment bank. This structure potentially offers better security than a traditional buy-in, however, since the assets which would have been passed to the insurer as part of a traditional buy-in arrangement are retained within the pension scheme.

The principal difference between a basic longevity swap and a synthetic buy-in relates to the fixed leg. In place of paying predetermined monthly amounts for a fixed period of time, the pension scheme pays amounts determined by the asset returns on its investment portfolio to the swap provider. Assets can be re-structured to the required risk/return/duration profile of the pension scheme.

The transactions are fully collateralised and, in the case of the synthetic buy-in, the pension scheme retains legal and physical ownership of its assets.

Executing a synthetic buy-in involves the following steps:

1. the pension scheme and the swap provider negotiate the nature of the assets that can be held within a ring-fenced portfolio (eg, asset classes, rating, liquidity and haircuts);
2. the swap provider determines what value of assets must be placed in the ring-fenced portfolio in order to meet the payments due under the fixed leg of the longevity hedge (ie, the buy-in premium);
3. the pension scheme places the required amount of liquid assets into the ring-fenced portfolio;

LONGEVITY RISK

Figure 9.7 A synthetic buy-in structure

```
Pension scheme                                    Investment bank
  ┌──────────┐    Return on ring-fenced assets  ───→
  │Ring-fenced│   Fixed leg                     ←───   Total return swap
  │portfolio  │   Top-up payments and haircut   ←- - -
  └──────────┘

                                                  Investment bank
                  Fixed leg                      ───→
                  Collateral                     ←- - →   Longevity hedge
                  Floating leg                   ←───
                  (ie, pension payments)
```

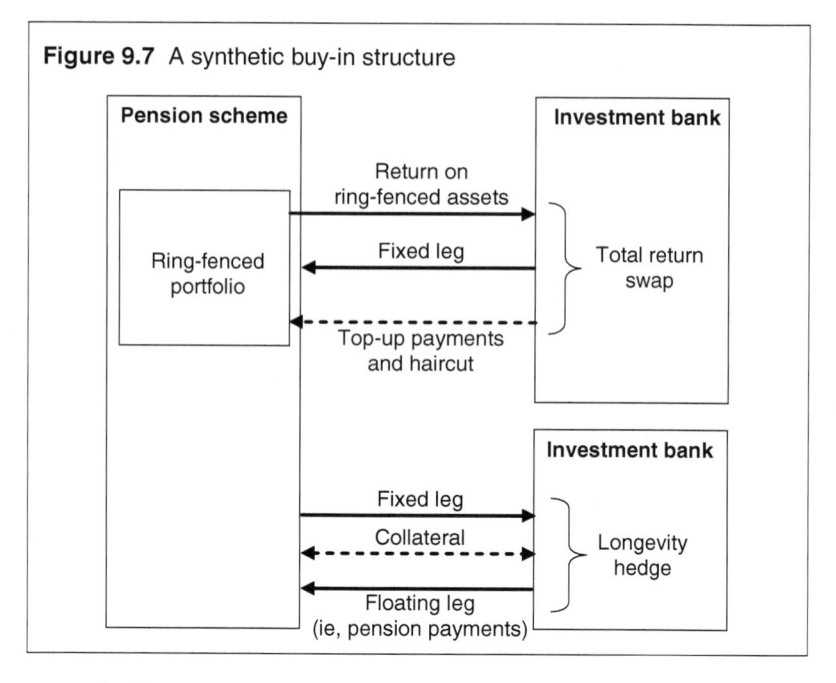

4. the longevity hedge and total return swap documentation are executed;
5. the swap provider places additional assets into the ring-fenced portfolio in respect of the agreed haircuts.

The economic impact of this structure is that the pension scheme has no exposure to pensioner longevity risk and has passed the risk on the assets backing the buy-in to the swap provider. Additionally, the pension scheme has significant security in the event of a default by the swap provider. An illustration of such a synthetic buy-in with an investment bank is given in Figure 9.7.

Insurance-wrapped longevity swap

In addition to being able to transact a longevity hedge in derivative format, some investment banks are able to offer the same product in insurance format by working with an insurance partner.

The steps to execute an insurance-wrapped longevity swap are illustrated for a UK transaction as follows.

1. The pension scheme transacts a longevity hedge in insurance format with a regulated insurer, for example, a Financial Services Authority-regulated (FSA-regulated) UK insurer.

2. The pension scheme also agrees to a longevity swap (ie, in derivative format) with the investment bank. This contract is held in escrow and may be enforced by the pension scheme on the event of insurer insolvency.
3. The regulated insurer may retain some of the longevity risk, but the majority of the risk is passed to the investment bank.
4. The investment bank identifies a number of reinsurers and capital markets investors with which to hedge its longevity risk.

Facing an FSA-regulated insurer gives the pension scheme access to the FSCS in the event of the insurer becoming insolvent. An illustration of an insurance-wrapped longevity swap for a UK transaction is shown in Figure 9.8.

Additional security may be provided by the investment bank, which could step in in the unlikely event of insurer insolvency, when the investment bank is willing to commit to step into the defaulting insurer's contractual obligations. Not all investment banks are willing to do so, but it is a feature offered by some banks.

SOME OTHER FEATURES OF RELEVANCE TO THE IMPLEMENTATION OF A LONGEVITY SWAP

In implementing a longevity swap, consideration should be given to a number of other features, such as novation and early termination clauses, quality of administration, overpayments and late notification, specific considerations for trustees and sponsoring employers and implementation issues.

Novation and early termination

The ability to alter hedging strategies over time is crucial for trustees, and a longevity swap can be structured to take account of a future novation to a buy-in or buy-out provider.

The arrangement ideally should be set up such that the pension scheme can transfer the swap to another counterparty or split the swap between counterparties. An investment bank would typically accept a new counterparty, provided they are deemed to be appropriate with regard to credit-worthiness and suitability after completion of due diligence. Existing collateral posted would enable the pension scheme to execute the new strategy, given that the market spread for

Figure 9.8 An insurance-wrapped longevity-swap structure

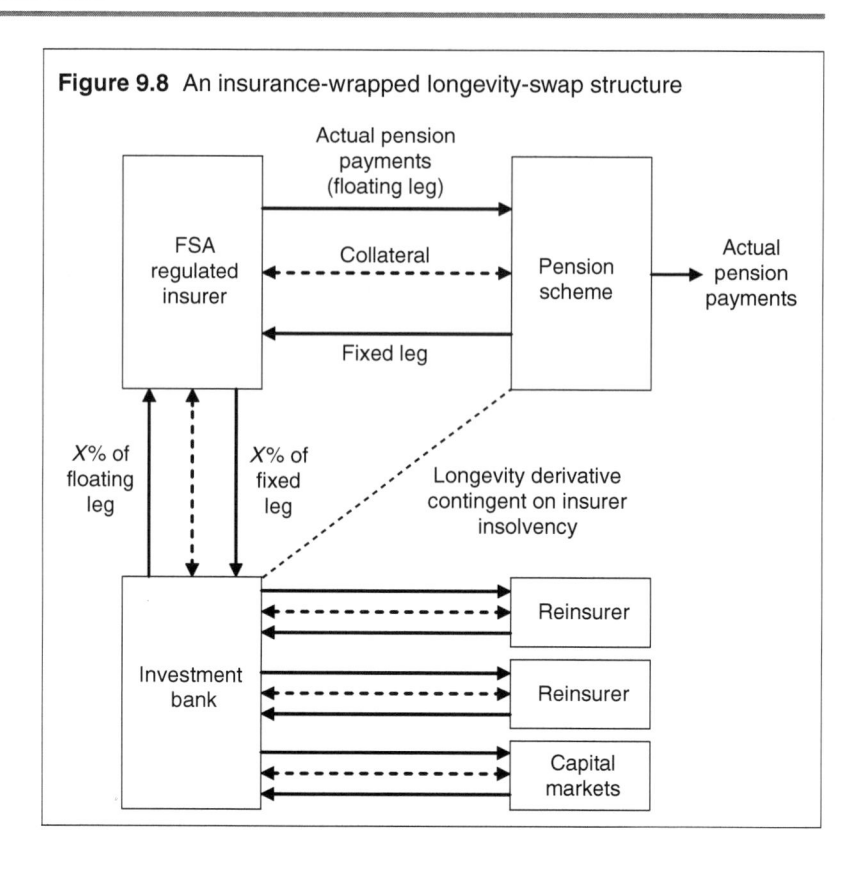

[Diagram showing: FSA regulated insurer exchanges Actual pension payments (floating leg), Collateral, and Fixed leg with Pension scheme, which makes Actual pension payments externally. FSA regulated insurer exchanges X% of floating leg and X% of fixed leg with Investment bank. A Longevity derivative contingent on insurer insolvency runs from Pension scheme to Investment bank. Investment bank connects to Reinsurer, Reinsurer, and Capital markets.]

transferring longevity risk and the performance of the portfolio are both inputs in the collateral model. Novation would be effected by transferring collateral posted to the new party, and amending the longevity swap so that it replaces the pension scheme.

Options for early termination should also be built into the structure to facilitate a close-out of the transaction in advance of its maturity. Such options can be inserted at regular intervals, for example, at the tenth anniversary of the transaction and every five years thereafter. A commitment should also be made to offer an unwind price on pre-determined dates. In the case of an investment bank, unwind terms follow standard ISDA swap mechanics, under which the principle is to compensate for replacement cost. In the normal course of events, the investment bank would expect to offer an exit on market terms, minus any reasonable cost for unwinding associated hedges. Exit terms with an insurer are typically negotiated on an individual basis for large schemes.

Although not guaranteed, the swap provider should also do its best to offer unwind terms at all times during the life of the longevity swap, which would enable the pension scheme to respond to unforeseen circumstances.

Administration of the longevity swap

A bank will typically engage a third-party provider to assist in the administration of the transaction, whereas whether or not an insurer does so will depend on whether or not it outsources its administration functions. The primary function of the administration is to track mortality in the portfolio and verify personal information in circumstances where such information is deemed to be impaired. When independence of the administrator is key to the transparency of the transaction, the parties will agree upon a suitable third-party provider prior to the execution date.

The administration of a longevity swap is effected using two separate methods for tracking the mortality experience of the portfolio.

- The servicer will undertake a monthly search of third-party sources, such as the UK's General Register Office, to determine which individuals within the portfolio have died.
- The pension scheme will provide the servicer with monthly information on the individuals within the portfolio that it believes have died. The servicer will cross-check these details with the data from the aforementioned third-party sources.

The pension scheme is able to contest any mortality information which it believes to be incorrect, and will have full access at all times to the results of portfolio tracking performed by the servicer.

A monthly net-settlement calculation will be generated, which may also be done by an independent calculation agent under the longevity swap. The monthly settlement will reflect the fixed expected longevity payment stream minus the floating actual longevity payment stream. The floating actual longevity payment will be calculated by reference to the mortality experience of each given month.

Overpayments and late notifications

In the event of an overpayment, the overpaying party will be reimbursed with allowance for an agreed rate of interest. Depending on the pension scheme's preference, adjustments for over- and underpayments can be made monthly, quarterly or annually. Some schemes hold the view that a monthly adjustment is administratively complex and has little value given that mortality data will always lag.

An adjustment is also made for late-reported deaths (the deaths that occur in the months prior to execution of the longevity swap but which have not been reported at the execution date). This involves the removal of individuals from the fixed leg who are reported as dead post execution but who died prior to execution.

The two major alternatives in relation to late-reported deaths are as follows:

- any floating amounts that have been paid in respect of such individuals are reimbursed to the swap provider and they are removed from the fixed leg;
- a lump sum is paid to the pension scheme in respect of these late-reported individuals and the individuals remain in the fixed leg for the duration of the transaction, but no floating leg is payable.

Considerations for trustees

The positive impact of implementing a longevity hedge can be seen in the fact that the pension scheme is no longer affected by the realised longevity of the pensioner members covered by the swap. However, there are a number of issues that the trustees should seek to understand and resolve ahead of transaction execution; we list some of these here as follows.

1. **Impact on scheme funding:** trustees need to understand how their scheme actuary will view the longevity-swap transaction for the purpose of the scheme's funding valuation. Will it affect the actuary's longevity assumptions? Will the actuary simply treat the swap as an asset of the pension scheme?

   There is no single correct answer to these questions and the views of the scheme actuary should be sought at an early stage. Many scheme actuaries will have already been asked to form an opinion on these points by other clients of the pension scheme.

2. **Collateral:** collateralising the longevity swap undoubtedly provides additional security for the pension scheme, but it potentially introduces an additional administrative burden for the scheme.

   The trustees should speak to their existing asset custodian to ensure that the custodian is able to deal with the collateral mechanisms underlying the longevity swap. The costs associated with provision of any collateral account mechanisms where these are optional extras, for example under insurance arrangements, should also be evaluated.

3. **Management information:** under the terms of the swap, the pension scheme's administrators are required to provide details of deaths which occur each month plus details of any contingent dependants' pensions which come into payment.

   This requirement should not present much of an issue for most third-party administrators (TPAs), but the TPA should be involved in discussions on management information to ensure that it is able to provide what is required.

4. **Buy-out/buy-in:** the trustees should seek to understand how the swap will be treated should a buy-out/buy-in subsequently be considered.

   Most investment banks would be happy to face an insurance company instead of the pension scheme if a traditional buy-out or buy-in subsequently occurred and the swap were novated from the scheme.

5. **Upsize/downsize:** certain events may mean that the trustees want to either include additional members within the swap, or reduce the level of benefits covered by the swap.

   Most swap providers should be willing to offer this flexibility, subject to certain constraints (eg, the pension scheme not selecting against the swap provider in deciding which additional members to include).

Considerations for sponsors

The corporate sponsor is likely to be focused on the accounting implications of the longevity swap. In practice, it is possible that the treatment may differ from scheme to scheme. To illustrate the potential

Table 9.3 Illustrative UK balance sheet impact

IAS19 liabilities	Asset value
No impact	The market value of the scheme's assets is adjusted by the following amounts:
	plus IAS19 value of hedged liabilities
	minus fixed leg of longevity swap valued using IAS19 liability discount rate and inflation assumptions

accounting implications, we set out our understanding of how a UK longevity swap might be treated as of the time of writing in Tables 9.3 and 9.4. In all instances, the corporate sponsor should seek advice from their own professional advisors.

The logic behind this approach is that the obligation to pay benefits to the current pensioners has been replaced by an obligation to pay the fixed leg of the longevity swap. In order to be consistent with the International Accounting Standard 19 (IAS19) treatment of the liabilities, both of these obligations are valued using IAS19 assumptions.

Putting in place a pensioner longevity swap has no impact on the non-pensioner liability value.

The accounting impact depends on the relationship between the fixed leg of the longevity swap and the IAS19 longevity assumptions underlying the pensioner valuation.

Implementation

We now turn to a discussion of the key stages in the execution of a longevity-swap transaction. In practice the time within which the transaction can be executed is likely to be dominated by two stages:

- the length of time it takes the scheme trustees and sponsor to become comfortable with the impact of the longevity hedge;
- negotiation of the legal documentation governing the transaction.

A summary of a typical process that an investment bank uses in entering into a longevity swap with a pension scheme illustrates the implementation stages in more detail.

Table 9.4 Illustrative UK profit and loss impact

Current service	Interest cost	Past service	Expected return on assets
No impact	No impact	No impact	The expected return assumption (ie, % pa) will not change, but the underlying asset value will be affected

1. **Price and agreement on preferred structure:** during the first stage of the process, the potential swap providers supply the scheme with indicative quotes for the execution of a longevity hedge. Several different quotes may be obtained to take account of the different structures discussed above.

   At the end of the indicative quote process, the pension scheme, in conjunction with its advisors, should have a clear idea of which structure (ie, unfunded longevity swap, bespoke fixed leg or synthetic buy-in) best suits its objectives. At this point, a mandate letter with the pension scheme is usually signed to formalise the terms of the transaction.

2. **Initial term sheet and data audit:** the objective of this phase is to establish an initial term sheet which includes structural details and collateral mechanisms. The term sheet forms a base document which enables the investment bank to develop the transaction in conjunction with the pension scheme and discuss risk participation with potential investors.

   At this stage, an audit of the quality of the data provided by the pension scheme is normally performed by, or on behalf of, the swap provider. If data quality is poor, a servicer is engaged to verify its accuracy. In practice, this process can take from a few weeks up to several months depending on the underlying portfolio.

   In the event that such a process is required, it can be conducted simultaneously with the closing of the transaction. It may, however, lead to a pricing adjustment post close if the audited data results in a materially different risk profile. Such adjustment is always performed according to pre-agreed formulae, and does not entitle either party to revise pricing in a discretionary manner.

3. **Structural refinements and documentation:** at this point in the transaction process, the structure and the legal documentation are refined. The pension scheme is now required to commit resources to the transaction including lawyers, actuaries and potentially asset managers, should the bespoke fixed-leg longevity-swap structure be used.

4. **Execution:** at the end of this process, the pension scheme is provided with a final price. Assuming no material change to the quality of the data, there is likely to be little variation between this price and the indicative price provided at the start of the process. Components that could induce variations in price are primarily structural changes, collateral terms and, should the synthetic buy-in be the preferred structure, asset price movements.

CONCLUSION

This chapter set out to summarise the main methods that have been adopted in the UK for de-risking longevity risk within employer-sponsored defined-benefit pension schemes. The discussion focused primarily on longevity swaps but also touched on alternatives such as buy-outs and buy-ins. The discussion was expanded to include an examination of relative advantages and drawbacks of the main de-risking tools and more sophisticated approaches. It can, however, only be considered an introduction to longevity risk transfer, since innovations are anticipated with market evolution.

> Copyright © 2011 Credit Suisse International. All rights reserved. This chapter reflects the assumptions, views and analysis of the authors. Credit Suisse may have issued, and may in the future issue, other reports that are inconsistent with, and reach different conclusions from, the information presented in this chapter.

10

Hedging Longevity Risk through Reinsurance

Gavin Jones
Swiss Re

Reinsurance provides a means for insurers to hedge their own longevity risk by complete transfer of a specified liability. Until recently, there has been comparatively little demand for the reinsurance of longevity risk, but interest in transferring longevity risk has increased at a time when capacity has similarly increased and is available. However, such conditions are unlikely to continue indefinitely.

For this reason, our discussion of the major types of reinsurance transactions available to transfer longevity risk (the focus of this chapter) has a special significance. Longevity risk transactions were initially taken up in Chapter 8 with the introduction of asset-backed risk transfer and longevity swaps. This chapter will consider these solutions in more detail and explore ways to mitigate counterparty credit exposure for these, as well as providing specific examples of some of the largest transactions that have occurred. The capacity of the market is also explored further, along with a focus on capital market solutions that may enable the insurance sector to manage its aggregate exposure and generate returns from its core function of managing diversifiable risks in the future.

First we look at asset-backed risk transfer and longevity swaps. Then we look at the issue of capacity, which was first discussed in Chapter 2 and, in particular, the volume of longevity risk that can be carried on global insurance and reinsurance balance sheets. Next we look in detail at the steps involved in a typical longevity reinsurance transaction and at further considerations around impaired and enhanced annuities, before concluding in the final section.

STANDARD REINSURANCE FORMS OF LONGEVITY RISK TRANSFER

The two standard forms of risk transfer discussed in this chapter are asset-backed risk transfer and longevity swaps.

Asset-backed risk transfer

These solutions reinsure a group of immediate and deferred lifetime annuities in a way that exactly matches the corresponding exposures of the insurance company's portfolio. The insurer makes a single payment that transfers to the reinsurer all risks, including exposure to longevity risk and asset risk but excludes the administration of the individual policies. Conceptually, an asset-backed transfer is similar to a "buy-in" for pension liabilities. It is also typically a necessary precursor for a full annuity portfolio transfer from one company to another, as, for example, is the case for UK insurance liabilities transferred via a Part VII transfer under the Financial Services Act of 2000.

Asset-backed risk transfer has the potential to create substantial counterparty credit exposure for the insurer because the single premium supports the liability over the lifetime run-off of the annuities. This exposure can be mitigated in a number of ways including assessing the level of underlying risk via credit rating and the robustness of regulatory regime or entering into more explicit risk mitigation strategies such as the following.

- Novate the liability: this approach extinguishes the underlying exposure by directly transferring the long-term liabilities to another party and is the underlying driver of the buy-out sector and full transfer (eg, Part VII transfer) of annuity blocks.

- Collateral arrangements: under these arrangements, the underlying assets are managed through an account over which the insurer has a floating charge in the event of default of the reinsurer.

- Deposit back: as the name implies, the underlying assets are deposited back with the insurer, creating a potential credit risk for the reinsurer which will need to be managed principally through a right of offset provision in the contract but also via a similar set of considerations to those discussed above.

Table 10.1 Illustrative large asset-backed annuity reinsurance transactions

Reinsurer	Cedant	Structure	Year	Size (£ bn)
Prudential	Scottish Life (Royal London)	Reinsurance to Part VII	2004	1.1
XL Re	CIS	Reinsurance	2004	1.0
Prudential	Phoenix Life & Pensions	Reinsurance to Part VII	2005/6	1.5
Canada Life	Phoenix & London Assurance	Reinsurance to Part VII	2005/6	2.2
Canada Life	Equitable life	Reinsurance to Part VII	2006	4.6
Swiss Re	Zurich Assurance Ltd	Reinsurance to Part VII	2007	3.7
Canada Life	Standard Life	Reinsurance	2008	6.7

CIS, Cooperative Insurance Services.

In reinsurance structures where the reinsurer is directly exposed to the underlying asset risk they will obtain more exposure to market and asset risk than they would if the longevity risk was transferred in isolation. Such structures provide scope for diversification of the reinsurance balance sheet but also create potential asset–liability-matching issues given the duration of the liabilities, particularly when the underlying liabilities are indexed. This is because indexed liabilities may extend the term and limit the instruments available for direct matching.

There have, however, been periods, such as in 2008 and 2009, when extreme levels of volatility and the absence of liquidity posed serious challenges to marking-to-market and hence transfer of certain assets as *in specie* premium. These challenges may have limited the ability to transact some asset-backed structures.

A summary of some of the largest asset-backed reinsurance transactions in the UK are shown in Table 10.1.

Longevity swaps

The indemnity longevity swap can be thought of as a bulk annuity but with the premium spread over 50 or 60 years rather than payable up front as a single premium as indicated in Figure 10.1. The actual

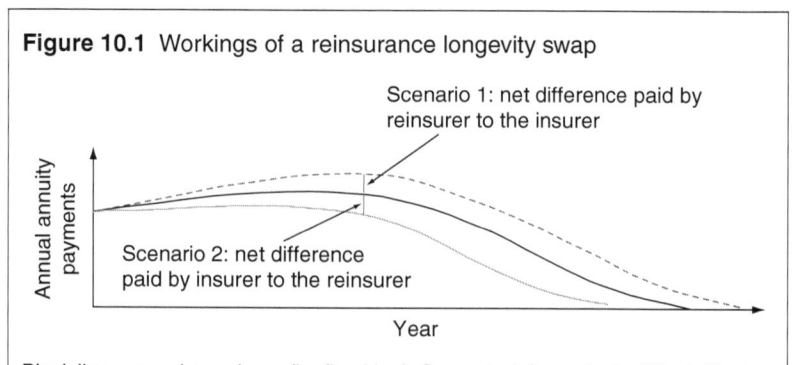

Figure 10.1 Workings of a reinsurance longevity swap

[Chart: Annual annuity payments vs Year. Black line shows annual premiums (fixed leg). Scenario 1 (grey dashed line) shows increased annual premium payments if life expectancy improves — net difference paid by reinsurer to the insurer. Scenario 2 (grey solid line) shows lower annual premium payments if life expectancy worsens — net difference paid by insurer to the reinsurer.]

Black line, annual premiums (ie, fixed leg). Scenario 1 (grey dashed line), illustrative increased annual premium payments if life expectancy improves; scenario 2 (grey solid line), illustrative lower annual premium payments if life expectancy worsens, ie, floating leg. Simulated figures, not based on any actual annuity portfolio.

annuity payments of the underlying annuity portfolio are met by the reinsurer, which fully mitigates the insurer's longevity risk exposure to the covered members. Under this arrangement, the underlying assets remain with the insurer, which retains the asset risk including any mismatch between assets and liabilities.

Only a small payment is typically exchanged between the parties each year because the "floating leg" (or the actual annuity payments) and the "fixed leg" (or the annual premiums) are netted off.

Despite the name "swap", longevity swaps are written as reinsurance policies with reinsurers or in derivative form with investment banking groups. To date, most transactions have been written via the insurance route, rather than in derivative format. But even when longevity swaps are written in derivative form, for example, where risk has been transferred from pension funds which cannot transact reinsurance directly, the risk written by the derivatives carrier has typically been simultaneously transferred to reinsurers, which are the end carriers of the risk. Under these arrangements, it is typically standard practice for longevity derivatives to have some features carved out from the risk transfer to ensure they are not classified as insurance. Examples of large longevity-swap transactions involving reinsurers are provided in Table 10.2.

Under a longevity swap, immediate counterparty credit exposure is negligible because the contract is an exchange of risk. However, small levels of two-way credit exposure can develop over time if

Table 10.2 Example large longevity-swap reinsurance transactions

Reinsurer	Cedant	Structure	Year	Size (£ bn)
Swiss Re	Friends Provident	Longevity swap	2007	1.7
RGA	AXA/ AXA Annuity Co	Longevity swap via an ISPV	2009	1.6
RGA/Pacific Life Re	Abbey Life	Longevity swap	2009	1.5
Hannover Re	Prudential	Longevity swap	2009	0.7
Pacific Life Re	Rothesay Life (RSA)	Longevity swap	2009	1.5
Hannover Re/Pacific Life Re/PartnerRe	Abbey Life (BMW)	Longevity swap (derivative)	2010	3.0

ISPV, Insurance Special Purpose Vehicle.

future longevity deviates significantly from expectations. This exposure may be managed via mechanisms such as collateral accounts discussed previously. In assessing the risk associated with a reinsurance arrangement, the parties should consider the strength of the counterparty as well as the materiality of their possible credit exposure. Counterparty risk should be assessed not only with regard to available credit ratings, but also with respect to the strength of the regulatory regime in which the counterparty operates and the strength of the underlying risk capital framework. In general, the counterparty credit risk associated with a longevity swap will be of a much lower quantum than an asset-backed transfer simply because the premiums are broadly aligned with the claims, provided appropriate offsets are allowed for within the treaty.

LONGEVITY: CAPACITY AND LONG-TERM RISK MITIGATION

We now turn to the issue of the limits on total volume of longevity risk that can be carried on global insurance and reinsurance balance sheets, a topic that was introduced in Chapter 2. The sheer volume of global longevity risk exposure, estimated by Swiss Re in 2007 at over US$20 trillion of pension assets backing the risk, is likely to require a greater capital resource than that currently available by the insurance industry.

The risks associated with longevity can be classified by type, for example,

- operational (eg, administration, validation of survivorship),
- base mortality (eg, white collar versus blue collar differentials),
- demographic risk (eg, existence of spouse),
- mortality trend risk.

With the exception of mortality trend, which is a systematic risk, each of these risks are diversifiable and fall within the core business model of insurance. For this reason, a natural business model forms around insurance which efficiently aggregates these diversifiable risks in the reinsurance sector. As a consequence, systematic longevity trend risk has accumulated on insurance balance sheet without diversification. This has some important implications, as global insurance capacity for the undiversifiable risk is used up.

As available mortality trend capacity diminishes, pressure on pricing increases. At the time of writing, nearly all of the new available capacity for longevity-risk-only transactions has come from the reinsurance market, which typically seeks to offset long-term mortality exposure. But as the benefits of the underlying anti-correlation fall, pricing must rise and new capacity must ultimately be found to fill the shortfall. One viable source is the further development of the capital markets for longevity risk, which is covered in considerable detail in Chapter 12.

Since 2006, a number of insurance companies have been formed in the UK to provide bulk de-risking transfer solutions such as buy-outs and longevity swaps to pension schemes. In these formations, the capital markets showed a potential appetite for the risk. However, many of the new insurance vehicles have made use of reinsurance capacity which will ultimately be limited. When this shortfall is encountered, the insurance industry will need to find a form of risk transfer that accesses the wider capital market, rather than seek the support of dedicated insurance capital.

For wider capital market participation, greater liquidity is required than that involved in individual insurance transactions with long durations. There are a number of prerequisites for a liquid longevity risk market to develop in the long term. These include

- increased market transparency through published, standardised longevity indices (covered further in Chapter 13),
- convergence of views on approaches to assess future mortality improvement trend risk,

- development of a standardised contract specification,
- the existence of secondary market liquidity for investor exit.

In the meantime, should a specific asset class in respect of systematic mortality trend risk appear, the insurance sector would be able to confidently manage its aggregate exposure and generate returns from its core function of accumulating and managing diversifiable risks.

Standardised (parametric) longevity swaps

As covered in Chapter 8, a parametric (standardised) longevity swap is a derivative contract whose payoffs depend on how future mortality in a standard population (index) develops. We now explore the use of these, especially from a reinsurance perspective.

In particular, these enable a standardised product to be used to hedge mortality trend risk, which typically results in higher levels of liquidity. Importantly, the payouts could refer to a different population (such as the population as a whole) to that of an underlying indemnity swap (which references the actual portfolio). There is unlikely to be significant market liquidity for underlying indemnity cashflows, but standardised contracts provide a means to manage the bulk of the capital and valuation exposure: key issues for the management of long-dated liabilities.

From a protection buyer's perspective, the derivative must be carefully calibrated in order for the payout to offset the impact of future changes in longevity. Basis risk is a consequence not only of the different populations, but also of other factors, including model risk (ie, a model is used to generate the calibration), other demographic risks (eg, uncertainty regarding proportion of lives that are married, for any spouse dependant benefits) and structural risks (eg, if the maximum tenor of the swap was 10 years, then the effectiveness of the hedge over the life of the underlying risk may be limited).

For a reinsurer the scale of existing longevity exposure provides an opportunity to underwrite a wide spread of longevity risk which should be closely correlated with the reference population index. As exposure to longevity risk transfer grows, market participants will look for greater price standardisation, increased transparency on credit exposure and the ability to novate contracts. The benefits of increased liquidity are not limited to greater capital and velocity of capital exposed to the risk, but also include greater market efficiency

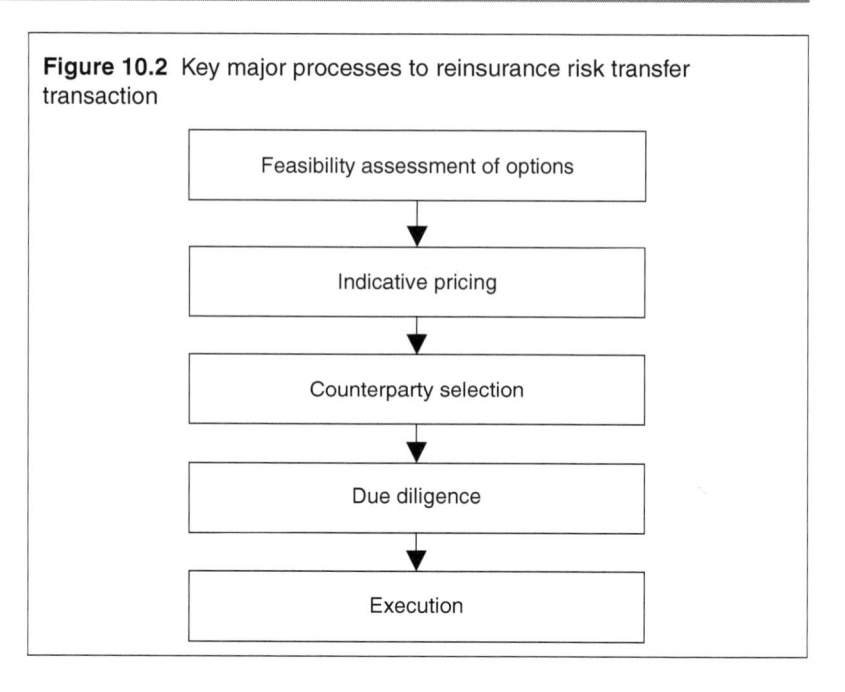

Figure 10.2 Key major processes to reinsurance risk transfer transaction

```
┌─────────────────────────────────┐
│ Feasibility assessment of options│
└─────────────────────────────────┘
                 ▼
┌─────────────────────────────────┐
│      Indicative pricing          │
└─────────────────────────────────┘
                 ▼
┌─────────────────────────────────┐
│     Counterparty selection       │
└─────────────────────────────────┘
                 ▼
┌─────────────────────────────────┐
│         Due diligence            │
└─────────────────────────────────┘
                 ▼
┌─────────────────────────────────┐
│           Execution              │
└─────────────────────────────────┘
```

and transparency, which increase the attraction for investors of the underlying risk takers. Over time we would expect to see increasing specialisation, as those entities dedicated to basis risk evaluation (such as large-scale annuity writers or reinsurers) capture value through this component, while the wider investor universe places capital at risk through more standard structures without the need to accurately manage indemnity specific cashflows. For this reason, reinsurance is likely to continue to have a significant role in the management of the risk, and if scale and liquidity for longevity risk transfer is not attained within the capital market, reinsurers are likely to be the main source of capacity for risk transfer for the foreseeable future.

CASE STUDY: STEPS INVOLVED IN REINSURANCE

We now turn to the steps involved in a typical reinsurance longevity swap. Transactions are usually structured around an initial feasibility assessment of the risk transfer options for an insurer and then move to a series of processes involving indicative pricing, counterparty selection, due diligence and execution as shown in Figure 10.2.

Indicative pricing is likely to be based on extracted data from the cedant's systems, enabling experience analysis and calculation of expected cashflow and liability based on the in-force exposure at a known date. Where there are published regulatory reserves, the claims can be reconciled on a common basis and pricing expressed with respect to a standardised benchmark: a step that enables a comparison of reinsurance terms on a like-for-like basis. To clarify the underlying details of the liability and enable more detailed per-policy evaluation which might have pricing implications, the process of establishing indicative terms can include a number of iterations for data queries and more granular and up-to-date data extracts.

After appropriate evaluation of the various counterparties, a decision will be made to move to exclusive negotiations with a single counterparty, where firm pricing and terms will emerge as a consequence of due diligence. This enables the reinsurer to fine tune the pricing and structure the risk transfer and align the arrangement with the underlying liability and administration system. Consideration may also be given as to whether any collateral mechanism needs to be included in the risk transfer.

Negotiation of final terms and conditions will include agreement on

- the exact liability transferred,
- treatment of data errors discovered after the treaty has been finalised,
- service standards for administration,
- survivorship validation (eg, certificate of existence),
- details for the settlement of the contract (including any update of claims and premium related to indexation),
- covenants, warranties and limitations,
- termination conditions.

With suitable levels of commitment on both sides, the reinsurance process involved in a longevity-swap transfer offers a quick, simple means for full indemnity risk transfer (including exposures such as to unknown spouse, inflation, data error and so on) to be transferred with cover given in a short legally binding document. These reinsurance arrangements are now relatively common transactions and current levels of market activity should provide comfort in terms of price discovery, flexibility in structuring and certainty of execution. Moreover, reinsurance arrangements can obtain full regulatory relief for the underlying liabilities because a precise liability is transferred.

IMPAIRED AND ENHANCED ANNUITIES

In addition to wholesale risk transfer on large blocks of annuities or underlying pension schemes, reinsurers have extended their life underwriting expertise to provide support to the underwritten annuity market which was introduced in Chapter 5. In markets with substantial levels of annuitisation, improved terms may be offered to customers with reduced life expectancy. These terms may be offered in either asset-backed or swap formats.

The potential for survivorship to deviate substantially from expected is greater for underwritten annuities than on larger volumes of more homogeneous standard annuity business. In addition, specific underwriting expertise is necessary to accurately evaluate differential mortality due to conditions as diverse as diabetes, multiple sclerosis and various cancers at different stages of their development.

Greater publicity in the UK and elsewhere around the open market option has spurred rapid growth in impaired and enhanced annuities which are strongly supported by the reinsurance market.

The aggregate risk considerations related to these products are similar to those of more standard annuities, but carry their own specific set of risks and have a business model that is more aligned with the protection market. For example, differential pricing by condition and the operation of competing pricing methodologies for factors such as postcode, smoker annuities, long- and short-form underwriting within the market may lead to concentration of specific underlying conditions within a portfolio. Consideration of mortality improvement is more complicated in situations in which the underlying exposure may be dominated by specific conditions.

The business model can vary from individually underwritten single life annuities (usually with very significant reductions in life expectancies) to more broadly based pricing at a portfolio level. As the primary annuity market becomes increasingly segmented, not only is the demand for pricing support from the reinsurance market likely to continue, but the basis pricing risk is also likely to increase: a trend that would drive further demand for reinsurance.

CONCLUSION

Reinsurance is a well-established method by which longevity risk has been transferred through both asset-backed and longevity-swap transactions. Each type of transaction has different levels of associated counterparty credit risk which can be mitigated through assessing credit rating, the robustness of the regulatory regime in which the reinsurer operates as well as through other mechanisms such as collateral accounts. Although longevity swaps by design tend to have lower credit and counterparty exposure risk than asset-backed transfers. Of those market transactions conducted via a longevity swap, the majority have tended to be issued as reinsurance policies rather than in derivative format, but even on transactions that have involved the capital markets reinsurers have typically sat alongside investment banks in some way. The capacity of the insurance market for longevity risk will be under increasing pressure, given the vast volume of global longevity exposure. Consequently, the ability of the industry to maintain pricing levels on longevity risk will largely depend upon the emergence of additional sources of capital such as from the capital markets. Asset classes that are developed for the transfer of systematic longevity trend risk, however, would offer the insurance sector a new opportunity to manage its aggregate exposure and generate returns from its core function of managing diversifiable risks while providing future investors the potential upside investment of an uncorrelated asset class.

11

Extreme Mortality Risk as a Natural Hedge?

Alison McKie, Nick Ketley

Swiss Re

Extreme mortality risk can be defined as the risk of financial loss in the event of sudden elevated levels of mortality experience. Life (re)insurers in particular are exposed to extreme mortality risk and are particularly vulnerable to sudden spikes in mortality through their life assurance portfolios. In practice this risk largely concerns the incidence and severity of lethal pandemics and other extreme mortality events like natural catastrophes and terrorist attacks. As longevity risk is essentially the risk of financial loss from lower than expected levels of mortality, it is intuitive to ask whether there is any offset between the two risks. This chapter explores the possibility of utilising extreme mortality risk as a natural hedge for longevity risk. Here it should be understood that the premise of the hedge is to use the income from underwriting extreme mortality as a buffer against longevity risk, with the expectation that, in the unlikely scenario of an extreme mortality event, any extreme mortality losses would be, at least partially, offset by mortality profits on the longevity portfolio.

We begin with an overview of extreme mortality risk-transfer techniques and illustrate how an institution with longevity risk can access this risk. We then consider the structural nature of extreme mortality risk and then contrast it with longevity risk, in order to identify any offsetting effect. We also discuss the impact of basis risk for both mortality and longevity risk transfer as well as the implications of duration mismatch. We demonstrate that a reliable offset between the risks is likely to be limited and that, even though most extreme mortality shock events are not likely to result in a significant reduction in value for survivorship liabilities, there may be circumstances in which financial offset will occur as well as outcomes with financial upside. We conclude that extreme mortality bonds are an asset risk class uncorrelated (or in certain circumstances negatively correlated) to longevity risk. Therefore, while it may be difficult to determine a reliable longevity liability hedging strategy using extreme mortality liabilities, there is a strong case for utilising extreme mortality instruments within an asset-allocation strategy.

EXTREME MORTALITY RISK TRANSFER

Extreme mortality risk can be transferred in either a funded or an unfunded format. An unfunded transfer is likely to involve a swap arrangement (either insurance or derivative based) between two specific counterparties. A funded transfer is generally through an insurance-linked securitisation and bond structure which can be sold to a number of investors. Although the market to date has developed mainly through insurance-linked securities (ILSs) referred to as "mortality bonds", both structures offer certain advantages. Swap structures allow risk taking without a commensurate initial financing requirement, but require collateral mechanisms to be put in place which are often bespoke and highly complex. Without standardised contracts or valuation techniques for exit and/or termination, this arrangement has resulted in low levels of liquidity of the underlying instruments. To date, the main buyers of ILSs (both natural catastrophe and mortality) have been investors, including institutional investors and specialist ILS funds that prefer to take on risk mainly through cash investments. While unfunded swap structures have been offered in the market, the inherent credit exposure and restricted tradability of these structures has limited the appeal of these instruments. However, the ability to tailor swap structures to meet specific risk transfer needs at a given point in time may lead to increased transaction frequency.

Given that the underlying mortality risk characteristics are independent of the risk transfer structure and the current market prevailing approach, in this chapter we focus on mortality bonds as the mechanism by which longevity risk holders can obtain extreme mortality risk.

Background

The first mortality bond, known as Vita I, was issued in 2003 by Swiss Re. Other (re)insurers that have sponsored mortality bonds are AXA (Osiris), Scottish Re (Tartan) and Munich Re (Nathan) and,

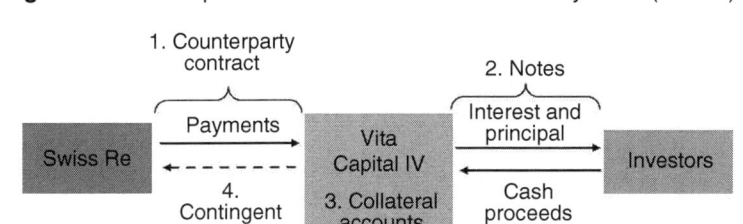

Figure 11.1 Example structure of an extreme mortality bond (Vita IV)

```
                1. Counterparty
                   contract                    2. Notes
              ┌────────┴────────┐          ┌──────┴──────┐
                     Payments                 Interest and
              ─────────────────▶    Vita        principal
   Swiss Re                       Capital IV  ◀─────────────  Investors
              ◀ ─ ─ ─ ─ ─ ─ ─ ─                    Cash
                    4.           3. Collateral   proceeds
                Contingent         accounts
                 payment
```

1. Swiss Re and Vita Capital IV (a special purpose company based in the Cayman Islands and set up specifically for the transaction) enter into an ISDA-based contract whereby Swiss Re makes payments in exchange for extreme mortality protection up to a specified notional amount. The payments to Swiss Re are based on the occurrence of certain mortality results (based on population data) above specified triggers.
2. Vita Capital IV issues floating rate notes to investors for the notional amount of the counterparty contract.
3. The proceeds of the notes are invested in collateral made up of World Bank issued debt securities (IBRD notes) on the initial issuance date. Coupons on the notes are paid from the counterparty contract payments received and investment earnings on the collateral held in trust.
4. If population mortality results exceed a specified trigger level for a given country during the risk period, the principal of the notes will be reduced by the calculated claim amount and the equivalent collateral is sold to make payment to Swiss Re under the counterparty contract. Otherwise the entire collateral is liquidated at the scheduled redemption date and the principal on the notes is returned to investors.

as of the time of writing, over US$2 billion mortality bonds have been issued, of which US$1.5 billion are from Swiss Re's Vita mortality bond programme.

Mortality bonds have evolved to facilitate the transfer of different subsets of extreme mortality risk, and have taken into account such factors as country of origin and riskiness of loss layer. For example, the Vita IV transaction (see Figure 11.1) is notable in that this is the first time the programme has been designed to be triggered on a single country (eg, US or UK) population extreme mortality event. Previous indices have used triggers on an aggregate of US, UK, Canada, Japan and Germany population mortality.

Why are mortality bonds issued?

Sponsors are motivated to issue mortality bonds in order to secure fully collateralised, multi-year protection from extreme mortality risk. This arrangement provides efficient risk capital relief through the transfer of a peak risk without introducing the credit exposure inherent in uncollateralised structures. Mortality bonds allow the sponsors to source capacity from the capital markets, which increases the overall capacity of the insurance industry to take on more mortality risk as well as further diversify the mortality risk accepted.

Mortality bonds can be issued at a range of attachment points (ie, the level of elevated mortality at which a payout is triggered, eg, 105% of expected mortality) depending on the relative level of risk which investors are willing to take. For the sponsor, economic value is a trade-off between the return paid to investors and capital relief achieved. A higher attachment point implies less risk and therefore lower compensation by the sponsor to investors. On an economic basis, a higher attachment also implies lower risk capital relief for the sponsor, although in practice this may not be recognised by some less sophisticated regulatory capital regimes.

The importance of indices

An important component of extreme mortality bonds is the use of indices based on population mortality data (parametric transaction), rather than an indemnity-based transaction that references a portfolio of specific named lives. Basing the transaction on publicly available population data enables investors to have access to exactly the same information as the sponsor and allows them to form their own view on the likelihood of an event occurring. As with other traded, index-based instruments, this transparency is important in promoting the liquidity of mortality bonds. In general, indices are also an efficient and scalable method of structuring a transaction.

The reference mortality index is typically tailored to provide the optimum mortality protection for the sponsor. This may involve weighting the index to the characteristics of the sponsors insured lives exposure, which in the UK would result in the majority of the index being weighted towards mortality experience between the average insured ages of 35 and 55 (the ages at which life assurance protection is typically most sought). Although an index could be tailored to reference any age range where there is suitable data available, the underlying data for the mortality index is generally population mortality statistics produced by the government of the relevant country(s), providing that a data source is consistent, transparent and publicly available.

Importantly, an index-based approach to issuing mortality bonds involves basis risk for the sponsor because of a possible difference between the mortality experience of the index and that of the underlying assurance portfolio. Consequently, under certain circumstances the sponsor of index-based bonds may suffer mortality experience on their portfolio higher than the bond attachment level (eg, 109% versus 105% of expected mortality) without an offsetting payout from the mortality bond. The basis risk is manageable for sponsors with large and well-diversified assurance portfolios, in which mortality experience in extreme events is likely to be highly correlated with population mortality. As such, sponsors of mortality bonds are typically risk aggregators such as reinsurers that provide indemnity cover to primary assurance companies and selectively hedge peak risks through, for example, parametric style coverage and other methods.

NATURE OF EXTREME MORTALITY RISK
Pandemic

The largest contributor to extreme mortality risk is probably the threat of a severe pandemic, which causes a large number of fatalities in a short space of time. A significant portion of the risk from infectious disease relates to pandemic influenza. In the 20th Century there were three major outbreaks, as detailed in Table 11.1, which shows estimated global deaths for each pandemic and the number of deaths. The excess mortality rate per thousand for the US is also shown in order to illustrate the impact for a single country.

The profile of influenza deaths by age has historically been "U-shaped" with peaks of mortality among infants and the elderly and comparatively lower mortality rates at the ages in between. However, this mortality curve was not the pattern for the 1918 pandemic, the most severe event of the last century, as illustrated by Figure 11.2. Instead the mortality distribution formed a "W-shaped" curve, with a middle peak in deaths among young adults between 25 and 34, which, as the graph shows, did not occur during the normal annual influenza seasons of the preceding years. The inter-pandemic years in the graph illustrate the "U-shape" normally seen in the distribution of mortality rates by age.

One striking feature of the 1918 pandemic is that individuals aged 65 or over accounted for less than 1% of all influenza-related deaths.

Table 11.1 Influenza pandemics of the 20th Century

Year(s)	Estimated global deaths (million)	Estimated US deaths (thousands)	US excess mortality (per 1,000)
1918–19 (Spanish flu)	40–50	500–550	5.30
1957–58 (Asian flu)	1–2	70	0.41
1968–69 (Hong Kong flu)	1	34	0.17

Source: Swiss Re (2007).

This figure is considerably less than the percentages for 1957 and 1968 pandemics, when this age group, generally thought to be more vulnerable to influenza, accounted for 64% and 52%, respectively. While mortality rates for infected people aged 65 and over were similar across the three pandemics, the incidence of infection in this group was much lower in 1918. A possible explanation for this phenomenon is that, depending on their actual age, those aged 65 and over may have been exposed to a similar virus in a previous pandemic, which may have given them a level of partial immunity to the 1918 strain. While the majority of deaths in 1918 were due to secondary bacterial pneumonia (since antibiotics were not then available), a significant minority, especially at ages below 65, died rapidly and violently soon after the onset of influenza symptoms. Why did so many of these apparently previously healthy younger adults die? One possible explanation is that the damage caused by an overreaction of the immune system resulted in the failure of multiple organ systems.

This type of analysis of a pandemic's trends is important to longevity risk holders who want to offset some of their exposure with extreme mortality risk, because future influenza pandemics may affect the distribution of deaths in diverse ways. These variations can have different consequences on the effectiveness of strategies to offset extreme mortality exposure. This analysis is particularly important in assessing the assumed impact on the different age groups.

EXTREME MORTALITY RISK AS A NATURAL HEDGE?

Figure 11.2 Impact on mortality of 1918 pandemic by age band

Source: Swiss Re (2007).

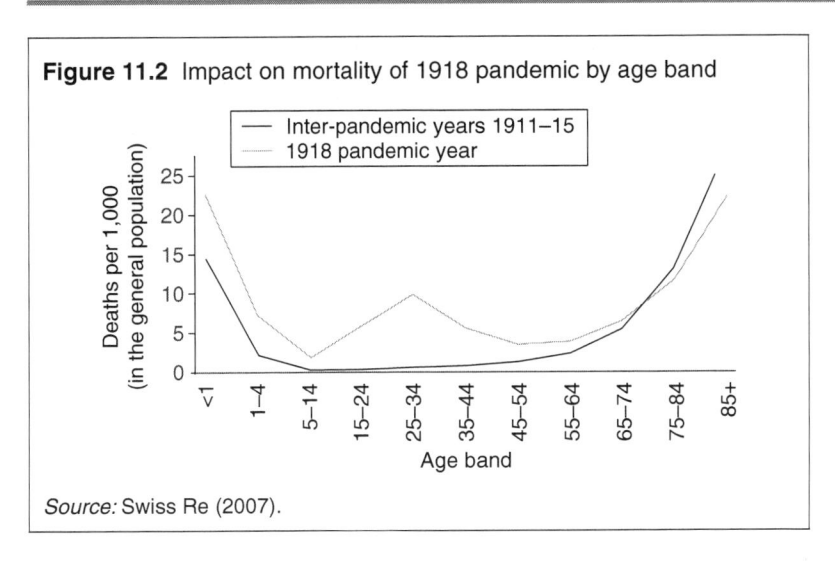

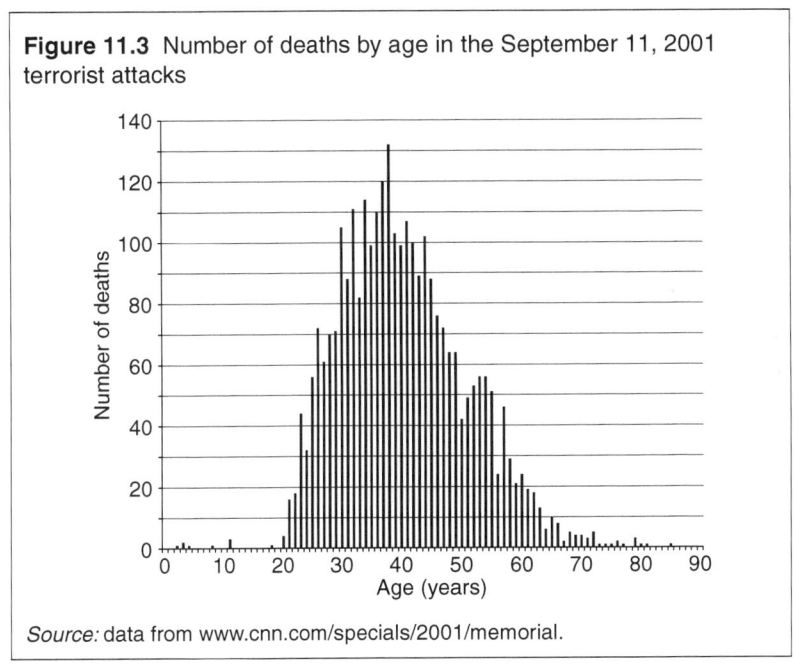

Figure 11.3 Number of deaths by age in the September 11, 2001 terrorist attacks

Source: data from www.cnn.com/specials/2001/memorial.

As challenging as it may be to evaluate the impact of an influenza pandemic on age distribution of fatalities, the issues raised by an outbreak of other infectious diseases are even harder to evaluate. It therefore seems reasonable to suggest that the impact would be fairly even or perhaps biased towards the younger ages and the elderly.

War or terrorism

An outbreak of war or an act of terrorism also raises the possibility of extreme mortality stemming from large numbers of fatalities. Although minor military conflicts and terrorist attacks occur relatively frequently, an act of war or terrorism on the scale required to cause a significant shift in population mortality appears to be considerably more remote than the threat from pandemics. In the case of war, fatalities are most likely to occur amongst those individuals involved in direct combat, ie, those between the ages of 18 and 45 (Obermeyer *et al* 2008).

While extremely unlikely, an act of terrorism severe enough to cause mass fatalities is perhaps most likely to target a city centre or busy transport hub, where most casualties would be of working age, ie, between 20 and 60. The type of impact such an event might cause is illustrated in Figure 11.3, which shows the number of deaths by age in the September 11, 2001 terrorist attacks in New York.

Other extreme mortality events

Natural catastrophes such as earthquakes or hurricanes and large-scale industrial accidents, such as the Bhopal toxic gas disaster in India in 1984, can also pose an extreme mortality risk. Their impact, however, would depend upon geographic location and could cut across all ages.

CONTRAST OF LONGEVITY RISK TO EXTREME MORTALITY RISK

Longevity risk can be divided into two main categories: the risk associated with in-payment annuities or pensions, and the risk associated with deferred annuities or pre-retirement members of a defined-benefit pension scheme.

Annuities and pensions in payment

In-payment longevity risk usually relates to active retirement benefits and as such generally involves older lives. Figure 11.4 illustrates the age distribution of the in-payment benefit for an example UK pension scheme. A logical pattern can be seen, where individuals begin to retire from age 50 onwards, with most benefits being drawn between the ages of 60 and 65. The exposure then runs off with age

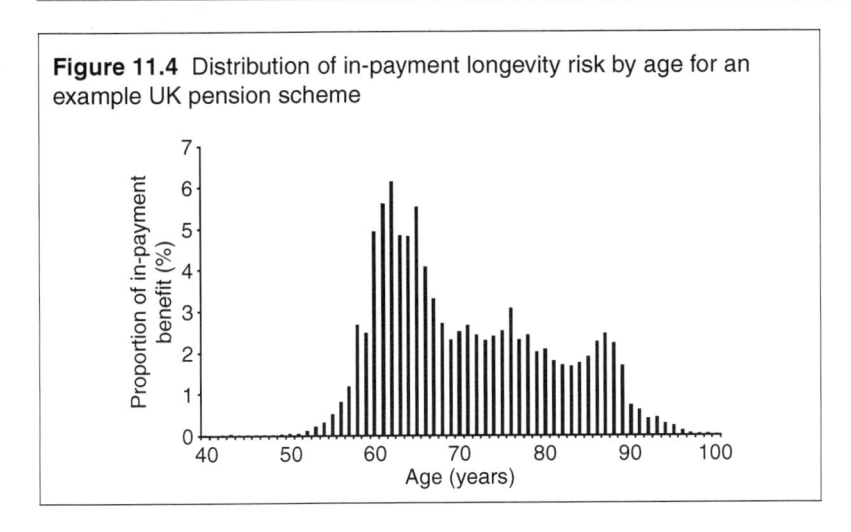

Figure 11.4 Distribution of in-payment longevity risk by age for an example UK pension scheme

as pensioners begin to die. A weighted average age of around 70 is typical for UK in-payment longevity risk.

Contrasting in-payment longevity risk with the components of extreme mortality risk described above, it can be seen that the majority of extreme mortality risk (which is currently transferred to the capital markets) generally relates to lives aged less than 60, while the majority of in-payment longevity risk generally relates to lives aged greater than 60. Therefore, extreme mortality risk is not necessarily a perfect offset for in-payment longevity risk. That is, in the event that a payment is required under the mortality bond (resulting in a loss to the holder) the reduction in liabilities (and resulting release of reserves as profit) on the in-payment longevity portfolio is likely to be small in proportion.

In theory, a mortality bond could be structured to reference an index relating to older lives to improve the reliability of offset. However, in this case sponsors would have less incentive to transfer this risk due to lower mortality exposure from older lives and the return to investors is likely to be lower due to the reduced risk.

Deferred annuities

The picture is considerably different for deferred longevity risk, however, because the populations that purchase these products are predominantly aged between 20 and 60. Acquiring extreme mortality risk from life assurance portfolios could effectively offset deferred longevity risk, because any payment under the bond would be potentially associated with significant reserve releases on the deferred longevity portfolio. In countries such as the UK, the majority of deferred longevity risk rests within defined-benefit pension schemes and, in particular, those schemes still open to new members. Therefore, this class of investors (ie, pension fund asset managers) would theoretically benefit the most from the offset between extreme mortality risk and longevity risk. In practice, the actual reduction in liabilities on the death of a pre-retirement member of a defined-benefit pension scheme could depend on features such as death-in-service benefits and other terms.

BASIS RISK

When assessing any reliable offset between different risk classes, it is important to consider any basis risk or heterogeneity between the reference populations. As pointed out previously, the basis risk between assured lives and the reference population data when discussing extreme mortality risk transfer may be effectively managed through the scale and diversification of the assurance portfolio. It is also the case that any sponsor of extreme mortality risk transfer may benefit from the structural difference between assured mortality experience and general population experience. In some countries such as the UK, the mortality rate for assured lives at key assured ages can be less than half that of the general population. This relationship reflects the high degree of socioeconomic selection amongst lives that have both the financial resources and underlying health status necessary to purchase life insurance. Although mortality experience for an extreme event such as those detailed above is likely to be highly correlated, the absolute impact from the major risk component of pandemics is likely to be lower for assured lives than for the general population. This is largely due to better underlying health status and other factors such as access to medical services.

In considering the offset between extreme mortality risk and longevity risk (setting aside complex indemnity risk swaps), any basis risk would be between the general population experience for the extreme mortality risk and working population experience for deferred lives (or pensioner mortality for in-payment lives) for longevity risk. In general, the population accruing and withdrawing pension benefits represents a considerably diverse mix of socioeconomic backgrounds, ranging from factory workers through to financial services employees. On average, mortality experience from pension beneficiaries would be expected to be fairly similar to population experience because of the wide social spectrum of underlying individuals.

There is, however, one notable distinction for those lives underlying longevity risk. By definition, these individuals have completed a significant period of time actively employed, a status that excludes the proportion of the general population who have never worked and are associated with poor health and low life expectancy. For this reason, the average longevity experience might be expected to be slightly better than population mortality (ie, have slightly lower mortality rates compared with population mortality). An individual pension fund or insurer would need to focus on the specifics of their own portfolio when considering any heterogeneity in the reference populations. However, this potential difference is likely to be relatively less significant than the structural age differences previously discussed between extreme mortality risk and longevity risk.

DURATION

Another important consideration in offsetting risk between extreme mortality and longevity risk is duration. Extreme mortality bonds have a much shorter duration (typically up to five years) than the longevity risk exposure. This mismatch implies a degree of sustainability or reinvestment risk around the use of mortality bonds to mitigate longevity risk. It could be argued that the impact of this mismatch could be significant or limited. On the one hand, despite the mismatch in duration, continued access to extreme mortality bonds is highly likely given that they are linked to capital relief for the sponsors. Increasing access to capital from outside of the insurance industry will also be a priority. Solvency II, the new EU capital framework for insurers, is expected to fully recognise the benefits of transferring peak risks such as extreme mortality in any format (including through the use of capital markets instruments such as ILSs). This recognition should incentivise sustained issuance. On the other hand, it could be argued that there is a significant asset–liability mismatch in considering short-term mortality bonds as an offset for longer term longevity liabilities. This is valid even though the projected costs and benefits could effectively be matched against each other through valuing on a present value basis. In practice, any purchase of mortality bonds is potentially more likely to be viewed on a fairly opportunistic basis versus the returns available from other investments, so the significance for asset–liability matching is perhaps reduced.

FINANCIAL CONSIDERATIONS

Extreme mortality risk is not necessarily a perfect offset for in-payment longevity risk, as the primary exposures to each occur at different age ranges. However, there is still a degree of financial offset. To demonstrate this point, let us consider a simple example in which the present value of benefits for an in-payment longevity portfolio is £3 billion and the age distribution is assumed to be typical. Applying a year-1 uniform extreme mortality shock assumption of 2‰ (ie, a weighted average mortality increase of roughly 10% for the portfolio) reduces the longevity liabilities by about 0.3% or £9 million. Assuming the mortality event were sufficiently onerous at younger ages to trigger a mortality bond, a bond investment of around £9 million would have an offsetting financial impact. It should be noted that this analysis does not account for the possibility of lighter mortality experience in the years immediately following the mortality shock, which would reduce the benefit to the longevity portfolio. On the other hand, there is also the possibility of an outcome in which higher than expected mortality on the longevity portfolio does not result in payout on the mortality bond. A heavy influenza pandemic with a disproportionate impact on older lives is one possible scenario that might result in such an outcome.

Applying a numerical example similar to that above to a deferred longevity portfolio is more difficult due to the subjectivity around the future accrual of pension benefits and the interaction with death-in-service benefits. While the death of younger members in the workforce may help to significantly reduce future funding requirements and reduce exposure to longevity risk, any immediate requirement to fund spousal pension benefits could result in additional financial strain.

CONCLUSION

Although there is clearly a degree of offset between extreme mortality risk and longevity risk, the two are not a natural hedge for each other due to the basic structure of each risk. This should be taken into account when developing a hedging strategy. Shock mortality events by definition affect only the number of deaths, which in many circumstances tend to affect a small proportion of the reference population. Longevity risk, however, is an exposure that pertains to the surviving individuals, which is by counterpart generally the majority of the reference population. Even in the event of an extreme pandemic of 10‰ extra deaths, for example, the expected impact on the valuation of a portfolio of survivorship liabilities would only be a reduction of around 1%. Therefore, the only truly effective natural hedge for longevity risk is through exposure to the opposing mortality trend (ie, mortality deterioration risk). (Re)insurers are perhaps best placed to take advantage of this natural hedge by underwriting both longevity and mortality trend risks, as well as managing mortality shock risk through extreme mortality risk-transfer techniques. This unified approach will provide a more complete hedging strategy and the potential for investors to access the benefits of an alternative asset risk class.

Although the natural hedge is not perfect, exposure to extreme mortality risk through mortality bonds (or other instruments) may provide attractive risk-adjusted returns when compared with vanilla corporate bonds. It can also sufficiently diversify against other asset classes such as credit, equity or property. Furthermore, the underlying asset risk of such instruments is likely to be at worst uncorrelated with longevity risk and at best negatively correlated. As such, extreme mortality instruments are likely to continue to have a strong case to form part of the asset-allocation strategy for both insurers with substantial longevity risk and defined-benefit pension funds.

REFERENCES

Obermeyer, Z., C. J. L. Murray and E. Gakidou, 2008, "Fifty Years of Violent War Deaths from Vietnam to Bosnia: Analysis of Data from the World Health Survey Programme", *British Medical Journal* 336, pp. 1482–86.

Swiss Re, 2007, "Pandemic Influenza: A 21st Century Model for Mortality Shocks", Report, URL: http://www.swissre.com/.

Part V

Capital Market Developments

12

Capital Markets and Longevity Risk Transfer

Guy Coughlan

Longevity risk – the risk that life spans exceed expectation – has become the focus of much attention for defined-benefit pension plans and life insurers with large annuity portfolios. Until relatively recently, the only way to mitigate longevity risk was via an insurance solution: a transaction in which pension plans typically bought annuities from, or sold their liabilities to, insurers which then bought reinsurance. This began to change in 2008, when the first capital markets solutions for longevity risk management were executed by Lucida and Canada Life in the UK. Both transactions were significant catalysts for the development of the longevity risk transfer market, bringing additional capacity, flexibility and transparency to complement existing insurance solutions.

This chapter focuses on solutions for transferring longevity risk via the capital markets from hedgers, such as pension plans and insurers, to end investors. We begin by reviewing the embryonic market for longevity risk transfer, the transactions that have been completed so far, the role of the capital markets and the primary participants. It is important that the longevity market is defined broadly enough to embrace both capital markets and insurance-based longevity swaps and includes longevity hedges implemented by insurers as well as those implemented by pension plans.

We then review the available longevity hedging solutions and their key characteristics, including their format in insurance or capital markets and design as customised (indemnity) or index (parametric) hedges. The discussion makes the point that customised hedges are often preferred because they provide an exact hedge of longevity risk, but that index hedges are particularly well suited for hedging the longevity risk of deferred pension plan members.

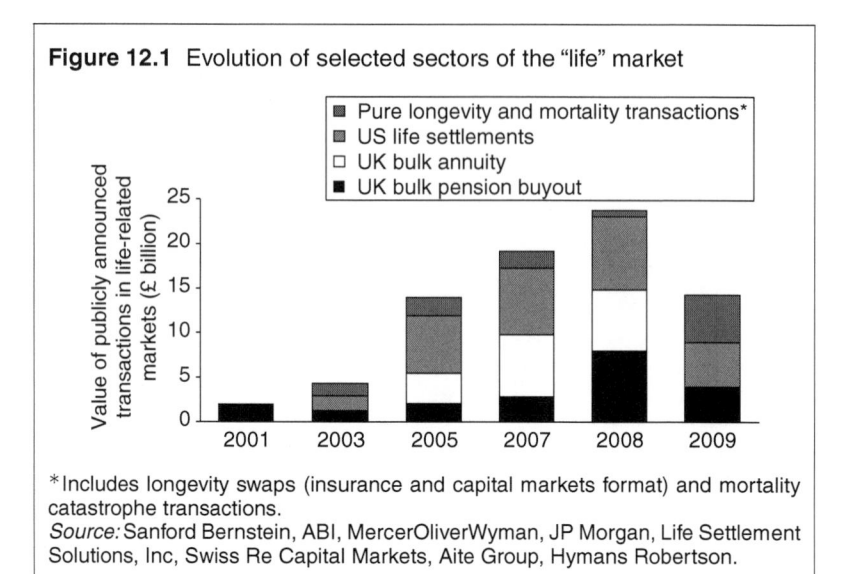

Figure 12.1 Evolution of selected sectors of the "life" market

[Bar chart showing value of publicly announced transactions in life-related markets (£ billion) from 2001 to 2009, with categories: Pure longevity and mortality transactions*, US life settlements, UK bulk annuity, UK bulk pension buyout]

*Includes longevity swaps (insurance and capital markets format) and mortality catastrophe transactions.
Source: Sanford Bernstein, ABI, MercerOliverWyman, JP Morgan, Life Settlement Solutions, Inc, Swiss Re Capital Markets, Aite Group, Hymans Robertson.

We also investigate the different types of hedges, including mortality forward-rate contracts known as "q-forwards", survivor forwards and survivor longevity swaps commonly known simply as "longevity swaps".

We highlight two significant initiatives, LifeMetrics and the Life & Longevity Markets Association (LLMA), designed to catalyse the development of the market. This discussion leads an examination of the important role that longevity indices have to play in market development and concludes with some brief summary comments.

THE MARKET FOR LONGEVITY RISK TRANSFER

The market for longevity risk transfer is a part of the broader "life" market that includes transactions of different kinds, many of which have existed for some time. These transactions include pension buy-outs (which transfer pension liabilities to insurers), bulk annuity deals (which transfer annuity portfolios between insurers/reinsurers), US life settlements (which transfer portfolios of US life assurance policies), embedded value securitisations, mortality catastrophe bonds and swaps, and longevity swaps. With the exception of 2009, the market for longevity risk showed impressive growth, as indicated in Figure 12.1, which shows the development of public transaction volumes for selected life market segments from 2001 to 2009. This growth, however, has been from a low base.

The pure longevity risk transfer segment of this broader market started in the UK, but in recent years there has been growing interest from pension plans and insurers in a number of other countries. Although a number of pure longevity risk transfer transactions took place as early as the 1990s, these deals were private, non-publicised insurance transactions and not part of a concerted effort to develop the longevity market. It was not until 2008, when momentum to develop the market began to build across the insurance and banking industries, that we saw the first such transactions announced publicly and the disclosure of many of their key details. It was these transactions that launched the market for pure longevity risk transfer in 2008.

The first such deal was a longevity hedge executed as a derivative in a capital markets format by Lucida, a pension buy-out insurer, in January 2008. The instrument was a q-forward contract linked to the LifeMetrics index of England and Wales mortality for a range of different ages. Following quickly on the heels of this deal was a second publicly announced transaction, by Canada Life in July 2008, but this time the instrument was a survivor longevity swap linked not to an index but to the actual mortality experience of the annuitants in the Canada Life portfolio.

In 2009, the market grew substantially and, although not shown in Figure 12.1, is now poised for significant future growth. However, given that Swiss Re estimates global longevity exposure at over US$20 trillion (Richardson 2010), it is clear that the market is currently minuscule relative to its potential size and could, therefore, grow enormously in coming years.

This market for pure longevity risk transfer has so far operated with instruments called longevity swaps, which have been transacted as both capital markets and insurance contracts. Of the nine longevity-swap transactions that were made public by August 2010 (Table 12.1), about half were executed in capital markets (ie, derivative) format and half in insurance format. Furthermore, about half have been executed by insurers and half by pension plans. Nearly all the transactions have been customised and undertaken on an "indemnity" basis, ie, where payments are linked to the actual longevity experience of the individuals concerned. By contrast, only one has used a longevity index to provide the longevity hedge. One-third of the deals have included capital markets investors amongst

Table 12.1 Publicly announced longevity-swap transactions

Date	Hedger	Size (£m)	Format	Term	Comments
Jan 2008	Lucida (insurer)	Not disclosed	Derivative	10 years	Index-based longevity swap First capital markets longevity hedge
July 2008	Canada Life (insurer)	500	Derivative	40 years	Indemnity longevity swap Distributed to capital markets investors
Feb 2009	Abbey Life (insurer)	1,500	Insurance	Run-off	Indemnity longevity swap Distributed to reinsurers
Mar 2009	Aviva (insurer)	475	Derivative	10 years	Collared indemnity swap Distributed to reinsurer and capital markets
Jun 2009	Babcock International (×3) (pension fund)	1,200	Derivative	50 years	Indemnity longevity swap First longevity hedge by a pension scheme
July 2009	RSA (pension fund)	1,900	Insurance	Run-off	Indemnity longevity swap Distributed to reinsurers
Dec 2009	Royal County of Berkshire (pension fund)	750	Insurance	Run-off	Indemnity longevity swap First longevity hedge by public sector
Feb 2010	BMW UK (pension fund)	3,000	Insurance	Run-off	Indemnity longevity swap Distributed to reinsurers
Jul 2010	British Airways (pension fund)	1,300	Insurance	Run-off	Indemnity longevity swap Distributed to reinsurers

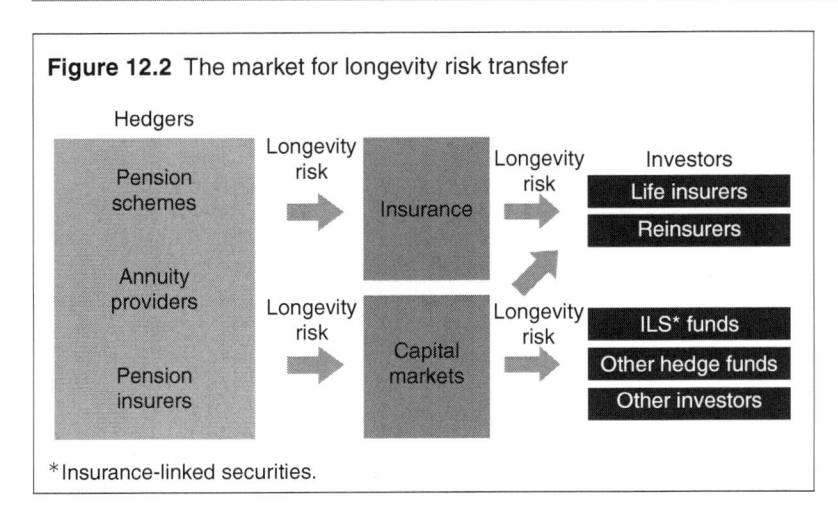

Figure 12.2 The market for longevity risk transfer

Hedgers: Pension schemes, Annuity providers, Pension insurers → Longevity risk → Insurance → Longevity risk → Investors: Life insurers, Reinsurers

Hedgers → Longevity risk → Capital markets → Longevity risk → ILS* funds, Other hedge funds, Other investors

*Insurance-linked securities.

the end holders of the transferred longevity risk, specifically the transactions involving Lucida, Canada Life and Aviva. Most of the transactions were designed as cashflow hedges, ie, they hedge the uncertainty in each of the liability payments. By contrast, the Lucida deal was designed as a value hedge, ie, it hedges the uncertainty in the value of the liability. The Aviva transaction included elements of both cashflow and value hedges.

Just as this book was going to press, the trustees of the Pall (UK) Pension Fund announced that they had completed an index hedge of their deferred pensioner longevity risk (Davies 2011; Mercer 2011). This hedge, the first of its kind, was executed with JP Morgan in January 2011 and based on the LifeMetrics Longevity Index. It involves a portfolio of q-forwards linked to male and female mortality rates for England and Wales, calibrated to hedge the value of the deferred pensioner liability over a 10-year horizon.

The role of the capital markets

In defining the longevity risk transfer market it is important to include transactions executed in both capital markets and insurance formats. These are alternative but complementary channels for achieving the same goal, as shown in Figure 12.2. Indeed, the capital markets bring several benefits, including the following.

- Additional capacity for bearing longevity risk: the universe of end holders of the risk is expanded beyond insurers and reinsurers to include financial investors.

- Greater diversity of counterparties: hedgers are not restricted to transact just with insurers and reinsurers, but can also transact with investment banks, exchanges and other intermediaries.
- Liquidity: appropriately designed capital markets contracts have the potential to be highly liquid which is not the case with insurance contracts.
- Fungibility: longevity hedges or investments transacted with one institution may be unwound with another institution.
- Potential for reduced counterparty exposure: longevity hedges transacted as capital market derivatives are required to be fully collateralised on an economic or marked-to-market basis to reduce counterparty credit exposure. In the past this requirement has generally not been the case with insurance transactions, although it is now changing for longevity transactions.

There are three main differences between capital markets and insurance longevity transactions. The first is obvious: the legal form of the contract. The second is the counterparty facing the hedger, which for insurance-based hedges must be an insurer, but for capital markets hedges there is no specific requirement. Finally, the nature of the end holder of the risk is different. With insurance-based hedges the risk will end up with insurers and/or reinsurers, whereas for capital markets hedges the end holders of the risk can include financial investors. Despite these differences, the two kinds of transactions, when appropriately structured, effectively achieve the same result in economic terms.

The development of a vibrant market for capital markets longevity risk transfer is widely seen as beneficial for the insurance industry in terms of facilitating optimal management of capital and building additional insurance capacity.

Market participants

Three primary kinds of participants are usually involved in capital markets' longevity transactions.

- **Hedgers:** insurers or annuity providers and pension plans that naturally have longevity risk and are seeking to reduce or eliminate it.

- **Investors:** financial institutions that are potentially end holders of the longevity risk; these include insurance-linked securities (ILSs) funds, hedge funds and endowments, as well as insurers and reinsurers.
- **Financial intermediaries:** banks and other financial institutions that facilitate risk transfer and, in many cases, stand between hedgers and investors.

Increasing numbers of investors of different kinds are in various stages of evaluating this asset class, which to them represents a new investment opportunity offering a positive risk premium and which is largely uncorrelated with traditional asset classes. At this stage many are focused on developing the skills and infrastructure to be able to invest in longevity exposure. In July 2008 JP Morgan placed the first pure longevity investments (originating from the Canada Life hedge mentioned above) with several capital markets investors via a 40-year survivor swap. This transaction was successful despite having many features that were not ideal from an investor perspective, such as very long maturity, customised longevity risk, lack of liquidity, uncapped downside risk and a requirement for complex analytical diligence.

Financial intermediaries can be useful for capital-markets-based longevity transactions for several reasons.

- **Liquidity provision.** By providing liquidity to both sides of the market it is unnecessary for hedgers to wait for interested investors to enter the market before hedging and vice versa. Moreover, the hedge remains in place if an investor redeems its longevity investment.
- **Credit intermediation.** By fulfilling the role of counterparty to both hedgers and investors, credit counterparty exposure can be left with institutions, such as banks, that are best equipped to manage it.
- **Repackaging.** Many investors want to take longevity risk in different forms from that in which hedgers want to shed it. By standing in the middle, intermediaries can slice and dice exposures into different parcels to meet the specific needs of different investors and hedgers.

It is important to note that financial intermediaries (such as banks) are unlikely to be long-term holders of significant amounts of longevity risk, but they may temporarily warehouse the risk to facilitate liquidity provision.

Other key players in the market include advisors and consultants, who perform various roles ranging from providing legal advice and detailed financial analysis to running competitive quotation processes. For example, employee benefit consultants have assisted UK pension plans in obtaining quotations from longevity hedge providers such as banks and insurers, performing due diligence and selecting the winning proposal.

Another emerging but important role of advisors and consultants is that of calculation agent for the mortality-related computations that feed into the ongoing determination of the value of a transaction and the payments that must be made. For example, Towers Watson acts as calculation agent for the LifeMetrics index on which the Lucida deal is based and Milliman acts in a similar capacity for the Aviva deal, listed in Table 12.1.

SOLUTIONS FOR HEDGING LONGEVITY RISK

The solutions currently available for hedging pure longevity risk can be classified broadly according to three characteristics.

- **Format:** insurance versus capital markets.
- **Design:** customised (indemnity) versus index (parametric).
- **Structure of instrument:** swap versus forward, among others.

As discussed earlier, the first characteristic pertains to the legal nature of the contract, which in the case of insurance contracts necessarily involves an insurer. Such legal considerations are explored further in Chapter 14.

The "design" characteristic reflects the nature of the longevity risk associated with the hedging instrument and for discussion purposes can be broken down into two categories: customised and index hedges.

A customised hedge is one in which the performance of the hedging instrument is linked to the actual longevity experience of the individuals associated with the exposure that is hedged. An example is the actual members of a pension plan or the actual annuitants in an annuity portfolio. By contrast, an index hedge is one in which the performance of the hedging instrument is linked to an index reflecting the longevity or mortality experience of what is typically a larger pool of lives, such as a national population.

Customised hedges have the advantage of providing a nearly perfect hedge, whereas index hedges will generally leave an element of residual risk, called basis risk, because the population associated with the exposure is different from the population associated with the hedging instrument. Index hedges, nevertheless, bring other advantages in terms of standardisation, transparency, greater appeal to investors and the potential for higher liquidity. Table 12.2 provides a summary of the key differences between customised and index longevity hedges.

Labelling instruments as either customised or index hedges, however, is perhaps too simplistic an approach for classifying the types of instruments that are in the market. Even at this early stage of development, hybrid hedges that combine some of the features of each have emerged. For example, hedges of pension liability value have been constructed using a specific bespoke index that is based on the realised mortality experience of the pension plan members.

The actual structure of the hedging instrument is the third characteristic of longevity risk deals. In general, hedging of longevity risk can be accomplished via many different types of instrument, ranging from the so-called q-forward used by Lucida to the survivor swap used by Canada Life and others. These different types of instrument are discussed in more detail in the next section.

Available hedging solutions

The availability of current longevity hedging solutions varies, depending on the type of longevity risk being transferred. As indicated by Table 12.3, which classifies the availability of hedging solutions by format and design, the solutions available for pensions in payment include customised hedges in either insurance or capital markets format, and index hedges available only as a capital markets solution. However, the choices are more limited for younger deferred pensioners (ie, those who are yet to retire and have not started drawing their pension). Customised hedges are generally not available for deferreds, except in special situations such as pensions that cover older deferreds whose retirement is relatively soon. For these portfolios, index hedges are extremely well suited to hedge the longevity risk associated with deferred benefits, as explained in the penultimate section.

Table 12.2 Comparison of customised and index longevity swaps

	Customised (indemnity) hedge	Index (parametric) hedge
Longevity risk indemnification	Total risk indemnification for portfolio of hedged lives	Not perfect hedge because of basis risk between index and underlying population, however expected to hedge majority of risk • Typically expected to hedge around 85% of risk
What is hedged	Hedge of pension plan cashflows	Hedge of liability value over life of swap
What structure is most suitable for	Customised solution typically only available for pensioner members • Optionality of deferred benefits makes it expensive to hedge and few investors want this risk	Deferred members • Typically longevity exposure not fully known for deferreds as members have options such as commutation of benefits that make it hard to accurately assess (ie, a perfect hedge is not needed) • No cashflows for deferred members which make hedge of value more appropriate
Data requirements	Requires pension plan to provide data over the life of hedge	Pension plan member data only required initially to structure hedge as payout of hedge is based on published index
Other	Bespoke contract tailored to structure of pension plan	Standardised contract • More attractive to capital markets investor base • Promotes secondary liquidity

Table 12.3 Available longevity solutions

	Pensioners' longevity risk (post-retirement)	Deferreds' longevity risk (pre-retirement)
Insurance:		
• Customised hedge	Yes	Limited
Capital markets:		
• Customised hedge	Yes	Limited
• Index hedge	Yes	Yes

STRUCTURES OF INSTRUMENTS FOR LONGEVITY RISK TRANSFER

We now turn to the key structures, or types, of instruments used to hedge longevity risk. The most common structure used to date has been the survivor longevity swap: an arrangement that is in fact equivalent to a portfolio of much simpler instruments called survivor forwards, or S-forwards. This, however, is far from being the simplest hedging instrument. For this reason, we begin our discussion with a different kind of forward contract: the mortality forward.

Mortality forward (q-forward)

A mortality forward rate contract, often referred to as a "q-forward" because the letter "q" is designated the standard symbol for mortality rates, is the simplest type of instrument for transferring longevity and mortality risk (Coughlan et al 2007a), and is the instrument used by Lucida in implementing the first capital markets hedge of longevity risk listed in Table 12.1 (Symmons 2008).

The importance of q-forwards rests in the fact that they form basic building blocks from which other, more complex, life-related derivatives can be constructed. When appropriately designed, a portfolio of q-forwards can be used to replicate and to hedge the longevity exposure of an annuity or a pension liability, or to hedge the mortality exposure of a life assurance book.

A q-forward is defined as an agreement between two parties in which they agree to exchange an amount proportional to the actual, realised mortality rate of a given population (or subpopulation), in return for an amount proportional to a fixed mortality rate that has been mutually agreed at inception to be payable at a future date (the maturity of the contract). In this sense, a q-forward is a zero-coupon

Figure 12.3 For a *q*-forward, cashflows based on fixed versus floating (or realised) mortality rates are exchanged only at maturity

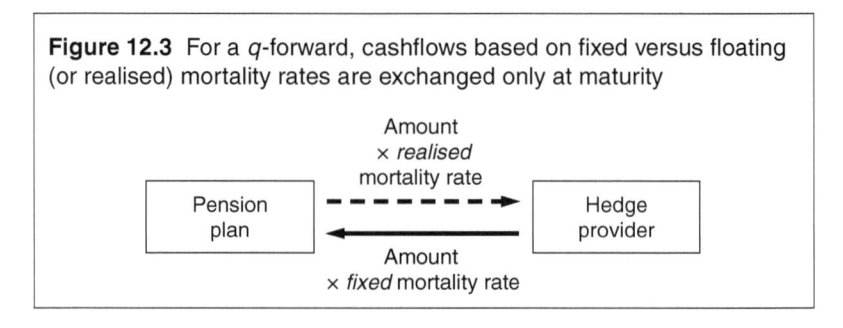

Pension plan — Amount × *realised* mortality rate → Hedge provider
Hedge provider — Amount × *fixed* mortality rate → Pension plan

Figure 12.4 Net payout from a *q*-forward at maturity

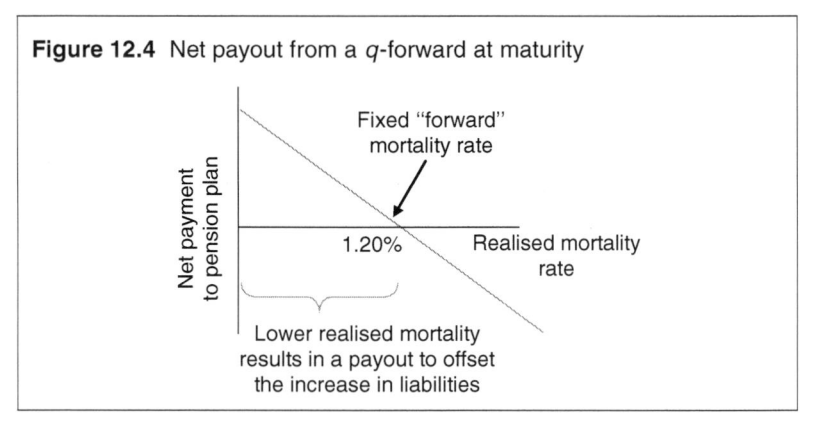

Axes: Net payment to pension plan (vertical); Realised mortality rate (horizontal). Fixed "forward" mortality rate at 1.20%. Lower realised mortality results in a payout to offset the increase in liabilities.

swap that exchanges fixed mortality for the realised mortality at maturity, as illustrated in Figure 12.3. The variable used to settle the contract is the realised mortality rate for that subpopulation in a future period.

In a fair market, the fixed mortality rate at which the transaction takes place defines the "forward mortality rate" for the population (or subpopulation) in question. If the *q*-forward is fairly priced, no payment changes hands at the inception of the trade. At maturity, however, a net payment will be made by one of the two counterparties.

The settlement that takes place at maturity is based on the net amount payable and is proportional to the difference between the fixed mortality rate (the transacted forward rate) and the realised reference rate. Figure 12.4 shows the settlement for different potential outcomes for the realised reference rate. If the reference rate in the reference year is below the fixed rate (ie, lower mortality), then the settlement is positive, and the pension plan receives the settlement payment to offset the increase in its liability value. If, on the

Figure 12.5 Survivor forward

```
                        Amount
                      × realised
                      survival rate
    ┌──────────┐   ◄──────────────   ┌──────────┐
    │ Pension  │                     │  Hedge   │
    │  plan    │   ──────────────►   │ provider │
    └──────────┘      Amount         └──────────┘
                   × fixed survival rate
```
Cashflows based on fixed v. floating survival rates are exchanged at maturity only.

Figure 12.6 Net payout from an S-forward at maturity

[Graph: Net payment to pension plan vs. Realised survival rate. Fixed "forward" survival rate at 87%. Higher realised survival results in a payout to offset the increase in liabilities.]

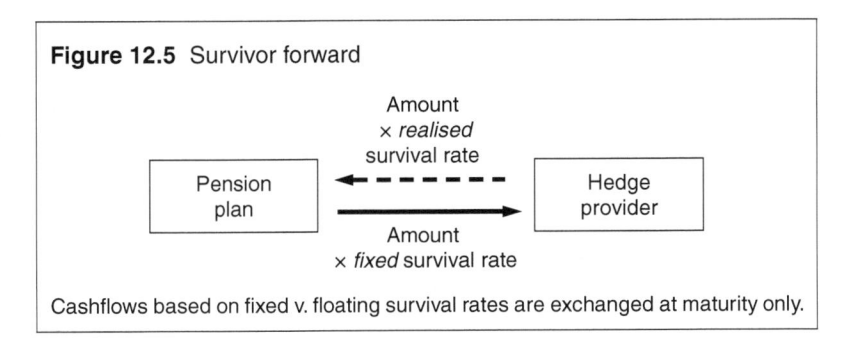

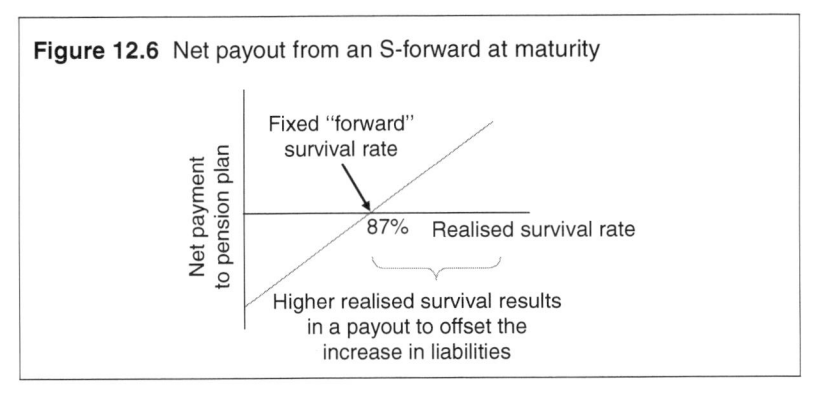

other hand, the reference rate is above the fixed rate (ie, higher mortality), then the settlement is negative and the pension plan pays the settlement payment to the hedge provider, which will be offset by the fall in the value of its liabilities. In this way the net liability value is locked in regardless of what happens to mortality rates. The plan is protected from unexpected changes in mortality rates.

Survivor forward (S-forward)

Another possible building block, which is slightly more complex than the q-forward, is what we call a "survivor forward". The S-forward resembles a q-forward in nearly every way, except that it is linked to a survival rate rather than a mortality rate. As such, it involves the exchange of a notional amount multiplied by a pre-agreed fixed survival rate in return for the same notional amount multiplied by the realised survival rate for a specified cohort over a given period of time. This S-forward structure is illustrated in Figures 12.5 and 12.6, where it should be noted that the fixed and floating arrows point in opposite directions to those for a q-forward,

Figure 12.7 Survivor longevity-swap cashflows

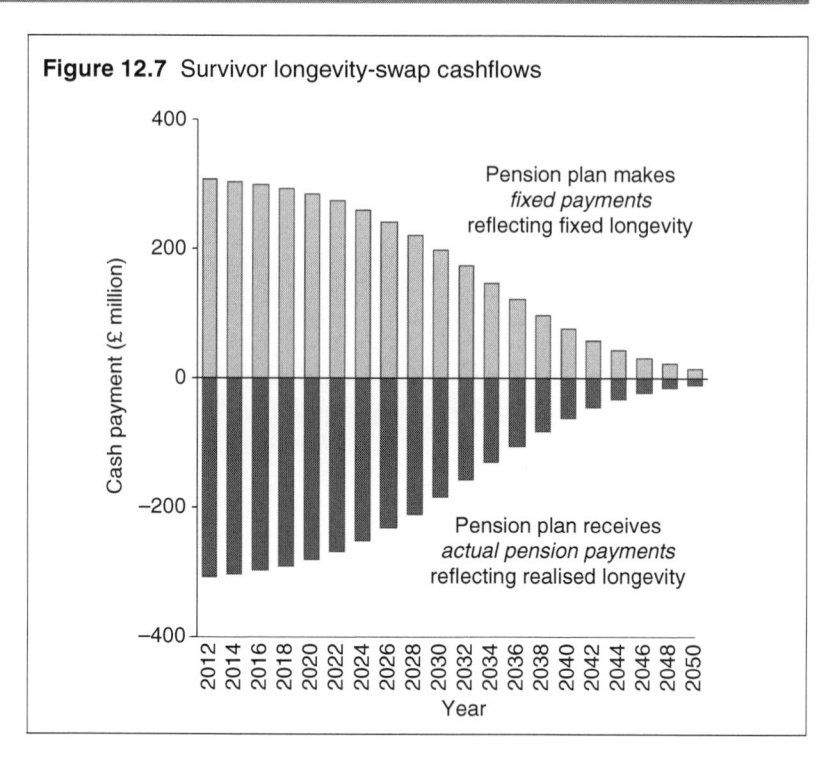

[Bar chart: Cash payment (£ million) vs Year (2012–2050). Positive bars labelled "Pension plan makes fixed payments reflecting fixed longevity"; negative bars labelled "Pension plan receives actual pension payments reflecting realised longevity".]

because paying realised survival is equivalent to receiving realised mortality.[1]

Survivor longevity swap

A survivor longevity swap is a derivative which involves exchanging a series of payments based on the actual realised survival in return for a series of pre-agreed fixed payments, as indicated in Figure 12.7. Because a survivor swap can essentially be thought of as a string of S-forwards with different maturity dates, the S-forward is clearly a building block for survivor swaps.

In practice, the survivor swaps that have actually been transacted (eg, in the Canada Life and Babcock hedges in Table 12.1) have cashflows for which the survival rate at each payment date is weighted by the pension amount. Therefore, each payment is based on an amount-weighted survival rate.

The Canada Life transaction was a 40-year maturity survivor swap designed to hedge, on a *pro rata* basis, part of the portfolio of annuities that Canada Life bought from Equitable Life in 2006.[2] In this survivor swap JP Morgan pays Canada Life the actual payments

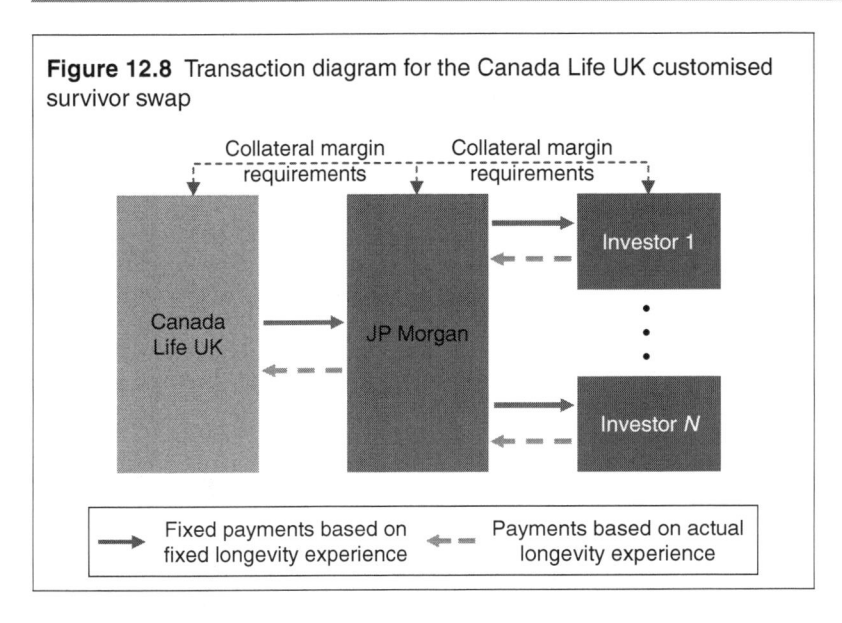

Figure 12.8 Transaction diagram for the Canada Life UK customised survivor swap

```
         Collateral margin          Collateral margin
         requirements               requirements

                                              → Investor 1
                                              ← - -
  Canada      →     JP Morgan                    ⋮
  Life UK     ← - -                           → Investor N
                                              ← - -
```

→ Fixed payments based on fixed longevity experience
← - - Payments based on actual longevity experience

due to annuitants based on their realised longevity experience and in return Canada Life pays a series of fixed payments based on the expected longevity plus a margin or risk premium. The swap therefore provides the insurer with a long-maturity, customised cashflow hedge of its longevity risk. The longevity risk transferred in this transaction from Canada Life to JP Morgan was then sold on to a group of investors with mirrored back-to-back survivor swaps (Figure 12.8).

INITIATIVES TO FACILITATE LONGEVITY MARKET DEVELOPMENT

There have been two major public initiatives aimed at facilitating the development of the longevity market. The first was the release of LifeMetrics in 2007 and the second was the launch of the Life & Longevity Markets Association (LLMA) in 2010. Both of these initiatives were aimed at promoting standardisation and education.

LifeMetrics

Launched in March 2007, the longevity toolkit called LifeMetrics[3] is a publicly available set of resources that includes longevity indices, analytics, frameworks and software for measuring and managing longevity risk.

The LifeMetrics longevity indices cover several countries, including the US, the UK (England and Wales), the Netherlands and Germany, based on national population mortality statistics. In the spirit of the longevity index principles that will be discussed in the next section, the LifeMetrics indices and toolkit are non-proprietary, fully transparent and freely available. They are fully documented[4] and include a framework for risk management, research publications, analytics and software for mortality forecasting and stochastic simulation. LifeMetrics index data, software and publications are available publicly from the website, with index data also available from Bloomberg (ticker: LFMT).

Life & Longevity Markets Association

The mission of the LLMA, a not-for-profit cross-industry trade association, is to promote a liquid, traded market in longevity and mortality related risk. Launched publicly on February 1, 2010, the organisation has 11 member institutions as of the time of writing, three of which joined since the launch, from across the insurance and investment banking industries. The current members are Aviva, AXA, Deutsche Bank, JP Morgan, Legal & General, Morgan Stanley, Pension Corporation, Prudential plc, RBS, Swiss Re and UBS.

The LLMA aims to "break down the barriers to market growth by supporting the development of consistent standards, methodologies and benchmarks".[5] The association is working to achieve this through a number of projects to develop and publish

- standardised longevity-swap structures,
- standardised documentation,
- LLMA-sponsored indices,
- a standardised valuation (pricing) model,
- a longevity risk management framework.

This initiative intends to deliver benefits to the market in terms of increased transparency and standardisation, which should lead to faster timescales for implementing longevity transactions because of an increased understanding and more streamlined due diligence. The result should be a larger and more efficient market for longevity risk transfer.

THE ROLE OF LONGEVITY INDICES

A longevity index is defined as a collection of data that relate to different life-related metrics such as mortality rates, survival rates and life expectancies, which are applied to a group of lives and various subgroups of those lives (such as age, gender, geography and socio-economic class).

Longevity indices have been integral to the development of the longevity market and particularly in the development of capital markets solutions as evidenced in the essential role they have in index hedges of longevity risk and also in certain customised hedge transactions. For example, Canada Life's customised longevity swap used several elements of the methodology and analytics of the LifeMetrics Longevity Index.

Longevity indices play an important role in market development in other ways. In the early stages of market development they increase the visibility of longevity and assist in the education of potential market participants who may be less familiar with this type of risk. They also provide a transparent benchmark for mortality rates, life expectancy, survivorship and longevity risk. Furthermore, the historical data embedded in longevity indices aids the pricing and risk assessment of longevity exposures and longevity hedges. Finally, they encourage standardisation, which is essential for building liquidity in any new market.

In order to become widely accepted and encourage transactions, a longevity index must be both objective and fully transparent (Coughlan *et al* 2007b, p. 9). Sweeting (2010) has recently discussed the importance of these properties and others in relation to longevity indices. Moreover, the LLMA has developed a set of 10 principles upon which any longevity index should be based:

1. tradability;
2. transparency;
3. robustness;
4. objectivity;
5. simplicity;
6. clear governance;
7. timeliness;
8. continuity;

9. consistency;

10. universality.

These principles are part of a publicly available framework for building and operating longevity indices published by the Life & Longevity Markets Association (2010). The LLMA encourages all market participants to adopt its framework in developing new longevity indices, including both public indices and private, proprietary indices based on customised pools of lives. The framework also proposes best practice guidelines on the methodology and governance of longevity indices.

The reason may be evident but it bears emphasis: appropriately designed longevity indices which conform to accepted principles and standards promote the development of the longevity market and facilitate longevity hedging and longevity investment transactions. Longevity indices and their ideal requirements are explored in further depth in Chapter 13.

Indices and hedging deferred longevity risk

Index hedges are particularly appropriate for hedging the longevity risk associated with deferred pension members and deferred annuitants, prior to drawing their pension or annuity, for several reasons. Firstly, the risk prior to retirement is a pure valuation risk because there are no payments. The uncertainty therefore affects only the value of the pension/annuity rather than cashflow. The value of the deferred pension/annuity is dependent on mortality improvement assumptions, which are generally determined with reference to mortality improvement forecasts for a broader population, eg, the population associated with a national longevity index. Hedging the value of deferred pensions/annuities with an index hedge is effective because it essentially hedges against unexpected mortality improvements. Secondly, the underlying longevity exposure of deferred members of pension plans is not well defined. This is because deferred members have several options that change the nature of the longevity exposure, in particular

- the option to retire early,
- the option to convert (part of) their pension into a lump sum,

- the option, in some cases, to exchange some of their own pension for a higher, spouse's pension in the event of their death.

These choices create significant uncertainty in the pension payment profile and in the amount of longevity risk. As a result, an exact hedge of deferred longevity risk is not really practicable or even desirable. But an index hedge provides effective reduction in longevity risk at an affordable cost, provided it is structured to minimise basis risk.

For a more detailed discussion of index hedges and their effectiveness as longevity hedges, see Coughlan (2009) and Coughlan *et al* (2010).

CONCLUSIONS

Longevity risk transfer via the capital markets is now a viable risk management option for defined-benefit pension plans, and for insurers and reinsurers with annuity portfolios. Longevity-swap transactions have been implemented using both customised and standardised index-based products. Moreover, longevity swaps have been implemented in both insurance format and in capital markets format. While most transactions in the public domain have involved customised swaps, there is growing interest in using index hedges to reduce the longevity risk associated with deferred pensioners and deferred annuitants. The market still requires further education and standardisation, but these shortcomings are now being addressed in a coherent and coordinated manner through the recently formed cross-industry trade association, the LLMA. The development of an active and efficient capital market for longevity risk transfer will bring substantial benefits to pension plans and their sponsors, as well as to insurers and reinsurers, through increased capacity and an enhanced ability to manage risk and capital.

> Additional information is available upon request. This chapter was prepared by the Pension Advisory Group and not by any research department of JPMorgan Chase & Co and its subsidiaries ("JP Morgan"). The information herein is obtained from sources believed to be reliable but JP Morgan does not warrant its completeness or accuracy. Opinions and estimates constitute JP Morgan's judgement and are subject to change without notice. Past performance is not indicative of future results. This material is provided for informational purposes only and is not intended as a recommendation

or an offer or solicitation for the purchase or sale of any security or financial instrument.

1 To understand this concept, consider that over a single year the survival rate for a cohort is equal to one minus its mortality rate. Exchanging survival rates therefore is equivalent to exchanging mortality rates with the flows in opposite directions.

2 For additional background on the transaction, see *Trading Risk* (2008) and *Life & Pensions* (2008).

3 See http://www.lifemetrics.com.

4 See Coughlan *et al* (2007b) and other related documents.

5 See http://www.llma.org.

REFERENCES

Coughlan, G. D., 2009. "Longevity Risk Transfer: Indices and Capital Market Solutions", in P. M. Barrieu and L. Albertini (eds), *The Handbook of Insurance Linked Securities* (London: John Wiley & Sons).

Coughlan, G. D., D. Epstein, A. Sinha and P. Honig, 2007a, "q-Forwards: Derivatives for Transferring Longevity and Mortality Risk", July 2, Report, JP Morgan, London, URL: http://www.lifemetrics.com.

Coughlan, G. D., D. Epstein, A. Ong, A. Sinha, I. Balevich, J. Hevia-Portocarrera, E. Gingrich, M. Khalaf-Allah and P. Joseph, 2007b, "LifeMetrics: A Toolkit for Measuring and Managing Longevity and Mortality Risks", Technical Document, March 13, JP Morgan, London, URL: http://www.lifemetrics.com.

Coughlan, G. D., M. Khalaf-Allah, Y. Ye, S. Kumar, A. J. G. Cairns, D. Blake and K. Dowd, 2010, "Longevity Hedging 101: A Framework for Longevity Basis Risk Analysis and Hedge Effectiveness", August, Pensions Institute Discussion Paper PI-1013, URL: http://www.pensions-institute.org/, forthcoming, *North American Actuarial Journal*.

Davies, P. J., 2011, "JPMorgan Strikes an Important Deal for Longevity Risk Trading", *Financial Times*, February 1, p. 32.

Life & Longevity Markets Association, 2010, "Longevity Index Framework: A Framework for Building Longevity Indices Developed by the LLMA", URL: http://www.llma.org.

Life & Pensions, 2008, "Canada Life Hedges Equitable Longevity with JPMorgan Swap", *Life and Pensions*, October, p. 6.

Mercer, 2011, "World's First Longevity Hedge for Non-Retired Pension Plan Members Completed", Press Release, February 1, URL: http://uk.mercer.com/press-releases/1406520.

Richardson, D., 2010, "Longevity Swaps: How They Fit into Your Longevity Risk Mitigation Strategy", Presented at the Marcus Evans Conference on Longevity and Mortality Risk Management, London, UK, June 22.

Symmons, J. 2008, "Lucida Guards against Longevity", *Financial News*, February 19, URL: http://www.efinancialnews.com.

Sweeting, P. J., 2010, "Longevity Indices and Pension Fund Risk", Working Paper, University of Kent, Canterbury, UK, February 18.

Trading Risk, 2008, "JPMorgan Longevity Swap Unlocks UK Annuity Market", *Trading Risk* September/October, p. 3 URL: http://www.trading-risk.com.

13

Longevity Indices

Paul Sweeting
University of Kent

As mortality and longevity risk becomes an increasing focus for pension schemes and insurance companies, the need to attract sufficient capital to enable the transfer of these risks is likely to gain urgency. One way of promoting this process is to encourage an element of standardisation, which can be achieved through the use of longevity indices.

In this chapter we first consider mortality and longevity risk, decomposing these risks into their component parts. Next, we examine some of the mechanics of longevity swaps and the ideal requirements of indices both in general terms and specifically for the transfer of mortality and longevity risk. The use of longevity index swaps in the transfer of both longevity and catastrophe risk is explored. We conclude with an examination of the long-term impact that market initiatives around publishing indices will have on the future growth of the market.

MORTALITY AND LONGEVITY RISK

The liabilities of defined-benefit pension funds have grown enormously since the 1980s due to falling interest rates and rising longevity. The impact of these trends on pension liabilities has been exacerbated by the fact that previously discretionary benefits have become guaranteed through legislation in countries such as the UK. What has resulted is a combination of forces that is driving a great deal of interest in selective pension de-risking.

Selective de-risking aims to reduce the risks for which the reward is limited. A prime example is in the management of interest rate risk, where there is little expected reward for unintended interest rate mismatch. This realisation has led to an increase in the use of liability-driven investment (LDI), implemented with interest rate and inflation swaps. Longevity risk has also become a target of those who wish to hedge their risk to the extent that it can be transferred for a reasonable premium.

Life insurance companies also face longevity risk, through the sale of annuities, and mortality risk, by writing life assurance policies, the most common form of which is term assurance.

According to the International Actuarial Association, longevity and mortality risks can be broken down into four separate risks (IAA 2004).

- **Volatility risk** arises because pension schemes or annuity portfolios cover only a finite number of individuals, each of whom will either die or survive over the period under investigation. The smaller the number of lives covered, the greater the risk that the actual number of deaths will differ significantly from the number expected.
- **Catastrophe risk** refers to a large short-term increase in mortality due to an event such as a pandemic. Given the fact that similar one-time drops in mortality rates do not typically occur, it is not usually used to describe longevity risk.
- **Level risk** stems from the volatility of past mortality experience. This is the risk that the current expected rates of mortality for a portfolio of lives are mis-estimated due to random variations in past experience.
- **Trend risk** stems from the possibility that future mortality rates will change at a rate different from that expected.

There are a number of ways of hedging longevity risk, the most obvious being to buy an annuity. However, as a fully funded solution, this option ties the reduction in risk to a reduction in expected return. An alternative that can have minimal funding requirements is to use a longevity survivor swap. As described in previous chapters, this arrangement is a contract in which one party commits to making periodic payments based on the expected mortality of a group of lives (the fixed leg), while the other party commits to making payments based on the actual mortality experience of that group of lives (the floating leg). A longevity survivor swap is useful if any deviation from the expected level of mortality is unwanted.

Some holders of mortality risk are concerned only with avoiding adverse results stemming from catastrophe risk. In this case, a mortality swaption might be more appropriate. For catastrophe risk protection, the buyer of the swaption would have the right to receive or make a fixed payment in exchange for making or receiving a payment based on the survival of the lives detailed in the swap contract. The exact structure of the swaption depends on whether the variable payment was based on the amount due to meet life assurance or pension payments. In the first case, the insurer would pay fixed and receive floating; in the second, the roles would be reversed.

As introduced in Chapter 8, a key question is whether to hedge on an indemnity or a parametric (index) basis. Under an indemnity-based arrangement, the exact longevity experience of the portfolio of lives is hedged, similar to the case of purchasing an annuity. For the pension scheme in question, this approach is attractive because the longevity experience of the lives in question will be replicated exactly by the contract in force. However, it may well be more expensive than a parametric solution because, from the point of view of the risk-accepting counterparty to the contract, the scope for using such risk to hedge, say, term-assurance business is potentially more limited, as the longevity experience will relate to a specific portfolio rather than, say, the general population. A scheme-specific contract is also less likely to be tradeable, as investors' knowledge of the scheme is likely to be less than that of a widely used reference population. This too would increase the cost. On the other hand, a contract based on a standardised reference population (a longevity index) gives rise to the prospect of liquid, tradeable mortality and longevity securities, swaps and other derivatives.

THE MECHANICS OF A LONGEVITY INDEX SWAP TRADE

A longevity index is an index that measures the survival of some reference population. It can take a number of forms, but the most obvious form is one that specifies the number of people from an initial group of individuals who are alive at a particular point in time. Such an index may also be quoted on a trading platform such as Bloomberg, giving market participants easy access to pricing information.

A longevity index swap trade is an over-the-counter (OTC) arrangement. Each of the counterparties to the agreement has a direct link to the other rather than counterparties to trades being linked indirectly through an exchange. OTC arrangements are typically more flexible than exchange-traded instruments, but, as discussed above, a significant degree of standardisation could emerge which would create a more liquid market for longevity transactions.

OTC arrangements for longevity swaps transacted in the capital markets require an International Swaps and Derivatives Association (ISDA) agreement. Among its other provisions, this agreement specifies the exact index on which payments will be calculated, when payments must be made and the rate of interest that must be paid between the effective date of a transaction and the date of payment. This final point is important, because there can be a time delay of many months between the effective date of a calculation of the size of a population and the payment of a swap based on that figure. This delay in payment could be worth a significant amount of money.

An important addition to the ISDA agreement is the Credit Support Annex (CSA), which details the terms on which collateral is paid. Collateral is important because if one counterparty to the swap becomes insolvent immediately prior to a payment being made, then the remaining counterparty may be left out of pocket. The solution is to calculate the value of the fixed and floating legs of the swap on a regular basis, and to ensure that there is sufficient capital paid across to meet the difference between the two amounts. The CSA records the frequency with which this calculation must be made and the *de minimis* change below which no additional transfer of funds is needed.

The CSA also details the way in which the two legs of the swap must be valued, including not only the interest rate to be used in discounting any payments, but also the way in which future mortality is estimated. Defining the approach to estimating mortality is problematic because, at the time of writing in 2010, there is no market-consistent view of the level of mortality improvements. As a result, models must be used. Potentially, this could be a source of disagreement because each counterparty is likely to prefer a projection that results in the payment of a lower level of collateral to be posted from its own perspective. One solution is for the investment bank that writes the swap to not only determine the rate of mortality improvement, but also give the counterparty the option to request independent arbitration that would allow for an alternative proposal to be put forward. If the arbiter is forced to choose between the two projections rather than a "middle way", then each party would be motivated to put forward their best estimate, since doing otherwise would only increase the risk that the alternative will be chosen.

IDEAL REQUIREMENTS OF LONGEVITY INDICES

A basic requirement of entering into a contract based on a standardised reference portfolio of lives is that the longevity index used in the arrangement is suitable. But what constitutes "suitable"?

A good starting point is Bailey (1992a). In the context of the (un)suitability of peer-group benchmarks for investment performance measurement, his ideal benchmark can be summarised by the criteria in Figure 13.1.

In this case, there is an implicit assumption that the benchmark is more specific than a more general market portfolio that contains all securities. The two criteria overlap, but useful additional points are made in the second list for criteria to assess benchmark quality.

How relevant are these general index requirements to the production of longevity indices?

A lack of ambiguity is still key. This criterion is important not only in describing the reference population on which the index is based in detail but also in explaining the treatment of ways in which the population will change over time through the deaths of individuals or the movement of individuals in or out of the population for reasons other than death. Populations that reference a country are not excluded from this requirement, because immigration and emigration may alter the composition of the population. For this reason, index definitions should explicitly describe the extent to which such population changes are allowed for when mortality rates are calculated.

Specificity is also needed in the period over which calculations are made, the calculation method and the degree, if any, to which the index values are smoothed. Smoothing mortality rates might give a better idea of the underlying mortality: the observed rates may differ considerably due to volatility risk. There are a number of approaches that can be used to smooth mortality rates, from simply taking averages to using a more mathematical approach such as kernel or spline smoothing across ages. Each technique could yield significantly different results.

This possibility suggests the need for two new criteria in longevity indices: objectivity and transparency. If mortality rates are

> **Figure 13.1** Bailey's benchmark criteria
>
> (a) Criteria for an ideal benchmark.
>
> - **Unambiguous:** components and constituents should be well-defined.
> - **Investable:** it should be possible to buy the components of a benchmark and thus to track it.
> - **Measurable:** it should be possible to quantify the value of the benchmark on a reasonably frequent basis.
> - **Appropriate:** it should be consistent with an investor's style and objectives.
> - **Reflective of current investment opinion:** it should contain components about which the investor has opinions (positive, negative and neutral).
> - **Specified in advance:** it should be known by all participants before the period of assessment has begun.
>
> (b) Criteria for assessing benchmark quality:
>
> - the benchmark should contain a high proportion of the securities held in the portfolio;
> - the turnover of the benchmark's constituents should be low;
> - benchmark allocations should be investable position sizes;
> - an investor's active position should be given relative to the benchmark;
> - the variability of the portfolio relative to the benchmark should be lower than its volatility relative to the market portfolio;
> - the excess return of the portfolio over the market should have a strong positive correlation with the excess return of the benchmark portfolio over the market;
> - the excess return of the portfolio over the benchmark should have no significant correlation with the excess return of the benchmark over the market;
> - the style exposure of the benchmark and the portfolio should be similar.

smoothed, then the method used should be as objective as possible so as to leave little or no scope for subjective opinion. Whether or not smoothing is used, the level of objectivity can be improved with the use of an independent calculation agent who further ensures the validity of index values for all users. The use of a smoothing approach also needs to be transparent and available for scrutiny by investors.

Some general concepts such as investibility cannot be directly applied to longevity indices; however, measurability can. The data used to construct an index needs to be capable of being measured. Meeting this criterion, however, is only half the battle, for while the data supporting an index may be easily made available, its timeliness may be harder to achieve in line with a prearranged timetable. For example, governments are unlikely to have fixed schedules for the issue of such data. Furthermore, subsequent amendments to data releases can pose challenges to index construction.

The timeliness of the data is also particularly important for longevity indices that rely on data collection and processing, which take a long period of time. The longer publication takes, the greater the risk of something happening between the effective date of an index and the publication of the index value. A pre-arranged timetable is also essential. Without it, accurate valuation of investments is impossible.

Even after the best efforts are taken to ensure timely data, there will always be a lag in the data. For this reason, any index-based product must consider the extent to which interest on payments has accrued over the period since the time covered by the data and the date of payment.

This discussion suggests that, in addition to measurability, two more criteria need to be met in the construction of longevity indices:

- the indices must be produced in a timely manner;
- they must be available according to a prearranged timetable.

A well-constructed longevity index also needs to be appropriate to the lives being hedged. One way to measure the appropriateness is by determining how closely the index follows the mortality experience of a particular pension scheme or annuity portfolio. While it is possible to get a near perfect match with an indemnity swap, such an instrument would not be particularly liquid, making it less attractive to potential risk-bearing counterparties such as hedge funds. At the opposite end of the scale, a population-based swap might be more liquid, but might provide a less exact match for most liabilities. Consequently, a compromise is needed between the extent to which an index reflects the experience of a particular pension scheme (with more indices providing more cover) and the number of schemes for which a particular index provides a reasonable reflection of experience. Viewed in this context, appropriateness can be recast as two competing characteristics: a need to reflect the nature of the portfolio of lives being hedged and a need to encourage liquid securities and derivatives.

This aspect of appropriateness, however, deals only with level and trend risks. When it is thought of in terms of volatility risk, the number of lives in a portfolio must also be considered. A suitable criterion might be for the difference between the value of liabilities and a specific customised survivor swap to be less volatile than the difference between the value of liabilities and an index population-based survivor swap. It also suggests that the difference in the performances of an index-based swap and a population-based swap should have a strong positive correlation with the difference in the performances of a portfolio of lives and a population-based swap.

Just as an investment benchmark should be reflective of current investment opinion, the structure of a longevity index should also reflect the use to which it will be put. Without going into a lengthy discussion of index structure, which is covered in the next section, this concept suggests that the criterion used for investment benchmarks also applies to longevity indices.

The criterion that benchmarks should be specified in advance also applies to longevity indices, inasmuch as the composition of the index should be known in advance. While meeting this requirement is straightforward in the short term, it is possible to guard against changes in the distant future. One way may involve the formation of an independent index committee to deal with any issues that arise.

Stability, in terms of low turnover of constituents, is important for performance measurement; however, it is also useful for the construction of longevity indices. Index criteria should change only infrequently. The remaining criteria have a less clear analogue in relation to longevity indices.

The following list summarises the criteria for longevity indices. That these criteria overlap in many ways with the 10 principles of longevity indices published by the LLMA as detailed in Chapter 12 suggests that a consensus is finally beginning to emerge on the market requirements for such indices.

- **Unambiguous:** the reference population on which the indices are based should be defined in detail, including the ways by which individuals can enter and leave the index (other than through death).
- **Transparent:** the methods used to graduate mortality rates should be clear.
- **Objective:** graduation or smoothing methods should have as little subjective input as possible.
- **Measurable:** it should be possible to measure the mortality experience of the reference population independently.
- **Timely:** the mortality experience of the reference population should be available shortly after the effective date of that experience.
- **Regular:** the indices should be produced in accordance with a prearranged timetable.
- **Appropriate:** the indices should reflect the composition of the populations requiring hedging.
- **Popular:** the number of indices should be held to a minimum, so that securities, derivatives and swaps based on them will be liquid.
- **Relevant:** the variability of the liabilities being hedged relative to the indices should be significantly lower than their volatility relative to population longevity.
- **Highly correlated:** the difference in the performances of an index-based swap and a population-based swap should have a strong positive correlation with the difference in the performances of a portfolio of lives and a population-based swap.
- **Reflective of current hedging needs:** the structures of the indices should reflect the needs of those using them to hedge.
- **Stable:** the criteria used to construct indices should change infrequently.
- **Specified in advance:** the indices should be defined in advance as far as possible, and there should be an independent committee to deal with issues when this is not possible.

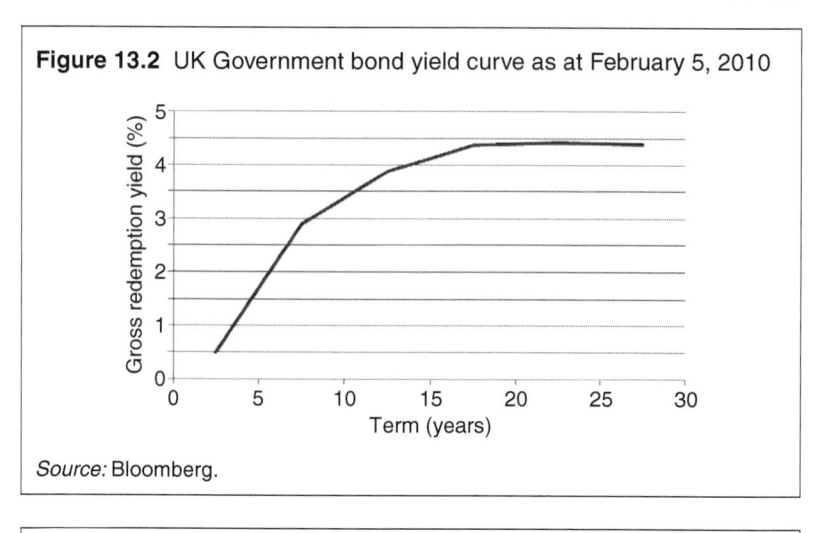

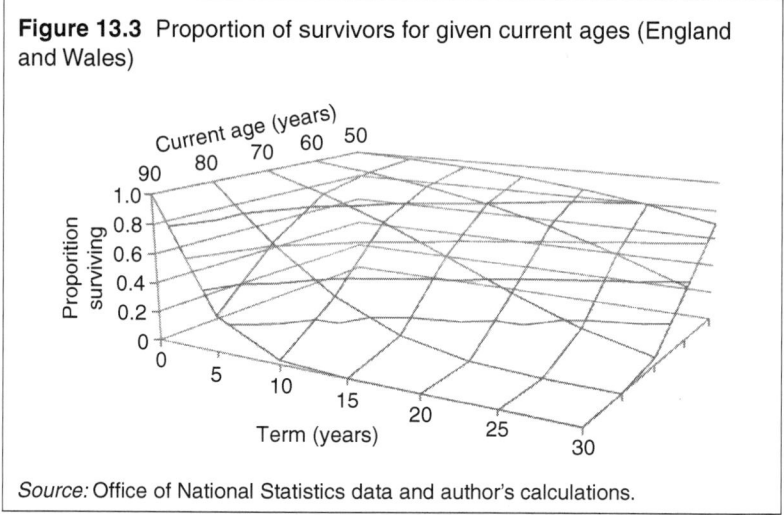

Figure 13.2 UK Government bond yield curve as at February 5, 2010

Source: Bloomberg.

Figure 13.3 Proportion of survivors for given current ages (England and Wales)

Source: Office of National Statistics data and author's calculations.

USING LONGEVITY INDEX SWAPS TO HEDGE TREND RISK

The reflection of current hedging needs by longevity indices raises a number of interesting issues, including the number of indices to be used in a strategy and therefore quoted. The question of index structure brings to mind the similarity between mortality rates and interest rates. Consider the rate of interest payable over different terms, shown in Figure 13.2.

If the probability of survival from a particular age to a range of future ages is analogous to this rate, then this line can be extended to a surface by considering the probabilities of survival for a range

Table 13.1 Swaps for which indices could be useful to hedge longevity risk

Term (years)	Current age (years)		
	60	70	80
10	✓	✓	✓
20	✓	✓	
30	✓		

of current ages. The resulting surface is shown in Figure 13.3. The third dimension in the figure is current age.

One swap strategy would be to try to match future cashflows with the floating legs of the swaps. However, such a strategy can require frequent rebalancing, which can be costly and time-consuming. As an alternative, LDI, mentioned earlier, might be used. In terms of interest rate and inflation risk, LDI is implemented through the purchase of a small number of interest rate and inflation swaps at evenly spaced terms. The result is that a change in nominal and real interest rates changes the value of the swaps by approximately the same amount as the change in the liabilities.

A similar approach can be used for survivor swaps. If these swaps were put in place for only a few ages, say current ages 60, 70 and 80, and a handful of future terms, say 10, 20 and 30 years into the future, then pension scheme liabilities could be hedged by using single payments for each of the current ages 60, 70 and 80 for a future term of 10, 20 and 30 years. Even within this range not all combinations would be needed. In particular, the maximum combination of current age and future term could be limited to 90 years of age. For example, this would leave the swaps for which an index would be required as listed in Table 13.1.

The proportions of the swaps would be adjusted and combined with cash so that the sensitivity of the swap portfolio to changes in future mortality expectations would be the same as that of the portfolio of lives. Having a small number of indices would also increase the liquidity in contracts based on these indices.

The next question is the metric of mortality on which the swaps should be based. Pension schemes should in theory prefer pension-based swaps based on the probability of survival, and swaps using

Table 13.2 Swaptions for which indices could be useful to hedge catastrophe risk

Term (years)	Current age (years)					
	20	30	40	50	60	70
1	✓	✓	✓	✓	✓	✓
2	✓	✓	✓	✓	✓	✓
3	✓	✓	✓	✓	✓	✓
4	✓	✓	✓	✓	✓	✓
5	✓	✓	✓	✓	✓	✓

this metric are often referred to as longevity (survivor) swaps. By comparison, those looking to hedge term-assurance portfolios should prefer life-assurance-based swaps based on the probability of survival to a particular point and then death. It is also worth considering a simpler metric, the probability of mortality in some future year and this is used in structures known as q-forward-based swaps In fact, pension-based swaps are the best option for pensioners and assured lives, with life-assurance-based swaps not far behind and q-forwards a relatively distant third. The suitability for pensioners is in line with intuition, but the suitability for life-assurance-based swaps requires further explanation. One way of rationalising this effect is to consider what happens to each type of swap if mortality rates fall. The pension-based swap will always be more sensitive to such changes than a life-assurance-based swap, since the fall in the final fall payment will be offset by the increase in the likelihood of survival to that date.

USING INDICES TO HEDGE CATASTROPHE RISK

The indices and swaps strategies described are aimed mainly at limiting the impact of mortality and longevity trend risk. However, the indices might also be helpful in creating a market for instruments aimed at protecting against catastrophe risk such as the pandemic risk instruments described in Chapter 11. While swaps are useful for removing risk in terms of variability, swaptions can be used to remove only downside risk: the risk of an adverse outcome rather than the risk that the outcome is different from that expected.

As described above, longevity trend risk can be mitigated using a small number of swaps spread over a small number of ages and a small number of future terms, although the terms would spread far into the future. This is because the main risk being hedged is that of a long-term rise (or fall) in mortality rates relative to the change expected. In contrast, catastrophe risk is more likely to be hedged over a much shorter time horizon (up to 5 years rather than 30) and protection would be needed in each of these five years. This would mean a larger number of swaptions would need to be bought. However, samples of ages could still be used, since increases in mortality from pandemics and even wars tend to affect relatively broad age groups. Table 13.2 gives an indication of some ages for which swaptions could be bought.

The cost of the protection under a survivor swaption depends on the extent of the cover: the more extreme the adverse outcome is, the lower the risk premium. Consider, for example, a life insurance company which wants to protect its term-assurance book against the adverse impact of a large increase in mortality beyond a particular level from, say, an influenza pandemic in a particular year. The insurer could buy a series of swaptions over a range of ages for each future year of interest. Each swaption would give the option to swap a single cashflow, with strike prices (the prices at which the swap would be exercised) set at appropriate levels.

THE GOVERNMENT AND LONGEVITY INDICES

A number of authors (see, for example, Blake and Burrows 2001; Brown and Orszag 2006) have suggested that governments might have a role in longevity markets as issuers of longevity bonds, although others (see, for example, Turner 2006; Antolin and Blommestein 2007) believe that certain governments already hold so much longevity risk in the form of public sector pensions that they should actually transfer some risk back into the market. In either case, longevity indices could help to facilitate such a transfer. If a government were to issue bonds, or simply act as a willing counterparty to swaps, then its participation might sufficiently increase liquidity to the point that its presence was ultimately not required. As discussed previously, the best way to increase liquidity is to provide a product that has the optimal combination of standardisation and diversity: a goal that can most easily be reached using longevity indices. This notion also holds true if a government wishes to transfer longevity risk back into the market, because suitable indices could help a government to find the widest market for its obligations.

MARKET PUBLISHED LONGEVITY INDICES

In the absence of government longevity indices, a number of longevity indices have already been created and published by the market, as covered in Chapter 12. These indices will undoubtedly help to build investor knowledge on longevity going forward and facilitate the longer-term growth of the mortality and longevity risk transfer market and we consider theses in the context of some of the criteria set out earlier.

Perhaps the most widely used indices can be found in the LifeMetrics[1] suite developed for the US, Germany, the Netherlands, and England and Wales. Rates are based on mortality of the entire population. For example, in developing indices for England and Wales, LifeMetrics takes raw data from the UK Statistics Authority and offers a crude central rate of mortality, m_x, and a smoothed initial rate of mortality, q_x.

The central rate of mortality gives the number of deaths as a proportion of the average number of individuals alive over the period. While this approach seems sensible, it is often more useful to have the number of deaths as a proportion of those alive at the outset of the period. This rate (the initial rate of mortality) allows an analyst to predict how many deaths are expected in the coming period given a population of a particular size. The initial rate of mortality is calculated by LifeMetrics from the central rate using the approximation $q_x = m_x/(1 + 0.5m_x)$. The initial rate of mortality is then smoothed using cubic splines.

This index satisfies many of the criteria described above. The data series is unambiguous, and the smoothing approach is both transparent and objective. However, because the index relies on externally produced raw data, there are no guarantees of regularity or timeliness. Also, since the population used is the entire country population, the relevance of this data to a specific group of lives such as a pension scheme or a book of annuitants is questionable.

The Credit Suisse Longevity Index uses similar data for the US only, but the version available on the public website quotes only a standardised measure of the US life expectancy. This therefore has the additional disadvantage that the sponsor (Credit Suisse) has to be contacted to obtain the age specific versions to customise the longevity exposure to different ages. However, it does contain both historical and forward index values.

The Deutsche Börse[2] Xpect Index produces a range of data in its cohort and age indices. The cohort indices give the remaining numbers of individuals surviving each month from cohorts born in a series of 20-year bands: 1900–19, 1920–39, 1940–59, 1960–79 and 1980–99. The age indices give the period life expectancy for each year of birth in the year for the age range 65–90. These figures are calculated annually. Both indices cover the populations of Germany, the Netherlands, and England and Wales. These indices score better in terms of timeliness and regularity, but are still only population-wide. However, Deutsche Börse also offers bespoke indices adjusted for socio-demographic characteristics.

Finally, Goldman Sachs developed the QxX index, which it offered until December 2009. This option was a longevity index covering medically underwritten US lives. This index had the advantage of being objectively calculated, as with the indices above, and was calculated more frequently (on a monthly basis). The number of lives covered was small (46,290 at the outset), and the class of business was not necessarily relevant for the hedging of pensions because it covered the life settlements market. However, it was perhaps more appropriate than an index based on a national population. As indicated above, Goldman Sachs decided in December 2009 to wind down its life settlements index (Goldstein 2009).

CONCLUSION

Longevity indices could serve a useful role in facilitating the hedging of longevity risk in pension schemes and life assurance companies. However, it is important that such indices are designed correctly and, while Bailey's criteria give a good starting point, the nature of longevity indices means that additional considerations are needed.

Good hedging results can be achieved using a relatively small number of pension-based swap contracts at key combinations of age and term. Such an approach would help to develop a liquid market in such swaps, which is important if the market for longevity swaps is to develop.

1   See http://www.lifemetrics.com.
2   See http://www.deutsche-boerse.com.

REFERENCES

Ansell, J., P. Moles and A. Smart, 2003, "Does Benchmarking Help?", *International Transactions in Operational Research* 10, pp. 339–50.

Antolin, P., and H. Blommestein, 2007, "Governments and the Market for Longevity-Indexed Bonds", OECD Working Papers on Insurance and Private Pensions, Working Paper 4.

Bailey, J. V., 1992a, "Are Manager Universes Acceptable Performance Benchmarks?", *Journal of Performance Management* 18, pp. 9–13.

Bailey, J. V., 1992b, "Evaluating Benchmark Quality", *Financial Analysts Journal* 48, pp. 33–9.

Blake, D., and W. Burrows, 2001, "Survivor Bonds: Helping to Hedge Mortality Risk", *Journal of Risk and Insurance* 68, pp. 339–48.

Blake, D., A. J. G. Cairns and K. Dowd, 2006, "Living with Mortality: Longevity Bonds and Other Mortality-Linked Securities", *British Actuarial Journal* 12, pp. 153–97.

Brown, J. R., and P. R. Orszag, 2006, "The Political Economy of Government-Issued Longevity Bonds", *Journal of Risk and Insurance* 73, pp. 611–31.

Cairns, A. J. G., D. Blake, K. Dowd, G. D. Coughlan, D. Epstein, A. Ong and I. Balevich, 2009, "A Quantitative Comparison of Stochastic Mortality Models Using Data from England and Wales and the United States", *North American Actuarial Journal* 13, pp. 1–35.

Coughlan, G. D., D. Epstein, A. Ong, A. Sinha, I. Balevich, J. Hevia-Portocarrera, E. Gingrich, M. Khalaf-Allah and P. Joseph, 2007a, "LifeMetrics: A Toolkit for Measuring and Managing Longevity and Mortality Risks", Technical Document, JP Morgan Pension Advisory Group, London.

Coughlan, G. D., G. D. Epstein, A. Sinha and P. Honig, 2007b, "q-Forwards: Derivatives for Transferring Longevity and Mortality Risks", JP Morgan Pension Advisory Group, London.

Cox, S. H., and Y. Lin, 2004, "Natural Hedging of Life and Annuity Mortality Risks", in *Proceedings of the 14th International AFIR Colloquium, Boston, MA*, pp. 483–507, URL: http://www.actuaries.org/AFIR/Colloquia/Boston/Cox_Lin.pdf.

Dowd, K., D. Blake, A. J. G. Cairns and P. Dawson, 2006, "Survivor Swaps", *Journal of Risk and Insurance* 17, pp. 1–17.

Goldstein, M. 2009, "Goldman Retreats from Life Settlements: Goldman Sachs Winding down Life Settlement Index", December 18, URL: http://www.reuters.com.

IAA, 2004, "A Global Framework for Insurer Solvency Assessment: Report of the Insurer Solvency Assessment Working Party", International Actuarial Association, Ottawa, ON.

NAPF, 2008, "NAPF Annual Survey", National Association of Pension Funds, London, UK.

Turner, A., 2006, "Pensions, Risks and Capital Markets", *The Journal of Risk and Insurance* 73, pp. 559–74.

14

Legal Considerations for Longevity Risk Transactions

Jennifer Donohue
Cadwalader, Wickersham & Taft LLP

In this chapter we address the legal issues that are central to longevity risk transfer, with a particular emphasis on capital markets. In addition, in the broader "life" market, transactions such as mergers and acquisitions activity and securitisation are also relevant to consider from a legal perspective because they provide a knowledge and experience base that can be leveraged when undertaking risk-transfer transactions.

Since the start of the 21st Century, the insurance sector has seen significant interest in consolidation activity. As the credit crisis placed increasing strain on precious bank capital, European banks sought to shore up their balance sheets by selling their non-core units, including insurance arms. This activity created opportunities for insurance companies to expand, and while several transactions (including Resolution's purchase of the life business of Abbey from Santander for £3.6 billion, Aviva's acquisition of AmerUS for £1.6 billion and Swiss Re's acquisition of GE Insurance Solutions) came to market, many others never amounted to more than speculation.

Even so, interesting innovations have developed around these acquisitions which use a mixture of internal resources, external debt and equity (ie, rights issues), each of which presents a new set of legal challenges. Private equity players have increasingly sought to enter the market for insurance through companies such as the Pearl Group and Resolution plc, which culminated in the £4.5 billion offer for Resolution plc in the period 2007–8. Notwithstanding the influx of this new money, the market has also witnessed pioneering developments in the area of securitisation, or "monetisation", as is the preferred term, of the on-balance-sheet value of a closed book of in-force policies. The Gracechurch transaction in 2003 and Box

Hill transaction in 2004 are two early examples. This capital-raising technique was refined and metamorphosed into a range of transactions including the Avondale securities issue in 2007 that involved the monetisation of a revolving book of policies, the private placed Portofinos loan notes in 2007 and the AEGON Scottish Equitable Zest transaction in 2008. These innovations, while not serving strictly to isolate longevity risk, involved significant elements of risk transfer and therefore provide an additional framework within which the legal issues in the area can be analysed.

Notwithstanding its potential as a source of capital, European insurers have taken a cautious approach to adopting monetisation, choosing to evaluate the performance of the pioneering transactions rather than immediately jumping aboard. Their caution, along with the concern over potential capital requirements under Solvency II, has left market participants jittery with regard to employing capital market solutions for effective longevity risk transfer.

With this discussion as a background, we can now begin a more formal exploration of the legal issues related to longevity risk. A recap of the primary sources of longevity risk and how market participants manage longevity initiates our discussion around longevity risk and we then explore the legal pitfalls of securitisation and, in particular, monetisation transactions.

WHAT ARE THE PRIMARY SOURCES OF LONGEVITY RISK?

Understanding the origins of longevity risk and the nature of its transfer is perhaps the best way to gain an appreciation of the legal considerations surrounding longevity risk transfer. As covered in Chapter 2, the two major sources of longevity exposure are found within annuities written by life insurance companies and corporate pension funds. Specific legal issues relating to the transfer of longevity risk from each of these entities will vary depending on the type of structure utilised to transfer longevity risk (eg, longevity swaps, buy-in, buy-outs) as well as the counterparties to the transaction (eg, pension schemes, insurers, reinsurers, investment banks) and will be discussed in more detail later in this chapter.

Annuities and pension funds, however, are not the only sources of longevity risk. Less obvious sources exist that have not yet been considered, such as the second-hand life policy market, which provides interesting opportunities and additional legal challenges. The risk arises because some life insurance policies carry a contractual term granting the policyholder the right to payment of an encashment or surrender value should the policyholder wish to cease paying premiums. This payment may not always reflect the full economic value of the policy at the time of encashment or surrender. In some cases, these policies may be assigned to a third party, which can take over premium payment obligations and the rights to receive the payments payable contingent on the death (or survival) of the insured life. Based on actuarial estimates, the third party may be willing to pay the policyholder an amount in excess of the encashment value in return for assignment of the policy. This arrangement may be in the economic interests of both parties, for example, if the policyholder is unable to continue paying premiums and wants an exit and the third party sees economic value in the trade.

In entering the second-hand market (the term typically used to refer to the market for such transactions), an investor may acquire a significant number of such policies that carry with them an exposure to longevity or mortality risk. Depending on the number and nature of the policies acquired in this manner, the exposures may be considered for securitisation. For instance, a sufficiently large market has allowed a number of brokers and financial institutions to become active in the US Life Settlements market, in which several high-value insurance policies written on older lives are sold in the secondary market. Securitisation of such policies embeds longevity risk in relatively medium-term notes but does not typically fully transfer longevity risk. This is because full transfer of longevity risk would generally require longer-dated securities and would also embed a number of other risks, including, for example, credit risk to the issuer of the insurance policy, legal risk in relation to the perfection of the assignment of the life policy and risks associated with potential challenge from the estate of the deceased policyholder.

Governments also tend to be exposed to longevity risk. State retirement provisions place obligations on central governments to make life-long payments to a large proportion of the population in many developed nations. Indeed, in the UK, one of the first longevity risk transfers to involve a local government authority's pension scheme has already occurred. Many, if not most, corporations are also exposed in some form to changes in longevity, not only as a result of pensions provision for their employees, but also because of the impacts of mortality on the potential size of their customer base. This latter source of risk may be very difficult to disentangle from other factors affecting the corporation, many of which will have a much greater immediate significance.

HOW DO MARKET PARTICIPANTS MANAGE LONGEVITY RISK?

Managing longevity risk involves making choices, each of which carries with it legal considerations related to the risk transfer.

Historically, there have been few ways for pension funds and insurance companies to hedge the longevity risks they face. But governments, pension funds, life insurance companies and individuals are under ever-increasing pressure to deal with the problem of longevity risk. The pressure to manage longevity risks of sophisticated annuity and pension products has spurred developments, which are being tested in the retail end and to a greater extent in the wholesale end of the insurance industry. For this reason some of the legal issues raised are cases of first impression often in the context of huge transactions.

As discussed in Chapter 9, one potential solution for a pension fund is a "buy-out". This route allows a pension fund to transfer its liabilities to a life assurance company. The conversion of defined benefits to annuities is, however, expensive and in the past insurance capacity has been limited, particularly when deferred annuities are involved. A buy-out also raises the issue of the transfer of the legal liability to pay pensions to an insurer. Trustees, for example, will seek to fully discharge duties to pension scheme members in the case of a buy-out. In this case, care must be taken over the difference between full and partial buy-outs and the details in the policy document (eg, the entity whose name appears in the policy document, the name of the trustees or members) as these may affect the discharge of legal liability on the scheme. The structure may take various forms; however, the key underlying model is that companies transfer the portfolio of pension contracts to an external investor that will assume the contractual obligations. In the past few years, the UK has seen the establishment of a number of new insurance companies specialising in these buy-outs, some of which have been funded by private equity.

Buy-outs are distinguished from "buy-ins", which allow trustees to purchase one or more insurance policies and use proceeds to meet liabilities. In this case, the trustees are not discharged from legal liability, but effectively hold the insurance policy as an asset of the scheme to meet the future liabilities.

Other legal issues that may need to be addressed in relation to pension scheme longevity risk transfers include areas such as preservation of benefits, consultations with and notices to scheme members, scheme member consent, the treatment of items such as transfer values that may be offered in conjunction with the transfer, the type of entity to which risk is transferred and the jurisdiction where the transfer is established (eg, in the European Union or outside its domain).

Reinsurers' appetite for longevity risk was not high towards the end of the 20th Century, unless the longevity deal was for an existing client, part of an overall package of risks and capped at a fairly low level. However, appetite for longevity risk has grown significantly since then and more significant volumes of this type of business have been transacted by reinsurers. Here the key legal considerations that are considered later in this chapter relate to the structure of the transaction and the form of the reinsurance treaty.

Alternatively, longevity risk may be hedged or reduced through balancing products. For example, the holder of longevity risk enters into a contract with another party in relation to, say, a term-assurance portfolio, thereby combining a conventional level of annuity with a life assurance to be broadly equivalent to the value of the annuity. The resulting combination (or homogenising) of the offsetting underlying risks (mortality and longevity risk) then reduces an insurer's exposure to future increases in longevity and in turn its need for capital reserves held in respect of this risk. Whilst there are no immediate legal considerations for an insurer balancing its own portfolio internally, there are regulatory considerations especially in terms of the capital benefits. When a transaction is enacted for the purposes of acquiring longevity risk or swapping mortality and longevity risk, the legal categorisation of the transaction as either reinsurance or capital markets transactions is of principal importance.

The capital markets have also developed "solutions" by providing a variety of vehicles hedging longevity risk effectively, and in this way have assisted insurers and reinsurers in achieving their objective of efficiently managing their regulatory capital. The first longevity-swap products transacted by the capital markets occurred in the early 2000s and while longevity bonds have also emerged as a potential strategy for managing risk, they have largely remained under development and not yet gained the same traction as longevity swaps.

As longevity swaps are effectively held as an asset of the insurer or pension scheme de-risking, the underlying liabilities are not discharged as they would be in the case of a buy-out. Further legal considerations specific to longevity are covered later in this section.

Indeed, all the precursors of an actively traded, longevity-swap market can be seen on the capital-market horizon and are driving the emergence of this market. It is likely to be only a matter of time before the product development emanating from a cast of major financial institutions takes hold of the market.

For the present, development has favoured indemnity triggers rather than parametric-based transactions. Parametric transactions, however, are likely to grow as insurers become more comfortable with managing basis risk between their own portfolios and population mortality. It is also probable that parametric solutions are more likely for deferred lives with pension schemes. The creation of an index and the structuring of deals based on an index raise a host of legal issues, which are beyond the scope of this chapter, but it may be useful to chronicle some of the indices discussed earlier in the book.

- In December 2005 Credit Suisse announced a longevity index based on US lives. The index aims to provide a benchmark against which longevity derivatives of various forms can be calibrated. The first of its kind, the Credit Suisse Longevity Index is designed specifically to enable the structuring and settlement of longevity risk transfer instruments such as longevity swaps and longevity structured notes. The index is marketed as "a standardised measure of the expected average lifetime for general populations based on publicly available statistics."

- In 2007, JP Morgan led the creation of LifeMetrics, a toolkit for measuring and managing longevity and mortality risk for pension plans, sponsors, insurers, reinsurers and investors. For the UK, LifeMetrics uses observed mortality rates as published by the government's Office for National Statistics

(ONS). It provides a standardised measure of risk aggregated across different risk sources and transferred to other parties. Longevity/mortality hedging strategies and the size of residual risk can then be compared with a base standard. As of 2010, it also includes index data for Germany, the Netherlands and the US.

- In the wake of LifeMetrics, Goldman Sachs Group, Inc announced the launch of a family of indices, called QxX, intended to allow participants to measure, manage and trade exposure to longevity and mortality risks in a standardised, transparent and real-time manner. The indices designed on a rolling annual basis have been reported to produce a continually updated reference pool, market evolution and underwriting trends. The product went live in 2008 but Goldman subsequently decided to stop supporting the index due to "poor uptake" and "a lack of commercial activity."[1]

- In 2008, Deutsche Börse launched a range of indices (Xpect Indices) tracking population mortality and longevity trends in Germany, with planned equivalents for other European countries. Deutsche Börse sources its own data from local municipalities and updates the indices monthly. The first expansion to other European countries included the Netherlands and as recently as 2010 the indices were expanded to include data from England and Wales as a consequence of interest in longevity risk transfer in these markets.

The impact of the development of longevity risk indices on the market has been significant, as evidenced by recent transactions covered earlier in this book. For example, in 2008, the closing of the first publicly acknowledged longevity-swap transaction between Lucida and JP Morgan took place. The deal involved a derivative contract linked to the LifeMetrics Index. The swap, called a q-forward contract[2] was in the region of £100 million and had a 10-year maturity. In 2008, the UK division of the insurer Canada Life entered into a swap transaction to hedge longevity exposure for £500 million with JP Morgan. This long-dated swap, with a maturity of 40 years, offers investors increased payment if the annuitants lived longer than expected. The swap also allows investors the option to resell the investment to JP Morgan at any time and the value of expected cashflows under the swap is assessed and updated month on month. Finally, the £1.7 billion deal between insurer Friends Provident and Swiss Re, using a reinsurance mechanism, was another UK transaction that closed out a successful 2008. Other examples of insured annuity, pension de-risking, reinsurance and capital market transactions are covered in Chapters 8–10 and 12.

WHO ARE THE INVESTORS IN THE LONGEVITY MARKET?

In addition to providing insurance companies and pension funds with a means of hedging longevity risk, longevity derivatives also offer speculative investors the opportunity to acquire longevity exposure. This possibility raises additional legal considerations because the type of the investor that becomes a party to the transaction affects the form of the transfer document as well as its character as either insurance or a derivative product and its regulation.

Investors in the capital markets, seeking to diversify their portfolios with an asset class disassociated from conventional risk factors, are the usual candidates. While the appeal of an asset class such as longevity hedges that are disassociated from investors' traditional risk factors cannot be denied, the market for the longevity risk products has not yet fully developed and many legal issues are being considered and addressed for the first time. There are still only a limited number of specialised investors in longevity risk. Attracting these investors requires the offering of competitive and sophisticated returns. The market is also in need of significant specialist education as to the meaning and legal analysis of these risks as there are few practitioners with the necessary transactional and regulatory experience in the area.

Even though longevity transactions have been limited, some encouraging signs have surfaced that indicate investors are currently taking a wide range of views as to future longevity experience. In particular, some investors are willing to invest without requiring a significant additional premium and are prepared to accept longevity risk at rates in line with those required by direct writers of annuity business. However, larger transactions still seem to need an additional premium to attract a wider range of investors even though they might be willing to accept the risk in more granular form.

One challenge to establishing a longevity bond market is that the underlying characteristics differ significantly from some of the more standard asset-backed issuances which often reference indicators that are more frequently updated than longevity experience, an advantage that makes these markets significantly more liquid and leads to greater pricing transparency for investors.

In recent years, hedge funds have also shown an interest in diversifying their portfolios by taking on longevity/mortality risk. Proprietary trading and asset management groups at investment banks have likewise begun to operate in this market. While the entrance of these new players is encouraging, the longevity market is highly regulated and therefore requires these new entrants to tread carefully or risk running foul of an often confusing and complex set of rules and regulations.

LEGAL CONSIDERATIONS FOR LONGEVITY RISK TRANSFER TRANSACTIONS

Many legal issues are common across the different types of longevity transactions, but there are important differences that arise due to structural differences in the transactions (eg, buy-out, buy-in or longevity swap) and the nature of parties involved in the transaction (eg, pension scheme, insurer, reinsurer or investment bank among others). For this reason, managing the legal issues of such transactions spans a wide spectrum of legal and regulatory issues from pensions to (re)insurance and capital markets and requires detailed knowledge of many areas.

Because some of the first longevity risk transfer deals were undertaken by reinsurance companies, we will first consider some of the legal implications associated with these transactions.

A key document in these arrangements is the "reinsurance treaty", which sets out in detail the terms of the transaction. Its drafting raises a number of key issues, which are considered below in no particular order.

- **Mitigation of credit and counterparty risk.** Owing to the extremely long duration of longevity risk transactions it is recommended that the parties carefully consider the long dated legal eventualities within the contract. Of particular importance is the potential default or deterioration in credit standing of the reinsurer. In order to mitigate this credit and counterparty risk, provisions are typically put in place for marking to market (marking to model) the outcome of the transaction. This provision is usually done through the combination of a collateral arrangement and clear definition of the way in which the contract would become unwound in the event of early termination. Such collateral arrangements are typically negotiated on an individual basis and therefore legal input is required to ensure that the language of the reinsurance treaty accurately reflects the terms of agreement between the parties. Parties to the treaty should also consider (and provide for) the impact of a "change of control" with respect to a party or changes in legal or regulatory requirements that would make the contract illegal or that would fail to meet the objectives of the parties at the outset (such as in relation to capital relief and risk transfer).

- **Data protection issues.** Data protection requirements need careful consideration, especially in situations in which, for example, data consents from pension members or policyholders of policies originated years ago were not obtained or do not comply with current requirements.

- **Cross-border considerations.** Cross-border transactions raise additional legal issues in terms of understanding the legislative and regulatory requirements of different countries and their impact on the transaction.

- **Ranking of recoverables.** Structuring the contract also has important legal implications from the standpoint of the ranking of the reinsurance recoverable not only at inception but also at any time that there are subsequent changes to the business of the reinsurer. Consideration of the ranking of reinsurance creditors relative to insurance creditors is particularly important in cross-jurisdictional circumstances.

- **Principle of *uberrima fides*.** Consideration should also be given as to whether the principle of *uberrima fides* (the doctrine of utmost good faith) applies to the contract of reinsurance in light of the extensive due diligence that is typically carried out by the reinsurer before entering into the contract. The principle of utmost good faith imposes positive obligations of disclosure. In practice, the principle permits either party to avoid a contract if one party either fails to disclose a material fact to the other, or is found to have made an innocent misrepresentation of a material fact, since statements made in the contract must be truthful.

We now turn to some of the legal considerations in respect of capital market longevity risk transfers, with a particular emphasis on longevity swaps (the primary type of capital market longevity transaction conducted) using the ISDA Master Agreement framework for our discussion.

Collateral mechanisms

Careful consideration needs to be paid to the language used to create and segregate collateral accounts or other mechanisms established for the posting of collateral in a longevity-swap transaction. Parties to the transaction must ensure that they fully consider the impact of insolvency on these provisions and the collateral that is held pursuant to these provisions. Before entering into these contracts, trustees and sponsors need a significant amount of education to understand the working of the transaction. The negotiation of these provisions should leave little, if any, doubt about the meaning of the contract's provisions or actions that might be needed in relation to the collateral. Precision in the collateral provision is particularly important so as to preclude situations in which the trustees are unwilling to act for fear of exposing themselves to liability to the detriment of all parties involved. The importance of clarity cannot be stressed enough in view of the fact that trustees are likely to change over the course of a long-term deal, requiring new parties to pick up where their predecessors left off.

While the ISDA Master Agreement is the preferred format for longevity risk transfer in the capital markets, the growth in the longevity-swap market has prompted the ISDA to develop a standard form document for longevity swaps to cater to their unique requirements. Under an ISDA Master Agreement, collateral mechanisms take the form of a Credit Support Annex, which operates considerably differently depending on whether it is governed by, say, English or New York law. For example, collateral posting under an English law Credit Support Annex involves outright title transfer to the holder of the collateral (an English law Credit Support Deed is used where the intention is merely to create a charge on to the collateral). Parties to a transaction might also want to carefully consider the appropriateness of incorporating a Credit Support Annex in their transaction based on the nature of the collateral involved. Given the potential complexities of collateral mechanisms, it should come as no surprise that these documents are often heavily negotiated and can be massive, as evidenced by the annex to the Babcock International Group's longevity swap with Credit Suisse, which was reportedly more than an inch and a half thick.

Exit terms

Provisions related to either party's ability to exit the transaction unilaterally also require careful legal review. In the traditional insurance world, exit terms take a number of different forms, including surrender clauses or recapture clauses. In the context of an ISDA Master Agreement the parties would have to consider early termination options or the ability to novate swaps upon buy-out of the underlying contract, where a longevity swap serves as a hedge. The parties may also want to keep the transaction outstanding notwithstanding the status of the contracting parties. In this case they would have to carefully exclude the ISDA Master Agreement's various early termination options.

Insolvency considerations

Insolvency considerations are extremely important to both parties to a longevity-swap transaction but can be especially critical to the party seeking to hedge or off-load longevity and interested in continuing the transaction to term notwithstanding the insolvency of the counterparty. Besides ensuring that the insolvency of the counterparty is not an early termination event under the ISDA Master Agreement, contracting parties will want to ensure that the transaction is fully collateralised and that the quality or rights with respect to posted collateral are not negatively affected by such insolvency.

Ability to demonstrate risk transfer

The ability to demonstrate that risk transfer has taken place may also be important for transactions that are required to be treated as reinsurance rather than a pure longevity derivative. The value of demonstrating that a risk transfer has occurred may come into play in a situation in which preferential accounting treatment is available for reinsurance relative to a derivative under local rules or vice versa.

For example, UK regulations allow a long-term insurer to take credit for reinsurance and arrangements that are analogous to reinsurance in terms of the risks transferred and the finance provided,[3] but only if there is effective risk transfer.

Administration

The details of the administration of transactions are also important and must be specified in the longevity-swap contract. When a third-party administrator or calculation agent is used, legal advisors will have to work closely with actuaries to ensure the clarity of definitions that are applied to the monitoring of data, calculation of cashflows and application of adjustments and corrections among other items. Responsibilities that cover a wide range of administration areas including, for example, administration of the policies, administration of assets and also of any trust or collateral arrangements need to clearly set forth for each party. This process can frequently become rather contentious when dealing with capital markets lawyers on one side and lawyers that work in the more traditional reinsurance space on the other. The latter are generally more comfortable leaving terms undefined because of the long history of custom and practise they can turn to when interpreting contractual clauses. This approach does not work in the context of capital markets, where longevity-swap transactions are novel and lack the legal precedent that parties to the transaction could fall back on when questions arise.

INSURANCE SECURITISATION

Insurance securitisation is well developed relative to longevity risk transfer transactions and, consequently, considering the legal issues associated with securitisation can assist in identifying further legal issues that may also be applicable to longevity risk transfers. However, in order to understand the legal implications associated with insurance securitisation, it is important to first understand exactly what monetisation is and the market drivers from a legal perspective.

What is monetisation?

Monetisation is a risk/capital management tool that allows insurers to release value from a pre-defined range of future accumulated profits on a life insurance portfolio through the contractual sale of such profits to third parties. This process is referred to as the release of value in force (VIF). As the term suggests, VIF is the value of an in-force portfolio of life insurance policies, which is the "economic value" of a book of in-force policies. Another way of thinking about this tool is to consider that monetisation is the value of the future profits anticipated to emerge in respect of such a book of business. Since regulatory regimes in the insurance space typically place conservative estimates on insurance liabilities and the assets held to support such liabilities, an insurer's assets are typically worth more than the corresponding liabilities. As such, the monetisation of "value in force" on a book of insurance policies (typically life policies) is the monetisation of the present value of the future regulatory surpluses expected to emerge on the book of business.

For example, public transactions that have been reported in the UK include NPI (1998), Gracechurch (2003), Box Hill (2004) and Avondale (2007). Portofinos (2007) and Zest (2008) are two private but reported transactions. Classic structures such as the Gracechurch and Box Hill transactions involved closed books of business, making the identification of the policies in the monetised pool relatively straightforward. The more recent market arrivals such as the Avondale Securities issue (2007) or AEGON's Zest transaction (2008) introduced new innovation. Gracechurch (Barclays Life) and Box Hill (Friends Provident) took advantage of a little-known provision in the regulations that enable life assurance companies to treat as equity capital borrowings which are of limited recourse to their VIF. Although popularly referred to as securitisations, transactions of this sort do not involve the transferring of title or the giving of security over third-party obligations in the way that traditional securitisations do. In effect, the life assurance company effectively pledges that the profits from its existing business, as realised each year over the term of the debt, will be used to service the debt obligations, making monetisation of the value of in-force business a more accurate description for these transactions. It is important to note that, where VIF has no regulatory value, it may have economic value and therefore can be monetised. The cash raised as a consequence of the monetisation may then be taken into account for the purpose of regulatory capital.

Transactions that are based on the monetisation of the VIF have been given various descriptors, including "VIF monetisation", "VIF securitisation" and "EV securitisation." EV refers to "embedded value", which is usually understood to mean the sum of the VIF and the net asset value of the insurance company; in this context the net asset value does not, in fact, play a significant role in the transaction. The result of the transaction is usually to exchange a portion of the shareholders' interest in the value of the in-force business for cash proceeds, giving rise to the term "monetisation". In this chapter, the term "VIF monetisation" is used for these reasons, but the other terms are also used in the market.

What are the market drivers of monetisation from a legal perspective?

Stricter capital adequacy regulation in the form of the Insurance Groups Directive[4] and the Solvency II reforms, as well as a general decline in equity values has forced European insurers to focus their attention on the need to raise capital, which in turn has prompted market innovations. Notwithstanding the regulatory impetus, the renewed interest in acquisitions further necessitates increased capital holdings.

The Insurance Groups Directive, for instance, has introduced arrangements that preclude the circumventing of solvency margin requirements under insurance directives by groups of insurance undertakings which could otherwise allow the same regulatory capital to be used more than once to cover the separate solvency margin requirements of different insurance undertakings of the group, a tactic referred to as "double gearing". Both the international initiatives Solvency II and Basel II require financial institutions to have a more risk-sensitive framework for the assessment of regulatory capital and generally involve increasing the amount of capital.

Life assurance companies are required to maintain a minimum level of regulatory capital against the risks to which their businesses are subject and to ensure that they are always able to meet their liabilities to policyholders as they fall due. For example, the UK Financial Services Authority (FSA) regulations set forth detailed rules regarding the amount and quality of capital that such companies must maintain, based largely on the developing rules for banks following Basel II. The capital requirements for life assurance companies involve the stratification of capital in tiers: Tier 1, broadly equivalent to equity capital, and Tier 2, broadly equivalent to long-term debt. This stratification mirrors the approach used by banks as far back as Basel I. The rules require that at least 50% of the capital is made up of Tier-1 capital. However, equity capital is expensive and the increasing demand for this form of capital has led life assurance companies to look for cheaper alternatives that nonetheless retain sufficient characteristics of equity for them to rank it as equity for regulatory purposes.

In the past, banks have succeeded in devising debt instruments that have had some equity characteristics, and a number have raised some so-called innovative Tier-1 or hybrid capital. However, certain regulations now significantly limit the extent to which banks and life assurance companies can use such instruments to raise capital that can be treated as equity for regulatory purposes. For example, at the time of writing, no more than 15% of the Tier-1 capital after deduction can be made up of hybrid capital in the UK. This restriction has led to the successful rehabilitation of an idea first tried (rather less successfully) by NPI in the late 1990s, the so-called securitisation of embedded value.

In undertaking monetisation it is important to consider not only the current regulatory environment but also potential changes to the regulatory environment which may have an impact on the transaction. A prime example is Solvency II, the new framework for risk-based solvency rules that is on the horizon for European insurance and reinsurance companies. In its efforts to address the criticism that traditional solvency rules for insurers are formulaic and ineffective in directing capital adequately in relation to risk, it is likely to spur changes in the capital-raising efforts of insurers. One of the key reasons is that (pre-Solvency II) regulatory capital is largely based on the volume of business written rather than its risk character. As covered in Chapter 6, the Solvency II regulations will force life and non-life (re)insurance companies to align capital requirements with their underlying risk and to develop a proportionate, risk-based approach to supervision. They are also designed to create a consistent regulatory framework across the EU and to recognise diversification and risk mitigation. The main outcome of this new risk-based regulatory approach is likely to be that European insurers will have increased regulatory capital requirements which could spur market innovations around insurance securitisation and monetisation that could be used as an effective mechanism to tackle issues around any onerous capital requirements and smooth the impact of Solvency II on European insurance companies.

Recent regulatory developments: ISPVs

In the UK, regulatory developments have emerged with the enactment of new rules relating to insurance special purpose vehicles (ISPVs).[5] These ISPVs assume risks from insurance or reinsurance undertakings, which can use these vehicles to fully fund their exposure through a debt issuance or another financing mechanism that is subordinate to their reinsurance obligations. Amounts recoverable from an ISPV by an issuer can be taken into account as an admissible asset and treated as reinsurance for the purposes of regulatory capital, but only with a waiver from the FSA. The Taxation of Insurance Securitisation Company Regulations 2007, which complements the new regulations, make securitisation, particularly regulatory approval, easier than it has been and demonstrates a regulatory willingness to consider securitisation.

LIFE INSURANCE SECURITISATION: LEGAL CONSIDERATIONS

Several legal issues need careful consideration when structuring securitisation transactions. Similar considerations can be applied to the transfer of longevity risk, whether by way of a simple longevity swap or a stand-alone structured vehicle. Listed below, in no particular order, are the primary areas of concern for the legal practitioners in the field.

What is being securitised?

In all transactions it is important to articulate clearly exactly what is being covered. Early monetisations, for example, dealt with closed books of business whose emerging VIF could be predicted with greater certainty because no new variables from new business entered the mix. The benefit here related to the modelling of the behaviour of the emerging surplus. Early transactions also focused on unit-linked policies as opposed to with-profits policies. Once again the predictability and accuracy with which the emerging surplus could be modelled was the rationale, as the inclusion of with-profits policies can make the VIF calculation subject to contagion from stock market fluctuations.

In the UK, Avondale (2007) was the first transaction in which a "dynamic" or revolving block of business was monetised with the provision that new business written for up to five years after the close of the transaction continues to be accepted into the "dynamic block" on which the VIF is being calculated. Putting aside the difficulties that a dynamic block brings to modelling the transaction, there are also important legal risks that relate to the documentation limiting the insurer's ability to write new business that will be included in its dynamic block. For investors, a key concern is a provision to ensure that any new business written by the insurer does not negatively affect the VIF of previously written policy. Careful drafting of the portfolio criteria with respect to new business being written by the insurer and monitoring of the dynamic block is therefore essential to preserve the integrity of the VIF as of the closing date for transactions involving a dynamic book.

Similar considerations need to be made in determining whether the plan is open or closed to new members for a portfolio underlying a longevity risk transaction.

What is the purpose of the transaction?

From a legal perspective, it is extremely important to be mindful of the intent for entering into the transaction. For example, if an insurer's intent is outright risk transfer rather than just regulatory capital relief, then careful drafting is required with regard to the risk transfer document and the reinsuring vehicle when structuring the transaction. As previously discussed, a key document in risk transfer is the reinsurance treaty ("the treaty"), which can be quite a complicated document and has been known to operate to transfer risk and to recapture it. In Box Hill, for example, the reinsurer provided reinsurance of certain liabilities and risks to Friends Provident Life & Pensions (FPLP), which, in turn, was required to pay an annual premium to the reinsurer in the event of a surplus on the defined book of business. This situation would occur if the premiums earned on the defined book of business were greater than the losses during a given calculation period. In addition to the annual premium to be paid, FPLP was required to recapture liabilities reinsured by the reinsurer, in an amount (the "recapture amount") corresponding to the amount of the defined book surplus calculated in a given year minus the annual premium. This ongoing recapture of liabilities allowed the reinsurer to release funds held as collateral and to repay principal under the reinsurer loan (ie, the loan being used to fund its reserves). This arrangement in turn allowed the issuer to repay principal on the notes. When setting up structures such as the one in Box Hill, it is important to ensure that the intended risk transfer has actually taken place in order for the parties to obtain that beneficial capital treatment under the relevant regulatory regime.

Under the Solvency II regime it is expected that capital relief will be given as a specific benefit in situations in which genuine risk transfer from the insurer is achieved.

Warranties

From a lawyer's perspective, the drafting of warranties related to monetisations and transactions that seek to off-load longevity risks to structured vehicles is extremely important. Warranties are critical to protect an independent investor's rights with respect to a ceding insurer even though no direct contractual relationship may exist. They also relate specifically to regulatory compliance and obligations that are specific to insurers and reinsurers. Warranties are a critical part of the triggering mechanism requiring the insurer to make payments to offset the impact of any breach.

Warranties that are typically seen on such transactions include those related to

- origination procedures and servicing of the defined book in a manner expected of a sound and prudent insurance company,
- the tax assumptions that are to remain unchanged,
- the responsibility for accuracy of all information,
- the requirement to act as a prudent insurer,
- the obligation to maintain an inflation hedge fully allocated to the defined book,
- maintenance of the reinsurer's regulatory surplus in an amount not less than the defined book surplus (the conduit covenant),

- provision for the reinsurer to meet regulatory capital requirements (the capital maintenance warranties),
- investment objectives and criteria for the reinsurer assets as per the reinsurer investment management agreement,
- investment of proceeds of the annuity book in accordance with the annuity-backed investment criteria and objectives,
- compliance with laws and regulations, including no mis-selling.

Rated debt

The market has seen a growing demand for rated insurance-linked securities. Much maligned for their ratings efforts in the structured finance space, rating agencies have nonetheless continued to retain expertise specifically relevant to the sophisticated risk modelling required for rating securities. The combination of these forces (a growing market demand and increasing expertise at rating agencies) has proceeded to meet this demand.

Mortality catastrophe bonds were the first group of products in this space to be rated. These ratings were followed by the Gracechurch and Box Hill transactions discussed earlier. Even though monoline insurance companies have been hit hard by the financial crisis, they had been used as the market for rated securities developed to provide an insurance company "wrapper" on transactions to insure against defaults, thus backing payment obligations and thereby allowing the rating agencies to improve the ratings offered on such securities. Rating of longevity-only deals has also continued to be extremely difficult, as "event risk" in these sorts of transactions is extremely large and difficult to model in the context of longevity-only transactions.

Recharacterisation risk

Recharacterisation risk is the risk that a longevity-swap transaction documented under an ISDA Master Agreement and intended to be a financial derivative is recharacterised by a court as a contract for insurance. Under Section 19 of the Financial Services and Markets Act 2000 ("FSMA"), any person who carries on a regulated activity in the UK must be authorised by the FSA or exempt (ie, an appointed representative or some other exemption). Breach of Section 19 is a criminal offence and punishable on indictment by a maximum term of two years imprisonment and/or a fine. Under FSMA, assisting in the administration and performance of a contract of insurance is defined as a regulated activity. As such, recharacterisation risk is a fundamental legal issue surrounding the character of the instrument issued by the note vehicle to the market. For the smooth and effective use of the instrument, it is important that it, and the trading in it, does not constitute the effecting or carrying out of contracts of insurance.

In the UK for example, the FSA notes in its Regulatory Guidance on the Identification of Contracts of Insurance[6] that the courts, in confining their decisions to the facts before them, have not fully defined the common law meaning of "insurance" and "insurance business". Even so, we have useful guidance in the form of descriptions of contracts of insurance. The best established of these descriptions appears in the case of *Prudential v. Commissioners of Inland Revenue* [1904]2 KB 658. This case, read with a number of later cases, treats as insurance any enforceable contract under which the insurer undertakes

(i) in consideration of one or more payments,

(ii) to pay money or provide a corresponding benefit (including in some cases services to be paid for by the provider) to an insured,

(iii) in response to a defined event, the occurrence of which is uncertain (either as to when it will occur or as to whether it will occur at all) and adverse to the interests of the insured (an insurable interest).

As the FSA points out,[7] the courts have adopted the following "principles of construction" to determine whether a contract is a contract of insurance.

(i) More weight attaches to the substance of the contract than to the form of the contract. The form of the contract is relevant, but not decisive of whether a contract is a contract of insurance (*Fuji Finance Inc. v. Aetna Life Insurance Co. Ltd* [1997] Ch. 173).

(ii) In particular, the substance of the provider's obligation determines the substance of the contract (*In Re Sentinel Securities* [1996] 1 WLR 316). Accordingly, the insurer's or the insured's intention or purpose in entering into a contract is unlikely to be relevant to its classification.

(iii) The contract must be characterised as a whole and not according to its "dominant purpose" or the relative weight of its "insurance content" (*Fuji Finance Inc. v. Aetna Life Insurance Co Ltd* [Supra]).

Pursuant to PERG 6.6, the following are factors that the courts have taken into account in deciding whether any particular contract is a contract of insurance.

- Case law establishes that the provider's obligation under a contract of insurance is an enforceable obligation to respond (usually, by providing some benefit in the form of money or services) to the occurrence of the uncertain event.

- Contracts under which the provider has absolute discretion as to whether any benefit is provided on the occurrence of the uncertain event are not contracts of insurance. This situation may be the case even if, in practice, the provider has never exercised its discretion so as to deny a benefit (*Medical Defence Union v. Department of Trade and Industry* [1979] 2 All ER 421).

- The "assumption of risk" by the insurer is an important descriptive feature of all contracts of insurance.

- The recipient's payment for a contract of insurance need not take the form of a discrete or distinct premium. Consideration may be part of some other payment, for example, the purchase price of goods. Consideration may also be provided in a non-monetary form, for example, as part of the service that an employee is contractually required to provide under a contract of employment.

- A contract is more likely to be regarded as a contract of insurance if the amount payable by the recipient under the contract is calculated by reference to either the probability of occurrence or likely severity of the uncertain event or both.

- A contract is less likely to be regarded as a contract of insurance if it requires the provider to assume a speculative risk (ie, a risk carrying the possibility of either profit or loss) rather than a pure risk (ie, a risk of loss only).

- A contract is more likely to be regarded as a contract of insurance if the contract is described as insurance and contains

terms that are consistent with its classification as a contract of insurance, for example, obligations of the utmost good faith.
- A contract that contains terms that are inconsistent with obligations of good faith may, therefore, be less likely to be classified as a contract of insurance; however, since the substance of the provider's rights and obligations under the contract is more significant, a contract does not cease to be a contract of insurance simply because the terms included are not usual insurance terms.

Even with the above list of factors, it may be difficult to predict whether or not the courts will characterise a particular contract as a contract of insurance rather than as an insurance-linked security. For this reason, in issuing any market instrument, the product structuring and the terms of the contracts ie, the documentation may have a significant impact on its characterisation. Since the categories of financial instruments covered by FSMA are extremely broad, and include a wide variety of structures and documentation, deal structuring and the terms of the bonds or notes issued need to withstand a significantly robust test.

MARKET OUTLOOK

With the advent of Solvency II, capital management techniques that are emerging in the banking sector following Basel II will inevitably arrive in the world of insurance. Financial institutions are becoming increasingly conscious of the cost of capital. By allowing insurers to use internal risk-based approach as opposed to the standard approach to manage their regulatory capital, these financial institutions will be able to simultaneously bundle and place risk in accordance with their needs and resources. For example, A–B loan structures that allow the risk inherent in a loan to be split between a senior and a junior piece, a feature well known in the commercial mortgage-backed industry, are becoming increasingly common for other asset classes. In doing so, this instrument allows the institution to retain an asset portfolio with a reduced risk profile while offering earnings potential to outside, unregulated investors.

Given the continuing consolidation drive in the European insurance market, monetisation may also emerge as an even more useful way of raising capital to fund acquisitions than it has been. In the future, its application can be either through the monetisation of existing books of business to raise finance for acquisitions, or partly funding an acquisition or refinancing a bridge loan by monetising some or all of the books of business gained under the acquisition. Going forward, new business generated by the life company may be used to repay other financings.

CONCLUSION

As we have seen throughout this chapter, the transfer of longevity risk to the capital markets is an area rife with legal pitfalls related to the nature of the transaction, the status of the parties and complexity of the products. While standardised documentation is on the horizon, it is extremely important that participants entering into these transactions seek advice from legal practitioners with both insurance/longevity and capital markets experience. The form and substance of the transaction documentation are extremely important to ensure the ongoing integrity of potentially long-term transactions. Given that the consequence of stepping into one of the many legal pitfalls related to market transactions may be a voided contract, there are far-reaching legal implications for all concerned. This possibility is particularly poignant at this nascent phase in the market's development, when negotiations are likely to be extended and the pressure to hastily close a deal may weigh on the prudence to see the deal done right. Experience has shown that constructing the deal properly is critical, as hastily constructed deals too often carry with them legal risks that the transacting parties had not considered and are unable to manage.

1   See "Goldman Pulls Plug on QxX Index", http://www.trading-risk.com/ (January 2010).
2   A term that derives its name from the symbol "q", which is used as standard actuarial notation for a mortality rate.
3   Prudential Sourcebook for Insurers: INSPRU1.1.19A.
4   Directive 98/78/EC of the European Parliament and of the Council on the on the supplementary supervision of insurance undertakings in an insurance group.
5   Prudential Sourcebook for Insurers Instrument 2006 (INSPRU).
6   PERG 6, FSA Handbook; see http://www.fsa.gov.uk/.
7   PERG 6.5.4, FSA Handbook; see http://www.fsa.gov.uk/.

Index

(page numbers in italic type relate to tables or figures)

A

AIDS, 9, 26, 36, 91
annuities, *75, 76, 83, 206, 207*
  basic types of, *50–1*
  commoditisation of, standardisation and strategies to deal with, 129–31
  compulsory, 126–7
  equivalence techniques, 169
  extreme mortality risk and, 274–6
  impaired and enhanced, 264–5; *see also* longevity risk: hedging of, through reinsurance
  insured portfolios:
    capital-market transactions, 218–20, *219, 220, 221*
    de-risking, 203–27
    recent market activity and, 221–3
    solutions, types of, 209–20
    UK market in, background to, 204–7, *206*
  large insured bulk transactions in, overview of, *223*
  portfolio cashflow profile, *51*
  regulation of, 125–6
  reserving and regulatory requirements for liabilities of, 147–73
    capital and, as economic valuation–correlation matrix, *150*
    capital requirements and, calculating, 149–50, *150*
    correlation matrices and, applying, *152*
    correlation matrices and, technical requirements of, *151*
    diversification framework and, validating assumptions, 153
    mortality and longevity trend risks and, combining, 169–70
    non-linearity and, allowing for, 153
    regulatory regimes affecting, 147–63
    Solvency I and, 147–8
    Solvency II and, 155–8, *157, 158*, 166
  risk-transfer transactions, *222*
  UK market in, background to, 204–7
  UK transfer market in, 208
  underwritten, 88, 123–43
    assessing longevity risk for, 131–2
    future market prospects for, 128–9
    lifestyle factors concerning, 131–2
    link between sales and process of, 132–4
    market and pricing of longevity risk and, 123–43
    medical factors concerning, 132
    sales of, 127–8, *128*
    UK market share of, *137*
  see also pension funds
arthritis, 24
asset-backed transactions, 256–7, *257*
  longevity swap versus, 224–7

Australia, 8, 13, 15, 23, 39, 101, 126
  compulsory pension plan in, 48
  smoking ban in, 94
Austria, 8, 22, 23

B

Belgium, 8, 23
Blackburn, Elizabeth, 30
blood disorders, 14
body mass index, 35

C

Caenorhabditis elegans 38, 38
Calment, Jeanne, 31
Canada, 23, 79, 101, 269
cancer, 14, 25, 28–9 35, 37, 94, 102, 123, 137, 171, 264
  colorectal, survival curve for, *139*
  risks of, 139–40
cardiovascular illness, 25, 29, 35, 94, 102, 137, 138–9
Carrel, Alexis, 30
centenarians, 15–16
  in England and Wales, *31*
  projected numbers of, *32*
changing demographics of ageing populations, 3–39
Chile, *116*
circulatory disease, 24, 25, 27–8, 93, 171
Continuous Mortality Investigation (CMI) 71, 72, 73, *83*, 91, 101, 102
  insured-population model of, 106–8
correlation matrices, *151*
credit risk, process correlation versus capital correlation, 151

D

death:
  age at, for women
    in Japan, *6*
    in Switzerland, 5

by cause, England/Wales, for, 60+ lives, 172
circulatory disease, 24, 25, 27–8
cancer, 28–9
  in European Union, *25*
historical causes of, 24–9, *26, 27*
historical developments, 26
present situation, 25–6
  in developed countries, 25–6
  in developing countries, 26
past evolution of causes of, 92–5
see also life expectancy; mortality
Denmark, 21, 23, 26
de-risking for pension schemes, 229–54, *243, 244, 245*
  main tools available for, 230–3, 244–7
    buy-in, 231–2, 236–8
    buy-in, synthetic, 245–6, *246*
    buy-out, 230–1, *231*, 236–8
    longevity swaps, 232–3 239–44, *240, 244*; *see also* longevity: swaps
    longevity swaps: bespoke fixed leg, 244
    longevity swaps: insurance-wrapped, 246–7, *248*
    more sophisticated variations of, 244–7
    traditional route, 231–2
    transferring risk, 230–1
  membership categories and, relation of solutions to, and risks transferred, 233–6
    main market and demographic risks, 235–6
    principal categories, 234
    solution comparisons, 236–8

INDEX

"progressive", strategy of, 238–9
pros and cons of buy-outs, buy-ins and swaps, 236–8
Deutsche Börse, 317, 325
diabetes, 24, 35, 94, 135
diarrhoea, 26

E

ECHP, *see* Eurostat European Community Household Panel
economic capital, modelling and longevity risk, 175–99, *190–1*
   applications, 185–92
   applications, specific: reinsurance, 193–5
   applications, wider, 192–3
   calibration and validation process for, 182–5
   cashflow models, projecting, *186*
   choices, comparing, 187–92
   fitting the model, *184*
   five simple steps for, *176*
   framework, 175–7
   internal model, delivering standard formula using, 185
   mathematical model for, type to apply, 181–2
      cashflow modelling, 181–2
      curve fitting, 181
      replicating portfolio, 182
   non-linearity, diversification and, 180–1
   other considerations concerning, 196–8
   payment obligations and, meeting, 197–8
   projected models and, use of, *192*
   projecting capital requirements, *188–9*
   projecting liabilities and capital, 185
   regulatory balance sheet and, defending, 198
   reinsurance and, 193–5
   risk margin and, calculating, *187*
   risk margin and, projected cost of capital, *187*
   Solvency II requirements, calculating, *178–9*
   speed and, need for, 177–80
economic-capital regimes, longevity stresses in, 165–6
EUROCARE-4 29
Eurostat European Community Household Panel (ECHP) 19
extreme mortality:
   basis risk and, 276–7
   bonds, duration of, 277–8
   bonds, example structure of, *269*
   bonds, reason for issue, 269–70
   financial considerations of, 278
   longevity risk contrasted with, 274–6
      annuities, pensions and, 274–6, *275*
   nature of, 271–4
      natural catastrophes and industrial accidents, 274
      pandemic, 271–3, *272, 273*
      war and terrorism, 274
   risk, as natural hedge, 367–79
   transfer, 268–71
      background, 268–9
      indices and, importance of, 270–1
   see also death; mortality

F

Financial Services Compensation Scheme (FSCS) 205, 238, 247
Financial Services and Markets Act, 209–10, 338

Finland, 23, 26, 28
flu, 5, 80, 91, 92–3, 271–2, 272, 278, 315
France, 4, 5, 12, 20, 23, 26, 28, 95, 106, 124, 125
   centenarians in, 15
   life expectancy at birth in, 4
   low mortality rates for advanced ages in, 7
   wine-and-fat diet in southwest of, 14
   women's cancer recovery in, 29
French Paradox, 14
FSCS, see Financial Services Compensation Scheme (FSCS)

G

German Socioeconomic Panel, 20
Germany, 4, 20, 23, 26, 106, 118, 298, 316, 317, 235
   Minimum Requirements for Risk Management issued in, 149
   Socioeconomic Panel in, 20
Greece, 8
Greider, Carol, 30

H

Hayflick, Leonard, 30
Hayflick limit, 30, 37
Human Mortality Database, 8, 91, 100, 101

I

INED, see Institut National d'Etudes Démographiques
influenza, 5, 80, 91, 92–3, 271–2, 272, 278, 315
Institut National d'Etudes Démographiques (INED) 7, 28
insured annuity portfolios:
   capital-market transactions, 218–20, 219, 220, 221
   de-risking, 203–27
   recent market activity and, 221–3
   solutions, types of, 209–20
   full annuity portfolio transfer, 209–10, 211, 212
   reinsurance, 210–18; see also main entry
   UK market in, background to, 204–7, 206
International Accounting Standard, 19 (IAS19) 154, 252
International Swaps and Derivatives Association (ISDA) 218, 233, 306, 329, 330, 338
Ireland, 26
   smoking ban in, 94
ISDA, see International Swaps and Derivatives Association
Italy, 8, 23, 26, 28, 106, 124
   male survival function in, 115
   national mortality tables in, 114

J

Japan, 4, 6, 12–13, 19, 23, 50, 125, 269
   centenarians in, 15
   female life expectancy in, 116
   life expectancy at age, 80 in, 7
   life expectancy at birth in, 8
   low mortality rates for advanced ages in, 7
   women's age at death in, 6

K

Kenyon, Cynthia, 38
Knauss, Sarah, 31

L

Life and Longevity Markets Association (LLMA) 56, 59, 226, 284, 297, 298, 300, 301, 310

INDEX

life expectancy, *11, 12, 38*
  aged, 65, by country, *10*
  annual gain in, 9
  at birth, 4–5
    by country, *10*
    for England/Wales, France, 4–5
  by country along best-practice line, 33
  centenarians and, 15–16, 31, 32
  challenges and opportunities concerning, 30–9
  changing demographics of, 3–39
  cohort effect and, 13
  expected versus maximum, explained, 135
  Hayflick limit and, 30, 37
  improvement of, past stages in, 5–7
  inter-country convergences in, 9–12
  inter-country differences in, 8
  lifestyle drivers of, 13–14
  limit to, 30–4
    biological, 30
    insight from oldest old concerning, 30
    two potential scenarios for, 34
  male–female, convergence between, 12–13
  Monte Carlo simulations for, 77
  period, aged, 65, England/Wales, *99*
  period and projected, 98
  possible improvements in, from the diffusion of good practices, 29
  previously underestimated evolution of, 32–4
  record, age-specific contributions to, 6
  significant global trend in, 7–8
  see also longevity

LifeMetrics, 91, 284, 285, 287, 290, 297–8, 299, 316, 324, 325
LLMA, *see* Life & Longevity Markets Association
longevity risk:
  assessment of, for an underwritten annuity, 131–2
  de-risking of, for pension schemes, 229–54, *243, 244, 245*; *see also main entry*: de-risking for pension schemes
    main tools available for, 230–3, 244–7
    membership categories and, relation of solutions to, and risks transferred, 233–6
    "progressive", strategy of, 238–9
    pros and cons of buy-outs, buy-ins and swaps, 236–8
  drivers for managing, 207–9
  economic capital, modelling and, 175–99, *190–1*
    applications, 185–92
    applications, specific: reinsurance, 193–5
    applications, wider, 192–3
    calibration and validation process for, 182–5
    cashflow models, projecting, *186*
    choices, comparing, 187–92
    fitting the model, *184*
    five simple steps for, *176*
    framework, 175–7
    internal model, delivering standard formula using, 185
    mathematical model for, type to apply, 181–2
    non-linearity, diversification and, 180–1

347

LONGEVITY RISK

other considerations
  concerning, 196–8
payment obligations and,
  meeting, 197–8
projected models and, use
  of, *192*
projecting capital
  requirements, *188–9*
projecting liabilities and
  capital, 185
regulatory balance sheet
  and, defending, 198
reinsurance and, 193–5
risk margin and,
  calculating, *187*
risk margin and, projected
  cost of capital, *187*
Solvency II requirements,
  calculating, *178–9*
speed and, need for,
  177–80
extreme mortality risk
  contrasted with, 274–6; *see
  also* longevity risk:
  mortality and
hedging of, solutions for,
  290–3
  available, 291–3
hedging of, through
  reinsurance, 255–65, *262*
  asset-backed transfer,
    256–7, *257*
  impaired and enhanced
    annuities and, 264–5
  standard forms of transfer
    for, 256
  steps involved in: case
    study, 262–4
  swaps and, 257–9, *258*,
    259, 261–2
key structural decisions for
  mitigation of, 223–7
  asset-backed transaction
    versus longevity swap,
    224–7
lifestyle factors concerning,
  131–2
managing, 57–8

market and pricing of; *see also*
  longevity risk: pricing of,
  123–43
  background, 124–31
  pension saving practices
    and, 124–5
  underwritten annuities
    and, 123–43
market investors, 326–7
market participants'
  management of, 322–6
medical factors concerning,
  132
mitigation of, key structural
  decisions for, 223–7
mortality and, 303–5; *see also*
  longevity risk: extreme
  mortality risk contrasted
  with
nascent market in, 50–1
pricing, 63–89, 131–42; *see also*
  longevity risk: market and
  pricing of; mortality: base
  level of, establishing
  adjusting for credibility of
    portfolio's experience,
    78–81
  adjusting for timing, 87
  complications concerning,
    87–8
  from experience, 65–81
  fully credible populations,
    65–71
  goodness-of-fit testing,
    70–1
  graduation methods of,
    66–7
  heterogeneity and, 87
  medium and smaller
    populations, 71–81
  overall approach to, 135–6
  predicting, by annuity
    amount, 82
  predicting, by
    geographical spread, 82–4
  predicting, by
    socio-economic class, 84–5

348

predicting, using postcode analysis, 85–7, *86*
predictive, and validation of experience results, 81–7
standard graduated tables for, 71, *72*, *73*
standard table and annuity portfolio, synchronising, 74
underwritten annuities and, 88
primary sources of, 320–2
sources of, 48–51
transactions, legal considerations for, 319–42
 administration, 331
 collateral mechanisms, 329–30
 exit terms, 330
 insolvency considerations, 330
 insurance securitisation and, 331–6
 insurance special-purpose vehicles and, 335
 market outlook, 341–2
 monetisation, explained, 331–3
 monetisation, market drivers of, 333–5
 rated debt, 338
 recent regulatory developments, 335
 recharacterisation risk, 338–9
 transaction's purpose, 336–7
 transfer, ability to demonstrate, 330–1
 warranties, 337–8
transfer approach for, key considerations in, *224*
transfer of, 52–8
 capital markets and, 283–302, *284*, *286*, *287*, *292*, *293*, *294*, *295*, *296*, *297*
 market for, 284–90

market participants, 288–90
sources of future capacity for, 54–7
see also life expectancy; longevity; mortality
longevity:
 assumptions of, in pension-scheme valuations, 166
 capacity and long-term risk mitigation, 259–62
 centenarians and, 15–16, *31*, *32*
 challenges and opportunities concerning, 30–9
 changing demographics of, 3–39
 consequences of, for dependency, 14–18
 credit risk and, process correlation versus capital correlation, 151–2
 dependency ratios and, 14–18, *17*, *46*
 diet and, 14, 36
 distributions, need to project, 170
 environmental and social changes and, 34–5
 financial impact of, 45–8
 fundamental research into, 37–9
 Hayflick limit and, 30, 37
 indices, 303–18, *308*, *312*, *313*, *314*
  deal requirements of, 307–12
  government and, 315–6
  hedging catastrophe risk and, 314–15
  hedging deferred risk and, 300–1
  market-published, 316–17
  mortality, longevity risk and, 303–5
  role of, 299–301

swap trade in, mechanics of, 305–7
swaps, trend risk and, 312–14
magnitude of issues concerning, 45–59
market development for, initiatives to facilitate, 297–8
   Life & Longevity Markets Association, 298
   LifeMetrics, 297–8
market issues concerning, 45–59
medical advances aid, 37
"mixed blocks" and, adjustments to assumptions concerning, 141–2
mortality trend risks and, combining, 169–70
new diseases and, 36; *see also* morbidity
phenomenon of, 15
possible improvements in, from the diffusion of good practice, 29
projecting, challenges to, 34–6
risk, *see* longevity risk
setting assumptions for, 163–72
   mortality improvement, 164
   opening (or base) mortality, 163–4
social and environmental changes and, 34–5
stress, calibration of the standard formula for, in Solvency II, 170–2
stresses, in economic-capital regimes, 165
swaps, 214–17, *217*, 232–3, 239–44, *240*, 244, 257–9, *258*, *259*
   administration of, 249
   asset-backed transaction versus, 224–7
   bespoke fixed-leg, 244–5
   cashflows payable in, 241–2
   collateral mechanics of, 242–3
   example structure of, *193*
   implementation, 252–4
   indemnity versus parametric, 225–7
   insurance-wrapped, 246–7, *248*
   novation, early termination and, 247–9
   overpayments, late notifications and, 249–50
   parametric (standardised) 261–2
   parametric versus indemnity, 225–7
   pricing of, 240–1, *241*
   reinsurance illustration of, 53
   relevant features concerning implementation of, 247–54
   sponsors and, considerations for, 251–2
   standardised (parametric) 261–2
   survivor, 296–7
   trade in, mechanics of, 305–7
   trustees and, considerations for, 250–1
see also life expectancy; mortality

M

MacArthur Foundation Research Network on an Ageing Society, 17
malaria, 26
Max Planck Institute, 7, 8, 18, 20, 23
Mexico, 127
   smoking ban in, 94

modelling, economic capital and longevity risk, 175–99, *190–1*
  applications, 185–92
  applications, specific: reinsurance, 193–5
  applications, wider, 192–3
  calibration and validation process for, 182–5
  cashflow models, projecting, *186*
  choices, comparing, 187–92
  fitting the model, *184*
  five simple steps for, *176*
  framework, 175–7
  internal model, delivering standard formula using, 185
  mathematical model for, type to apply, 181–2
    cashflow modelling, 181–2
    curve fitting, 181
    replicating portfolio, 182
  non-linearity, diversification and, 180–1
  other considerations concerning, 196–8
  payment obligations and, meeting, 197–8
  projected models and, use of, *192*
  projecting capital requirements, *188–9*
  projecting liabilities and capital, 185
  regulatory balance sheet and, defending, 198
  reinsurance and, 193–5
  risk margin and, calculating, *187*
  risk margin and, projected cost of capital, *187*
  Solvency II requirements, calculating, *178–9*
  speed and, need for, 177–80
morbidity, 18–24
  compression or expansion of, 22–4
    future trends, 24
    past trends, 23–4
  disability-free life expectancy and, 18–19
  inter-country comparisons of, 19–22
    age groups and socioeconomic factors, 21–2
    male–female, 19–20
    new diseases, 36
mortality:
  allowing for improvements in, 140–1
  base, estimating, 136–7
    to reflect impairment, 137–40
  base level of, establishing, 63–89; *see also* longevity risk: pricing
    calculating q_x from μ_x, 70
    Gompertz–Makeham (GM) method, 67–8, *67, 69*
    goodness-of-fit testing, 70–1
    graduation methods, 66–7
    P-spline method, 68–70, *69*
  crude rates of, 65–6, *66*
  England/Wales, male, by major cause, 93
  England/Wales regional differentials, 84
  excess winter, 81
  extreme; *see also main entry:* extreme mortality
    basis risk and, 276–7
    bonds, duration of, 277–8
    bonds, example structure of, *269*
    bonds, reason for issue, 269–70
    factors influencing, *64*, 64–5
    financial considerations of, 278
    longevity risk contrasted with, 274–6
    as natural hedge, 367–79
    nature of, 271–4
    transfer, 268–71

forward rate contract for, 293–4, *294*, *295*
future developments in study of, 116–18
future, projecting, 91–121, 107, 109–10
  communicating about, 95–9
  deterministic models, 106–8
  deterministic versus stochastic models for, 104–8
  expectation approach to, 103
  explanatory approach to, 104
  extrapolative approach to, 103
  future, projecting, 95–9
  methodologies and techniques available for, 103–8
  other influencing factors concerning, 108–13
  past evolution of, 92–5
  sense checks on, 118–20
  stochastic models, 108
graduated rates of, *67*
heat maps of, 96–7, *97*
improvement assumptions concerning, 164
key data types available for projecting, 99–102
key indicators to direction of changes in, 96
longevity trend risks and, combining, 169–70
male, by major cause, England/Wales, 93
male–female divergence in, 94–5
older ages and, considerations at, 113–16
predicting, by annuity amount, 82
predicting, by geographical spread, 82–4
predicting, by socio-economic class, 84–5
predicting, using postcode analysis, 85–7, *86*

price, calculating from geographical distribution, 83–4
reaction of key indicators to direction of changes in, 96
regional differentials, England/Wales, 84
smoking prevalence and apparent changes in rates of, 111
standard graduated tables for, 71, 72, 73
see also death; extreme mortality

N

natural catastrophes and industrial accidents, 274
Netherlands, 23, 26, 47, 298, 316, 317, 325
New Zealand, 33
  female life expectancy in, *116*
Norway, 26, 28
  female life expectancy in, *116*

O

obesity, 3, 24, 36, 123, 138
  body mass index and, *35*
  clinical, 36
  in younger population, 94
OECD, *see* Organisation for Economic Cooperation and Development
Office for National Statistics (ONS), UK, 7, 21, 45, 83, 84, 103, 106–7, 111, 324–5
  cancer trends studied by, 28, 29
old-aged dependency ratio, changes in, 14–18, *17*
Olovnikov, A. M., 30
ONS, *see* Office for National Statistics
Organisation for Economic Cooperation and Development (OECD) 12, 23

P

pandemic, 271–3 272, 273
PAQUID survey, 19, 20, 21, 24
pensions and pension schemes/funds:
   corporate/occupational, as source of longevity risk, 49
   de-risking of, for pension schemes, 229–54, *243, 244, 245*; *see also main entry*: de-risking for pension schemes
   main tools available for, 230–3, 244–7
   membership categories and, relation of solutions to, and risks transferred, 233–6
   "progressive", strategy of, 238–9
   pros and cons of buy-outs, buy-ins and swaps, 236–8
   financial and regulatory regimes for, 154–5
   longevity assumptions in valuations of, 166
   longevity de-risking solutions for, 229–54; *see also main entry*: de-risking for pension schemes
   private, estimated assets in, 47
   reserving and regulatory requirements for liabilities of, 147–73
   buy-out, 155
   capital and, as economic valuation–correlation matrix, *150*
   capital requirements and, calculating, 149–50, *150*
   correlation matrices and, applying, *152*
   correlation matrices and, technical requirements of, *151*
   diversification framework and, validating assumptions, 153
   funding basis, 154
   International Accounting Standard 19 (IAS19), 154
   mortality and longevity trend risks and, combining, 169–70
   non-linearity and, allowing for, 153
   regulatory regimes affecting, 147–63
   Solvency I and, 147–8
   Solvency II and, 155–63, *157, 158,* 166
   as risk issue, *see* longevity risk
   saving practices and, international differences in, 124–5
   state, as source of longevity risk, 48
   see also annuities
population:
   ageing of, *see* longevity
   of centenarians (2007) 16
   in developing and developed countries by age and sex, *16*
   Human Mortality Database's data for, 8, *101*
   life expectancies in, *see* life expectancy
   UK projection of, *46*

Q

QxX index, 317, 325

R

regulatory regimes and
   annuities, 125–6, 147–63
   economic-capital, 148
   German Minimum Requirements for Risk Management, 149
   Individual Capital Adequacy Standard (UK) 148–9
   Solvency I, 147–8
   Solvency II, 155–8, *157, 158,* 166
   Swiss Solvency Test, 149

reinsurance, 52–4, *53*, 55, 56, 156, 159, 193–5, 196, 210–18
   hedging longevity risk through, 255–65, *262*
   asset-backed transfer, 256–7, *257*
   economic capital, modelling and longevity risk and, 193–5
   impaired and enhanced annuities and, 264–5
   standard forms of transfer for, 256
   steps involved in, case study, 262–4
   swaps and, 257–9, *258*, *259*, 261–2; *see also* longevity: swaps
   risk-transfer transactions for, 222
   single-premium annuity, 213–14, 214, 215, 217
Retail Distribution Review, 126
Russia, 9, 95

S

Sanborn, Eunice, 31
SHARE, *see* Survey on Health, Ageing and Retirement in Europe
smoking, 24, 31, 35, 52 93–4
Solvency I, 147–8, 164–5
Solvency II, 104, 105, 125, 147, 149, 155–6, 176–7, 208, 237
   calibration of standard-formula longevity stress in, 170–2
   longevity within, 166–72
      current mortality risk, 167–8
      trend risk, 168–9
   Pillar I of, *158*, 168
   Pillar II of, 160–1
   Pillar III of, 161
   previous economic capital regimes compared with, 162–3
   structural overview of, 156–7
   three pillars of, overview of, 157
South Africa, 124, 125, 126, 127
   smoking ban in, 94
Spain, 8, 26, 28, 95, 106
   Civil War in, 95
Supercentenarian Research Foundation, 31
Survey on Health, Ageing and Retirement in Europe (SHARE) 19
Sweden, 23, 26, 28
Switzerland, 6, 26, 28, 148, 149
   Financial Market Authority in, 149
   Solvency Test (SST) 149
   women's age at death in, *5*
Szostak, Jack W., 30

T

terrorism, war and, 274
tuberculosis, 92

U

United Kingdom, 26, 45
   annuities market in, background to, 204–7, *206*
   annuity pricing by postcode in, 13
   cancer trends studied in, 28, 29
   circulatory disease in, 28
   death of, 60+ lives in (England/Wales), 172
   dependency ratios in, 46
   disability-free life expectancy in, 21
   Individual Capital Adequacy Standard in, 148–9
   INED survey concerning, 28
   large pensions market in, 46
   population projection in, 46
   underwritten annuities in, 137, 137

United States of America, 4, 8,
    17, 22, 33, 35, 101
  Census Bureau of, 9, 15
  female life expectancy in, *116*
  life expectancy surpasses
    78 years in, 8
  obesity in, 36
  stagnant older-age
    mortality in, 7
  underwritten annuities sold
    in, 128
United States Census Bureau, 9, 15

W

war and terrorism, 274
WHO, *see* World Health
    Organization
World Health Organization
    (WHO) 13, 14, 36

X

Xpect Index, 317, 325